SHIP SS JEREMIAH O'BRIEN

Londonderry

London

Portsmouth

Lo Havre

Roen

Cherbourg

WITHDRAWN

Atlantic Ocean

☐ Outbound voyage
▣ Return voyage

APPOINTMENT

IN

NORMANDY

by
Walter W. Jaffee

Copyright © 1995 by Walter W. Jaffee
Published by The Glencannon Press
P.O. Box 341, Palo Alto, CA 94302

First Edition

Library of Congress Catalog Card Number: 95-076272

ISBN   0-9637586-4-0

Photos without credit are from the author's collection.

Dedication

To those who built the Libertys and those who sailed them,
To the volunteers who brought the *Jeremiah O'Brien* back to life,
To the friends and supporters who made the voyage possible,
To the veterans and seamen of the U.S. merchant marine, and
To all whose imagination and dreams rode along with us on
"The Voyage of a Lifetime."

By the same author:

The Last Liberty
The Last Victory
The Last Mission Tanker

. . . in my mind the image of life's need,
Beauty in the hardest action, beauty indeed.
They built great ships and sailed them, sounds most brave
Whatever arts we have or fail to have;
I touch my country's mind, I come to grips
With half her purpose, thinking of these ships.

— John Masefield

ACKNOWLEDGEMENTS

One of the most rewarding aspects of writing *Appointment in Normandy* was the opportunity to relive the whole, wonderful experience and savor again the unique camaraderie of shipmates on a long voyage — the stories, views and ideas on many subjects, from the pre-*O'Brien* lives of the crew to why we wanted to do this to philosophies about war and history and English beer and French wine to why the engine crew (or the deck crew) are such weird types (depending on who's talking).

Rather than a wearisome listing of names to "acknowledge," the reader will meet the characters, and some of them really are "characters," in the course of the book. Crew and volunteers "come alive" in the talks, discussions, debates and incidents scattered through this account of the great voyage; in my view, the best kind of acknowledgment.

A special note of thanks to the *San Francisco Chronicle* for allowing me to reproduce portions of columns, articles and editorials and Carl Nolte's great series, and to Phil Frank for his permission to include Bruce the Raven on our crew list. Bruce is actually one of only two permanent crew of the *O'Brien* (the other is Miss Jerry O'Brien who occupies the forward guntub). Bruce is berthed in the crow's nest on the foremast.

One member of the crew needs special acknowledgment. With his knowledge and skill in programming and problem-solving, Bob Black rescued me (and the book) innumerable times from the problems and frustrations presented by the monster named "Computer," which is at once the greatest tool in the world and, at times, the most baffling. Ellen Wallis was of immeasurable help in acquiring the appropriate hardware and software and generous in providing information and advice. To them both, my sincere thanks.

I'm very grateful to Jim Conwell, Bob Gisslow and Marci Hooper for their proofreading skills. Their meticulous attention to detail and knowledge of different aspects of the voyage saved me a great deal of embarrassment.

Finally, my thanks to my editor, R.B. Rose, for her support, her enthusiasm for the project, the uncountable hours she put in slogging through the various drafts, her editorial eye and suggestions, and her constant encouragement.

Contents

FOREWORD

"The trip of a lifetime," was the almost universal reaction to the idea of the *Jeremiah O'Brien*'s return to Normandy. As the proposal evolved, plans were laid and ports of call suggested. Just hearing the names was thrilling — Panama, London, Edinburgh, Liverpool, Glasgow, Normandy.

Normandy! The name carried an almost electrical charge. It conjured a vision of thousands of ships covering the ocean from horizon to horizon, and the greatest maritime invasion in history. Cardiff, Portland, Cristobal, Boston, Le Havre, Normandy. We savored the names. New Orleans, Rouen, Cherbourg, Portsmouth, Normandy. It always came back to Normandy. Normandy and D-Day, Normandy and Operation Overlord, Normandy and the longest day in history, Normandy and the greatest gathering of ships since the beginning of time. And the *Jeremiah O'Brien* had been there, and would be again.

There were those who, from the first, believed in it, those who didn't think it could be done and those who thought it a foolish idea, a waste of time and money. But no one could deny it would be the trip of a lifetime, a voyage back — and forward — into history. Except for the *O'Brien,* not one ship from the thousands that served on D-Day 1944 was capable of returning to Normandy on June 6, 1994. If she went, the *Jeremiah O'Brien* would again make history. We were determined that the *O'Brien* would keep her rendezvous if hard work and determination could do it.

Until the very last, no one was sure the ship would actually go. Nevertheless, with the support of their families, volunteers made the necessary plans to be away from spouses and children, homes and jobs, in some cases for as long as six months.

The course was fraught with obstacles, difficulties and problems, but, one by one, each hindrance was overcome and on April 18, 1994, the *SS Jeremiah O'Brien* cast off her lines and departed San Francisco for her appointment in Normandy. Fifty-five volunteers were on board. Twenty-seven would make the entire voyage while others signed on for various "legs" of the trip.

We felt ourselves among the most fortunate of people. We also felt an obligation to all the volunteers who worked on the ship, to friends of the ship who went out into the community for help, to the families without whose encouragement and support none of us could go, to our sponsors and well-wishers, and to the worldwide brotherhood of World War II veterans and seafarers whose hearts and dreams rode along with us.

Two years ago, I wrote *The Last Liberty*, the history of the *Jeremiah O'Brien* from her launching in 1943 to summer 1993, when plans for the Normandy voyage were taking shape. From the epilogue to that book: "It is not an easy task to take a fifty-year-old ship crewed with volunteers halfway around the world. Will the volunteer crew, with an average age of 71, be up to the voyage? Will the country's leaders support this historic voyage?"

Appointment in Normandy answers those questions.

One other quote from that epilogue was an expression of hope and belief in 1993. On June 6, 1994, it became a reality. "The task ahead is formidable, but the *SS Jeremiah O'Brien*, her friends and her volunteers are up to the challenge. Over and over they have proved their perseverance and determination. The ship will sail to Normandy and once more do her part. But this time the cause is not war but a celebration of the triumph of freedom and liberty. Jeremiah O'Brien would be proud."

Walter Jaffee
Menlo Park, California
March, 1995

1

THE IMPOSSIBLE DREAM

Chief Engineer Ernie Murdock's suggestion had a simple title: "Proposed Anniversary Voyage of the *SS Jeremiah O'Brien*." It was an eight-page document suggesting that the ship take part in both the 500th anniversary of Columbus' landing in the Americas in 1992 and the 50th anniversary of D-Day at Normandy in 1994. He presented it to the Board of Directors of the National Liberty Ship Memorial (NLSM) on December 10, 1987. (See appendix A.)

Ernie's plan was thorough and well thought-out. It addressed financial planning, drydocking, logistics, supply, crewing, shoreside support, coordination with government agencies and myriad other details. Fifty-four ports of call were suggested. It was endorsed by Capt. George M. Tuttle, Jr., the ship's master in 1987, Marci Hooper, who then was second purser and storekeeper, Kevin T. Kilduff, a volunteer third assistant engineer, and Susan Krelle, a volunteer member of the engine department. But it involved taking the ship, almost 50 years old, on a voyage halfway around the world and back. Many on the Board thought it impractical, if not downright foolish, to even think of taking the vessel outside the Golden Gate, much less on an 18,000-mile voyage.

Capt. Ernie Murdock sailed on Liberty ships during World War II. After serving as an oiler on the *Janet Ward Roper* and the *Margaret Brent* where he saw action in Great Britain, he attended the maritime training school at Fort Trumbell, New London, Connecticut. Graduating with a third assistant engineer's license, he sailed on the *William Few* and went in that capacity to Southern France. After the war, he joined the U.S. Coast Guard where he attained the rank of Captain and served as Captain of the Port in both Jacksonville and San Francisco. Following retirement from the Coast Guard, Capt. Murdock devoted his energies to restoring a C1-M-AV1, the *Lock Knot*, and the *Jeremiah O'Brien*. He has served as Chief Engineer of the *O'Brien*, was Marine Superintendent for "Normandy '94," and is presently on the Board of Directors of the National Liberty Ship Memorial.

"To say it was met with derision would be an understatement," recalls Marci Hooper, now the NLSM business manager.

Bob Burnett, *Jeremiah O'Brien* shipkeeper: "Most of the Board was negative. I don't recall anybody being particularly interested, but several of them were definitely against it."

The proposal was tabled.

The seed was actually planted in mid-1986. Marci Hooper and Ernie Murdock sat talking after dinner in the shipboard gunners' mess one evening. Lee Iacocca's fund-raising efforts for the centennial of the Statue of Liberty were in the news and while discussing that much-anticipated event, the notion of taking the *Jeremiah O'Brien* back to Normandy for the 50th Anniversary of D-Day came up. Almost instantly, a fever of enthusiasm began to burn and soon Marci and Ernie were writing out the names of potential crew members on paper napkins.

Jack Loomis, a longtime volunteer, came by, overheard the discussion and sat down.

"Well, if you go," he said, "and I'm dead, I'd like you to take my ashes along with you."

"No problem," said Ernie. "Where would you like us to scatter them?"

"Oh, I don't want you to scatter them. I just want to go along for the ride."

During the next few weeks Marci and Ernie wrote down more ideas, expanding the concept to include the quincentennial of the arrival of Columbus in the new world, scheduled for San Juan, Puerto Rico, in 1992. In October 1987 Marci invited Ernie Murdock, George Tuttle, Kevin Kilduff and Susan Krelle to a dinner party at her home. By the end of the evening, they had a draft of the proposal which was researched and refined into the formal document presented on December 10.

Dick Brannon, chief engineer, Normandy '94: "He passed that around to those of us in the crew and that's the first that I, personally, had any inkling that a voyage was proposed. Ernie Murdock gave a lot of thought to this. It was quite detailed."

At the next board meeting, the proposal was again tabled. And at the next one, and the next, for almost four years.

Dick Brannon: "Doug Dickie was chief at this time. So he said, 'Well, the engineer's job is still open. You come back and be nominal first assistant, although there is no title connected with it, you would be doing the job of first assistant.' That was in 1990. By this time, this Normandy idea had become more and more viable and so I became more and more interested in the trip while Doug Dickie became less and less enthused about the trip, fighting against it the whole way. Nothing sudden happened, but the crew themselves, the dedicated black gang, were all for it. They thought, hey, that's a neat idea, a neat idea. On deck the same way, Bob Burnett and all the dedicated guys, they were all for it."

In November 1991 Marci Hooper was contacted by Professor Andre Delbecq of the Business School at the University of Santa Clara. He was a member of a "sister city" association between San Jose and Rouen — home of *L'Armada de la Liberté*, a gathering of tall ships which was to take place in Rouen, France in July 1994. It would be part of the celebrations commemorating the 50th anniversary of the liberation of France. At his request a meeting was called of the NLSM board members. In attendance were Rear Admiral Thomas J. Patterson, founder of the organization, Capt. Carl Otterberg, staff captain of the *O'Brien,* Robert Blake, Chairman of the Board, Capt. George Jahn, master of the *O'Brien,* Marci Hooper, and Donald Watson, medical officer. Mr. Delbecq brought books and posters depicting the previous Armada, *Les Voiles De La Liberté*, which took place in 1989. Passing the literature around, he said Rouen wanted the *Jeremiah O'Brien* to attend the 1994 gathering, and the ship would have a place of honor. He asked the critical question, "Do you want to go?" And now, the years of patient lobbying finally bore fruit.

"Let's go around the table and see what everyone says," said Tom Patterson, later to be commodore of the voyage.

One by one, each person in the room was asked the question and, one by one, each agreed. It was a turning point. Normandy was now more than just a dream.

In March 1992 John Boylston, the head of Project Liberty Ship, which operated the *John W. Brown* in Baltimore, called and requested a meeting of representatives from the three World War II museum ships, the *Brown,* the *O'Brien* and the *Lane Victory* of San Pedro. He said, "I think there's a way to get the kind of money we need to get our ships in shape for the next century."

At a subsequent meeting held in April aboard the *O'Brien*, he proposed that the three ships travel in convoy to Europe for the commemoration of D-Day on June 6, 1994. Suddenly, everyone was very interested.

But weeks passed with little action. The events for the quincentennial of Columbus' landing were dropped because of a lack of time and funds. This had the positive effect of allowing everyone to focus on getting the ships to Normandy. All three ships had served during World War II and their presence at the 50th anniversary would be more than appropriate.

Marci Hooper had long planned a vacation to England and France. With the impetus of the interest on the part of Rouen and the *Armada* and the growing enthusiasm for what was being called "The Last Convoy," her vacation quickly became a business trip. November of 1992 found her visiting authorities in ports of England and France where she presented press kits, including ship photos, advertising brochures, histories, letters of commendation and certificates of merit for each of the three museum ships. The effect was dramatic. To the British and the French, the proposed convoy was no longer a mere notion. Here was a real person, directly representing the *Jeremiah O'Brien* and the other ships, assuring them that three American World War II veteran ships were doing everything they could to attend the D-Day commemoration.

THE SHIPS ARE COMING
UNITED STATES SHIPPING BOARD   EMERGENCY FLEET CORPORATION

This World War II poster captures the spirit felt by the crew when the convoy was announced.

In December 1992 things really began to happen. First, the *O'Brien* went into drydock. Among other things, it was time to have the tailshaft pulled for inspection. But as Marine Superintendent Ernie Murdock went through the ship with Coast Guard officials and American Bureau of Shipping (ABS) representatives, he was concentrating not only on this routine drydocking but on the one to come — the all-important drydocking that would take place just prior to sailing for Normandy sixteen months hence.

The Department of Defense (DOD) issued a certificate to the *O'Brien:*

Department of Defense, World War II Commemoration Committee designates National Liberty Ship Memorial as a Commemorative Community. Awarded in recognition of support for the 50th Anniversary of World War II remembrances during the period 1992-1995, having agreed to develop annually three or more educational programs, commemorative activities or events to honor World War II veterans, their families, and those who served on the home front. Done this 9th day of December 1992.

signed, Dick Chaney
Secretary of Defense

Retired Brigadier General R. C. Tripp, the *O'Brien*'s liaison with the Army, received a draft copy of the Army's concept plan for the D-Day ceremonies. Even a year-and-a-half before June 6, 1994, most of the final events for the ceremonies were anticipated. The theme was to be "A Grateful Nation Remembers — Honoring Those Who Served." The DOD Anniversary of World War II Commemoration Committee was given responsibility for overall planning guidance, coordination and support for all commemorative events. The concept plan set out several key assumptions: the President would attend, as well as the Secretary of Defense, the Chairman, Joint Chiefs of Staff, the Secretaries of the Army, Air Force, Navy and the Commandant of the Marines; veterans' groups and foreign dignitaries would take part. The planning objectives were noteworthy in their simplicity and their focus with key elements being: 1) To keep the WWII veterans central in all events, including planning and execution and, 2) to make all events meaningful, dignified and basic. Other sections of the overall plan dealt with logistics, timing and areas of responsibility.

At about this time the Normandy '94 Committee was formed. Tom Patterson: "I had been asked by the Board of Directors if I would serve as the chairman for the voyage. I accepted and started to put together a committee that would be able to handle all the parts of the planning and the conducting of the voyage itself. This continued into the beginning of 1993 and we finally ended up with thirty-three people on the Normandy voyage committee. This committee was meeting on the first Thursday of every month and then as the year progressed we had to have special meetings for such subjects as fund raising and meeting the regulatory bodies — U.S. Coast Guard, American Bureau of Shipping. These fell into special meetings." [See appendix B for listing of committee members]

In that same month, Adm. Patterson asked the author to be historian for the committee. The first meeting I attended was on January 7, 1993. It was held at the ship's shoreside office at the end of Pier 1 at Fort Mason in San Francisco. It was a familiar location. The Maritime Administration (MARAD) had operated its radar school there for several years. Many of us had renewed our radar certificates in the same room. The few seats at the conference table were taken well before the meeting started at 10 a.m. Soon we were dragging chairs in from adjoining rooms and the last to arrive had to stand. Twenty-two people attended the meeting.

A wide range of topics relative to the coming trip were discussed, many of them foreshadowing problems that would plague us throughout the voyage. Probably the most important was the budget. Art Haskell, a recently-retired executive from Matson Lines, handed out copies of his financial forecast. [See appendix C for the budget] Although we knew the trip would be expensive, the bottomline figure of $2.6 million came as something of a shock. This was softened to a degree by the explanation that $1.6 million was already in hand or would come "in kind." The budget generated more questions than it answered but, as Mr. Haskell said, "Its purpose is to serve as a point of departure and raise questions." And it put the trip into financial perspective.

Tom Patterson: "We looked at the budget that had been prepared by Mr. Haskell which amounted to two million six hundred seventy-five thousand dollars and we realized the Herculean task we had committed ourselves to."

One anticipated source of funds was the eagerly-awaited legislation that called for selling six scrap ships from the National Defense Reserve Fleet, two for each of the museum ships: *Jeremiah O'Brien, John W. Brown* and *Lane Victory*. Patterson said that Congresswoman Helen Bentley's (D-Maryland) staff reported the "Scrap Ship Bill" was ready to submit and that Capt. Warren

Leback, the Maritime Administrator, expected the legislation to pass on the next effort. This was in part due to several new friends in Washington such as Dianne Feinstein, Barbara Boxer and Nancy Pelosi (all D-California), all sympathetic to our efforts. The amount netted would depend on the demand for scrap steel and the value of the dollar on the world market, but many thought $750,000 was a realistic amount to expect from the sale for the use of each museum ship.

Besides funding, one of our more enduring problems in the project would be the need for ship ballast. The optimum figure was 3,000 tons. Tom Patterson reported that 5,000 tons of lead was available from the Navy in Bremerton, Washington. The difficulty would be getting it from Bremerton to San Francisco. A later problem would be that there was far less than 5,000 tons. But, as we quickly learned, most plans were subject to change.

Other issues arose. Bill Duncan, representing the crew, raised the question of crew licenses and certificates. Many of the volunteers had expired documents or never had documents to begin with. Would the Coast Guard waive requirements?

Duncan expressed the concern on the part of the crew that outsiders and newcomers might be given precedence over the longtime volunteers. Adm. Patterson emphatically said, "It always has been and always will be the policy of this committee that the volunteer crew comes first." He closed the meeting with this reminder, "It's the work that's done before you leave that brings you home."

In February 1993 Tony Seideman, a New Yorker, formally approached the three museum ship organizations during a meeting at Fort Mason. He rode the *John W. Brown* on one of her earlier cruises and was enthusiastic about representing the ships in fundraising efforts. He proposed that his organization, America Works, raise funds nationwide for the convoy. The representatives of the three ships agreed to his proposal. Being represented by a national, rather than regional, organization, it was hoped, would make major corporate donors more approachable. But from the viewpoint of the *Jeremiah O'Brien,* there was a serious question of how effective they could be operating through a New York office 3,000 miles and three time zones away from the West Coast. The NLSM opted to continue their own fund-raising on a more local level while America Works would concentrate on the national level. The others concurred. The result was that the idea of the convoy was still alive, there was hope for high-level national funding, but each organization would also pursue its own avenues of financial support.

Subsequent committee meetings covered an ever-expanding range of plans, problems, crises, logistics, and funding, funding, funding.

As the project grew it attracted the interest of outsiders, all willing to help, some with their own agenda. Adm. Patterson asked pointed questions and made short work of professional fundraisers masquerading as friends of the *O'Brien.*

The concerns over funding were overriding. At this point the NLSM was almost broke. It barely had enough funds to meet the next few months' expenses, yet it was boldly planning to raise and spend another $2.6 million in the next eighteen months. Meetings went on for hours, with obsessive talk about (the lack of) money. Tom Patterson: "The initial response was discouraging but we had expected that and it didn't really turn us aside."

One disappointing fact was that the federal budget for 1993 was already in place so we could not expect funds from that quarter, and even if the scrap ship bill passed, it probably wouldn't be until the Fall, so funds would not be available from that source until 1994. Ernie Murdock reminded the committee that the ship must be drydocked in October 1993 if the Normandy voyage was to be made. At $500,000, it was the single most costly line item in the budget. Where would we get the money?

Everyone had ideas for fundraisers — from bake sales to cruise-ship tickets. One of Don Watson's fund-raising efforts that did work, to an extent, was an automobile raffle. He arranged for a Chrysler/Jeep dealer to donate a new vehicle, at cost, to the ship. We sold tickets and raffled it off. After paying the $23,000 "dealer cost" we realized a profit of $6,500 — a welcome amount but somewhat disappointing compared to what we had hoped.

Ernie Murdock, left, and Bob Davidson, engineer, discussing the early stages of the Normandy voyage. Photo by Mike Emery.

Capt. Sandy Jones of American President Lines put fifty-two immersion suits* on board the *O'Brien.* They cost the ship nothing and eliminated a $100,000 line item from the budget.

A "Crab Feed", a San Francisco tradition, was held in the ship's no. 2 'tween deck, an area set up as a meeting, conference and party room. Volunteers set up tables and chairs, plates, bibs, napkins and tableware. Others went to work melting butter, making salad, cutting San Francisco's famed sourdough French bread, breaking dungeness crab into manageable pieces and brewing coffee. By the end of the evening, appetites were well satisfied, the committee netted $3,700 for the effort, and everyone left with a sense of accomplishment.

As the weeks went by, more ideas were floated. One was the possibility of producing a video featuring the *Jeremiah O'Brien* to market to major corporations to solicit corporate support. Another idea that appealed to many was the "infomercial." All of us had seen the late night efforts at selling beauty products, car polish, vegetable slicers, psychic services and "How to Get Rich in Real Estate." Paul Reyff suggested we make our own infomercial

---

* Sometimes called "Gumby suits" because they give the wearer the appearance of that cartoon-like character, immersion suits are similar to a skin diver's dry suit, covering the entire body and protecting the wearer from exposure if forced to abandon ship. Immersion suits are required on all ships traveling above 35 degrees north or south latitude.

and show it on television during cheap, late night hours.   He calculated that such a commercial would reach 25 million people in six months, generate 200,000 responses and gross $5 million with a net of $3 million.   Here, in one effort, we could have an income greater than our entire budget!   A motion to proceed was raised, seconded and passed in a flash.   It was an idea with some promise, but, like many notions in those early days of the committee, it never happened.   Some efforts were made to get historical film to use in the project and then it simply died.   Everyone was in favor of it but no one wanted to do anything about it.

About this time we learned that the President would ask for a 5-10% reduction in federal spending.   This did not look good for our prospects of getting money from the federal government. Then we received word that "America Works" was folding, another potential source of funding gone.

New issues and problems continued to surface.   One of the more controversial discussions at these early meetings centered around uniforms.   In general, the attitude of the crew was anti-uniform, anti-regimentation, anti-anything military.   It was a matter of professional pride.   The crew felt that American merchant mariners had no need for uniforms.   They were the best seamen on earth and no uniform was necessary to advertise or prove that fact.   On the other hand, traveling into foreign cultures, we needed to respect the expectations of those cultures.   Also, the *O'Brien* represented a unique, historic endeavor, and it was important that the public be able to recognize officers and crew.

Just as emphatic, however, were people such as Don Watson, who <u>like</u> to wear uniforms.   At one Normandy Committee meeting he presented a professional-looking display of merchant marine uniforms and proposed standards of dress for the three ships participating in the voyage.   An ex-Navy man, he envisioned different uniforms for officers, petty officers and crew. "Would the ship pay the cost of attiring the whole crew?"   The issue was tabled until we had a better handle on funding.   And so it went — eventually every issue, proposal, problem came back to the question of funding.

Even the most dedicated, die-hard enthusiasts occasionally need some encouraging news, some sense that they are not alone in their vision as they encounter one obstacle after another, trying to gather support from those who applaud the project but find reasons why they cannot help, or, worse, who promise help, then reveal the self-aggrandizing string attached. Even more discouraging are the prophets of doom who mock or scorn the "grandiose scheme" and can momentarily dishearten the staunchest optimist. But not Adm. Patterson. I remember a popular bumper sticker saying, "What part of 'NO' don't you understand?" Tom Patterson, in effect, said, "I don't understand that word at all." And on he charged.

Now, we began getting interest from overseas. The first came from Brigadier T. Longland, OBE, of the British Ministry of Defence. It was addressed to Adm. Patterson and dated 26 March 1993:

Dear Admiral:

COMMEMORATION OF THE D DAY LANDINGS JUNE 1994

During a recent visit to Washington LTG Kicklighter mentioned that it was hoped to refurbish and then sail two Liberty ships and a Victory ship across the Atlantic in time to take part in the ceremonies commemorating the 50th Anniversary of the D Day Landings.

I have been appointed to lead the team responsible for the planning and coordination of the British Government's commemorations for D Day and my team are now putting together an outline of the events proposed for June 1994.

One of the ideas being worked upon at present is the concept of a flotilla of ships sailing from Portsmouth and Southampton to the Normandy coast on June 5th 1994. The outline plan would be that the flotilla, consisting of a mixture of commercial vessels and warships would congregate first off Portsmouth and then, led by the Royal Yacht, sail across the Channel before dispersing to their various ports. While they were sailing across we would hope to fly the Royal Navy's and the Royal Air Force's Historic flights overhead to add a little more atmosphere to the occasion.

Clearly the addition of your ship to the flotilla would be most welcome and would add a touch of authenticity that would be much appreciated by all the veterans taking part.

Should you be able to take part I would be grateful if you would get in touch so that we could discuss the project in more detail.

I have also written to Mr Johnson [*Lane Victory*] and Mr Boylston [*John W. Brown*] concerning their vessels.

Yours Ever,
Tom Longland

The Last Convoy was becoming a reality in the minds of the British. At home, the meetings continued and the main problem was still money. Adm. Patterson reported some good news. The Bentley, or Scrap Ship, Bill would pass in the Fall. The second part of fund-raising, after the Bentley Bill, was corporate sponsorship. Capt. Otterberg, Adm. Patterson and NLSM board member Capt. Henry Simonsen were working on the oil industry for donations of money and oil. A maritime auction was planned as a fund-raiser. Adm. Patterson also suggested to General Tripp that he, General Kicklighter and Patterson work on DOD support, developing a list of the ship's needs, "in kind" items that could be obtained through the Department of Defense.

Admiral Thomas J. Patterson graduated from the Merchant Marine Academy at Kings Point, New York in 1944. While still a midshipman he sailed on his first Liberty ship, the *SS Jim Bridger*. Upon graduation, he served in the merchant marine, then went on active duty in the Navy in 1950. While there he commanded a Liberty ship, the *USS Guardian AGR-1*, ex *James G. Squire*. Joining the Maritime Administration in 1962, he became Western Region Director in 1970. He founded the National Liberty Ship Memorial and was responsible for selecting the *O'Brien* to be a museum ship. In 1982 he was appointed as Deputy Superintendent to the U.S. Merchant Marine Academy. He retired in 1985 and now devotes his full attention to the *Jeremiah O'Brien*.

Tom Patterson: "We knew that there were alternative ways of putting this voyage together and that's what we were mainly experienced in doing. For example, getting the Maritime Administration and the U.S. Navy to transfer to us the outfitting gear that we needed for the ship. And by going to the various vendors and various steamship companies we were able to get contributions of what we needed. This was the main way the voyage was put together."

Adm. Patterson emphasized the need for action. "It is time to get this thing moving," he said. The meeting ended after almost three hours with his final words, "Do It."

Now came an important communication from France. Marci Hooper received a letter from Yves-Asseline, vice-president of *L'Armada de la Liberté*.

Dear Marci,

It was a pleasure to have you on the phone yesterday.

About the Liberty ship, we could propose you to be a "star" on the french TV on Saturday 9th or Sunday 10th July 1994.

We would like your ship arrives in the harbour of Rouen in the middle of the Armada.

Tall ships and moderne war ships could "welcome" the "*Jeremiah O'Brien*". All the event broadcast "LIVE ON TV", we have a contract with the state TV channels covering all France. I think this sort of support could help you in finding sponsors.

Do you think possible to sign a contract between your association and the Armada in order to make these things sure.

Please be so kind to let me know your opinion on this and please give me your schedule.

Best Regards,

In April a sale of Vintage Model Kits was held. Ed Von Der Porten, our museum director, had recently discovered an old barn full of model kits of ships, airplanes, jeeps, and amphibious vehicles, all made before and during World War II. The *Jeremiah O'Brien* acquired them hoping to use them as a "draw" in the never-ending fund-raising. What happened was beyond their hopes. A press release brought local TV stations to the ship to film setting up for the sale. Then a local radio station heard about the sale, put it on the air, and demand exploded. Entry to no. 2 hold had to be restricted and people were limited in the number of models they could buy. It was a stunning example of the power of publicity.

The *O'Brien*'s annual Maritime Day Cruise took on added significance in 1993. In an open letter to the public, Chairman of the Board Robert E. Blake said, "Our salute this year has double meaning, for we are preparing our ship for steaming to her commemoration of the 50th year in celebration of Operation Overlord, when the *Jeremiah O'Brien* participated eleven times in delivering supplies to our armed forces across the English Channel at the Normandy beaches."

The program contained a special letter from Adm. Patterson: "Now we are committed to take the *O'Brien* on her eighth voyage. Destination — Normandy. Of the thousands of ships that were at the beaches in 1944, *Jeremiah O'Brien* is the only original Liberty ship that was there and is capable of returning."

Taking place on May 22 and 23, the cruise included the transfer of simulated cargo to amphibious vehicles, a rehearsal for an event to take place in Cherbourg, France, the following year. On board were seven of the ship's original crew members: Rosario Carista, messman; Charles Hord, fireman-watertender; Daniel Bandy, Coxswain of the Armed Guard; Carl Scharpf, third assistant engineer; Morgan Williams, seaman in the Armed Guard; Hank Kusel, deck cadet; and Robert Milby, radio operator. They had been part of the crew on her first seven voyages during World War II.

Important members of the maritime community began to publicly support the voyage. Capt. L. M. Pivonka, COMSCPAC (COmander Military Sealift Command PACific) wrote:

> I recently had the privilege of spending the day on board the Liberty ship, *SS Jeremiah O'Brien*, as she steamed in San Francisco Bay. I was truly impressed with the dedication of her all-volunteer crew and with the superb condition of this 50-year old living memorial to merchant mariners. I was inspired by the crew's commitment to take the ship to Normandy for the 50th anniversary of "D-Day." MSCPAC is supporting this goal in every way possible.

Friday, June 18, 1993 was the 50th anniversary of the launching of the *Jeremiah O'Brien* in Portland Maine*. A black-tie dinner-dance was held at the San Francisco Presidio Officer's Club to commemorate the occasion. The South Portland [Maine] Shipyard Society sent a representative. Coleman "Coke" Schneider,

---

* *The Last Liberty* by the same author is the history of the *Jeremiah O'Brien* from her launching in 1943 to her 50th anniversary.

deck cadet on the first three voyages, flew in from New Jersey. He would join us as a messman for the first part of Voyage 8 — the return to Normandy. An undercurrent of anticipation and excitement was keenly felt by everyone attending. Where would the ship be on her next birthday? Would she be at anchor in an English port, basking in the glory of an historic return to the beaches of Normandy, or would she be tied to the pier in San Francisco? Where would everyone be a year hence? Aboard ship in a place of honor at a great naval review, or watching the event on TV? There were as many opinions as there were people, but overall they fell into two groups: those who thought the ship would make it to Normandy and those who thought it wouldn't. But the excitement and sense of anticipation were there. The word "Normandy" was on everyone's lips.

Adm. Patterson took the floor. His first words were, "The *Jeremiah O'Brien* is a lucky ship. She has been lucky all her life, and now she stands on the threshold of her greatest adventure." The audience broke into applause.

The next day the 50th Anniversary Celebration continued aboard ship. Special events highlighted the weekend. The Navy Band of San Francisco played a concert on deck. A special stamp cover ceremony was held in no. 2 hold.

The euphoria was short-lived. In July the Coast Guard issued inspection requirements for the three vessels of The Last Convoy. To comply with regulations, the ships would have to obtain: the Certificate of Inspection issued by the Coast Guard, a Loadline Certificate, issued by the ABS, an FCC (Federal Communications Commission) Radiotelephone certificate, an FCC Radiotelegraph certificate, a Safety Equipment Certificate, a Safety Construction Certificate and a SOLAS (Safety of Life at Sea) certificate. Getting the certificates required inspections by various regulatory bodies, predominantly the Coast Guard, ABS and FCC. The ten page Coast Guard document further detailed the types of inspections and requirements: lifesaving equipment, fire protection equipment, operations, electrical systems, machinery, drydocking, manning, rules of the road, stability and general items. For 50-year-old ships staffed by 70-year-old volunteers and funded by donations, these were major hurdles.

Dismay at the magnitude of the tasks facing the crew was eased somewhat by the realization that the *Jeremiah O'Brien* was moving up in the British hierarchy of planning for the commemoration. In July, a letter addressed to Tom Patterson arrived from the Chief of Naval Staff and First Sea Lord:

My dear Admiral,

I understand from the British Naval Staff in Washington that you are the head of an exciting project to bring the Liberty ship *Jeremiah O'Brien* to the United Kingdom in 1994 to take part in the commemoration of D Day.

Certainly the participation of a Liberty ship would be highly appropriate. Many will vividly recall the enormous contribution made by the Liberty ship in World War II, and the thousands of brave men who sailed those ships from the USA to the various distant theatres of war.

I can well imagine the immense challenge which such a project represents but I know that it will mean a considerable amount to the veterans gathering in the UK and France to see a Liberty ship at the commemorations. May I wish you and your colleagues every success in your venture.

The crew paused to savor the encouraging tone of the letter, then turned back to their tasks.

For many years the volunteers on the *O'Brien* worked one day a week. The deck department came in on Wednesday and the engine department on Thursday. The third weekend of each month was set aside as "steaming weekend," a chance to operate the main engine for the benefit of the public. Steaming weekend became something of a social occasion with some crew arriving Friday night and staying aboard until Sunday afternoon. Often, breakfast, lunch and dinner were prepared on the coal-fired stove in the galley. In the evenings there were cocktails, old movies and stories, some of them true. But now, with the Coast Guard requirements and deadline approaching, a sense of urgency set in. To keep her appointment in Normandy, the *Jeremiah O'Brien* would have to leave San Francisco in April 1994. That was only a few months away. The volunteers began coming to work two and three days a week. The chores multiplied and the social hours diminished.

Publicity was important and the NLSM was pleased to see their ship receive increasing attention. In October 1993 Jerry Carroll, of the *San Francisco Chronicle*, described his trip aboard the *O'Brien* during the annual Fleet Week cruises.

> I boarded the gallant *Jeremiah O'Brien* on Sunday with 250 other sea dogs. It's the only Liberty ship of 2,751 built still able to get about under its own steam. It was saved from the breaker's yard thanks to the efforts of hundreds of volunteers. It took them 14 years, but they scraped the rust off the *O'Brien* and coaxed the frozen engines back to life.
>
> Next year is the 50th anniversary of the Normandy invasion, an event that wouldn't have been possible without the Liberty ships. The volunteers hope to raise enough money to sail the *O'Brien* to France for the big D-Day celebration. If the *O'Brien* volunteers can raise the $2.5 million needed for the voyage, the crew sailing her across the Atlantic will average 71 years old.
>
> They are silver-haired, when there is hair at all, and more than a few are gimpy and hard of hearing, but these Liberty ship veterans still have the kind of quiet capability once the marvel of the world. Yankee ingenuity, it was called, a can-do spirit that moved mountains if they got in the way. Hands-on guys spare of speech, they did their work and moved on to the next job.

The magazine *Steamboat Bill* published a summary of our plans in its Fall 1993 issue:

> Plans and preparations to send *Jeremiah O'Brien* and *Lane Victory* to participate in the 50th Anniversary of the invasion of France are well advanced. The venture, officially known as the "Normandy '94 Convoy Project" now has full support of the Department of Defense World War II Commemoration Committee. The two West Coast ships will leave their home ports in April, 1994, and will meet the Baltimore-based Liberty ship *John W. Brown* in New York for a parade in the harbor before the three-ship convoy leaves for Europe by way of Halifax on May 17. A Canadian naval escort will accompany the ships on their voyage to Southampton for their June 6 trip across the Channel. Amphibious troops aboard the ships will reenact the landings at various beaches. After the ceremonies the three ships

will visit 45 European ports. Cost of the project is estimated to be around $5 million.

That same week, Adm. Tom Patterson, Bob Blake and François Le Pendu, a French-speaking volunteer, went to France and England.

Tom Patterson: "Marci Hooper had made a trip out to England and France in 1992. She met people out there that she had stayed in contact with like Len Sawyer (author of *The Liberty Ships*), and a Frenchman who owns a DUKW*, named Jean-Paul Caron. So, in the summer of 1993, the committee decided that we should go over to meet all these people and make the arrangements for the ship to get there."

They began with a rendezvous in Paris on October 12 with the Minister of France for the — wonderfully named — Ancien Combatants, Monsieur Coesse, and Comtre Amiral (RADM) Pierre Argousse.

Tom Patterson: "Through Jean-Paul Caron, we had asked for an endorsement from the Minister of France, actually from the President, François Mitterrand, that he would invite President Clinton to send the *Jeremiah O'Brien* over there. Well, the way it finally turned out, we got to the third-ranking Minister of France, who is the equivalent of our Vice President. Monsieur Monory issued a letter to Vice President Gore in which he invited the ship to come over, so we did have an official endorsement from the French government."

While in Paris, the *O'Brien* group met with Col. Benedict in the American Embassy who presented them with a list of key people to see and provided an introduction to the American Embassy in London.

The next stop was Arromanches, the focus of the British D-Day landings and site of a commemorative museum, where they met the mayor and other dignitaries. In the D-Day museum Adm. Patterson showed the *O'Brien* film, a video taken during some of

---

* DUKW is one of the few military abbreviations that is not an acronym. The letter D represents the year of the vehicle's design, U indicates it is amphibious, K signifies front-wheel drive and W means rear-wheel drive.

the ship's bay cruises, to an enthusiastic audience. Everyone was eager to see the *Jeremiah O'Brien* arrive for the fiftieth anniversary commemoration.

The American Cemetery at Colleville, near Omaha Beach, was the next call. This was the scene of one of the bloodiest battles of the D-Day landings. Interred there are some 10,000 American servicemen and fourteen American merchant seamen. Superintendent Phil Rivers was highly interested in seeing our ship participate, and pointed out the anchorage at Pointe du Hoc where President Clinton would make his address at the commemoration ceremonies.

The group then went east to Rouen, where they met officials from *L'Armada de la Liberté* and the port. There they received their warmest welcome of the trip. Rouen wanted to make the *Jeremiah O'Brien* the centerpiece of the commemoration, at which they expected 5,000,000 people. The *O'Brien* would hold the position of honor in the center of the line of tall ships from all over the world that would be there for the historic occasion.

From Rouen, our envoys went to Cherbourg, then Adm. Patterson continued to England on his own. On October 20th he met with the First Sea Lord, Sir Benjamin Bathurst, his deputy, Captain Harris, and Commander David Alexander of the British Commemorative Team. Patterson briefed them on the prospective voyage and asked for their help. Sir Benjamin endorsed the voyage and said he would help with every means at his disposal. At every stop copies of *The Last Liberty*, the history of the *Jeremiah O'Brien,* were given to local dignitaries as a souvenir — and a reminder.

Next, Patterson called on Shell Oil Company's operating manager, Capt. David Smith, who agreed to assist in locating fuel in England. There followed a meeting with officials from the Port of London concerning berthing. D. J. Jeffrey, the chief executive, promised his help. The trip was far exceeding the committee's hopes and expectations and morale soared with each report received.

We learned that the British Broadcasting Corporation (BBC) was very interested in covering the arrival of the *O'Brien* in London. The plan was for the *O'Brien* to come alongside *HMS Belfast,* moored in the Thames. Veterans from the British cruiser, which also served at D-Day, and ours would man their respective rails. It promised to be a dramatic event as the two ships tied up side by side, two survivors of the Normandy invasion 50 years past.

The reports got better and better. Patterson met Capt. Allan Swift of the Southampton Institute of Navigation, Her Majesty's equivalent to a U.S. port captain. He confirmed the following itinerary: On arrival from New York, the *Jeremiah O'Brien* would come into Southampton. All the ships of the commemoration ceremony, including fifteen U.S. Navy ships, would assemble on the 4th of June at anchor. The Queen, in a time-honored tradition, would review the gathered fleet from the Royal Yacht *Britannia*, traversing from Spithead into the Solent. On June 5 the ships would sail for Normandy, arriving the following morning. June 6 and 7 would be devoted to 50th Anniversary ceremonies which would be televised around the world.

Returning to London, the admiral met with the United States Naval Forces in Europe, Public Information Officer, Capt. Chuck Conners and Operations Officer Capt. Steve Tinsley. They promised to run interference for the *O'Brien,* help make advance arrangements and get us written into the operations order. This would ensure that the Navy included the *Jeremiah O'Brien* in their plans.

The results of the trip were almost immediate. On October 18 the committee received a copy of a letter from the mayor of Arromanches to the United States Ambassador to France, Mrs. Pamela Harriman:

Madam Ambassador,
I had the great pleasure to meet with the Admiral Thomas J. Patterson; he came to Arromanches to inform us of the project of the participation of the Liberty Ship "*Jeremiah O'Brien*" with its World War II crew in the D-Day 50th Anniversary ceremonies.
The City of Arromanches finds the idea remarkable.

We are extremely enthusiastic about the coming of the "*Jeremiah O'Brien*," a historical monument in the United States, and are certain of the immense success of this operation.

To sight anew on our Normandy coast, a Liberty ship loaded with war history and its crew of veterans that took part, with bravery and generosity in the liberation of our homeland. How symbolic!!!

I have accordingly, the honor of extending an official invitation to this Liberty ship to join for our June 1994 celebrations.

The City of Arromanches would be particularly touched, if Madam Ambassador could be present at the time of the ceremonies, between June 4 and 7, 1994, to honor our Liberators.

Very truly yours,
The Mayor
Dr. Jean-Paul Lecomte

And later that same month:

To: Captain of Vessels Tomanelli
Naval Attache
U.S. Embassy
2 Avenue Gabriel
75008 Paris

Paris, the end of October

Commandant,

I recently received an American Delegation, who came to present the project of the participation of the *Jeremiah O'Brien* in the commemorative ceremonies of the 50th Anniversary of the Allied Landings.

I wish to make known to you how perfectly essential the presence of this Liberty ship during these demonstrations are, with regard to the historical symbolism and to the quality of the conservation of this ship.

I hope that the coming of the *Jeremiah O'Brien* will be assured.

Very Truly yours,

Louis de Catuelan
Senator of Yvelines
Co-President

And from the Port of London Authority, dated November 2, 1993:

Dear Adm. Patterson:

My attention has been drawn to the commemoration next year of the landings on the beaches of Normandy and the proposed visit of the *SS Jeremiah O'Brien.*

I am pleased to say that we not only welcome the visit but will wish to do all that we can to facilitate it.

I note that you have already had preliminary discussions with my staff in regard to the likely berthing requirements and of course navigation through our waters to a central London berth. I have asked my staff to do all that they can to accommodate the *Jeremiah O'Brien* to meet your wishes as far as we can.

Turning to costs, I am aware that you have been quoted our normal charges for commercial vessels visiting the Pool of London. However, the 50th Anniversary is a timely reminder of the sacrifices that those directly involved, as well as the people of London, made in bringing a successful conclusion to the war. I am therefore delighted to be able to offer to waive all of our pilotage, conservancy and berthing charges for the proposed visit.

My staff are ready to do all they can to help but if any fundamental problems do arise that you feel should be drawn to my attention then please feel free to contact me.

D J Jeffrey
Chief Executive

The letters were eloquent affirmation, on the highest levels of these nations, of the great vision that began at the table in the gunners' mess seven years before.

Meanwhile, back home, most of the funding hopes for the voyage rested with the "Scrap Ship Bill." As the bill worked its way through Congress, the committee's hopes rose and fell with every rumor but by November 5 a cautious sense of optimism began to be felt. HR-58, as the bill was known, finally passed out of the Merchant Marine and Fisheries Committee of the House of Representatives and was reported to the House floor. David Richardson, special assistant to Helen Bentley, confidently said it would pass. The companion piece, Senate Bill 1605, was being introduced by Senator Barbara Mikulski of Maryland, the Senate

Democratic leader. Senator John Breaux from Louisiana, who chaired the Subcommittee on Commerce, Science and Transportation, had pledged his support.

Almost all the volunteers were eager to be on the trip, but some were against it. Dick Brannon: "Doug Dickie [the ship's chief engineer] asked me some weeks before, when the talk got very, very hot about the ship going to Normandy, about the plan. You know, Marci and all the shoreside people had gone to Europe and laid all the groundwork, really actively planning for the trip. So everybody knew that it was getting red-hot but nobody knew firm. And Doug told me, he asked me, he says, 'If they make that trip, do you really want to go on that trip?'

"I said, 'Doug, I'm a completely open mind. If they want me to go, I'll go.'

"And he says, 'My God', he says, 'I'm so opposed to this trip,' and 'it's terrible.' All the negatives, all the negatives. And he said, 'Boy, if this ship has to go, I will not be aboard. I'm not going to make the trip. I don't approve of it. I think they're nuts, absolutely nuts to do it.'

"He fought every step of the way, every way he could to discourage us. And the guys, you know, the crew that's still here today, they said, 'Doug, why don't you wake up to reality.' They're pushing for this trip.

"NO, blah, blah, blah, And somebody, I think it was Richard Hill, jokingly, he said, 'Doug, you're against this, you're against that. Oh, but you want to stay on the ship, you like the job, but you're fighting against the tide. When are you going to retire anyway?'

"And Doug says, 'I'm never going to retire. They're going to have to haul me off this ship feet first and put me in a coffin. I'm never going to retire.' Next breath he tells me if it goes to Europe he will not be on the ship. The thing was on a very iffy state of thoughts at the time."

As we drew closer to the "Go-No Go" decision date crew speculation increased. Will we? Won't we? Who? What? When? Adm. Patterson decided to put a stop to all the rumors.

Dick Brannon: "On November thirteenth at a big meeting in number two hold there was announced a special crew meeting, bring your family, bring your friends and everything. Tom Patterson got up and addressed the crew; there must have been about two hundred people there. Number two was jam-packed 'cause the talk had been so much, it was so, God, it was a common topic of conversation. All '93, talk, 'I was going, are we going, if we're going,' etcetera, conversation up the ying-yang, every coffee session, every bullshit session, are we going or aren't we. And November thirteenth Tom set it all to rest. He said, 'I want to announce to you now that the trip to Normandy is on, it's firm. It's no longer If we're going to go or When we're going to go, the trip is on. Gear your thinking to the fact the ship will go to Normandy. Clear the air.'"

Spirits lifted once the decision was made we were definitely going to Normandy. Here Charley Mooney, right, seems to be pointing to Clarence Rocha, far left, saying, "He's going." Ken Murray in the center looks for Clarence's reaction. Photo by Mike Emery

2

GREAT
EXPECTATIONS

Tom Patterson's announcement released a maelstrom of activity. That same afternoon the first department head meeting was called. It was held in the officers' saloon, or messroom, the largest room on the ship, located on the main deck, forward in the midships house. The saloon contains a long, green settee on the forward bulkhead under three portholes which overlook no. 3 hatch. Lengthwise against the settee are three tables, each with two swivel seats, allowing four people to sit at each table, two on the seats and two on the settee. Against the after bulkhead of the room, just inside one entrance is another table, set fore and aft, with four swivel seats. On the same bulkhead at the other entrance is a wooden buffet. All sixteen places were occupied and even the in-between areas on the settee were taken. Capt. George Jahn opened the meeting by announcing that Doug Dickie had resigned as chief engineer and was being replaced by Dick Brannon.

The new head of the engineering department recalled it this way: "To this day, I don't know what actually happened 'cause I wasn't involved in the administration but Doug Dickie was no longer chief engineer and George Jahn asked me. Very briefly he said, 'Are you available, you want the job?'

"And I couldn't believe it. What, what, what? Yeah, sure, well, OK. Dickie is out and I'm the chief engineer. So, that's all I know. What happened behind closed doors, I have no idea. I didn't ask for it, I didn't make an application, nothing. They looked around, there was literally no retired chief engineer locally in San Francisco. They didn't want to advertise nationwide, they wanted a guy, a local guy who was familiar with the ship. So I said, what the hell, I guess I better go along with it. Captain Jahn wants me to take the job, OK, who am I to argue. So it was very low key, undramatic. It's just that there was a vacuum here, they had to have a guy. And the rest is history."

"So Doug came up here, packed his personal gear, drove his car down to the gangway, and moved off and didn't say good-bye or nothing. He was just extremely bitter and crushed and unhappy.

George Jahn started his seagoing career as a cook's helper on tugboats with his father. After high school he sailed as ordinary seaman, AB and quartermaster in the Sailor's Union of the Pacific. Receiving his mate's license before World War II, he was torpedoed on the Matson ship *Manini* just a few days after Pearl Harbor. He was later master of the Liberty ship *William Matson* and took part in the Normandy invasion. After working for Matson he became a tug master, then pilot, for Red Stack Towing Company. Eventually his career took him to independent piloting, where he achieved a reputation for skill unsurpassed on the West Coast. Capt. Jahn and his wife, Pat, reside in San Francisco.

"He fought it to the bitter end. He fought the trip but he fought to stay on the ship. That placed him in a very untenable situation."

Doug Dickie was perhaps more vocal than some others but enthusiasm among the crew for the voyage was not universal. There were some who firmly believed the ship would never leave San Francisco Bay. But even among the detractors, many set aside their opinions and willingly worked long hours right up to the time of sailing.

Bob Burnett, carpenter: "There were times I absolutely thought we wouldn't go. There we were talking the story, but I think there was always room for doubt. We had such incredible obstacles ahead of us, not the least of which was finances. And I had a lot of concern about getting things done in the time we had to get them done. We were not seeming to resolve the problems that needed resolving, putting things off until almost too late, things that needed to be done. The main concern was about the uncertainty of money. We would have been a lot better off if things were done ahead of time, but the lack of funding didn't allow for that."

Russ Mosholder headed up the steward's department, accepting the position of chief steward. Capt. John Paul, who as chief mate had headed the deck department for a number of years, continued in that capacity. Everyone knew that from this point on "business as usual" would have to give way to "get the job done."

For years the crew had stockpiled spare parts, unused equipment and replacement machinery in the *O'Brien*'s lower holds. They had become expert "scroungers," collecting no-longer-produced ship parts from wherever they could beg, borrow or steal, stockpiling them for future use. But now, most of the hoard had to be removed. The lower holds were needed to stow ballast and while it was perfectly fine to leave things sitting loose in the holds when the *O'Brien* cruised the protected waters of San Francisco Bay, the open seas encountered on an 18,000-mile trip were another matter. An inventory was requested from each department listing all items to remain aboard ship, those to be stored ashore and those to be disposed of.

> Dick Brannon graduated from the California Maritime Academy in 1938. Sailing as a licensed engineer for American President Lines, he worked his way up from third assistant to chief engineer in their around-the-world and transpacific services on everything from Liberty ships to passenger liners. Retiring from APL in 1981, he became an active volunteer with the *Jeremiah O'Brien* and, except for serving two years as a consultant to the Del Monte Corporation on a shipbuilding project in Seville, Spain, has been with the ship since. He has a life-long fascination with all things Spanish and when interviewed during the voyage for this book, was reading the biography of Gaspar de Portola in Spanish. He and his wife live in Pacifica, California.

Department heads were told to interview their personnel to find out who could make the voyage. The entire trip would take approximately six months and be divided into five legs.

Ernie Murdock issued a worklist of items needing attention. Clearly, he knew about the announcement beforehand. His worklist was dated two days earlier.

Deck Department

1 Prepare lifeboats for examination and inspection by USCG including the following:

   a. Testing of air tanks.

   b. Weight testing of boats and davits.

   c. Inventory and assembling of all gear and fittings.

   d. Prepare listings of any missing equipment, repairs or replacements required on air tanks, fuel tanks, and provision storage tanks.

2 Assist in inventory of all loose gear in former cargo spaces.

3 Remove all excess items from #3 Upper Tween Deck except spare shaft.

4 Remove all unserviceable non USCG-approved life ring buoys from ship. Stencil all serviceable ring buoys as required by USCG. All ring buoys to be properly mounted and maintained. (Engine Dept involved in procuring and mounting ring buoy brackets).

5 Complete an updated ship's Emergency Plan and post as required.

6 Strip and paint out #2 Hold Upper Tween Decks.

7 Prepare listing of parts and supplies needed for 6 month voyage.

Engine Department

1 Repair all required reach rods for remote activation of valves.

2 Remove all boiler mountings for examination by USCG Marine Inspectors. Prepare boilers for internal and external examination. Apply hydrostatic test pressures on the boilers and piping as required by the Coast Guard regulations. Prove proper operation of safety and relief valves.

3 Hydrostatically test all other pressure vessels as required by the USCG.

4 Make permanent repairs to any defective bilge piping.

5 Prepare all cofferdams and void tanks for internal examination.

6 Prepare inventory of all spare parts.

7 Prove proper operation of bilge system serving cargo spaces.

8   Open all overboard discharge valves above the waterline for inspection.
9   Procure or fabricate ten (10) each holders for 30" life ring buoys. Install holders in locations as designated by USCG.
10   Prepare list of parts and supplies as needed by USCG.

Stewards Department
1   Paint the Galley.
2   Prepare current inventory of supplies and equipment.
3   Prepare list of items needed for 6 months voyage.

Obviously Ernie had been thinking about this for some time.

The voyage itinerary given out at this time was: April 14, depart San Francisco. May 20, arrive Portsmouth. June 4, arrive at Spithead anchorage. June 5, depart for Normandy beachhead. June 6, commemorations at Pointe du Hoc and Omaha Beach. June 7, demonstrate loading cargo into DUKWs. June 8, arrive at Chatham. June 15, arrive in London. June 22, arrive at Fowey, Cornwall. July 2, arrive at Cherbourg. July 10 arrive at Rouen. July 17, arrive at Le Havre. July 21, arrive at Londonderry, Northern Ireland. July 25 depart for Portland, Maine. August through September, visit ports on East and Gulf Coasts. October 8, enter San Francisco Bay.

In auspicious timing Adm. Patterson received a response to a letter written months before. Dated November 16, 1993 it was from General Kicklighter:

Dear Admiral Patterson:
Thank you for your letter of June 3, 1993 to President Clinton concerning your plans to represent the United States Merchant Marine at the 50th Anniversary of D-Day being held in England and France June 1994. Your efforts on behalf of the United States Merchant Marine are most welcome. As the SS *Jeremiah O'Brien* made eleven channel crossings in support of the invasion, it is important that the *O'Brien* represent the U. S. Merchant Marine at Portsmouth, England, on June 5, 1994.

As you seek assistance for your Commemorative Convoy, remember the SS *Jeremiah O'Brien* is a federal vessel owned by the Maritime Administration, on loan to the Department of the Interior, and is entitled to transfers of excess government property. In addition, the expected passage of HR-58 will provide you much of the funds needed to repair the *O'Brien* for the voyage.

I look forward to the *SS Jeremiah O'Brien* representing the U.S. Merchant Marine at the D-Day Commemorations in England and France in 1994.

Very Respectfully,
Claude M. Kicklighter
Lieutenant General, USA Retired
Executive Director

"Excess government property" was a possible source of "in kind" contributions of equipment. This is a provision in federal law whereby one government agency can transfer supplies and equipment to another. It would eventually save us over $100,000 in expenses.

References to the ceremonies for the 50th Anniversary of D-Day began appearing in news articles and periodicals, heightening the crew's anticipation and spurring their efforts. Maupintour's 1994 catalogue for Continental Europe (published in late 1993) included a "World War II: The Western Front" tour "Commemorating the 50th anniversary of D-Day." Cruise lines advertised cruises to the English Channel for a front seat view of "D-Day Plus 50 Years."

Interviews were already well underway of volunteers wishing to make the Normandy trip. The word was out and eager future crew members burned up the telephone wires. The trip would be a major commitment for up to six months away from home and family with hard work and no pay. Most of the volunteers were retired and had the time, but problems of age and health had to be considered. The younger volunteers had jobs and other responsibilities. For everyone, the unqualified support of their wives was vital. Their families, too, would be making a major commitment. Yet, the inquires and applications flooded in. Initially, first priority was given to those who had the most amount of volunteer time and were willing to make the entire voyage.

More work projects surfaced that weren't on Ernie Murdock's original list: clean out the deep tanks, install gaskets for all watertight doors, make operational the bridge deck toilet, backflush the bilges, inspect and replace the hatch boards, put the evaporators into service, secure all water sources, repair ceilings in the lower holds, repair the feed water regulator, be sure the paint lockers meet Coast Guard requirements, determine license requirements for all hands. . .

The trip to the Suisun Bay (California) Reserve Fleet to identify and remove ship parts under the "excess government property" provision was fruitful. The crew brought back or set aside for future use: lifeboat gear, a wood vise, light sockets, rigging, ring buoys, oars, provision tanks, a battery tray, lifeboat transmitter, tachometer gear, fathometer spare parts, two shots of anchor chain and a connecting link, linens and utensils for the steward's department and 28 cots. It was a good "haul."

As preparations for the great voyage continued, I cast about for a way to become part of the volunteer crew. My book on the O'Brien's history from her launching in 1943 to the summer of 1993 included an epilogue describing the plans for the Normandy trip. It would be "a dream come true" to make the voyage, both personally and professionally.

At the 1993 crew Christmas party, I asked Adm. Patterson the fateful question, "What are my chances of making part of the voyage?"

"How much of the trip could you make?" he asked, but turned to look at my wife, who was standing beside me. She, bless her, said, "the whole voyage, if he wants." From that moment, in addition to being historian, I was officially second mate for the voyage.

Ballasting for the trip continued to raise questions. Where would we get it? In which holds would it be placed and from what dock would it be loaded? Will our cargo gear be certified for this purpose or will a barge crane be needed? Will lead ballast come from Bremerton? Would the commanding officer at Bremerton release it? Ballasting was a major concern. A totally empty ship will snap and bounce viciously in a rough sea. Ballast was essential to pull the ship down into the water, so it could ride more as part of the ocean rather than above it. Someone jokingly referred to the problem as "getting the lead out."

The work list got longer: install temporary radar mast, prepare oil tanks, clean and inspect void compartments, clean no. 1 and no. 2 deep tanks, prove the salt water circulating system operable, remove and examine the anchor chain, repair interior gussets and stays on the stack, inspect boiler mountings. . .

In December the pace quickened. On the 10th a memo went out from Ernie Murdock, "In the new year we will have work parties lasting several days and people will be staying on board."

Donations for everything from fuel oil to pilot ladders to toothpicks to brooms to stores to valves to satellite communicators were sought. In the NLSM office, Marci Hooper, the business manager, Karen Kamimoto, the interim bookkeeper and the volunteers began the complex project of ensuring that donors were recognized and thanked and their donations logged so that we would know what and how much we had, what we still needed and how much more we had to find, raise, borrow and beg.

The local PBS station's December Pledge Drive was one example of volunteers helping each other. Sandy Shaw, manager of KQED volunteer services, said the *O'Brien* crew manning the phones helped raise more than $10,000 for the station. In return, the station broadcast interviews with the crew about the voyage which drew attention to the ship, bringing in additional funding.

Ballast remained a big problem. How would we get the promised lead from Bremerton to San Francisco Bay? By truck? By MSC ship? By barge? The lead was awkward to handle, being stored on standard 4' x 4' pallets in 3-1/4" x 3-1/4" x 17" ingots, and weighing one ton per pallet. Prices quoted ranged up to $150,000, far beyond our means.

. . . clean port and starboard potable water tanks, repair bilge piping, make operable the after house hot water system, repair valves on the no. 1 and no. 2 DC generator, megger all generators, install two mast lights for canal passage, install rudder angle indicators, obtain a satellite navigation system, radar, and weather fax, three 25-person life rafts with quick-acting releases and ring buoys. . .

Bill Duncan, crew chairman, pointed out that we had only eighty-four work days remaining, but just the projects already lined up totaled 373 man-days. This list did not include the unforeseen problems that would inevitably arise. To finish on time would translate to five men working every day, six days a week. He suggested that groups begin staying overnight to lengthen the work day. Chief Steward Russ Mosholder agreed to be available after the first of January to feed those who remained on board.

And again the ballast problem. If the financing problem could be resolved, it was estimated that at 172 lifts per day, 161 hours would be required to complete the task, which converts to ten sixteen-hour days. A berth would be needed which had available cranes and longshoremen. While we worked on the problem, alternate plans to get the needed weight were suggested. We might carry cargo — government or commercial. Chevron at Le Havre could perhaps provide a cargo of oil drums for the return trip. Four-ton loads of keel blocks, located in a nearby abandoned shipyard, were mentioned.

Interviews of volunteer crew continued, including medical history and clearance, then their ability to get required documents. Capt. Murdock had prevailed with the Coast Guard to be lenient in issuing crew certificates for the voyage. Training programs, including classes in cargo loading, lifesaving, lifeboat handling, firefighting, damage control and radar were developed.

. . . prepare the galley for major meal service, emergency lighting, gasoline for lifeboats, inspect and clean port boiler, get navigation charts, hatch tarps, ring buoys, install revolution counter, repair sound-powered telephones, test general alarm, inventory lifeboat gear, get spare piping, steel stock, threaded stock, boiler tubes. . .

Even as the crew and office staff worked, however, an undercurrent of anxiety was always present. The "Scrap Ship Bill" seemed to be stalled in Congress. The Fall months had passed and the bill was still stuck in committee while the Congress struggled with the budget and cutting the deficit. Now, they were to adjourn for the holidays. Without the funds from sale of the scrap ships, the whole project was doomed. Appeals and entreaties flooded our representatives in Congress.

Finally, with an eleventh hour press from Representative Helen Bentley with California Senators Dianne Feinstein and Barbara Boxer, the bill made it through. On December 23, 1993, Tom Patterson announced that President Clinton had signed into law the Liberty Ship Memorial Act of 1993. [see appendix D]. The *Vallejo* (California) *Times-Herald* was first to carry a report on the significance of the Act to the voyage.

SAN FRANCISCO -- The countdown to D-Day has started again for the *SS Jeremiah O'Brien*, the only operating survivor of the fleet of 5,000 that took part in the epic Normandy invasion of World War II.

President Clinton has signed the Liberty Memorial Act, legislation designed to help the *O'Brien* and two other ships sail to France to take part in festivities commemorating the 50th anniversary of the June 6, 1944 invasion that was the beginning of the end of Hitler's Third Reich.

During the invasion in 1944, the *O'Brien* hauled troops, cargo and the K-9 corps to Omaha and Utah beaches.

The rest of the ships in the invasion fleet have either been broken up for scrap or serve as museums and are not operational. In contrast, the *O'Brien,* a tourist attraction near Fisherman's Wharf, occasionally sets sail on San Francisco Bay.

The *O'Brien* had been docked in Suisun Bay's Mothball Fleet until October 1979 when a grassroots campaign to return it to sailing status began with its transfer to the Bethlehem Steel Corp. yard in San Francisco.

Selling off other ships for scrap is exactly what the law signed last week by the president will do to get the *O'Brien* off the French Coast by June 6, 1994, according to Marci Hooper, spokeswoman for the ship.

The legislation authorizes the federal Maritime Administration to donate surplus ships to groups that maintain the *O'Brien* and two other World War II merchant marine vessels, the *John W. Brown*, a Liberty ship in Baltimore, and the *Lane Victory* in San Pedro. Neither of the other ships served at Normandy.

The groups must sell off the old ships for scrap to raise funds to get the *O'Brien, Brown* and *Lane* in shape so they can be among the backdrop of ships assembled for Clinton's commemorative speech at Normandy.

"In Europe, June 6 is a very big day," said Donald MacLean, office manager of the *Lane Victory*. "It's the day their liberty started. Unfortunately, it's not a big day here."

Backers hope to raise a total of $2.5 million for the trip.

The fund raisers include a New Year's party aboard the Liberty ship that's billed as a trip to the past. "At midnight, you'll wonder if it's 1994 or 1944," said Hooper. "A big band will be jumping with songs of the '40s. We'll even have crooners, jitterbuggers and an old-fashioned radio show."

Preferred dress, of course, is military.

The next department head meeting was abuzz with the news. The bidding for the sale of vessels from the Reserve fleet would open on the 11th of January and close on the 17th. Cash from the sale could be expected around the end of the month, only ten weeks before the ship must sail.

. . . new wiring for the gyro and emergency light system, keys for crew members to secure personal belongings in cabins, a slop chest to supply crew necessities en route, a means of handling crew money, get cleaning supplies, rags, sawdust, paper, staples, detergent. . .

With time remaining becoming more and more of a factor, we began looking for additional labor. The California prison facility in the nearby community of Dublin was suggested. It was thought they might supply workers for some of our heavier and dirtier projects.

At the January 4 Normandy Committee meeting, Tom Patterson handed out additional committee assignments. His list of who was to do what covered ten pages. Crew chairman Bill Duncan issued a memo advising everyone which forms and documents they would have to have on the voyage. The deadline to accomplish all requirements was March 1, 1994. Included were:

Complete a current Physical Examination using USCG form #719K, REV5-87 (Supporting document requesting a waiver for a disqualifying condition must be attached). Provide a current "Drug Free" certificate, as required by USCG. Complete all training/exams, etc. required for certification. Have all current documentation, license, etc. required by USCG for your current position. Provide two copies of each document to your dept. head for your personnel files: U.S.

Merchant Mariners Documents, Licenses, Certifications, Physical Exam, Drug Free Certificate, Medical History from your Physician, Complete a "Personnel Information Summary" form whenever you have completed all USCG requirements and have all documentation needed. Provide a duplicate of the completed form for your personnel file. Upon completion of the items above, review and finalize the sections of the voyage you are requesting. This will be a firm and final commitment to your dept. head for the voyage. Have a current U. S. passport for travel to foreign ports.

Coast Guard requirements and SOLAS limit the size of the crew to the capacity of the lifeboats on one side of the ship. The *O'Brien* has four lifeboats, two on each side. The forward one is a motor lifeboat. Since part of the space in the forward boat is taken up by the motor, it has a smaller capacity than the other, twenty-five. The after boat is propelled by oars and rated to carry thirty-one. This set the size of our crew at a maximum of fifty-six.

Despite a volunteer list of more than two hundred and another two hundred that submitted applications for the trip, we had a hard time filling some jobs that required special skills. The only previous cooking on board had been by volunteers on steaming weekend so there wasn't as large a group of experienced stewards and cooks to draw from as there were sailors and black gang.*

> Bill Duncan's father was a chief engineer for Napier Line in the British merchant marine. Bill was born in Linden, New Jersey. In 1943 he went into the National Guard and was assigned to the 69th Infantry Division. Entering the European theater at Rouen, France, in January of 1945, he went into the front lines at the Siegfried Line, Malmedy, Belgium. Recalled into the Army for the Korean war in 1950, he was discharged in 1953, then was recalled again for the Berlin and Cuban missile crises. Bill was discharged from the Army in 1976 as a Lt. Col. He went to work for the Merck Company, retiring in 1987. Bill moved to California where he became a volunteer on the *Jeremiah O'Brien* and is now on the Board of Directors for the NLSM. He and his wife, Dottie, reside in Alameda, California.

---

*The term "black gang" comes from the days of coal-fired ships when the stokers' shovels kept a constant cloud of black coal dust suspended in the engine room. Anyone working there came up covered with coal dust. Occasionally the term is used to refer only to unlicensed engine room personnel, but in this case it refers to all ratings.

Other crewing problems were developing. Because some were taking leaves of absence from jobs or because of medical restrictions or financial considerations, many could not make the entire trip. Additional volunteers would also be needed at various ports to run the ship's gift shop, which was expected to be a strong profit center for the voyage. Where would these people sleep if all the accommodations were taken by the on-board crew? Also, in consideration for age and the extreme temperatures in the engine room in the tropics, the engine department decided to stand 3-hour watches instead of the traditional 4-hour watch. This meant we would be carrying an additional watch of engineers, consisting of a licensed engineer, a fireman/watertender and an oiler. Where would they sleep? Someone had to start assigning cabins, bunks and lockers. Everyone agreed that, yes, someone should do that, then went on to other topics.

Meanwhile, Tom Patterson and Ernie Murdock had business in Washington, D.C. On January 10 they had a conference with the new Maritime Administrator, Vice-Admiral (Ret.) Albert J. Herberger and his staff. They reported the *O'Brien*'s progress and asked him to expedite the papers that would transfer the Victory (scrap) ships under the Liberty Ship Memorial Act.

On January 11 Patterson, along with Clint Johnson of the *Lane Victory* and Capt. Brian Hope from the *John W. Brown,* met General Claude M. Kicklighter for a conference with the *USS George Washington* battle group, commander RADM Albert Kredich, USN, and the commanding officer of the nuclear carrier *USS George Washington.* Capt. Charles Connors, representing U.S. Naval Forces in Europe briefed the group:

On June 3 President Clinton would come aboard the *USS George Washington* at Portsmouth. Then the ships would shift out to anchorage on the Solent off Spithead. On June 5 the *Royal Yacht Britannia* with the queen of England, the president of the United States, the president of France and other dignitaries would review veterans assembled aboard the anchored fleet. This fleet would include the units of the *USS George Washington* battle group, the *SS Jeremiah O'Brien*, the *SS John W. Brown*, and the *SS Lane Victory*. At 1700 the ships would get underway and proceed to the Normandy beaches. The *George Washington* battle group, the two Libertys and the Victory would be anchored off Omaha beach on a line of bearing with Pointe du Hoc. On the morning of June 6, the 50th Anniversary of D-Day, there would be a sunrise ceremony held aboard the *USS George Washington* with American WWII veterans, presided over by President Clinton. Then the president would fly to Pointe du Hoc for a memorial service in honor of American forces buried in the nearby Colleville cemetery. The president would speak at a joint U.S. and French memorial service at Utah beach. The United States Merchant Marine would be included with all of the armed forces at each of these memorial services.

The crew aboard the *O'Brien* eagerly received Patterson's reports and pored over the schedule of ceremonies. This was really going to be a great historic occasion, and they were more determined than ever that their ship was going to be there.

. . . install washing machines, renew gaskets, run new piping to sanitary tank, install wiring, test oil-water separator, repair lifeboat air tanks, locate flags, test refrigeration system, run wiring and piping to generator. . .

In Maine, the *O'Brien*'s birthplace, the following article, dated January 16, appeared in the *Sunday Sun-Journal,* published in Lewistown:

He was a Mainer and a Revolutionary War Hero. A Maine State Park at Machias is named for him, and his name lived in the history of World War II. This year his name will live again in the 50th anniversary observance of the Allied liberation of France. He was Jeremiah O'Brien, and a ship bearing his name and built in Maine participated in the June 1944 Normandy invasion and is expected to return there this year. O'Brien was a staunch Revolutionary War patriot. He and other men of the Machias area won what is called "The First Naval Battle of the Revolution." They captured the British ship "*Margaretta*" in Machias Bay on June 12, 1775. O'Brien was chosen to supervise preparation of an earthen gun battery on the river below Machias in anticipation of British retaliation. The Machias men did not have long to wait. The month after the loss of their ship, the British sent the "*Tatmagouch*" and the "*Diligence*" to retake the captured ship. Without resisting, the vessels surrendered — to Capt. Jeremiah O'Brien. That was the start of O'Brien's trek through history.

Produced in South Portland

During World War II, workers at 18 U.S. shipyards built 2,751 Liberty ships to carry troops and supplies to theaters of operations around the world. The Liberty ship was born of the wartime need for vast fleets of cargo vessels. It was a workhorse, no great speed, designed to be built fast from the keel up, no luxury, just space for cargo (human or machine) and power to get there. The South Portland Shipyard built 236 of the vessels during World War II. One of them, launched June 19, 1943, was christened the *SS Jeremiah O'Brien.*

After World War II, the *O'Brien* was mothballed in Suisun Bay near San Francisco until 1979, when it was reconditioned by a volunteer group of merchant mariners. Congress made the ship a National Historic Landmark in 1980 and it has been berthed at Pier 3 on the San Francisco waterfront at the National Liberty Ship Memorial.

Marci Hooper of the Liberty Ship Memorial says the *O'Brien* "is the last unaltered operational Liberty ship in the world." Now, the Liberty Ship Memorial at Fort Mason in San Francisco hopes to raise enough funds to send the ship back to Normandy this year.

When a fleet of ships from what were the Allied nations of World War II sail across the English Channel this coming June 5 as part of the anniversary observance, if the *O'Brien* is there, it will be the only vessel in the fleet that was part of the Normandy operation a half-century ago, says Hooper. The *O'Brien* is scheduled to sail from San Francisco April 2 and dock at Portsmouth, England, about May 20. British and French authorities have indicated their cooperation in making the *O'Brien* a "star" in the anniversary observance.

Ed Langlois, president of the South Portland Shipyard Society, says there is a possibility the *O'Brien* may sail into Portland on its return trip, but at this point the visit is uncertain.

A history of service

Just as Jeremiah O'Brien served the fledgling nation during the Revolution, the ship bearing his name served the country in the invasion of France. The *O'Brien* sailed from New York April 12, 1944, and docked at Newport, Wales, 16 days later. After a trip to Scotland, it went to Southampton and on June 9, 1944 (three days after D-Day), it sailed across the English Channel, anchoring off Omaha Beach the next day. The ship carried troops and trucks on 11 shuttle trips back and forth across the Channel before eventually leaving Europe for home. Off Omaha Beach, the vessel came under fire at night, said Thomas McGeehan of Mountain Top, Penn. "The Navy ordered merchant ships not to fire," said McGeehan, "because the Navy gunners on board would fire too low and shoot away their ship's rigging. That didn't happen to the *O'Brien*," he said in an interview last week, "but a lot of ships had to return to England for refitting. You can't unload cargo with no rigging." McGeehan was a student at the King's Point Merchant Marine Academy and served as a deck cadet on the *O'Brien*. He left the sea after the war and took up a career in railroading.

Ballast continued to be the no. 2 topic *du jour* (no. 1 was always funding). In late January it was reported that an MSC ship, the *Wabash,* was loading lead pallets for the *O'Brien* in Puget Sound. The quantity, originally thought to be 5,000 tons, was later reduced to 3,500 tons and now, in actuality, was 1,000 tons. It was being loaned to the ship and was scheduled to arrive on the 28th. The use of shore cranes and Maersk Line (a Danish-flag steamship company and one of the largest in the world) stevedore labor to remove and store the lead until the *O'Brien* was ready for it was arranged, another generous donation. We were now "only" 2,500 tons short of the optimum amount of ballast needed for the voyage. Ideas popped up at every department head meeting: cement blocks from Hunters Point Naval Shipyard, bagged rice, sugar and potatoes for the 'tween deck space, sand in open hoppers, propeller shafts and anchor chain. Given our financial status, each suggestion had to meet the criterion of cheapness. Even "free" ballast had money attached in the form of labor and machinery costs to transport and load it.

Tom Patterson: "Every project that we took on became its own separate challenge. For example, the ballasting of the ship. We went all over trying to find the right kind of ballast. There were keel blocks from Hunter's Point Naval Shipyard, but they were too big. We had information about the Navy having surplus lead, and that took a couple of months to resolve. It took calling back to Washington, D.C., to the rear admiral in charge of Naval Sea Systems command, who was in charge of installation and logistics, to find out where the lead resided up in Puget Sound Naval Shipyard. Then we didn't get the amount that we requested. We had to settle for 1,000 tons instead of 3,500 tons. Then we had to arrange for transportation down which we ultimately got from a Navy ship from Logistics Group One. That was another separate effort, to get the transportation . . ."

We were now past the January drydock date. A new pre-voyage schedule was put out. Drydock was scheduled for the 24th of February, continuing for two weeks. The inclining test was scheduled to occur early in March and, afterward, a tour of the Bay to adjust the compass. The fuel, coming by barge, was scheduled for approximately the 13th, 14th and 15th of March. Then would follow sea trials with the ship scheduled to depart San Francisco April 14.

On January 26 we shifted the ship to one of the government piers at Alameda, across the Bay from San Francisco. The Navy supplied two pilots to move the ship and the services of two Navy tugs, free.

. . . door keys. Crew rooms were fastened with locksets that took large, old-fashioned brass keys, the kind you see jailers using in western movies. To preserve historical accuracy, we had to order spares so the crew could lock their doors when they went ashore in foreign ports. The cost was estimated at $850. . .

At one of the department head meetings, I was suddenly made safety officer. By now, despite my best attempt to shrink into the woodwork when Tom Patterson and Ernie Murdock looked around for volunteers, my second mate duties had expanded to include safety, keeping a historical record and training. The others fared no better. We all had added responsibilities.

We made progress in some areas and none in others. It's one of the facts of working with volunteers that they have to be willing to do a job. For example, cleaning out the forward deep tanks was a dark, dirty, thankless task, yet the tanks had to be cleaned for the ship to pass inspection and to carry water ballast and drinking water. On a Navy ship, you would simply order some sailors to do the job and it would get done. On a merchant ship, the crew would have to do it or be fired. But in a volunteer organization, you have to ask, beg, cajole. If no one wants to do it, it doesn't get done. We decided to contract out the work on the forward deep tanks.

A different problem concerned the generators. Alternating current was needed to operate the radars. The ship's obsolete system was set up for direct current. We would solve this prob-

Bill Bennett, left and Bob Burnett, center, removing hatch beams to give access to extra equipment going ashore for storage in Alameda.   Photo by Bruce McMurtry.

lem later, in an unforeseen manner, through the efforts of someone most of us had never heard of before, a dynamo named Anna Falche.

Anna Falche: "What really got me interested in the *Jeremiah* was that Tom Patterson had asked me to help on getting ready for this voyage. I said I would help as much as I could, but I was just really too overworked in my own business. He had said, 'Lend a little help,' and I said, 'Fine.' So I came down to the ship one day with the Texaco rep and watched the crew come up for lunch with their brown paper bags and saw the commitment these men have. And I thought, here are these guys that are really dedicated. I just thought, you owe it to them. These are men that have never asked us to help. They have never really done anything but put into the system and never taken out anything in return, and never expected anything in return. I said, 'It's time that we give them the dignity

them the dignity that they've really justly deserved and we should be very proud of all they stood for and what they've done.'"

. . . drydock, inspect fire and safety equipment, cargo handling equipment, cargo spaces, communications equipment, main propulsion, auxiliary equipment, fuel capacity, refueling points, water capacity, stewards stores, officers' names and experience, number of junior officers, number of crew, rotation plan, other persons aboard, waivers, medical provisions, general specifications, cargo to be carried, where loading and discharge would take place, cargo plan, intended stevedores, emergency plans — watch, quarter & station bill, drills, towing plans, convoy plans, navigation and mooring plans, communications plan, stores and replenishment, agents, in-port security, lists of other agencies involved with the voyage, coordination with the *Lane Victory,* Certification from the Coast Guard, ABS and FCC. . .

On February 2, the National Maritime Historical Society, publisher of *Sea History* magazine, sent a letter to its entire mailing list encouraging them to support the *O'Brien:*

> The National Maritime Historical Society invites your attention to the enclosed invitation from the *SS Jeremiah O'Brien.* "The spirit and pride of America" is what the *Jeremiah O'Brien* people say is at stake in the voyage of their ship to the Normandy beaches to mark the 50th anniversary of D-Day on 6 June this year.
>
> Our Society says that the *O'Brien*'s people are right! And they've earned that right, through their dedication, drive and nearly half a million hours of freely donated labor to keep their vessel open to the public and steaming San Francisco Bay as a living memorial to the merchant seamen of World War II, and to the seafaring heritage of the United States.
>
> Let me urge you to accept the invitation they extend to join them in this venture, via the enclosed memorandum. I can hardly think of a better investment in our heritage — can you?
>
> Yours sincerely,
> Peter Stanford
> President

The accompanying flyer offered to immortalize donors by inscribing their name on a bronze plaque on board the ship.

Help began to arrive. Proper training of our crew was a concern. Many of them had no seagoing experience and others were rusty, not having sailed for 30 years or more. Firefighting training was donated through the good graces of the Maritime Administration and MSC (Military Sealift Command).

The crew of the *USNS Mercy*, the hospital ship, was a big help. They offered to assist with lifeboat training and invited department heads to visit their ship the following week to select any equipment they might need. They offered the services of a stove and sheetmetal man to help repair our coal-fired stove in the galley, something Russ Mosholder had been trying to accomplish for weeks.

Tom Patterson: "The Military Sealift commander in Oakland, Commodore Mike Pivonka, showed a great interest in the ship and in the voyage. He opened his inventory up, both in his warehouse and in his fleet. Ships that were being decommissioned were made available to us to look for the type of equipment we needed."

The *USS Arkansas* came to our rescue by supplying skilled engine room personnel to help with the boiler. Bank of the West contributed $10,000. Members of the maritime community contributed nautical items for a maritime auction. Donations ranged from ships' running lights to shipboard china to a lifetime membership in the Glencannon Society to a gourmet dinner for 12 aboard the *O'Brien* to a sailboat to a ship's chronometer to ship models to a large oil painting. Mr. & Mrs. John A. Traina, Jr., prominent San Franciscans (she is bestselling author Danielle Steel) graciously agreed to serve as hosts.

PG&E (Pacific Gas and Electric Co.) included a feature on the ship and plans for Normandy in its monthly newsletter.

"The *O'Brien* is now abuzz with volunteers preparing to depart April 15, with a crew with an average age of 71. It will steam through the Panama Canal, cross the Atlantic and arrive in Normandy by June 6, the 50th anniversary of D-Day. If you want to tour the ship soon, call 415-441-3101."

It was a small item, but because it went to every household in Northern California it generated a great deal of interest.

No detail was too small to argue. At a department head meeting on February 11, the discussion of crewing centered around the concept of whether or not to have a bedroom steward, known as a "BR," for the officers. This was a position on merchant ships in World War II and is carried even today. The BR makes beds and cleans all the officers' staterooms. Bill Duncan, representing the crew, passionately argued against it. He said that in the United States no man should be subservient to another, especially on a volunteer crew. Against his protests, it was decided to have a BR to preserve the historical accuracy of the trip. As the discussion shifted on to other topics, he said, "In that decision, two hundred years of progress in human rights just gave way to tradition."

Adm. Patterson had some good news: American President Lines would install a 10 cm radar and an ARPA (Automated Radar Plotting Aids) radar, and Anna Falche, owner of Independence Petroleum Company, who had recently joined the organization, was working with Caterpillar to donate a generator.

The Coast Guard officer in charge of licensing and certification, Lt. Cdr. Robert E. Davila, arranged a program whereby the Coast Guard would come aboard the ship to examine crew members for their merchant mariners documents. This was a great help, allowing the crew to continue working while they were examined. It was gracious of Cdr. Davila to do this when normally exams are given at their office.

The hospital ship *Mercy* continued to be a benefactor, offering to sort and correct for us the charts coming from an East Coast MSC ship, the *Meyer*. Through Chief Mate Bob Holley, they also sent life preservers, refrigerant, mattresses, a galley steam kettle, plastic trays and galley uniforms.

In the first part of February Chief Mate John Paul announced he wasn't making the trip. The author was promoted to Chief Mate, Ray Conrady, who had been third mate, became second mate, and we began looking for a new third mate.

A fine article by Eric Brazil appeared in the *San Francisco Examiner*, San Francisco's afternoon newspaper:

> *Jeremiah O'Brien* is heading to 50 year D-Day ceremony. Alone
> among the armada of 5,000 ships amassed for the D-Day landings in

Normandy, France, the *S. S. Jeremiah O'Brien* survives — ship-shape. On April 14, the Liberty ship will steam through the Golden Gate en route to Omaha Beach and Point Du Hoc to participate in the 50th Anniversary commemoration of D-Day, June 6.

The voyage, under command of Capt. George Jahn, 78, with a crew of old salts — average age about 70 — will climax a remarkable volunteer effort launched 15 years ago.

Volunteers have logged more than 425,000 hours reconditioning the ship. [Tom] Patterson, a San Rafael resident who chairs the 'Normandy '94' campaign, expects the ship to pass its Coast Guard inspection for seaworthiness for the trans-Atlantic voyage via the Panama Canal by mid-March.

The reconditioning project has captured the interest of an astonishingly broad spectrum of volunteers, from 90-year-old deckhand Clarence Rocha, a retired longshoreman, to Port of Oakland engineer Hans Miller, who had just graduated from high school when he volunteered a dozen years ago; to Anna Falche, president of Independence Petroleum, a bunker trader who has taken on the responsibility for figuring out how to fuel the Normandy voyage.

"I'm retired, but I'm working harder now than I ever did," said Jahn, a San Francisco native (Mission High 1933), who spent the last years of his active sea career as a bar pilot. Jahn captained a Liberty ship on the perilous Murmansk run to Arctic Russia as well as at Normandy and had a freighter torpedoed under him shortly after Pearl Harbor and spent 10 days in a life raft before being rescued.

Jahn and Ernest Murdock, 66, of Tiburon, a retired Coast Guard captain, who was an oiler on Liberty ships during World War II, will select 45 crew members from among nearly 400 applicants to take the ship across the Atlantic.

One sailor already assured of a berth is Coleman "Coke" Schneider of Tenafly, N.J., who as a merchant marine cadet made six Atlantic crossings on the *Jeremiah O'Brien* during the war. He'll be shipping out from San Francisco in April as an assistant mess steward — a far cry from his job as chief executive officer of AA World Class Inc., the nation's largest manufacturer of embroidered emblems.

Financing for the $2 million Normandy voyage is still a bird in the bush.

Special legislation dedicating $765,000 from the sale of scrap ships to the *Jeremiah O'Brien*, in kind donations of equipment and fuel have put the volunteers within sight of their goal. Even the Navy has pitched in: A team of sailors from the nuclear cruiser *USS Arkansas* is working aboard the ship daily at its temporary berth at the U.S. Naval Supply Center dock in Alameda.

"We're going to sail. We owe it to the crew. They've put their lives into fixing this ship up for the voyage," Patterson said.

The wheelhouse of the Jeremiah O'Brien. *The ARPA radar donated by American President Lines can be seen in the right background, just inside the door.*

In a nifty piece of diplomacy last fall, Patterson and Robert Blake, president of General Engineering and Machine Works in San Francisco, won plaudits and promises of cooperation from both the British and French governments for the *Jeremiah O'Brien*'s participation in the D-Day commemoration.

Free dockage, fuel and tugboat

"The enthusiasm of the French is terrific," said Blake, who served aboard Liberty Ships in the Pacific. "When we said 'Liberty ship' their eyes lit up and they said, 'We'll do anything we can to help.'

Timetable for the 20,000 mile voyage, believed to be the first of its kind for an all-volunteer crew aboard a government-owned vessel, calls for the *Jeremiah O'Brien* to arrive in Portsmouth, England, May 20, where it will be reviewed by Queen Elizabeth.

Although the *Jeremiah O'Brien* is old, none of the volunteers who have had a hand in reconditioning it are worried about her seaworthiness.

Engineer Bob Davidson, 73, said that the Liberty ships' triple expansion steam engines, built to an 1890 British design, were made to last 100 years. "They went back to the archives for these," he said, gesturing at the *Jeremiah O'Brien*'s engines. "They knew what they could do and the abuse they would take. They're big and they're heavy and slow speed, but if you take care of them, they'll do the job."

Room assignments. Who would sleep where? Tom Patterson: "We were looking for a volunteer crew, and we offered it first to our wonderful volunteers over the last fifteen years who had worked this ship, brought her to such an immaculate state. There weren't enough that were able to make the voyage, so then we opened it up to those in the industry with proper experience and health. This was placed mainly under Captain Otterberg [staff captain] and he worked through the department heads on the ship, with the master, in assembling the first crew which numbered fifty-six."

The chief mate had to fill the twenty-three positions in the deck department (including purser, gunners and day-working ordinary seamen) while the chief engineer did the same for the engine department. One afternoon I went around and counted all the bunks. There were 77. That's easy, I thought, fifty-six people should fit into 77 bunks. But it wasn't that simple. In some rooms the bunks were three and four high, designed during World War II when nimble kids of 18 and 19 manned the gun crew. But we had a not-so-nimble crew with an average age of 70. Some assignments were obvious — the master had his own stateroom and office as did the chief engineer. The chief steward and chief mate had office-room combinations and no one argued the point. But beyond that, it got complicated. From the time the ship came out of the reserve fleet fifteen years earlier, crew who worked on the ship more than one or two days a week had simply taken rooms in which to sleep while they were on board. Over the course of the years they brought in personal effects, kept their work clothes in lockers and came to feel proprietary about their rooms. There would be some resentment at being "kicked out" to make way for some comparative stranger who was making the trip. "Extra" people not normally carried on a Liberty Ship, such as Adm. Patterson, a doctor, the extra watch for the engine room and a few others, would also have to be housed.

. . . plan for expected crowds of 4,000 a day during ship's visit in European ports (one day we actually logged in more than 10,000 visitors), docents to explain the ship, brochures, inventory for the ship's store, which we set up in no. 3 'tween deck and which we hoped would earn good revenues from sales, find and contract with vendors for scores of items from heavy sweaters embroidered with the ship's name and logo to commemorative medals, caps, watches, flags, pencils, T-shirts, maps, books . . .

A large problem was lack of communication. The volunteers working the ship thought the office was notifying everyone. But Marci Hooper was frustrated because department heads weren't supplying her with lists of people to notify. The NLSM office attended to thousands of details with two paid staff and a few volunteers. Making and answering phone calls, writing and responding to hundreds of letters, they were the nerve center linking the ship with agencies, government, donors, vendors, volunteers, news media — so many projects that did or did not work out. Their responsibility was enormous. Norm Schoenstein and Ray Palacin were volunteers who helped in any way they could. Any other help came from catch-as-catch-can volunteers who donated one or two days a week.

Karen Kamimoto: "Mary Woodward, 80-something years old, came in every day because she was needed, answering letters, opening mail, working full-time. She was really a trooper."

. . . ballast, ballast, ballast. With only 1,000 tons of lead coming from the Navy in Bremerton, more was needed. Ideas were thrashed out at department head meetings.

Tom Patterson: "We identified ballast up at Rough and Ready Island, anchor chain. It turned out that it had been preferredly given to the State of California. But that was erroneous, it actually belonged to the Navy's Superintendent of Salvage. So we had to go to them in Washington. They finally gave us the chain, and then we found out that the chain had to be loaded up there. We had a tremendous amount of logistics getting this chain down to the yard."

On February 18 we shifted to San Francisco Drydock. Ray Conrady, second mate, supervised tying up and letting go on the bow, Joe Milcic, a longtime volunteer third mate who couldn't make the voyage because he didn't have a radar endorsement, did the same on the stern and the chief mate took the bridge relaying orders from Capt. Jahn and the pilot to the mates by walkie-talkie and to the engine room by engine order telegraph. Our pilot was again Capt. Terry Ruff, and he and the two tugs we used were provided gratis by the Navy.

It was a wet but calm day with intermittent rainsqualls and sunshine. After days and days of discharging excess equipment, loading new equipment and vans, with people swarming the decks and interiors, inspecting, visiting, checking, viewing, asking questions, wanting directions, it was relaxing to have the ship returned to us, even just for a few hours.

As always, there was something grand about being on a ship moving across the water. You feel you are at the center of the universe and everything revolves around you. You become

The beginning of a tradition. We flew our corporate sponsors' flags any time we moved the ship. Later in the voyage we flew them all the time we were in port. Photo courtesy Ed Langlois.

part of that great living being that is the ship, feeling the hum and vibration of living machinery, as you watch the world pass in calm delight. We looked at several ships at anchor in the Bay, some of them empty, their rusty bulbous bows protruding awkwardly above the water. The chief steward brought hot coffee and pastries to the bridge. For a few moments all was at peace with the world as we sipped coffee and watched the shipyard grow larger and larger.

Then it was back to reality. Capt. Ruff skillfully turned us at the edge of a yacht basin and we backed alongside pier 70. We were in a "wet berth" (as differentiated from a dry dock). The first order of business was cleaning out the double bottom tanks. And that was just the beginning.

During our shift to the drydock, Capt. Jahn, left, explains some of the finer points of piloting to Adm. Patterson. Photo by Mike Emery.

3

NORMANDY OR BUST

O n March 1 the *Jeremiah O'Brien* was pushed by tugs into drydock. There she was carefully positioned by the docking master over a series of keel and bilge blocks. The dock's ballast tanks were pumped out and the dock rose, the ship settling on the blocks, until the ship and the floor of the dock were out of the water.

To the crew, drydocking is a special event. It gives them the rare opportunity to walk under the hull and a chance to see the entire ship with its huge rudder and propeller exposed. Several volunteers came to see the ship out of the water. Tony Rapp, who would join us in the latter part of the voyage, asked a yard worker to take his picture with the propeller and rudder in the background. Bob Burnett helped one of our volunteers, Bob Hiller, who is almost blind, to find the ladder to the dry dock. Hiller simply wanted to be there with the ship. It was a very tender moment.

Even before the hull was dry the Coast Guard and American Bureau of Shipping began inspecting the *Jeremiah O'Brien.* Whenever they came to a welding seam they scraped, probed and beat on it with pointed hammers and scratch awls. If they thought the seam weak, they marked it with a can of spray paint to indicate the area should be sandblasted and inspected further. By the following day the *O'Brien's* hull looked like an abstract tiger. White and red paint marks were everywhere, even under the bottom.

After Coast Guard and ABS inspectors finished, the hull was striped like a cat. Photo by George Bonawit.

The pressures of not enough money, too many expenses, too much work, not enough time, too many opinions, inspections, repairs, preparation and meeting the April 14 sailing deadline began to affect the crew. Ernie Murdock was upset about the marked seams — so much more welding than he anticipated. Tom Patterson, normally so determined and optimistic, was worrying about the hurricane season that would come in the Caribbean just as we passed through on our return in October. He wanted to eliminate scheduled ports and get home before the hurricanes hit. He called a special meeting to discuss the matter. The immediate results were that the ship would reduce the number of East Coast ports and arrive back in San Francisco in September instead of October. He was somewhat reassured by the representative of our weather routing service who said they could give three days' warning on any hurricane or weather condition, but still he worried. Our lifeboats and the lifesaving equipment they contained were an ongoing project that seemed never to end. Phil Sinnott, a longtime volunteer, spent all his time working on them and said he was staying awake nights worrying about lifeboats. Ernie Murdock was irritable. Patterson looked tired. The crew was grousing about their berths and all the "strangers" who were going on the trip. The fact that we were out of local, qualified volunteers did not appease them. Both the chief mate and the chief engineer were trying to fill positions in their respective departments and updating the list almost daily as, one after another, volunteers who had signed up to go dropped out for various reasons. In my journal one day I wrote in large letters, THESE ARE THE TIMES THAT TRY PEOPLE'S SOULS.*

With only five weeks to find a third mate, we got lucky. Pete Lyse, who had submitted an application, was able to drop everything on short notice and fly out from Michigan to help us out. He turned out to be an excellent shipmate and officer. There was some other good news. Anna Falche came aboard one day with the news that the Otis Spunkmeyer Corporation was interested in helping us. She said they would sponsor a farewell party for the *O'Brien* in San Francisco and a party in London for dignitaries aboard the ship. They had a DC-3 which they would make available to us in Europe. Best of all, they would give the ship all the cookie dough, muffins, bagels, bread and coffee needed for the voyage. Of all the generous corporate sponsors the ship had, Otis Spunkmeyer was one of the more "fun" organizations. The notion of stocking enough frozen cookie dough to last six months brought to mind visions of tons of Chocolate Chip, Double Chocolate Chip, Peanut Butter, Oatmeal Raisin and White Chocolate Macadamia Nut dough lying deep in the holds of the ship, perhaps even serving as ballast until it was used.

Then, in early March, disappointing news. Patterson announced that we had realized only $588,000 from sale of the two Victory ships, not the $750,000 we expected.

---

*I am learning politically correct terminology.

Things got worse. Arriving aboard about 0800 one morning we found out the Coast Guard was expected and the weekly department head meeting was canceled. From this moment on, the Coast Guard caused nothing but problems for us. The Captain of the Port, A. H. MacDonald, was aboard inspecting everything. Capt. Jahn escorted him partway through the ship, then came storming into the saloon. "That does it! I had to walk away from him. Just who the hell does he think he is?

"What happened?"

"That Coast Guard captain. He looks in number four 'tween deck and he says, 'well, this all has to be secured before you can go anywhere. You're not ready for sea.'"

"Jesus, I KNOW that! We're more than a month from sailing yet. OF COURSE it's not ready for sea!"

Another Coast Guard inspector happened to come in at that moment. "And where the hell was the Coast Guard during the War?" shouted Capt. Jahn. "Who needs them. They don't know anything anyway. What the hell good do they do?"

Capt. Jahn had a chance to let off steam but it wasn't the best way to handle the situation. In the days ahead we all made efforts to keep our captain away from the Coast Guard inspectors and vice versa. Every time he saw one we would hear, "What good is the Coast Guard? What do they know? They should turn it back over to the Steamboat Inspection Service."

Tom Patterson was more diplomatic: "We didn't see Capt. MacDonald every day, but we did meet with him over in his office. We didn't always agree but we were able to find a way to keep the work going ahead."

Bob Burnett: "They were just trying to do their job and cover their perception of what they had to do. I was frustrated with some of it because it seemed they had so many requirements that were so totally unnecessary and picayune. And they were ignoring the number one priority of the preservation of a National Historic Landmark. I know they were concerned about the safety but I hated seeing the destruction of some of the internal fabric of the ship."

But the inspectors working for Capt. A. H. MacDonald had to do what he said. As inspector Guy Therriault said one day, "He's the boss. When he says 'Jump,' I have to ask how high."

One of the problems with the first Liberty ships built during World War II was that, because welding was a new technology, the ships had a tendency to crack. Cracking always occurred in conditions of extreme cold and deep loading. A few even broke in half. Statistically, this only occurred about ten times and there was never a loss of life due to a Liberty breaking in half. But a ship breaking in two is a dramatic event, one that stays in the public memory for decades. The cracking problems were corrected and by the time the *Jeremiah O'Brien* was launched, they were no longer a factor. Nevertheless, Capt. MacDonald got hold of some information regarding cracking and, in a remarkable exercise in convoluted logic, applied it to our ship. His parting shot that first day was to deliver a letter requiring "cargo carrying Libertys" to have crack arresters, hatch stiffeners, and several other extras that were added on when the early Liberty ships broke up during the war.* The fact that our ship was already modified, would not carry cargo, and would not be sailing in extreme cold mattered not a whit to him.

The result was consternation, anxiety, frustration, anger and more stress. The next several days were taken up with phone calls to Washington by Murdock, Patterson, and Fred Kaufman, our naval architect.

Dick Brannon: "Being a marine engineer by profession, I was well acquainted with the mechanical condition of the ship. At no time did I have any doubts that the ship would present any problems. The unknown is always there. The unknown can always happen. Shit can happen. No one knew, literally, twelve hundred, thirteen hundred miles from San Francisco, anything could happen, we may go in deep shit. We could crap out off of Catalina Island and be towed into San Pedro. We don't know those things,

---

*A crack arrester consists of steel plating riveted to the main deck and sometimes the sheer strakes (uppermost row of hull plating) whose purpose is to prevent cracking or, if it occurs, prevent it from spreading.

but experience and my years at sea indicated to me that the ship was in damn fine condition.

"John Pottinger [former superintendent of the Suisun Bay Reserve Fleet and past chief engineer of the *O'Brien*] gave me personally and privately a hundred percent support. He said, 'You've got a beautiful ship there. I know that ship inside and out. From the layup fleet I know the care it's been given. I've been working my butt off ever since it was hauled out of the layup, I know that ship is a good ship. You got no problems.'

"So the thrust of the opinion was that people knew that the ship could do it. They had confidence in the ship, And that's my viewpoint, I was supremely confident in the ship itself, mechanically, boilers and engine, piping, bilges, hull."

The chief engineer was one of the busiest people aboard, but he never let the demands on his time depress him. In fact, if anything, his disposition improved with pressure: "The boilers are the heart of any ship no matter whether it's Robert Fulton's north river steamboat. The *Great Eastern* had boilers, prime movers. Everybody, every steam engineer in the world, would say the ship isn't going anywhere unless it has good boilers. So my first thought was, can the boilers of the *Jeremiah O'Brien* stand up to the unknown stresses of making a twenty thousand mile, five to six month voyage after being laid up for 30-some years. Can it do it? Big question mark. This ship was singled out for preservation at the layup fleet. John Pottinger, being the superintendent engineer during a lot of its layup time, saw to it that this ship got extra special TLC.

"Mechanically, they laid this ship up in superb condition. Mechanically, they did a magnificent job and the same way with the main engine. So I'd been aware of the program of preserving this ship and everybody from Harry Morgan, Doug Dickie, John Pottinger, they were utilizing these hundreds of years of skill in preserving this ship, making it ready to operate. So when they firmly announced it's going to make the trip to Europe, I had no qualms whatsoever.

"A very good friend of mine, Volning Jullienell, was a retired inspector/surveyor with the American Bureau of Shipping. He volunteered his services to gauge the hull during our drydocking in ninety-two. He personally gauged the whole hull, took his figures back to the laboratory, ran them through the machine, and found the hull was in superb condition. So we had experts pronounce their opinions. The ship was physically ready. And I, of course, having lived with ships for quite some time, knew this ship reasonably well. The ship itself was no problem. It was just the mentality and the thinking and the logistical support and the insurance, the fuel, the cost, the storing and shit, the crewing, those were ancillary. I never had the slightest doubts about the ship itself."

Ships that belong to the United States Government, known as public vessels, are technically exempt from regulation and inspection by other government agencies. One proposal to circumvent the Coast Guard problem was to declare ourselves a public vessel.

Tom Patterson: "That's a good, valid question but the answer is No. The Maritime Administration has always had its ships classified and with the Coast Guard certificate of inspection. Although legally they don't have to do it, they have always obtained the classification. We felt that we were breaking out a fifty-one-year-old ship to go on an eighteen thousand mile voyage and therefore we should have all the proper certificates. That way nobody could ever accuse us of jeopardizing the lives of the crew that sailed on the ship. And we still feel that was the right way. Probably the Maritime Administration wouldn't have allowed us to take the ship if we hadn't obtained the certificates necessary. It's arguable whether all the things we did were necessary but that's what we had to do, get the certificates and we got them. Even the Public Health Service said it was the cleanest ship they had inspected for a long time, the FCC, Panama Canal Certificate, Load Line Certificate, every certificate was obtained, so we were fine."

Anna Falche showed up late that same afternoon. She thought the crack arrester issue could be handled with a waiver which her attorney could get in a matter of days. We could only hope.

Work continued without letup. Besides what the shipyard was doing, we still had far more jobs than people to do them. Confusion reigned. We would get forty sailors from the Navy to help, what qualifications did these people have? When would we get them? What would they do? Everyone was talking and asking questions but nobody was listening.

Amidst all the turmoil this cartoon appeared in the crew messroom. It captured the indomitable spirit of the crew. Drawing courtesy of Jean Yates.

The day after being promised all the Navy help, we learned no one was coming. The only thing that did arrive were the forty box lunches ordered for the sailors. They were given to the crew who seemed to enjoy the change from their usual home-packed lunch.

A great help to the deck department was a list of "Sailors Duties" put out by bosun Rich Reed. In it he detailed the intricacies of standing each watch, what time to relieve the watch, go on lookout, call the next watch, how to stand lookout, what kind of clothes to pack and "do's and don'ts" on how to be a good shipmate. [See appendix E for the complete list].

It was now the middle of March, one month to our departure date. Adm. Patterson said, ". . . it has gotten down to a seven-day-a-week job." Still, our tried-and-true volunteers showed up when they could, some every day, others not so frequently. The oldest was Clarence Rocha, who had just turned 90. A retired longshoreman, he ran the deck winches for us. His doctor wouldn't let him make the long voyage but he helped every day.

Carl Nolte, a reporter for the *San Francisco Chronicle*, described the enormous task in one of his stories.

> . . . But there is only so much volunteers can do; shipyard crews have to do the rest, including about 3,500 linear feet of welding to tighten seals and 2,000 new rivets need to be driven. Andre Lopez, the riveting subcontractor, is looking for a few good riveters. This sort of work is not done much any more, he said.
>
> All this is not cheap; the shipyard bill alone is expected to be about $600,000. The National Liberty Ship Foundation figures that it has received $2 million in cash and in-kind contributions so far. The biggest chunk was $588,000 the government provided from the sale of two old ships that were sold for scrap.
>
> The *O'Brien* sails April 14, takes two weeks to get to the Panama Canal and a little over a month to get to England. It's a long voyage in a ship designed to be slow but reliable.
>
> "We're going," said Robert Blake, a veteran of World War II merchant ships and now chairman of the National Liberty Ship Foundation. "We're going," said Norm Burke, a retired banker who will work in the engine room. Even if we have to go out on Market Street with a tin cup, we're going."

The work, problems and fund-raising efforts on the *O'Brien* were duplicated a few hundred miles south where the *Lane Victory* was preparing for the trip to Normandy. The *O'Brien* and the *Lane* are sister ships in spirit, if not in fact, and they like to help each other out when they can. But by this point, there was no time or energy to spare and the two ships labored individually at putting their voyages together.

The two West Coast ships were to rendezvous with the *John W. Brown* somewhere off Bermuda in mid-May in "The Last Convoy" across the Atlantic to England and France. Capt. Brian

Hope, of the *John W. Brown*, called it convoy HX-355 (HX-354 sailed from Halifax in May of 1945).

The weekly department head meeting covered a typical agenda; good, bad or humorous: Although the port anchor chain was all right, we needed two shots for the starboard chain which would be forthcoming from the Reserve Fleet. Two Kings Point cadets would come aboard in April. We had cut doorways in the 'tween deck bulkheads to give easy access to the interior of the ship. Now the Coast Guard insisted on watertight doors in those areas. A fire plan was required so that if there was a fire in foreign ports the local fire brigade could come aboard and see at a glance how our firefighting system was configured. The steward's department had almost finished painting the galley. The port sanitary tank had not yet been cleared, pending the replacement of two rivets. Someone suggested getting Bob Hope and Gene Autry involved as their names would attract donations. The tanks were sounded showing 1890 barrels of fuel oil aboard. MacKay Radio was assisting with labor, material and advice in the radio room. Contacts with the FCC in Washington had been established. A total of 57 rivets were replaced, far fewer than anticipated. The cutting and welding of bulkhead 88, one of the items required in Capt. MacDonald's letter, was a problem because it added to the costs. Chief Steward Russ Mosholder was ordering supplies for the trip.

Adm. Patterson closed the meeting with a frank discussion of the marine safety requirements insisted upon by the Coast Guard. "The Coast Guard wanted us to put a crack arresting strap around the ship. This would have been over a million dollar job in itself. We didn't feel that it was necessary." This was protested to the Coast Guard Admiral in Washington.

"Will we sail or not?" Patterson was asked.

"I don't know," was the reply. "We will not sail without Coast Guard approval."

"How about a percentage? What are the odds?"

"I won't guess."

The meeting ended and we went back to our jobs feeling discouraged.

Bill Duncan, crew representative-deck engineer: "I had great expectations about the trip. It was a very exciting prospect but then when the reality set in, there were times I felt that we would never make it. There were times I was <u>sure</u> we would never make it. And there were times when that feeling was reversed. It was a very fluid, fluctuating time, with all the preparations of the ship and the requirements of the Coast Guard, and seemingly lack of direction on the ship at that time, made it a very uncertain period. But in the back of my mind I used to visualize the actual departure. I could see it in my mind, but then when I went on board I would say, no way."

Around this time the April issue of *Sea Classics* magazine hit the stands with an article, "D-Day Plus 50 Years: The Last Convoy." A full-color photo of the *Jeremiah O'Brien* passing under the Golden Gate Bridge was featured as the centerfold. Our spirits rose again and we fell to with new determination.

Some of the crew scheduled for the first leg of the voyage, to Portsmouth, England, began showing up. This helped somewhat with the labor problem and, more important, was good for morale. The newcomers were fresh, positive and enthusiastic. They were a badly-needed boost to our spirits.

Then, more good news. Fred Kaufman, our naval architect, came up with proof that we were well under the required 2,571 pounds per square inch deck stress figure. This meant the crack arrester was not required. While he worked with the Coast Guard in Washington and Anna Falche and her lawyers worked on the local level, word finally came down for the San Francisco Coast Guard to drop the issue.

The welding process continued, 2.56 miles worth.

Chairman of the Board Bob Blake was frequently on hand, offering encouragement, solving problems, acting as an industry liaison. His contributions cannot even begin to be listed. Next to Tom Patterson, Blake was probably the major ball-carrier and that the trip happened was due in large part to him. His favorite expression was, "Don't give me problems, give me solutions." He owned a large, black female dog named George. We could always tell when Bob had come aboard because George would come

After the hull is spray-painted the draft marks are put in by hand.

Just before going in the water, the final result.

Yardworkers apply a primer coat before putting on the final boot-topping.

nosing through the passageways, her toenails click-click-
ing on the hard surface.

We became resigned
to the fact that each morning
would present a new "crisis
du jour." The promised generator from Caterpillar hadn't
materialized. Testing one of
our lifeboats, a yard worker
stepped into it, his weight
causing the boat to tilt so that
the test weights all shifted to
one side and the boat sank.
In the process of raising one
of the cargo booms at no. 2
hatch, Clarence Rocha lowered when he should have
raised, and bent it. Clarence

*Chairman of the Board, Bob Blake, in a
rare quiet moment with George.*

felt terrible about it, but it was a simple mistake, the kind of thing
that could happen to anyone. With so much to do, these minor
crises were inevitable.

Phil Sinnott: "There was a terrible amount of pressure,
last-minute pressure, in getting the ship past the Coast Guard
requirements and insuring that all needed equipment was on board.
The game plan changed from day to day which often made everything that was done before of no use. It must be said that the
fellows in the crew were splendid, as always, those guys rose to
the occasion."

Warren Hopkins, NLSM Board of Directors: "It was like
during the war when everybody had a cause. Patterson was the
enthusiasm. Blake was the hard worker, he was down there every
day and he just worked like a dog. They held up marvelously
well."

Good things also happened. Capt. H. W. Simonsen generously donated a yacht to the ship which produced a handsome
return in the form of a lease-purchase. The Foster Wheeler Corporation, a manufacturer of marine boilers (and the *Jeremiah*

O'Brien's boilers), donated $5,000. Thanks to negotiations by Art Haskell, the ABS waived the $12,000 in fees due for their inspections.

Capt. MacDonald had been co-opted on the crack arrester, but in the days ahead there would be additional requirements: welding shut the newly-installed watertight doors between the holds in the 'tween decks, adding about six inches of lip, or sill, to the companionways leading into no. 2 hold, adding eight inches to the coaming leading to the bosun's stores in the bow, etc., etc., etc. There was a sense that although MacDonald couldn't stop us, he would exert his authority in every way and make our task as difficult for us as he could.

On March 28 the dock was flooded at 0900 and the ship returned to the water. John Paul and I had agreed that he would step down when the ship went back in the water. It was a relief to everyone. Having two chief mates on a ship is awkward. "You can't work for two bosses," the old saying goes.

Tom Patterson: "One of the largest jobs that we faced was putting the vessel in class and obtaining the Coast Guard Certificate of Inspection. We recognized from the beginning that this was going to mean a tremendous amount of money. We had estimated our shipyard repairs plus the Coast Guard and ABS requirements at over nine hundred thousand dollars and ultimately it went over one point two million dollars."

With three tugs assisting (provided at no charge, thanks to their owners), the *Maggie* and *Benicia* from Bay and Delta Towing and the *Sea Duke* from Red Stack, the ship was quickly returned to the wet berth at pier 70.

The remainder of the day was spent preparing lifeboats for inspection and preparing for the inclining test the next day. Fred Kaufman was aboard. This was his hour. The purpose of the inclining experiment is to determine the height of the ship's center of gravity above the keel. It is performed by moving a known weight a known distance across the deck, determining the angle of heel the vessel assumes and, with these values, solving for metacentric height. To measure the angle of heel a pendulum is hung in the lower hold. When the weight is shifted, the deflection of the pendulum is measured. This distance is then used in a trigonometric formula to determine the ship GM or metacentric height. From this, various calculations can be made to determine the ship's stability and, consequently, safety.

The inclining experiment is a surprisingly delicate procedure. Among other things, all the vessel's tanks must be either empty or full, otherwise as the ship starts to heel the center of gravity of the liquid would shift, causing exaggerated readings. The vessel must not have a list to start with. The formula for calculating GM is based on a right triangle. If there is a list, the triangle is not right, hence inaccuracies. Balance is so delicate that Fred Kaufman needed to know the weight of each person on board to include in his calculations and they had to all stand on the centerline of the ship while the test was being conducted.

Journal entry: "A little over two weeks to go."

The Coast Guard was aboard on almost a daily basis now, nosing into everything. The long hours and hard work were taking their toll. Ernie Murdock, who spent every day on board, seemed constantly on edge.

March 29 was another hectic day. As I walked aboard with Capt. Jahn, Murdock met us with yet another list of Coast Guard requirements. The deck department, with Rich Reed, who would be bosun for the voyage, and Per Dam, who was bosun-shipkeeper from the time the ship came out of the Reserve Fleet, supervising, spent the morning cleaning the decks preparatory to doing the inclining test. For the test to be accurate everything had to be in place as if the ship was at sea. At 1230 everyone who wasn't absolutely essential to the inclining test was sent home. Any extra weight, even that of a human body, could upset the calculations.

The following day we learned the inclining test was passed. We shifted to the Naval Air Station in Alameda to load lead ballast which had finally arrived from Bremerton. Our berth was directly across the pier from a massive aircraft carrier, the *USS Abraham Lincoln.*

Dick Brannon: "On one of our many trips around the Bay, Gene Anderson, who is a very fine, older type gentleman, looked at me. I was handling the throttle because there were so many new people on the ship. So Gene looked at me and he says, 'How in the hell can you make it look so easy. You just do this and do that and the engine works.' He says, 'Other people are always fighting the controls and this and that.' I said, 'Gene, you got a hundred seventeen tons of cold, cast iron and steel here. And you want it to go full ahead, and do this and that. Just pretend that you're making love to a woman. You want to warm up this hundred and seventeen tons of cast iron and steel. And you want it to do anything you want it to. Take it easy. You tweak it a little bit here, a little valve there, a little steam here, get lots of lubrication . . . give it a lot of TLC. When you've got that engine thoroughly warmed up, it'll do anything you want it to.'"

We finally started loading the ballast in the late afternoon and finished the day at 1800 with 87 tons aboard. It was a start.

Voyage 8 commenced at midnight on April 1. The deck log simply says, "0000 Begin Voyage 8." [Voyage 7 ended on February 8, 1946].

Later in the morning, the DUKW, our one piece of deck cargo for the voyage, belonging to Jean-Paul Caron, arrived alongside. It had quite a story. According to Jean-Paul, he was a small boy when the D-Day landings took place. As he walked near the Normandy beaches a DUKW with American soldiers in it came ashore. They saw him and gave him some chocolate. He was so taken with the machine, the GI's and the candy that he wrote the serial number of the vehicle down. Returning home, he asked his father if he could buy it some day. Years later he and his father tracked the vehicle down and bought it at a surplus sale.

As usual, to everyone's frustration, the Coast Guard was all over the place, inspecting, demanding, insisting. Part of the problem was that on a voyage such as this, on a 50-year-old Liberty such as the *O'Brien*, it was not realistic to simply "go by the book." Some initiative was required to assess the situation and find practical solutions that accomplished the objective. This put some inspectors in the difficult situation of working with the

"Getting the lead out."   Joe Spears' crew places lead ballast in no. 4 lower hold. Photo by George Bonawit.

This is the way the main deck looked a few days before departure. What a mess! Photo by George Bonawit.

A small part of the food stores for the six month voyage.

Potatoes, a staple of any sea voyage, stowed on the boat deck.

Fresh vegetables and canned goods to carry us through the long days at sea.

Cots, for sleeping on deck in the tropics — and for guests.

crew to resolve problems and yet satisfying their superior, Capt. A. H. MacDonald.

Tom Patterson: "We got excellent help, particularly from ships like the *Samuel Gompers.* They sent over three boiler technicians first-class, Steven Keely, Mack Zedmans and George Smith. The professional expertise of these men was outstanding. They really helped the chief engineer get those boilers done. The Sailor's Union of the Pacific sent down some sailors to help us get our stores aboard. We had great help from the U.S. Navy and from the maritime industry."

One week.

The ship swarmed with Coast Guard inspectors. Lt. Cdr. Davila was aboard helping the crew with final documentation. The din increased and continued around the clock. On deck, welders' blue arcs flashed everywhere. The yard continued shifting ballast into the holds. The huge cranes traveled on their rails, lifting pallets of lead and dropping them into the hatches where forklifts ran the heavy loads into corners and inaccessible underdeck areas, distributing the weight evenly. The decks were cluttered with lead ballast, pieces of pipe, hatch boards and beams. Miles of welding cable and air hose snaked over and under and around everything. On top of it all came the stores — sacks of coal for the galley, cots for the tropics, bags of potatoes, boxes of bananas, onions, cases and pallets of canned goods — peaches, mayonnaise, tuna, fruit cocktail, prunes, juices — roasts, steaks, sausage, bacon, ice cream, flour, spices, yeast, fish, fresh fruit, toilet paper, soap, detergent, disinfectant, eggs, fruit juice, melons, apples, oranges, peanut butter, butter, relish . . .

Bev Masterson, ship's store: "I went down to the ship while it was at the drydock. It didn't seem like the old *Jeremiah.* It was quite dirty and things were all over the deck. It didn't look like the ship I knew."

April 7 we continued clearing old gear out of the holds, moving things about the decks, and moving ballast to correct the list and get it off deck and into the hold. The deck crew concentrated on the lifeboat requirements. The galley crew rigged a chute down one ladder and, one by one, slid the boxes and crates of stores down to the dry stores and refrigerated areas, where other volunteers lifted them off and stacked them. It was all very low tech. The engine crew continued working on boilers, piping, wiring and tanks.

As departure date drew closer and closer, we had even more frequent Coast Guard inspections. One result was a slip of paper called an "835" because that was the form number on it. It's similar to a "fix-it-or-else" ticket issued by the Highway Patrol. The Coast Guard writes up an item such as, "provide two Coast Guard approved lifejackets for navigation bridge," and keeps a copy. When the item is fixed it is inspected, crossed off and initialed by the inspector on the original and the copy. We received quite a number of 835s during February and March. After a lengthy discussion of them one day, the chief engineer said, "Well, that's nothing. I got a sixteen-seventy once."

"A sixteen-seventy," said Ernie Murdock, frowning, "I never heard of such a thing, What's that?"

"Two eight thirty-fives," said the chief, laughing.

Most of the next day was again spent moving things around the deck. We were able to close and secure no. 5 hatch for sea. We finished relocating the lead ballast. Coal was loaded for the galley and the crew continued working on the lifeboats. We tried to clear as many of the Coast Guard 835s as possible, but for each one cleared they seemed to find two more.

The AC generator from Caterpillar arrived on the dock. Anna Falche had worked long and hard on this project and it finally paid off. "We are proud to be a part of this historic voyage," said Caterpillar Vice President Richard L. Thompson, head of the company's Engine Division. "When Admiral Patterson, chairman of Normandy '94, said he needed a 'Cat Generator Set' to make this trip to France possible, I felt honored that we would have a part in commemorating the contributions that these ships and these men made."

The Caterpillar generator set would provide the electricity to operate navigational, medical, lighting and other modern electronic equipment. It would provide the precisely controlled power required by today's integrated circuit electronics, and be fuel efficient, clean-running and quiet.

More miscellaneous equipment and material came to be loaded aboard: stores and supplies, spare parts, machinery. The cranes operated on double shifts. The crashing and banging sounds never ceased. By this point, many of the crew were working almost literally from dawn to dark, seven days a week. Some gave up on trying to commute from home and just stayed on the ship. The stamina and dedication of the volunteers was almost beyond belief. Seventy- and eighty- and, in the case of Clarence Rocha, ninety-year-old men put in days of labor that could shame men who were decades younger. Clarence, along with Joe Milcic, Bob Davidson, and others, although not making the trip, showed up, day after day, to do their part.

The Stan Flowers Company went to work shoring the lead ballast in no. 4 lower hold. They are one of the oldest and best companies on the West Coast at this type of work. We could be assured that when they finished, nothing would shift in rough weather at sea.

On April 9 we began taking on fuel. The Shell Oil Company in Martinez, California, had generously donated 5,000 barrels of fuel, in effect topping off our tanks.* The Tosco Oil Company in Concord, California, gave the equivalent of another 1000 barrels, and ultimately Chevron Oil Company gave us $25,000 to purchase oil.

We began clearing the decks and were able to close and cover no. 4 hatch. When the tarps were in place, the generator was set on top of it.

Sea trials were run on April 10. It seemed as if everyone and his brother was on board. Sea trials are to prove to the Coast Guard and the American Bureau of Shipping that all the systems work and, in particular, that the boilers can hold a sustained load for a period of time at full speed. One boiler was ready, the other wasn't. Nevertheless, we crisscrossed San Francisco Bay at full speed (10 knots) for a couple of hours and were back alongside by 1130 with the traditional broom flying at the mast showing a clean sweep of all trials. Capt. Jahn did a masterful job of handling the ship and we all felt that things were starting to settle in.

---

*A barrel is 42 gallons.

But the gods weren't going to let us get through the day without another trial. That evening an Anchors Aweigh crew party was held at the San Francisco Maritime Museum graciously sponsored by the Episcopal Homes Foundation's San Francisco Towers retirement community. Changing from our dirty work clothes, the crew and our families enjoyed a champagne buffet, swing music donated by the "Toot Sweet Band" and old World War II films, or walked along the museum's bayfront promenade looking at the sea and enjoying the respite from the noise and clamor of the ship. Then the word spread that there was a fuel oil leak in no. 4 lower hold. This was a serious problem and conjecture ran wild — rupture of the plating at the bottom of the hold because of the weight of all the lead? Rotten piping? Bad gaskets on the manhole plates that lead to the deep tanks? No one slept well that night.

The next day we discovered there were also oil leaks in no. 2 deep tank and no. 3 lower hold. The deep tank had a couple of feet of oil. Capt. MacDonald was in his glory with four inspectors triumphantly viewing the leaks. There was talk of another two weeks of repairs and even canceling the trip.

Dick Brannon: "During this agonizing five months preparation period from November to April, Bob Burnett came to me a couple of times with a very long, serious expression on his face expressing doubts, asking me, 'Do you really think we can make it.' 'Of course we can do it, of course, no problems, all we need is the support, the money. The ship itself can make it. Absolutely, we're going to make it. Of course we're going to make it.'

"There were times when certain regulatory body people were giving us an extremely hard time and it reflected all through the attitude of the crew and I says, 'Bullshit, don't worry about it. They'll pipe down at the last minute. They <u>know</u> they don't know. They're smart enough to know they don't know. They're just trying to prove something and they can't back up. The ship is in perfect condition. We'll make it. We're going to do it. Absolutely, no question.'"

The media glare increased. Our decks swarmed with TV crews, radio interviewers and newspaper reporters from local, national and foreign stations and papers. These in addition to the daily turmoil of welders, riggers, electricians, crew, ship chandlers, deliverymen, Coast Guard and American Bureau of Shipping inspectors and curious visitors.

From USA Today:

SAN FRANCISCO — A half-century after the D-Day invasion of Normandy, a crew of dream-driven old salts — average age 70 — has embarked on what some might call an assault on common sense. Their mission: to restore a ship that's 10 times older than its life expectancy and sail it halfway around the world through some of the roughest seas on Earth to join D-Day's 50th anniversary party June 6.

But $2.4 million and 500,000 volunteer hours later, here it sits in a shipyard berth, aswarm with crew members, yard workers, financial backers and Coast Guard inspectors — all working feverishly to ready the *O'Brien* for a voyage once considered impossible.

"O.K., so we're all a little crazy," acknowledges Coleman "Coke" Schneider, 70, an original *O'Brien* sailor and among 56 crew members for this trip. "But, hey, we're reliving our youth, so who cares? This is something we have to do. And we'll make it there, I guarantee it — *if* the Coast Guard lets us."

He's impatient. To arrive at Portsmouth, England, the beginning of festivities by June 3, the 12-knot-an-hour *O'Brien* must ship out this week. But it still hasn't passed inspection.

"There's nothing we want more than for this ship to get there," says Coast Guard Petty Officer Gary Openshaw. "It's part of history. But, unfortunately, there are still problems. . . . We don't want any disasters."

Still to be done: loading and securing tons of lead weights as ballast to keep the *O'Brien* from capsizing. "Obviously, that's pivotal," says Openshaw. "But we do believe they can finish by the end of the week."

Not, however, without considerable mayhem and round-the-clock work schedules. These passageways bustle with sweaty-faced men in their 70s carrying boxes, huffing up ladders hauling tools, toiling in 130-degree heat below decks as they fire up the boilers.

The physical toll is substantial. "I guess three hours of sleep a night isn't enough," concedes Jim Wade, the *O'Brien*'s graying purser and chaplain, who was ordered to take the rest of the day off after growing dizzy. A half-hour later, he was back at work. "There's too much to do," he mumbles.

There are a few youngsters to help, two merchant marine cadets elated to go along but struggling with the complications of running a ship lacking computerized systems. "You have to do everything by hand," sighs Dirk Warren, 20. "It's going to be a long trip."

But the old-timers are untroubled by obstacles. For them, the *O'Brien* is precisely what a ship should be.

"She's a fine ship," says Capt. George Jahn, 78, the *O'Brien*'s commander. "Old or not . . . (she's) as seaworthy as they come."

Coleman Schneider, steward utility: "Upon coming aboard the *O'Brien,* I stepped into a beehive of activity. People were climbing all over the ship, sparks flew from welders, cables were strewn all over. The Coast Guard was here with the American Bureau of Shipping. The Navy was lending a helping hand."

On April 13, we shifted to San Francisco's Pier 35 for the big party sponsored by Otis Spunkmeyer. It was a grand bash but we weren't ready for it. Anna Falche with Kenneth R. Rawlings and Linda E. Railings, of Otis Spunkmeyer, Inc., did an outstanding job arranging for a beautiful buffet on the upper level of the pier while below was decorated in a carnival atmosphere complete with popcorn and soft pretzel wagons and Otis Spunkmeyer's celebrated cookies. Frank Jordan, the mayor of San Francisco, was the host. Guests of honor were Antony Ford, the British Consul General and Yvon Roe d'Albert, Consul General of France. A band played swing music. It was a gala affair and we wanted nothing more than to take a few hours to enjoy it. But . . . on our way over from the shipyard some fuel oil "burped" out of the air vents to the forward double-bottom tanks leaving a black, gooey mess all over the foredeck. As we tied up alongside, the foredeck was roped off, the band was told to stay on the pier, and visitors were restricted. The admiral, the captain, the chief mate and the second mate donned their dress blue uniforms and went ashore to meet the press on the pier while the engine department went to work on the mess.

Dick Brannon: "That was something. I can laugh about it now. Here they're throwing this big party right next to us and I'm out there on deck in coveralls, with sawdust, cleaning up fuel oil. And a couple of the Coast Guard inspectors, I gotta hand it to them, they pitched right in and got down on their hands and knees with us and helped wipe it up. So here's this party, everyone dressed up and us right alongside cleaning up fuel oil."

April 14 arrived — our departure date. Instead, we returned to the San Francisco Dry Dock. Every moment was occupied trying to clear off the items on the Coast Guard 835s Nils Anderson, who is a retired professional firefighter, gave a fire lecture and demonstration in the morning. His presentation was up-to-date and knowledgeable. The Coast Guard was visibly impressed. We conducted a fire drill. Everyone passed except the engine room which was told to try again the following day.

One of the few pleasures at this time was working with Joe Spears, the rigger foreman. He had a good sense of humor and was very knowledgeable. In charge of the dockyard cranes, he was the one we called on to shift loads of ballast from the deck to the hold or position liferafts for welding or load stores for the voyage. With a few simple instructions over the walkie-talkie to his crane operators Lee Burnett, Tom Watts and Gary Sproles, he could solve almost any problem that required the movement of something heavy. Then it was up to the riggers themselves, Tony, Tupa, Scott, Paul, Pimental, Jones, Carter and M. Thomas to sling, unsling and stow the load. This was usually done with a few simple gestures, telling the crane operator "boom up, swing right."

Ron Robson brought aboard a potted palm tree and set it on the deck just outside the captain's cabin. It was a humorous reference to an episode in the classic movie, "Mr. Roberts" and we all appreciated the allusion — all except the admiral. Second Mate Ray Conrady confided that the admiral didn't understand or see the humor in the palm tree! I made a promise to myself that, admiral or no, I would throw that tree over our last night out before returning to San Francisco.

Now, for some reason, the Coast Guard inspectors became easier to work with. It may have been a sense of mutual understanding; they respected how hard we were trying and we understood that they must answer to their boss. There was also a sense of so much energy and momentum moving us forward that they were simply worn down by it. The inspectors began trying to help, rather than hinder us. For several days they and, in particular, Guy Therriault, stayed late, spending extra time checking items.

One of the final touches before sailing was planting a palm tree. Ron Robson plants the tree, appropriately, outside Capt. Jahn's cabin.

Then Guy would go home and work on projects to help us, such as making copies of a required SOLAS safety book which Pete Lyse, the third mate, put together under his direction, or working out calculations for engineering items that had to be checked off the next day.

Someone asked Chief Engineer Dick Brannon how he was. His reply was, "Worse than I was yesterday, not as bad as I'll be tomorrow."

Since returning from the party we had been loading the anchor chain ballast which, surprisingly, arrived from Stockton on landing craft as promised. Joe Spears' crew set it in no. 2 lower hold and Stan Flowers' men built a wooden crib around it to keep it from shifting.* That night the last of the ballast was blocked in place. The deck log entry read, "2100 — Shipyard riggers completed blocking and securing ballast in forward holds."

Carl Nolte, of the *San Francisco Chronicle,* now came on as part of the crew. I had an extra slot for a midshipman, so, in lieu of that, Carl was made a day-working ordinary seaman, the same as our ship's photographer, Mike Emery. Carl would work as part of the crew and file reports to the *San Francisco Chronicle.* On April 16, the first of his articles as a crew member appeared:

> The Liberty Ship *Jeremiah O'Brien*, one of the oldest operating merchant ships in the world, is getting ready to sail from San Francisco on an epic voyage to yesterday. If all goes well, the trip will

---

*Our total ballast on board, sailing, was less than half the "optimum" 3,500 tons.

The day we all waited for approaches. The sailing board shows the next port (country, in this case) and the date and time of sailing. "Call back" means the time everyone must return to the ship.

make history, because the *O'Brien* will be commemorating the 50th anniversary of D-Day, the Allied invasion of France. It will also be an adventure, because most of the volunteer crew are veterans of World War II, steaming the old ship back to their own youth.

The *O'Brien* was there on June 6, 1944, carrying troops, then tanks and supplies. It is the only ship that was in the invasion armada — the largest in history — that is capable of making the trip back to Normandy.

The crew has already gotten a taste of the old wartime cliche that told people to hurry up as fast as they could so they could wait around as long as necessary. So far the sailing date has been postponed twice because the Coast Guard wants more work done to be sure the old ship is absolutely seaworthy. With any luck, the *O'Brien* will sail during the weekend.

"This is the last big adventure in a guy's life," said Ralph Ahlgren, who is 72 and served in the South Pacific. He is a retired printer, has not been to sea for more than 40 years and is shipping on the *O'Brien* as an oiler in the engine room.

For more than six weeks the old sailors have been working on the ship, getting it ready, loading fuel, meat, potatoes, beans, butter, paint, tools, brooms, toilet paper, soap, and the thousands of things that will be needed for a 20,000 mile voyage down the Pacific Coast to Panama, through the canal, across the Caribbean and the Atlantic to Portsmouth, England and France and then back to San Francisco.

"We will proceed to sea as soon as we are ready," said Captain George Jahn, the 78-year-old master of the ship. When is that? "As soon as we get certified," he said.

The crew has been put on six hour notice. On board, there is a kind of optimism and enthusiasm that only comes when volunteers overcome those who said it couldn't be done. They have waited a lifetime for this, a few extra days do not matter so much.

Every member of the crew has had to take a physical exam and all were certified fit. However, they all have been told in writing that "a significant risk to life and limb exists, and the usually expected measures may not be available, with potentially dire consequences, especially in the age group expected."

A doctor will be aboard, and so will the Rev. Jim Wade, an Anglican priest, who is doubling as the purser. Just to be on the safe side, the veterans have been augmented by some younger hands. Some of the less senior engineering officers are younger men. The kid in the engine room will be Dirk Warren, 20, a cadet from the U.S. Merchant Marine Academy at Kings Point, N.Y.

"This," he said, "is a great historical opportunity. I'm just gonna love it."

Money is still a problem. Nobody is getting paid, but the voyage is costing $2.4 million, and all but $300,000 has been raised. "We have good credit and have always paid our bills," said retired Rear Admiral Thomas Patterson, who is heading the effort and sailing with the ship.

"But with credit, you have to pay it back."

The debt aside, Patterson has high praise for the help the *O'Brien* got from the San Francisco maritime community. "You couldn't do a job like this anywhere but on the San Francisco waterfront," he said. "When you need them, they are there."

It will be a triumph if the ship makes it. Even sailing day will be a small triumph.

A nearly identical ship, the *John Brown*, was also planning to go from Baltimore to France for D-Day but the voyage was canceled Thursday, almost at the last minute. An inspection of the hull showed that the rivets on about half the length of the ship had to be renewed; the ship was not seaworthy. The cost of repairs, said Captain Brian Hope, who headed the project, "was beyond belief."

He called it "a terrible disappointment. We were done in by rivets."

One other old ship, the 1945 vintage *Lane Victory*, based in Los Angeles, is also expected to sail, perhaps in company with the *O'Brien*.

Almost everyone was living aboard. The crew began gathering in the messroom and the officers' saloon after dinner to talk and swap sea stories. A good sense of camaraderie was developing.

April 16 was another hectic day. We started the morning with 69 outstanding items on 835s. After three meetings and working at it all day, we reduced that number to 38.

Tom Patterson: "The work kept going but we also had many uncompleted items, 835s and other outstanding items that they wouldn't let us sail unless they were corrected. This was in all departments, deck department, engine department, stewards department, and radio shack, every place had things that we had to get done. And the 14th·crept up and we could not sail due to the outstanding items, then the 15th, the 16th, the 17th. Now we were really getting short. The Military Sealift Command director of engineering, Jack Sisson, happened to come over to the ship to bring us some artifact instruments for the reciprocating engine, and he said, 'Can I help you?' We said, 'Yes, you can help us. What we need you to do, Jack, punch this list out and organize a system here for us to get this work done.'"

Somehow, through all the turmoil, Capt. Jahn kept a pleasant, reassuring demeanor — except, of course, when there was a Coast Guard inspector in the vicinity.

April 17, the list of uncleared items was down to sixteen and many of those were partially complete. Again the Coast Guard stayed late to check off 835s.

Tom Patterson: "By the seventeenth we had the items under control and then the captain set the sailing board and we announced that we were going to leave." Late in the day Patterson pleaded with everyone to stay aboard to help finish correcting Coast Guard items, asking them to work into the night if necessary. Then he went home.

Tom Patterson: "There was only one other problem that we faced. We hadn't passed the four-hour sea trial in the Bay due to the fact that one boiler was down for cleaning. So we asked the Coast Guard for their concurrence to hold our sea trial on the way out with their inspectors on board. On that morning of the

Sailing day at last. François Le Pendu, Sam Wood and Pat McCafferty watch as shipyard workers bring the gangway aboard. Family, friends and well-wishers watch from the dock. Photo by Bruce McMurtry.

eighteenth all our families and friends and industry and everybody was down, and we left the dock."

Carl Nolte described it:

> This ship's voyage into history began just after noon yesterday, a nostalgic trip from San Francisco back into the world of 50 years ago.
>
> The *Jeremiah O'Brien*, the last seaworthy World War II Liberty ship, is on its way back to France to commemorate the anniversary of D-Day, June 6, 1944, and it sailed from the city that has been its home port with style and a little sadness.
>
> A crowd of friends and relatives cheered and waved as the *O'Brien* let go its lines at Pier 70 and slowly got under way at 12:05 p.m., four days and five minutes late.
>
> "Good-bye, good luck, and Godspeed, be careful," others called out, just like all the ship sailings in the old movies about wartime.
>
> Lunchtime crowds sitting in the sun at barside restaurants raised their glasses. On board, one could still hear the faint cheers.

Bev Masterson: "I felt sad in one way that the ship was leaving and this was the first time I couldn't be on her. Sad in one way and yet happy to see her go. I was so proud of her and the crew. Words can't express it, really."

Karen Kamimoto: "It almost seemed impossible and along the way different people were discouraged off and on but they'd get a second wind. It was a gorgeous sight to see that ship leave the dock."

Bill Duncan, deck engineer: "It was a wonderful feeling to see everyone on the dock waving good-bye. This was the second time on a Liberty for me, the first was coming from Europe after World War II. It was a strange sensation, like picking up fifty years later from where I left off."

We took on board several inspectors from the Coast Guard, FCC and ABS in addition to pilots, a compass adjuster, a Mackay radio technician and members of the press. Yachts and small boats milled around just off the pier, waiting to see us off. Finally, just before noon, we let go the lines and slowly eased away from the dock. Whistles and horns blew. One boat had a small cannon on board which it fired several times. Picking up speed, we headed toward the Oakland-Bay Bridge, there were more whistles — the traditional three long blasts, which we answered with the *O'Brien*'s deep-throated, authoritative foghorn, then a short blast followed by our own short blast. As we passed under the bridge and crossed toward the Golden Gate, the San Francisco fire boat *Guardian* joined us spouting gushers of red, white and blue water in arcing geysers that reflected rainbow prisms in their mist. Several yachts came along, then helicopters from local television stations appeared, hovering first above the ship, then at wheelhouse level. The beautiful skyline of the city passed on our port side, bright geometric blocks of glass and color in the periphery of our vision.

Even while all this was going on we continued working on those last 835s. Engineers welded the 'tween deck doors shut, showed the Coast Guard that each boiler, each system was working properly. On deck we broke out fire hoses and, with an inspector inside the 'tween deck, sprayed the hatches to prove their watertightness.

As we passed under the Golden Gate Bridge a thick fog set in. Suddenly the aircraft and small boats disappeared. Third Mate Pete Lyse began blowing the required fog signal, one long blast every two minutes. We were on our own except for the pilot boat following along to take off the inspectors, the media and the pilot. Up in the wheelhouse I turned the radar on. It didn't work. Well, no problem, I thought, we'll use the backup, a small yacht radar on the flying bridge. Racing up the ladder to the next deck I turned on the standby set. It wasn't working either. Well, I thought, at least we have the gyrocompass. The pilot knows the courses, he can get us out. Keeping a calm demeanor, the second mate, Ray Conrady, and I sent the nearby Coast Guard inspectors off with the bosun to check off another 835 item, one as far away from where we were as possible.

"Gyro's not working," said Capt. Pat Butner, the pilot, when everyone was out of earshot.

"How about the magnetic compass?" I asked hopefully. We both looked at the compass adjuster who was busily taking readings and making calculations. He shook his head no.

Oh, Lord, I thought.

"Don't worry," said Capt. Butner. "I'm on the radio to the pilot boat. He's got us on his radar. He'll guide us out."

With crossed fingers, we managed to distract the Coast Guard's attention from the problems on the bridge and quietly followed the pilot boat out through the fog.

Then the final moment came. The Coast Guard and ABS gave Capt. Jahn our certificates and agreed we could go. Guy Therriault, of the Coast Guard, held out his hand. "All right, Mate. We're leaving," he said.

I shook his hand and said, "Good." Realizing how it sounded I said, "I didn't mean . . ." Then we both laughed.

As the last pilot boat departed Capt. Jahn ordered a southerly course (the gyro, which takes more than an hour to warm up, was working now) and full ahead on the engines. At last, we were on our way.

4

A Downhill Run

A nd so, once again, to sea.

Now, the ship was ours. Gone, at last, were the Coast Guard, FCC and American Bureau of Shipping. Gone were the TV cameras and news photographers. Gone were the shipyard workers, deliverymen, inspectors, chandlers, visitors and officials. We could finally settle in and get on with our voyage to Normandy.

The intense effort of the last few weeks left us exhausted. A passage in Melville's *Moby Dick* sums up how many of us felt, "Whenever I find myself growing grim about the mouth; whenever it is a damp, drizzly November in my soul; whenever I find myself involuntarily pausing before coffin warehouses, and bringing up the rear of every funeral I meet; and especially whenever my hypos* get such an upper hand on me, that it requires a strong moral principle to prevent me from deliberately stepping into the street,

---

*Short for 'hypochondria," a state of depression somewhat more chronic and morbid than modern day "blues."

and methodically knocking people's hats off — then, I account it high time to get to sea as soon as I can." Doctors once prescribed "a long ocean voyage" as therapy. We were ready for it. It was good to be at sea again, on a ship rolling gently to the grey northwesterly Pacific swell coming in on our starboard quarter.

Rich Reed, bosun: "The best part was getting away. You know, finally leaving after all the bullshit we went through, running around with the Coast Guard and everything, the sea trials. To me one of the real high points of the whole trip was the getting away."

Jim Conwell, AB: "When we sailed on April 18th, I wasn't certain that we were really going. We were kind of on the ragged edge. We still had Coast Guard inspectors on board. The rumor mill was, well, we're not really going, we're just on a sea trial, we'll return. But then we put the Coast Guard folks on the pilot boat and off we went. So that was certainly a very positive experience."

Hans Miller, third assistant engineer: "As soon as the last pilot boat left, I was happy."

Most of our electronics problems soon resolved themselves. The magnetic compasses were accurate by the time the compass adjuster left the ship. The gyro settled onto the correct heading by the time we cleared the pilot station. And the smaller of the two radars was working. That left the ARPA radar. It took another day for Ed Smith, our electrician, to solve the electrical problems which caused it to receive the wrong amperage. It worked perfectly the remainder of the trip. Oh, and the fog lifted by the time we cleared the Farallons, the barren rock islands that lie off the entrance to San Francisco Bay, so we didn't need the radar immediately anyway. But for a while it was almost as if the old ship was protesting all the newfangled equipment.

As we steamed south, a few miles offshore, some of the steward's department, Ron Smith, Al Martino, Eddy Pubill, Rudy Arellano and a few off-watch members of the black gang, Gene Anderson, Bill Concannon, Richard Hill, Arnold Sears, Dirk Warren and Jim Gillis, stayed on deck, watching the California coast pass.

Most of us went to bed and slept as long and deeply as the shipboard routine would allow.

The next day, April 19, was spent securing and clearing the decks. Assisted by the watch-standers who weren't on duty, our deck department day workers, Joe Callahan, Mike Emery, Bruce McMurtry and Carl Nolte turned to under Rich Reed's guidance lashing the gangways and booms in place, making up guys, preventers and runners, and making sure the spare parts and equipment in the lower decks were secure. By noon, engineer Bob Noiseux had the welds on the 'tween deck watertight doors cut and the added lips on the companionway entrances removed. We gave the ship a thorough washdown, from flying bridge to main deck and from bow to stern, sluicing her with salt water from the fire hoses. Some people call it getting the "land" off the ship.

Most of the crew spent their off-watch hours sleeping and stowing personal gear in their rooms, something we had little time for in the turmoil of the last few weeks. I had packages of cookies, chips, candy and other munchies my wife packed for me. As I was stowing them in a locker under my bunk, Dr. Haslam knocked on my door offering cookies that his girlfriend sent along. We soon learned that almost everyone on board had extra bags of cookies, tins of nuts, chips, soft drinks, liquor and other goodies, all sent by loved ones from home.

This first full day out was a grand mix of feelings. We — or most of us — felt twinges of guilt mingled with regret at leaving our wives and families behind, gratitude to them for letting us go, excitement at being away on our own, yet missing them to share in the exhilarating experience. But overlaying it all was the thrill of the voyage. Being at sea again was exciting. We were on a great adventure, the adventure of a lifetime.

Tom Patterson: "We were all so happy at that point to be at sea."

Norm Burke, oiler: "It was a fantasy for all of us old timers that worked on the *O'Brien* for 10 or 12 years to take it out the Gate, and go out to sea for three or four days. Now it came to pass. And not just three or four days but for several months. It was almost too good to be true."

Phil Sinnott: "The sun and the moon and the stars were all in the right configuration for this thing, and I was part of it. It's amazing how quickly you can fall back into the old patterns of sailing. It amazed me how quickly the crew dropped so easily back into that after so long, no doors slamming, the quiet. . ."

On the port side of the main deck are located the two crew messrooms, one forward of the other, separated by a pantry. The forward one was originally the gunners'* mess but now served the black gang. In it two tables run fore and aft with rows of swivel seats welded to the deck on either side. This was Jack Carraher's domain, he being the messman assigned to that room. Greg Williams worked in the pantry, washing dishes and silverware and helping in the messrooms. The after messroom contained two fore and aft tables with swivel seats and a small two-man table. Bosun Rich Reed (later, Marty Wefald) and Bob Burnett, carpenter, sat at the two-man table while the rest of the deck department shared the remaining tables and seats with the gunners. This was the realm of Rudy Arellano, messman. Meals were always served on time: breakfast from 0730 to 0830, lunch from 1130 to 1230 and dinner from 1700 to 1745. When not used for meals, the messes served as recreation rooms. During these times it was common to find Otto Sommerauer, gunner's mate, reading a magazine, Alex Hochstraser, fireman/watertender, writing a letter home, Dick Currie playing solitaire at one table, Sam Wood and Bruce McMurtry playing chess at another, a political discussion between Jim Miller, Marty Shields and Ron Smith at still another. The crew constantly wandered in and out to see who was there and visit if they weren't working.

In the saloon, tradition has the officers taking the same seat at each meal. At dinner that evening Capt. Jahn established the seating for the officers' mess: he, the admiral and the chief engineer sat at the center table. The mates took the starboard table and the engineers the port one. The radio operator, doctor

---

*During World War II merchant ships carried U.S. Navy gunners as part of their regular crew. A freighter such as the *O'Brien* carried up to 27 enlisted men and a gunnery officer. Their sole purpose was to man the guns and protect the ship.

Part of the steward's department getting ready for dinner. Left to right, Coleman Schneider, Jack Carraher, Pat McCafferty and Russ Mosholder. Photo courtesy of Coleman Schneider.

and purser sat with either the mates or the engineers, depending on where there was an empty seat, and the cadets sat at the aft table. Tom Patterson sat at dinner wearing his admiral's stars on

Rudy Arellano stokes the galley range for another day of gourmet cooking. Photo by Bruce McMurtry.

his collar. Everyone else dressed as they do on most merchant ships: khakis without insignia or civilian clothes.

Al Martino was the head cook, and responsible for preparing main courses and planning meals. Jimmy Farras was the second cook and baker. He prepared breads, pastries, rolls, vegetables and main courses. Eduardo Pubill was the third cook. His task was to assist in any way. Between them, they immediately demonstrated to everyone that we had signed on a "feeder." Breakfast consisted of juice, melon, toast, muffins, hot and cold cereal, bacon or sausage, scrambled eggs, hot cakes or French toast. Lunch was often chicken, pasta, or sandwiches with a vegetable such as cauliflower, or potato chips or coleslaw or a green salad, with cake and/or our famed Otis Spunkmeyer cookies for dessert. Dinner would be salad with a choice of dressings, steak, fish, pork or lamb with potatoes, green beans or some other vegetable and cake or pudding and again cookies for dessert.

In the evening many of the crew repaired to no. 2 hold which became our theater. Five hundred videos and two television sets with built-in VCRs were loaned to the ship by the Norway House of San Francisco, a charitable organization that also provides newspapers, magazines, books and "home away from home" services to merchant ships. If two films were shown, the second would be in the officers' mess. As we got farther into the tropics, the movies moved out onto the deck. On this first leg Coke Schneider masterminded the movie schedule. Our first screening was "The Cruel Sea."

On April 20 we went through the Santa Barbara Channel. It was a beautiful sunny day with blue skies. The ship rolled gently to a moderate following sea. Everyone on board was so familiar with the appearance of the *O'Brien* that we never gave it a second thought. But as we rounded Point Concepcion, Phil Sinnott, the AB at the wheel, pointed out a large containership traveling northbound. Drawing nearer we saw it was American President Lines' *President Adams*. They called on the bridge-to-bridge radio and wished us well, commenting on how good we looked. The mate on watch knew all about the voyage, hoped we made good speed and said he wished he was there with us.

Suddenly we realized the world had not seen an armed merchant ship in the open ocean since the late 1940s. We were a floating time capsule. Our voyage had received wide coverage, and we learned that it was being followed with avid interest and enthusiasm. The old-time camaraderie of the sea came back to the industry for this voyage. Modern maritime commerce has become a routine, undramatic, uninteresting business that all but ignores the old-time brotherhood of the sea. But mariners everywhere seemed to yearn for that lost camaraderie and all through the trip, ships of all types — cargo vessels, Navy ships, boats, yachts, tankers — greeted us, blew their whistles in salute and took pictures, often changing course to do so.

The entry in the deck log simply read: "1135 Spoke the *President Adams*, northbound."

On the evening 8-to-12 watch, we entered the Long Beach Traffic Control Zone. The Coast Guard tracks all ships approaching and leaving the Los Angeles/Long Beach area on radar and by bridge-to-bridge radio. Although we were simply passing through, we were in the zone. They followed us on their radars as we passed outside the main traffic lanes and between Catalina Island and Long Beach. Leaving their area of control it was apparent they recognized the name of the ship, they wished us a pleasant voyage and good luck.

A few minutes later we sighted a bright stationary light in the darkness just ahead and to the right of our course. As we drew nearer, the light separated into several and it became clear a dredge was working the area. The dredge called on the bridge-to-bridge radio and advised how much clearance to give as we passed. When he learned the name of our ship the dredge captain's conversation changed from business to an interested discussion of who was on board from which maritime schools (he was a California Maritime Academy graduate), the nature of our voyage and how fortunate we were. Signing off he, too, wished us good luck and God speed.

It wasn't long before we realized there are actually some advantages to sailing an old Liberty ship over modern ones. Modern ships are air-conditioned, all the rooms, passageways and entrances have airtight doors. There are no smells outside your own room. On the *O'Brien,* the doors aren't sealed. They have louvers at the bottom and portholes are left open for ventilation and every time the cooks began working in the galley the smell of food permeated the ship. It was wonderful, the mixed smells of chocolate chip cookies, bacon, bread, pancakes, sausage, chicken, more cookies,

One morning's baking by the galley crew and one reason for so many good smells throughout the ship. Photo by Bruce McMurtry.

roasts, potatoes, muffins and more cookies. Even the simple, pungent smell of coal burning somehow added to the feeling of traveling back in history to a better time.

The atmosphere lulled us all into reminiscent moods. At lunch Capt. Jahn talked about working for United Fruit Company just after the strike of '34. He was an AB on one of their ships. After the ship arrived in San Francisco and discharged its cargo of bananas, it was his job to sweep out the refrigeration compartments in which the bananas were stowed. They contained a few loose stalks and bits and pieces of dunnage. Because the bananas were refrigerated, the snakes and tarantulas that came along with them went dormant, sleeping most of the way. With the cargo off and the refrigeration shut down, these creatures slowly came back to life. Young George Jahn suddenly found his broom alive with slithery, crawly things. "I didn't stay there long," he said. "Those things gave me the willies."

After lunch those of us off-watch would sometimes go for a brief rest in our bunks, drifting off to the mild sound and vibration of the engine's thump, thump, thump as it pushed us on our way. It was a curiously soothing and quiet sound, so different from the harsh, mechanical high-pitched whines and explosive roars of modern diesel engines. Later, everyone was pleasantly surprised to learn we made 12.4 knots for our first twenty-four hour run from noon to noon. We had cautiously projected nine knots for the trip.

After all the pre-departure turmoil, we had a chance to settle into our rooms. In part, this meant cleaning out the accumulation of the previous fourteen years. I had no use for most of the charts, books, keys, extra blankets, ashtrays and miscellaneous junk in my cabin. But it wouldn't do to throw it away, someone might have a use for it. While the second and third mates were on watch, I gave them each several armloads of "stuff" by setting it on their beds. When I came off watch myself, there was a similar pile of junk in my bed. After a day or two of this round robin, I noticed some familiar items, the stuff I tried to get rid of was coming back to me.

Left to right, Joe Callahan, Coleman Schneider, Sam Wood, Jim Wade, Tom Patterson and Pete Lyse attending the burial at sea.

That afternoon we conducted two burials at sea. Relatives of Capt. McMichael, former master of the Nuclear Ship *Savannah* and the *O'Brien's* first peacetime master, arranged for his ashes to be scattered at sea. We also buried the remains of an aged San Franciscan. It was our first opportunity to see purser/padre Jim Wade in his Anglican finery. He gave a long-winded but very appropriate service.

The ship steamed on, rolling gently on a slight swell. In the distance we saw whales. Nearby, porpoises playfully swam ahead of the ship, cutting back and forth in front of the bow.

During the day we received the following radiogram:

TO: CAPTAIN GEORGE JAHN, OFFICERS AND CREW
    SS JEREMIAH O'BRIEN

FROM: SS LURLINE

I TAKE THE GREATEST PLEASURE AND SATISFACTION IN HEARING OF YOUR SUCCESSFUL DEPARTURE FROM SAN FRANCISCO, COMMENCING YOUR HISTORIC RETURN TO THE BEACHES OF NORMANDY. MAY YOU HAVE A SMOOTH PLEASANT PASSAGE AND A SAFE RETURN.

ON BEHALF OF ALL MY OFFICERS AND CREW - GOOD LUCK AND BON VOYAGE!

CAPT ROBERT BUELL
MASTER, SS LURLINE
MATSON NAVIGATION CO.

We also received welcome word that Norton, Lilly and Co., who would be our ship's agent in the Western hemisphere, had arranged to have some of the charges for going through the Canal waived in each direction, $3,750 worth of line handling, admeasurement, tug fees and other items. The fees for the transit itself could not be waived due to a treaty between Panama, Colombia and the United States that allows for such a contingency for Panamanian and Colombian warships only. The transit would now cost $9,680.

Much of the more lengthy communications between the ship and shore was done by SITOR, a computer-to-computer satellite system. This included Carl Nolte's dispatches to the *Chronicle,* Second Mate Ray Conrady's to the *Examiner* and the nightly "Crew's News."

Bill Bennett, AB on the 12-to-4 watch, took on the task of writing the crew's news. It was dispatched daily and read into a telephone message by Gary North of KFS World Communications* in Half Moon Bay, California, (a marine radio station handling traffic from ship-to-shore and vice versa) which generously donated all the official communication charges for the ship. Gary North became known as "The Voice of the *Jeremiah O'Brien*." The number was called scores of times each day by crew families and interested members of the public.

Marci Hooper: "Thank heavens we had the hookup with PacBell [Pacific Bell] and KFS. Bennett, the pen, and Gary North, the voice, to the public, took a great deal of heat off of us as an everyday chore. People could call and hear how the ship was doing without calling us."

Gary's speaking voice, rich, deep and expressive, couldn't have been better if we requested it from central casting. Bill's first enthusiastic message went out on April 20 and read:

This is the Voice of the *Jeremiah O'Brien.*
Good evening San Francisco and greetings from the *Jeremiah O'Brien* — day three of our voyage back to the beaches of Normandy. Our vessel entered Mexican territorial waters at 0330 today and our noon position is 40 miles south of the port of Ensenada. Ship's speed the past 24 hours averaged 11.4 knots at 68 revolutions per minute. Chief engineer Dick Brannon is all smiles. When asked about the operation of his giant, triple-expansion steam engine, his response was just one word: "Excellent!"

The message traffic went both ways.

THIS IS TO CAPTAIN GEORGE JAHN AND CREW OF THE JER O'BRIEN EN ROUTE TO FRANCE AS A YOUNG 17 YEAR OLD

---

*KFS World Communications recently changed its name to Globe Wireless

Even the political pundits were aware of our voyage. This cartoon by the San Francisco Chronicle'*s Tom Meyer suggests an alternative use for the ship. Cartoon courtesy of the* San Francisco Chronicle.

ABLE-BODIED SEAMAN I SAILED 5 LIBERTIES FROM 1943-45 I AM ENJOYING VOYAGE AS IF I WERE WITH YOU. HAVE A SAFE TRIP AND GOD SPEED WATCH OUT FOR U BOATS IN THE ATLANTIC. WARM REGARDS
JOE AND JUDY MC REYNOLDS

By April 21 we were off the coast of Baja California and 800 miles into the voyage. The sky was overcast in the morning and cleared in the afternoon and the ship sailed on, surrounded by a calm blue sea. There was a growing feeling of bonhomie as everyone got more rest and fell into the routine of day-to-day ship operation. For the present, this meant chipping, scraping and painting areas repaired in the shipyard that were left unpainted in the rush to get us out; re-stowing gear in the 'tween decks; making sure all mechanical and electrical systems were working properly.

Today was the first laundry day. The washing machines were located in no. 5 'tween deck, three old Maytag wringer-type washers that were scavenged from Victory ships at the Reserve Fleet. The engineers got them working and visions of washing clothes by hand in buckets of salt water thankfully vanished. Of course there were no dryers. This was not a modern ship. Drying lines were run in no. 4 and 5 'tween decks and in the fidley (the upper engine room casing). Clothes dried overnight in the 'tween deck or in about four hours in the fidley, although there were times in the tropics that clothes dried even before we finished hanging them out. Today, carrying my bag of dirty laundry aft, I went through the companionway at the after end of no. 5 hatch and down into the 'tween deck. A few others were there, doing the same chore. It was a reeducation in a process most of us hadn't been part of for thirty years, but we gradually reached a consensus on how to do what. Separate whites from colors. Wash whites in one tub, colors in another. Put one cup of soap and a splash of bleach in each. Run for twenty to thirty minutes. Pump water off, take clothes out and run them through wringer, refill with fresh water, rinse soap out by running each load another 10 to 15 minutes. Run clothes through wringer again. Carry wet laundry to fidley and hang anywhere there's space and it won't interfere with the engineers' duties. Remove laundry as soon as dry so someone else can use the fidley. A sense of affinity developed in sharing our newly-acquired knowledge on how to use the old wringer machines.

Ironically, most of the mechanical problems we encountered were with the new equipment. The Inmarsat system (a satellite telephone system) came with a backup, battery-operated, power supply if the main power supply failed. For some reason this prevented the Inmarsat from operating. Finally Bob Gisslow, the radio operator, figured out that by by-passing the backup, satellite communications would be restored. When disconnected however, the system sent out an "A" (dit-dah) in Morse code, presumably to warn the operator that it was disconnected. There was no way to shut the sound off. We heard dit-dah, dit-dah, dit-dah, for the next several days, becoming slightly weaker and more plaintive each day, until the battery was drained.

Bob Gisslow: "In the very initial portions of the voyage I was completely new to lots of the equipment that I was using, and still reviewing the use of the old stuff that I hadn't used in so many years. The difficulties that occurred in the equipment in the initial stages was tiresome. But after awhile it all seemed to straighten out so that I was comfortable with our means of communication."

On this day, we resumed the old tradition of ringing each half hour of time as the watch progressed. There is a bell outside the wheelhouse with a lanyard that leads to the helmsman. As the ship's clock struck each half hour, he rang the same number of strokes on the bell. It was a carryback to years ago and another pleasant reminder of the historic nature of our voyage.

Tom Patterson: "We were running into wonderful weather and the ship, instead of making the ten knots that we had counted on, suddenly started to build up eleven knots and twelve knots."

Someone asked the captain how we could be making such good time, averaging almost twelve knots. Common wisdom was that Libertys could only go eight to ten. "We're going down hill, that's why," Capt. Jahn replied. In the sense that our latitude was constantly decreasing, he was right.

The next day the weather was even warmer with a gentle following sea and the wind astern. Now and then, a flying fish leapt out of the water, and the crew conjectured on the wonderful sportfishing in these waters, if only we had the time. Breakfast was melon, cereal, pancakes and sausage. Except for the melon, we all knew what was cooking hours ahead of time from the aromas permeating the ship.

A particular atmosphere developed as we sailed the calm blue seas under azure skies, both mellow and playful, like the porpoises that kept us company.

Bosun Rich Reed pulled a classic practical joke on novice seaman Mike Emery. He said, "Hey, kid, I need something. Grab a bucket here and go down in the engine room and get the engineers to give you a bucket of steam."

Mike went down below, going from one man to another until he caught on. "So I drew a bucket of water," he said, "and went back on deck and gave it to the bosun. 'Jeez,' I said, 'it was steam when I started. It must have melted.'"

Carl Nolte: "On the oldest ship in the American Merchant Marine, they play the oldest jokes in the steamship business."

Back in San Francisco, our shoreside office was having a difficult time handling the admiral's messages and everything else that was going on. Marci Hooper: "Once the ship departed we were dealing with shipping pieces of machinery to Panama and we were still trying to arrange things in the European ports. Also, we had to deal with all the things that got put aside. Everything that was done in those last three months before sailing was extraordinary. We fought fires, we were fire-fighters of the highest degree. Everyone who called had a problem, whether it was when we were going to cruise again to how do I reach my father. From January to November [1994] the office went from a mode of dealing with things in a routine manner to a standard pattern of firefighting. Our little office with a handful of people and only two phonelines had become the operations center for a major steamship company."

The volunteers that stayed behind continued their efforts, relieving some of the pressure. Karen Kamimoto: "Some of the crew that didn't go would come to the office and hang out. They felt lost without the ship there. Fortunately we had a whole compendium of volunteers, Norm Schoenstein and Ray Pallacin were a big help. They came in every Tuesday. The volunteers are a great group of people."

Adm. Patterson spent every waking moment sending and receiving letters, messages and faxes. It was as if he never slept. The radio operator, Bob Gisslow, was constantly in the radio shack sending and receiving the admiral's radio traffic. After three days of this he asked at dinner one night, "Why didn't the admiral just meet us over there?"

One side effect of all the electronics traffic was apparent to everyone. Many brought portable radios along for entertainment. But each time our radio operator sent a message his transmissions were so powerful they drowned out any incoming signals. It was frustrating to tune in to a station then have your program vanish in a loud caterwauling of dots, dashes and electronic noise.

Tom Patterson: "I sent an invitation to President Clinton inviting him to come aboard with Mrs. Clinton and meet our crew while we were at the Commemoration. I sent this in through the Military Sealift Command network and asked them to get it to the White House, which they very nicely did."

When Patterson wasn't sending or receiving messages, he spent much of his time examining the chart, worried about being within two or four miles of shallow areas. Capt. Jahn, having spent much of his life on tugboats, liked to pass close to shore, "to see what it looks like." With the Global Positioning System donated by American President Lines, we could pinpoint our position to within a few feet. The admiral, schooled in older types of navigation where a position within five miles was considered decent accuracy, simply couldn't abide what he considered "getting too close." He didn't want to interfere, after all, as he told us before the trip, he was only the "owner's representative," not the captain. Complicating the issue was the fact that the ship and the whole voyage was really his baby. It, and we, wouldn't be there but for him. In the end Capt. Jahn prevailed, but the admiral did a lot of checking.

There was a sense of mission on the part of the crew. On deck one frequently heard, "We have a job to do." It might seem a subtle difference but unlike other merchant ships, our job was not getting a cargo on a ship somewhere, but getting the ship itself somewhere. Yet everyone easily and comfortably fell into the routine of a past lifetime of experience. If you added up the seagoing experience of those on board, it would probably total a millennium.

We passed Cabo San Lucas after dinner. Capt. Jahn brought the ship within a half mile of the beach to see the sights. Everyone was on deck. We saw modern houses and resort hotels, dune buggies running up and down the brown sand hills, a few roads and little traffic. The hotels were gleaming, bright, modern buildings. A few small boats came out loaded with tourists, waving and shouting as we steamed past.

Saturday, April 23 was another beautiful day. The air was warm and balmy with blue skies and tranquil seas. Since all the crew — from captain to wiper — were volunteers, no one was paid, so no one watched the overtime, weekends were just ordinary days and work went on as usual. No one minded. We moved the deck watch from the wheelhouse up to the flying bridge. Here one really felt close to nature — nothing but sky overhead, the living sea all around, and the ship gently rolling and yawing under your feet.

Bruce McMurtry, deck utility: "Actually I did get paid for a while. I'm in the Naval Reserve and requested non-pay orders to active duty on the *O'Brien*. They were turned down. I mentioned it to Adm. Patterson and he interceded with Adm. Tadeshi. The next thing I know I received orders assigning me as First Class Master-at-Arms on the *SS Jeremiah O'Brien* in a pay status. I was probably the last active-duty U.S. Navy sailor to serve on a Liberty ship. I was attached 14 April 94 and detached 13 May 94 at which point we were in the middle of the North Atlantic."

Everything wasn't blue skies and roses. Bill Duncan: "We had a few problems on the way over, minor problems. A lot of the facilities had not been used in fifty years, sewer drains, shower drains, and little by little they blocked up. We had to take them apart and clear them. It was a very awkward position for old guys when these pipes were in hard-to-reach places. When we were younger we could just hold on with one hand, but now it was different. One shower line blocked up right over the engine, and we had to climb up over pipes, strap ourselves in with ropes, cut the pipe and replace it. We were swinging there like monkeys. But we did it."

The Pabst Brewing Company and the Olympia Brewing Company donated several pallets of beer to the ship and that afternoon, at 1600, Russ Mosholder broke out a case of beer on the after deck. It was an instant attraction and the beginning of a tradition that would last the entire voyage. It gave the crew a chance to unwind and let down after a hard day of chipping, painting, oiling, repairing and cooking.

But the beer almost didn't make the voyage. Russ disliked drinking aboard ship: "I didn't want that beer on the ship. Well, the crew had other ideas. I think one of the funnier things was the morning I was going to have all the beer unloaded back on the dock. The beer was on pallets over there and I got permission from the admiral and Anna Falche to take the pallets off. By the time I got up in the morning it was all gone. It was already stowed below decks. I had to laugh about that."

Rich Reed: "Yeah, you know, on the old stick ships like this, the crew, they gathered around after lunch or after dinner at number four hatch. They swapped sea stories. They got to know each other. That's a thing of the past. Now there's no camaraderie. Ships are all container cells and narrow decks. There's no place to gather. And the crews are a lot smaller, so you work and you get off watch and there's nobody around 'cause the crew's so small. The last ship I was on, an eight hundred fifty-foot tanker, had a crew of sixteen on there. And you just don't get the camaraderie. You know, it's just that everybody's asleep. There are not enough guys to sit around and when you are you're usually so dog-tired anyway but here, it's just right aft of the house, right outside everybody's room.

> Bosun Rich Reed began sailing in the Sailor's Union of the Pacific immediately out of high school in 1965. Working in all capacities from ordinary seaman to bosun, he served in the merchant marine in Vietnam, carrying supplies and ammunition to our fighting forces. For the past several years he has captained the pilot boat for the San Francisco Bar Pilots. He has been a volunteer with the *O'Brien* for fourteen years. He and his wife and children live in Novato, California.

"That's where I learned to tie probably half the knots I know. You sit around after supper out there on the hatch and the stories start to go, and somebody gets a line out and starts showing the guys how to tie knots, and it's just a good way to get things going. I mean, everybody has a good time out there and they razz each other and tell sea stories, none of which are true. When I was around the SUP hall, talking to guys about making the trip, one thing everybody brought up, and everybody misses, is that. They really do."

Tonight's movie was "Action in the North Atlantic," with Humphrey Bogart. If ever there was a training film for the merchant marine, this is it. Made during World War II, it tells the story of the crew of a merchant ship sunk by a German submarine. They return to sea and sink a submarine themselves. It's the type of story that fires you with patriotism and makes you want to go out and fight Nazis, even fifty years after the fact.

On Sunday it was again calm and warm, although overcast. Schools of grey dolphins lazily turned and jumped around the ship during the 8-to-12 watch. We raised the church pennant, a blue cross on a white triangular background, for Jim Wade to hold church services in the morning. Although Anglican, he had arranged permission to conduct Protestant and Catholic services. Someone jokingly said, "Why didn't he talk to a rabbi? Then he could have covered all the bases."

Sunday dinner, in keeping with tradition, was a treat: cucumber and onion salad, steak, baked potatoes, cauliflower, homemade rolls and rice pudding. It was followed by a double-feature, "Patton" and "Tora, Tora, Tora." The next night's double feature was aimed at submarine aficionados, "Das Boot," and "The Hunt for Red October." Our taste in movies was certainly becoming predictable.

The next day the weather turned from comfortably beautiful to hot and beautiful. The sky was clear, the seas a flat, calm, deep blue. We passed Acapulco in the early morning and entered the Gulf of Tehuantepec and the thermometer began to rise.

Adm. Patterson made a curious remark. He said, "The ship just gets better all the time, but all we do is get older." Looking around, though, it appeared that everyone was getting younger. People walked with a bounce in their step. Animated chatter, laughter and jokes filled the messrooms. Good will abounded. Everyone seemed to be reliving his youth and the spirit was infectious.

Jim Conwell, one of the ABs on my watch, said that a few days earlier he asked Second Mate Ray Conrady if he would help him learn to take star sights. "He gave me two copies of Bowditch, the Star Almanac, a Nautical Almanac, and two or three other references."

"Well, that's a good start."

"Yes, but now I'm afraid to ask him the time. He'll probably give me a book on how to make a watch."

Journal entry for April 26: "Hot, hot, hot."

Heat permeated the old steel ship. Everyone outside was working in shorts and T-shirts or just shorts. The crew broke out the cots and began sleeping on top of the hatches and on the main deck.

> During World War II Norman Burke went through the maritime school in Catalina at the age of 18 and three days later was assigned to the Liberty Ship *William Proust* as an oiler. He later sailed on a T-2 tanker, ocean-going tugs and finally on a C-2 where he was an electrician. Coming ashore he became president of his own rubber company. Active with the *Jeremiah O'Brien* for more than a decade, he is retired and is on the Board of Directors of the NLSM. He and his wife reside in Los Gatos, California.

Passing by the chief engineer's room one day, I saw Dick Brannon at his typewriter dressed in shorts with a red bandanna wrapped around his head, looking for all the world like an Indian. Third Mate Pete Lyse said the thermometer was at 98° in the afternoon. Sam Wood, 8-to-12 ordinary seaman, was working on deck dressed in shorts with a blue bandanna wrapped around his head. All he needed was an eyepatch and a cutlass to look like a pirate.

If it was "hot, hot, hot" on deck, conditions in the engine room were hellish. Its only "air conditioning" was the adjustable cowl ventilators on the flying bridge and the open sky lights at the top of the fidley. Temperatures soared to 110°, 120°, even 130°.

Oiler Norm Burke's job was to squirt oil into the piston bearings of the three-cylinder steam engine every thirty minutes. Then he oiled the moving crossheads, running the oil can up and down in time with their movement. Norm Burke: "The working conditions in a Liberty ship in the engine room are very severe. I was concerned because at my age of sixty-nine, I didn't snap back as a young kid would do under the temperature extremes. It was very hard for me to get enough fluids in over a twenty-four hour period to survive the heavy perspiration and the work down there. It was difficult, but I felt comfortable that I'd make it all right."

Bill Duncan: "The biggest problem in the engine room was the heat. When the weather was hot outside it was thirty degrees hotter in the engine room. If the ship was moving and the funnels were turned in the right direction you got some air, if not, you didn't get any. The heat was the big problem."

Steve Worthy, first assistant engineer: "When I volunteered, I said I was only going to work for three weeks. I was up to six weeks and I told them I wanted to get off in Panama. I was looking forward to it. The engine room was hot. But the biggest aspect was your room, the conditions. I missed the air conditioning. There wasn't any place to cool off. But at least no one was shooting torpedoes at us either."

Despite the heat, the sense of adventure was real. In the crew mess at night, one often saw three or four people sitting at tables writing. Everyone seemed to be keeping a journal of the voyage. Our purpose, our ship, and the historic "once in a lifetime" voyage seemed to inspire everyone to record this bit of living history. Carl Nolte and I pestered everyone with questions and interviews. Mike Emery was usually found with three or four cameras dangling off him, even when doing his regular chores on deck. There were frequently two or three camcorders going at any one instant. This would be the best-recorded voyage in history.

On the night watch we saw distant faint flashes of heat lightning but it was much too far away to hear, shimmering

Phil Frank's Farley and Bruce the Raven, long popular in the Bay Area, took on added interest with the crew when Farley became envious of Carl Nolte. Courtesy Phil Frank and San Francisco Chronicle.

occasionally in a cloud bank hovering along the Mexican Coast. Around 2300, the lookout reported a ship's light forward. Then it rose, a dark orange ball of a full moon, directly ahead of the *O'Brien.* The night became bright with pale moonlight. The sea ahead was a path of silver and gold. The masts and booms were outlined with moonlight and dark shadows. On deck, a few of the crew leaned on the rail, watching the silvery water; the orange glow of a cigarette arced into the sea. Behind them, someone tossed in their cot, a sheet billowing momentarily, ghostlike. A bird, a booby, landed on a light standard on the bow and, tucking its head under its wing, went to sleep.

Herb Caen's celebrated column in the *San Francisco Chronicle* carried the following item on April 27:

> A bit of humor *noir* from Richard Knight about our gallant Liberty ship, *Jeremiah O'Brien.* As she draws ever closer to the open seas, Knight envisions Germany's last restored U-boat 238 slipping silently out of its pen at Bremerhaven and — . . . Satellitem: After reading here that there are 250 cases of Pabst Blue Ribbon and 50 cases of wine aboard the *Jeremiah*, Bernard Kaplan wants to know if the crew has a designated helmsman.

Phil Frank's popular cartoon strip, Farley, runs daily in the *San Francisco Chronicle.* One of its main characters, Bruce, a talking raven, sophisticated far beyond his position on the evolutionary ladder, decided to join the *Jeremiah O'Brien* on its adventure. He immediately became the crew's alter ego. Copies of the

Here Farley languishes for the "long sea voyage" he imagines Carl Nolte enjoying on the O'Brien. *If only he could see Carl with a paint scraper. Courtesy Phil Frank and* San Francisco Chronicle.

The newest and the oldest American-flag ships meet at sea off Central America. Photo by USNS Yukon.

strip (sent by fax) went up on the bulletin boards in both mess-rooms and the saloon. Later, a more tangible association would develop.

The *USNS Yukon*, newly-launched and on her maiden voyage from Mississippi to San Diego, contacted us. She wanted to rendezvous and changed course to meet us. Shortly after midnight the newest ship in the merchant marine and the oldest met in the open ocean off Mexico. The *Yukon* turned, following us until well after daybreak. She put over a small boat to take photos of the two ships traveling together.

That day we saw our first turtle floating in the ocean. A muddy green color, its flippers paddled aimlessly, making it appear awkward and ungainly. A school of about a hundred dolphin heard us and came toward the ship, their grey backs lazily breaking the surface as they dove under and around the ship. Eventually they left, searching for a new diversion.

Radio messages were a welcome tie to the outside world. From Don Watson at our shoreside office in San Francisco:

WE ARE RECEIVING DAILY REPORTS BY PHONE FROM THE CHRONICLE ALSO DAILY CHRONICLE NEWSPAPER REPORTS FROM CARL NOLTE. ALSO PHIL FRANK WHO DOES THE CARTOON FARLEY IS HELPING OUT AS WELL AS KCBS AND KGO. CARL AND I TALK DAILY ALL IS WELL IN THE OFFICE, BILLS BEING PAID, MONEY IN THE BANK, DONATIONS COMING IN. SO, TELL THE CREW ALL IS WELL.

DOC WATSON
CHIEF OF STAFF AND SO FORTH

And this from complete strangers:

TO: CAPTAIN AND CREW
FROM: CHRISTOPHER J GUIDI AND JONATHAN GUIDI

WE ARE REPRESENTING TAY KAPPA EPSILON FRATERNITY
WE THE BROTHERS OF THE FRATERNITY OF SAN FRAN-
CISCO STATE UNIVERSITY WISH YOU LUCK ON YOUR HIS-
TORIC VOYAGE BACK IN TIME
TO US YOU REPRESENT MORE THAN A MARITIME MEMORY,
YOU REPRESENT AN IDEOLOGY LONG LOST
PRIDE AND REVERENCE FOR THE MANY WHO HAVE
FOUGHT FOR OUR LIBERTY
GOD SPEED
CJG, JG, TKE

The Crew's News this day, sent by Bill Bennett to KFS and read by Gary North to an ever-expanding following of callers:

This is the Voice of the *Jeremiah O'Brien.*
Good evening San Francisco from the crew of the *Jeremiah O'Brien.* Day 10 of our voyage back to the Normandy coast. The past 24 hours we have traveled 284 miles. Our average speed was 11.8 knots. Sea water temperature is 82 degrees; on deck it is a toasty 90 degrees with about 95% relative humidity. We deck people are cool in comparison to the engineers. They must tolerate temperatures of 125 degrees plus, during their three hour watch. We are about to enter Nicaraguan waters today and ETA Panama is Saturday. *Jeremiah O'Brien* — out."

Much of the conversation at coffeetime dealt with other ships and days gone by. It was common to hear Bill Rowlands, Ed Lingenfield or Dick Currie swap stories:
"I was on a 535 as AB. . ."
"I was on a C-4 one time. . ."
"There was this Liberty I was on. . ."
Or the perennial, "This is no shit, . . ."
Carl Nolte's column for April 28 dealt with the engine room.

It was 92 degrees in the crew's mess room on the *Jeremiah O'Brien* at noon, and the ship's people have taken to sleeping on deck these past few steamy nights. But now in the engine room of the last seagoing Liberty ship, it is hotter than the hinges of hell. Even the ladders going down to the main engine platform are too hot to touch. In the fireroom, next to the two boilers, it is 120 degrees, day and night.

Carl Nolte at the keyboard, typing out one of his ever-popular tales of the O'Brien. *Photo by Mike Emery.*

"What are we doing down here?" fireman water tender Dick Currie, 55, told a visitor. "We're sweating."

The *Jeremiah O'Brien* is 50 years old and is not air-conditioned. Norm Burke is 69 years old, and he spends six hours a day down in the heat, oiling the engines. And he is not the oldest man — chief engineer Richard Brannon is 75. For these men and others, it is a labor of love. Without them, the *O'Brien* would never be able to keep its appointment in Normandy for the 50th anniversary of D-Day.

Burke has the 3-to-6 watch, which means he is at work in the late afternoon and before dawn. He is a successful retired businessman from Los Gatos, but when he was a kid, he served on merchant ships. "They told me, 'You're an oiler, oil the engine.' I didn't even know where they stored the oil. He knows now.

The engine itself is like something out of the Smithsonian Institution. All of it is easy to see. Big connecting rods flash up and down, making a steady noise like the footsteps of a dinosaur. This engine was built in Hamilton, Ohio, in 1943, but the design is from the 19th century. Looking at it, said Currie, "is like standing inside the crankcase of your car, watching the engine run."

"This is history here," said Worthy. "As much American history as Gettysburg."

The engine is powered by steam, water heated beyond the boiling point by burning oil. The oil fires turn the water to steam, then the steam, at 200 pounds pressure per square inch, pushes the pistons, which push the rods which turn the crankshaft, which turns the main shaft, which turns the propeller.

The *O'Brien* burns Bunker C oil, "thick, ugly, nasty stuff, practically the lowest rung on the petroleum ladder, like crude oil," said fireman Alex Hochstraser, at 35, one of the kids aboard. "These old guys trained me to be a fireman," he said, "because they didn't have enough time to train me to be an oiler and because they thought I had enough stamina to stand the heat." Hochstraser offers a glimpse into the firebox through a peephole. You can't look at the fire directly, it's too bright. "How hot is it in there? Hot enough to get rid of you like that," he said, and snapped his fingers.

It's hot below now, but it will be worse in the Panama Canal because the only ventilation is air brought down from on deck. These are the large curved tubes on every ship that look like question marks. As long as the ship is moving there is air. In the canal, when it is going slowly, there is no wind, no air. On deck, the canal is wonderful to see, they say. Down below, it will be hell.

Norm Burke: "I had some misgivings. I knew this leg of the trip would be very difficult because the ship had not been really tested before and we could expect a variety of problems with all of the equipment. Surprisingly we've only had minor problems but I have to consider that some of the experience and knowledge I have is very helpful in overcoming these problems. I think it was certainly worth the effort to come aboard."

Steve Worthy: "It was very unique in the sense of volunteerism versus professionalism. The volunteers have a better attitude, they're more eager to help. However, when they do help they don't report to you and they have much more independence than I'd like to see. I'm a much more regimental, structured individual. I don't like surprises, I like to know what was planned, not necessarily in concrete, but to get a plan of what we're going to do, who's going to do it and if they have trouble they report to department heads or figureheads, whoever's handling the job, go right on up the line. So I enjoyed some aspects of the *Jeremiah O'Brien* as far as the eagerness and the nice attitude but on the other hand they weren't professional in the sense that if they have problems, I didn't hear about it. No one hears about it and all of a sudden it just didn't get done and then someone else had to take up the slack. So there was good and bad. Overall it was good. Overall I liked it. I liked the attitude."

Norm Burke: "I think that if any ship returned to Normandy it should have been this ship. To my understanding, it was the only ship in service today that actually participated in the invasion. I was surprised that our government didn't take a stronger interest earlier in seeing that we put our best face forward in showing the 'can do' spirit of the American people. Resurrecting a ship of that era and bringing it from San Francisco to England and Normandy with old, tired men and doing it successfully and the men paying their own freight, demonstrated that this country still has what it takes to be a leader in the world. I hope that through the human interest that this ship created, perhaps the need of a strong merchant fleet would start to become better understood by the public at large. In time of need, the merchant fleet of other countries will not participate in military situations. We must have a fleet of civilian-operated ships that can carry our goods in time of peace and take care of our needs in time of conflict."

The movie that evening was "Captain's Paradise." Long a favorite in maritime circles, it stars Alec Guinness as the master of a ship that runs a liner service between Gibraltar and Morocco. He has a wife in each port, one a staid, proper English lady, the other a firebrand. This old favorite drew one of the largest audiences of the voyage.

A few hundred miles to the north, the *Lane Victory* prepared to join us. From one of Carl Nolte's columns:

> The *Lane Victory* will leave port with a similar crew of volunteers who restored the ship for a cruise to Normandy. The Victory, which is 50 feet longer and is powered by engines twice as powerful, was built later in World War II. Its crew, whose average age is 72, plans to rendezvous off Bermuda with the slower *O'Brien*. The Victory is the last operating ship of its class and served in the Pacific in World War II, Korea and Vietnam.

The day before our arrival in Panama, April 29, the weather cooled down a little. Tall grey thunderheads with almost black rainsqualls under them marched across the horizon, periodically drenching and cleaning the ship in heavy, cooling downpours as we passed points on the Panamanian Coast with interesting names like Islas Ladrones (Thieves Islands) and Morro de las Puercas (Castle of the Pigs).

Bruce leaves in pursuit of the O'Brien *and a chance to make a quick buck. At this point everyone on board adopted him as the ship's mascot. Courtesy Phil Frank and* San Francisco Chronicle.

All day long, the crew were in and out of the wheelhouse and chartroom wanting to know when we would arrive. It was a little distracting, yet symbolic of the collegiality on board. On regular merchant ships the navigation bridge would be off limits. But on the *Jeremiah O'Brien* we were volunteers together, equals, peers. (Of course, some, like the captain and the admiral, were a little more equal than others.)

As we drew closer, great white liners disappeared and reappeared in the mist as torrents of rain beat down on us. Ships exiting the Panama Canal blew whistle salutes as they passed in the opposite direction. Third Mate Pete Lyse was able to talk to the captain of a Norwegian cruise ship on the bridge-to-bridge radiophone in his native tongue.

The engineers turned the steam on for the first time since before leaving San Francisco and suddenly the "WHAM, BANG, CLANG" of steam pipes resounded throughout the ship. Called "steam hammer," the sound is exactly like that of a heavy hammer hitting steel. We needed the steam to operate the winches when we tied up the following day.

The messages continued coming into the radio shack. Bob Gisslow printed them out and passed them on for posting on the bulletin boards:

TO: CAPT. JAHN AND CREW OF SS JEREMIAH O'BRIEN

HOPE AND PRAY THAT OUR AMERICAN SS O'BRIEN WILL BE ACCORDED THE HONOR FIRST SHIP IN AT OMAHA BEACH

AT THE HEAD OF THE INTERNATIONAL FLOTILLA. YOU
SHOULD BE. WE ARE SO PROUD OF YOU. THREE CHEERS
FOR OUR STARS AND STRIPES FOREVER.

ROSAMOND AND MAURICE CASTLE
OAKLAND, CA.

TO: ADMIRAL TOM PATTERSON
CAPT JAHN AND ALL CREW

ON YOUR HISTORIC VOYAGE. ALL LIBERTY SHIP SAILORS
WISH YOU ALL THE BEST. SIGNED
DON BARKER PRESIDENT US MERCHANT MARINE VETER-
ANS NORTHERN OREGON.

The morning of April 30 we slowly eased our way into the
harbor approaches to Balboa, on the Pacific side of the Canal.
Balboa was once a sleepy old city with low buildings. Now it
bristled with skyscrapers and office complexes. We picked up the
pilot, Capt. Ove Hulin, and the customs and immigration officials.
Then, with a tug as our escort, we passed under the "Bridge of the

*Entering the Canal Zone with the "Bridge of the Americas" just off the
O'Brien's starboard bow. Photo by Bruce McMurtry.*

Americas," the graceful, arching span that connects the continents of North and South America. Within a few minutes we were tied up to pier 2 South at Rodman Naval Base. The last time the *Jeremiah O'Brien* had been in Panama was 1944.

The captain's arrival message sent to the *O'Brien*'s home office in San Francisco read:

ARRIVAL REPORT
APRIL 30, 1994

ARRIVAL 0918 AT SEABUOY
TOTAL DISTANCE 243 MI AV SPD 11.7 KTS
TOTAL DISTANCE 3253 MI AV SPD 11.64 KTS
TOTAL STEAMING TIME 11 DAY 15 HR 18 MIN
WEATHER ON ARRIVAL
    HIGH UNBROKEN CLOUDS
    BAROMETER 1010
    TEMP 80F SEA WATER 85F
FUEL ON HAND ARRIVAL 6290 BLS
    TOTAL CONSUMED ON VOYAGE 1780 BLS

1005 PILOT CAPT. OVE HULIN ABD
1156 FIRST LINE PIER 2S RODMAN NS
1209 FWE
1215 PILOT AWAY

5

THE CONTINENTAL DIVIDE

Well, actually, it was 1115, Panama time. Someone miscalculated the time zone. It little mattered. The first item of business was mail. We eagerly tore open the letters from home. It had been only twelve days but they — or we — seemed a world away.

The Norway House thoughtfully forwarded a box of magazines and recent newspapers. What a welcome touch of home and boost to the morale. After the mail, we got a chance to catch up on the arguments, whims and vicissitudes of the press.

From Herb Caen's column of April 28.

NOW THEN: Gary Paul Gairaud has a late update on Richard Knight's fantasy that as the Liberty ship *Jeremiah O'Brien* nears the open seas, on her way to Normandy, the restored German submarine, U-238, slips silently out of her pen at Bremerhaven. 'Actually,' contends Gairaud, "it's the famous U-69, a notorious raider, that has been hidden in a mixture of sauerbraten and red cabbage near Bahia Bianca in Argentina. Once the pickled pigs feet were removed from

Bruce begins his quest. Would he make it to Panama on time? Would the crew want the brandy? For the answers to these and other burning questions, stay tuned. Courtesy Phil Frank and San Francisco Chronicle.

the torpedo tubes, a crew-cut crew set sail on April 21st. They should intercept the *O'Brien* in mid-Atlantic late in May." Isn't there enough here, Mr. Coppola, for at least the first draft of a movie?"

And:

MEMORABLE newsfoto of the wk.: Russell Yip's in the Chron of the Liberty ship *SS Jeremiah O'Brien* outward bound under the Gate Bridge and heading into a fog bank as she begins her voyage back to Normandy for the 50th annvy. of D-Day. This adventure, already being deliciously reported by Carl Nolte, is gripping the city to the point where there are office pools on how far she'll go before breaking down. Those who drew "Monterey," have already lost. . .

Interest around the nation, but especially in the San Francisco Bay Area, was high. Articles and letters to the editor brimmed with enthusiasm. But, as always, there were the few who took a different view.

From the *Chronicle* on April 25:

Editor — Contrary to Carl Nolte's report, (Chronicle, April 18) those of us who opposed sending the Liberty ship *Jeremiah O'Brien* to Normandy did not argue that the ship "would never make it." Instead, we contended that she would "never try to make it."

Venturing a 50-year-old emergency-built vessel that spent 33 years in lay-up on an arduous voyage with an inexperienced crew is laden with high risks. Why place a national treasure that should be preserved for future generations in harm's way unnecessarily?

Many cities across the country are honoring D-Day with local ceremonies. The same could have been done in San Francisco with the *O'Brien* as the centerpiece, and without the costs and perils of a long ocean voyage. When the *O'Brien* returns let us hope that she will never leave the Golden Gate again.
William Jardine
Redwood City

Much more surprising, and very disappointing, was another letter which appeared on April 23 in the *Chronicle:*

Editor — To sail a World War II Merchant Marine cargo ship back to the scene of a crucial Allied battle she helped to win, half a century ago and half a world away — WOW! Exciting? Of course. Romantic? Ah, yes. A wise and worthy project? Well, maybe not.

The Liberty Ship *Jeremiah O'Brien*'s return to France for the D-Day commemoration (covered with commendable glimpses of realism by Carl Nolte in last Saturday's paper, April 16) is truly a captivating idea. To oppose such a scheme is to risk being labelled "super-grouch." We'll risk that label because we do oppose this excursion — as far too risky, too expensive and potentially counterproductive.

In the hands of project managers who have sought to bypass both repair procedures and test requirements commensurate with good marine practice, the 50-year-old *Jeremiah O'Brien* and her crew have been put at enormous risk — a level of risk which is unacceptable now and will remain unacceptable, no matter how the voyage happens to turn out. And the level of debt with which the project managers have saddled the National Liberty Ship Memorial is also unacceptable, and will become increasingly burdensome. Sadly, the *Jeremiah*'s Normandy project puts the future of this national memorial in jeopardy — too steep a price to pay for a moment's glory which is, at best, elusive.

Harry Morgan
Volunteer Chief Engineer
Joanie Morgan
Volunteer Purser
Jeremiah O'Brien
Sonoma

We were dumbfounded at this unnecessary, unconstructive and misleading letter. Harry and Joanie were not Volunteer Chief

Engineer and Volunteer Purser. They both resigned from those positions in 1986, before the Normandy voyage was even proposed. Neither of them had any firsthand knowledge of what the ship was doing since that time. More shocking was the fact that this came from Harry Morgan. Most of the crew had a great deal of affection and respect for Harry. It was like being slapped in the face by a favorite uncle.

Then, Dick Brannon revealed something that made the whole issue even more confusing: "Harry Morgan and Joanie, while they were broadcasting to the public, negatives, they fed me, privately, very good advice. Harry on the mechanics of the ship and Joanie on the social aspects, they fed me at the same time they were publishing the negatives. They gave me all kinds of encouragement. Harry, mechanically, was a big help." Some things are unfathomable.

Even as we finished reading our mail a military brass band was assembling on the pier alongside the ship. We dressed the ship, festooning it from stem to stern with brightly-colored signal flags strung together. At each halyard we raised the flags of our corporate sponsors: Chevron, Shell, Caterpillar, Foster-Wheeler, the City of San Francisco, The San Francisco Maritime Museum and Crowley Maritime, who had provided their corporate flags for this purpose.

Tom Patterson: "The Military Sealift Command had arranged a wonderful reception for us. Rodman Naval Station had a big cake and lunch for our crew. And they gave us fresh water." The water replenished that which was used on the way down for boilers, showers, drinking and cooking.

The band played rousing marches. Ceremonies commemorating our successful arrival were held on the pier. Later in the afternoon, the Navy sponsored a barbecue. It's surprising how good a hamburger tastes, grilled outdoors on a smoky fire, with the jungles of Panama providing background greenery. This enthusiastic welcome gave us the first hint of what might be in store for us. It was all quite exciting.

Rich Reed: "That was our first contact, and especially for a lot of the guys, our first response to some of the receptions that we were going to get."

Some of the younger, unattached crew spent the night on the town. Mike Emery, photographer-ordinary seaman: "Some of us grabbed a cab and went bar-hopping. We ended up in a strip club, I forget the name, but we got seated at this bar, right next to the stage. The highlight was a beautiful woman from the Dominican Republic, wearing only a *Jeremiah O'Brien* hat. Tall and tan and young and lovely, with nothing on but the hat. We walked up the gangway at four-fifty-eight for a five o'clock call-back."

Carl Nolte: "That was great fun. Whatever stories you heard are all true. We were upholding the tradition of the ship."

The sailing board was posted for the *O'Brien* to sail Sunday, May 1, at 0600 "ship's time." We were all up and ready, anxious to experience what many consider the "eighth wonder of the world." The ship was dressed with signal flags from bow to stern, the deck officers wore white uniforms.

The pilots came aboard. There were four, the senior pilots on the list: Captains Chamberlain, Pascavage, G. Smith and Mahar. Each of them were in the merchant marine during World War II, some on Liberty ships, and each wanted a chance to pilot the oldest American-flag ship through the Canal. They generously donated their services and would take turns, relieving one another every couple of hours during the transit.

Tom Patterson: "We took 85 military and their dependents through the Canal at the request of the commanding general of Southcom [Southern Command]." It was a courtesy that would raise the specter of our old adversary, the Coast Guard.

The last line was thrown off the dock at 1000. We slowly backed away from the pier, turned in a northwesterly direction and headed for Miraflores locks. As we neared the lock entrance, an exiting ship passed and blew the traditional salute of three long blasts. Because of the warm climate and for better visibility we navigated from the flying bridge. This put us directly under the *O'Brien*'s steam whistle. I looked at Capt. Jahn. He nodded. "Go ahead," he said, covering his ears with his hands. "Cover your ears," I warned loudly. Then we answered with the *O'Brien*'s authoritative steam whistle, three deep, resonant, loud WHOOOOOSH's. The ship blew a short toot and we responded with the same. Everyone took their hands from their ears, laughing.

Now we turned our attention to the locks before us. Transiting the Canal is an experience that never pales, no matter how many times one does it. Every crew member not on watch was up on deck to see it all. Approaching the first lock, a boat came alongside and several line handlers came aboard. As we neared the massive gates at the entrance, already open to let us enter, two small boats rowed toward us — one to the starboard bow, one to the port bow. Two heaving lines snaked out from the foredeck, landing within easy reach of the boats. The line handler in each boat grabbed the line and was rowed back to the concrete lock wall where he handed the line to a waiting compatriot. The lines were tied to a wire rope dangling off two waiting "mules" (electric locomotives). The linemen on the bow pulled on the heaving lines until the wire ropes were aboard the *O'Brien*

Miraflores locks, the first set entered from the Pacific side. The ship in the background is going in the same direction as the O'Brien. *Note the date on the control tower — and it all works perfectly. Photo by Jim Conwell.*

where they threw them over a set of bitts. With a clang of their bells, the mules started moving in the same direction as our ship even as they pulled the slack out of the wire ropes. Once the bow entered the lock we were close enough for the linehandlers on the stern to throw lines to two additional mules that were paralleling us. When we were completely in the lock, the mules slowed down, taking tension in their lines, while the ship's engines were put in reverse to stop the forward motion. The ship was held stationary in the middle of the lock by the four mules as the lock gates were closed and the water rushed in.

The gates at Miraflores are the tallest in the Canal because of the extreme tidal variation of the Pacific Ocean. The entire operation was orchestrated, and that really is the word for it, by the pilot, who "conducted" with a hand-held walkie-talkie and commands to the ship's helmsman and the engine room. There is a second set of locks at Miraflores so the mules stayed with us and the process was repeated. We entered the mile-long Miraflores locks at 1108 and departed at 1132, a very efficient operation.

Marty Shields, ordinary seaman: "What really stood out on the trip over was steering under pilotage which was something I had never, never done."

It was a short run across man-made Miraflores Lake to Pedro Miguel locks, the second set on the Pacific side. As the gates closed and the ship was raised the final thirty-one feet to the level of the interior of the Canal Zone, we marveled at the surroundings. Passengers and crew mingled, talking and pointing, cameras and camcorders going. The white stucco buildings with their red-tiled roofs at the center of each lock system, dating from the original construction in 1914, looked freshly white-washed. The grassy areas around the lock systems were neatly manicured. The mules hummed efficiently as they moved us, with the occasional clang of a bell acknowledging the pilot's command.

The locks are massive grey concrete structures, spotted here and there with dark green blotches of marine growth. At each end was a set of massive steel gates, so delicately balanced that they could be swung with forty-horsepower motors. On first entering, you look up at the mules and the control building, but as water is pumped into the lock the ship rises so that by the time the gates open you look down on the locomotives and work areas.

Twenty-two minutes after entering Pedro Miguel locks we began our transit of the Canal proper, exiting into Gaillard Cut, named for Col. David Dubose Gaillard, the engineer responsible for its construction. About eight miles long, the cut was carved through rock and shale for most of its distance. This is where most of the excavation in the construction of the Canal took place, with devastating slides occurring frequently, even after the Canal opened. More than any other area, Gaillard Cut gives the impression of the waterway as an enormous ditch. To our right was Gold Hill, at 587 feet, the highest promontory along the channel. To the left was Contractor's Hill. As we passed through the 500-foot-wide channel, we felt dwarfed by the steep slopes. Here and there, where there was enough soil, pampas grass and low tropical vegetation had taken hold. We crossed the Continental Divide, the only place in the world you can do so by ship. Someone observed that we were actually crossing two divides simultaneously — West/East and North (America)/South (America). As we left Gaillard Cut, we saw to our right the Gamboa area, where the Chagres River flows into the Canal channel.

The tropical heat was formidable, especially in the engine room and the galley. Jimmy Farras, second cook: "The heat going through Panama, that wasn't too fun. I recall coming through the Canal, the galley got so hot I was cooking hamburgers and one of the pie tins that we had a frying pan on, cooking the hamburgers, melted like solder. Yeah, it turned like, mercury. It just scchhhgsssskkk [makes melting noise]. I should have saved that tin."

Carl Kreidler, gunner: "I been in Panama a couple of times during the war and it was about a hundred fifty percent better during the war than it is now. All the unemployment, and so forth. And, I guess I didn't remember when I was so young, but I didn't remember the tropics being quite that hot, but it was."

Rich Reed: "It was hot but I think everybody really endured really well despite the heat."

We entered Gatun Lake. The channel became much wider with low islands covered with thick jungle growth. The passengers and crew pointed excitedly at each new vista: iridescent butterflies fluttering across the ship's path, brightly-plumed birds flittering from tree to tree, animal calls in the jungles, an occasional crocodile sliding into the water. And almost every ship we met saluted us by whistle. "Hold your ears," was no longer necessary. Passengers and crew did it automatically as the mate on watch reached for the whistle pull.

At 1545 we anchored in Gatun Lake awaiting Pacific-bound traffic to clear the Atlantic locks before moving on. Rain squalls passed over, drenching everyone with cooling water, then the sun came out, drying us almost instantly.

Dick Brannon hardly got out of the engine room: "Going through the Canal eastbound, I was at the throttle probably eighty to ninety percent of the time because everybody was new. I was the only guy that ever handled one of these engines before."

Bill Bennett sent his Crew's News for the day while we were at anchor:

> This is the Voice of the *Jeremiah O'Brien*.
>
> Good evening, San Francisco. At noon today the *Jeremiah O'Brien* was Europe-bound under the command of a Panama Canal Commission pilot. Captain George Jahn, Master of our vessel, had the ship dressed in maritime fashion. All of our licensed deck personnel also were in their formal dress white uniforms. *Jeremiah O'Brien* looked very classy. We have as our guests today representatives from the military enjoying our trip through the Panama Canal. The weather is a comfortable 82 degrees with clouds and a

Bruce arrives. Never let it be said that the ship's gunners don't have their priorities straight. Courtesy Phil Frank and San Francisco Chronicle.

welcome rain. At present we are anchored in Gatun Lake waiting
our turn to exit the waterway in three steps via Gatun Locks. The
attitude is still very positive aboard ship. Keep us in your thoughts
and prayers. America is returning to Normandy.
Jeremiah O'Brien — out.

Heaving up the anchor, we slowly approached Gatun locks,
the final set of locks that would lower us to the level of the
Atlantic Ocean. To our left we could see the top of the earthen
dam which was built across the Chagres River to form Gatun
Lake. The two wings of the dam and the spillway have an aggre-
gate length of about 1½ miles. Nearly a half mile wide at its base,
the dam slopes to a width of 100 feet at the crest, 105 feet above
sea level and twenty feet above the normal level of Gatun Lake.
It was an impressive sight.

Gatun locks at 1-1/8 mile are the longest in the system.
Containing three lock chambers measuring 110 feet wide by 1,000
feet long, they lowered the *O'Brien* a total of 85 feet in three

"Mules" carefully guide the O'Brien *through the locks. Photo by Bruce McMurtry.*

Looking astern toward Gatun Lake, we see the gates closing before the O'Brien *is lowered to the next lock. Photo by Bruce McMurtry.*

steps. Then it was a little over a six-mile run through a 500-foot-wide channel, cutting across a mangrove swamp to Limon Bay and Cristobal. We tied up to Pier 16 and rang off Finished With Engines at 2020 (8:20 p.m.).

Jim Conwell: "Something I had been looking forward to with my civil engineering background was transiting the Panama Canal. That lived up to its expectation. That certainly is one of the engineering achievements of the century."

Phil Sinnott: "This is the stuff dreams are made of."

Not everyone thought the Canal was the eighth wonder of the world. Greg Williams, steward utility: "I'd never been through it before. It was a lot smaller than I thought it would be. You always see things on TV or in the movies and they probably use a wider angle lens so it looks like it's smaller in contrast and I had the same feeling going through the Canal."

Our berth was concrete over hard-packed dirt on a barren pier usually occupied by other ships while awaiting a discharge or loading berth or having repairs done. There was a small, ramshackle shed at the seaward end and little else. The lush tropical

Entering the last lock at Gatun. Beyond the gate lies the entrance to Limon Bay and the Atlantic Ocean. Photo by Marty Wefald.

vegetation that covered every spot of bare ground in the Canal Zone seemed to stop at the gate to Pier 16, several hundred feet from the bow of our ship. It was desolate. As we rigged a gangway from shore, which our crew did simply by lifting it up to the side of the ship, a peddler set out a few T-shirts for sale on the dock, then sat down and went to sleep. We were warned to be careful. Cristobal was a gutted remnant of American Colonialism with seventy-five percent unemployment. Crime was rampant. Most of the crew gravitated to the nearby Panama Canal Yacht Club, where it was safe, beer was cheap, and they could see the ship from the window.

From Carl Nolte's column: "The club was full of yachties, generally a class of sailors avoided by merchant seamen since yacht sailors are merely amateurs. But such is the cachet of the old Liberty ship that everyone was welcome at the yacht club yesterday. Toasts were drunk, boats were toured, and sea stories were swapped."

We began taking diesel fuel the next day, May 2. The sailing board was posted for that morning, but it soon became apparent we'd be there longer. The meter on the dock showed the diesel coming aboard at a rate of thirty-two gallons per hour and we were slated to take on more than a thousand gallons for the diesel generator which burns about a barrel a day.

Most mariners consider themselves citizens of the world. They have a special allegiance to their own country, of course, but seamen of all countries and ethnic backgrounds usually find a common bond in their love of the sea and things maritime. Capt. Jahn and I stood on the dock talking when a group of sailors from a nearby ship wandered over. After a few hesitant words in different languages, they realized we spoke English and began asking about the ship. Soon Capt. Jahn was telling them about the *Jeremiah O'Brien* and the purpose of our voyage. They were nonplussed when he said, "We're all volunteers. We work for nothing."

"Nothing?" one of them asked incredulously.

"No pay."

"No pay?" From the looks on their faces, it was clear they thought they hadn't heard correctly.

"That's right. Volunteers. Nothing. No money."

"No money?" they echoed. Now they looked suspicious, as if expecting us to try to con them out of something but they weren't sure what, yet.

Just then François Le Pendu walked up. He said something in French. The sailors' faces showed instant comprehension. Soon they were rattling away in French, comparing ships, and again being told we were volunteers and what that meant.

Capt. Jahn explains our voyage to the crew from a Cameroon tanker.

"They're from Cameroon," said François, in an aside. "The French is native to them. That is their ship over there," he said, pointing to a modern tanker across the quay. The conversation progressed to a tour of the *O'Brien*'s engine room and an exchange visit.

Jean Yates was our resident artist. An art teacher in the Santa Rosa (California) junior college system, he had a definite talent for painting, drawing and all things artistic. Rich Reed convinced him we needed to leave a calling card on the dock, something to commemorate our visit. Jean swept an area clear and, with chalk, laid out a design that dramatically displayed the date and the name of the ship. The hot tropical sun had him soaking with sweat by the time he had the outline chalked in. As he carried the paint down to fill in the chalk lines, the chief mate offered to help and picked up a brush. Then Sam Wood came down from the main deck where he was watching, picked up

Jean Yates, backside to camera, creating a "calling card" on the dock at Cristobal. Photo by Marty Wefald.

another brush and started on a different color.   Soon there were five or six crew taking turns painting in Jean's logo, a working example of the *Jeremiah O'Brien* spirit of volunteerism, friendship and good shipmates.

Rich Reed: "The Canal, the transit through the Canal, especially for the guys that haven't seen it before, I mean that's, you know, that speaks for itself.   What a thrill that thing is to go through. I think it was a turning point. Everybody, even myself, we had a little anxiety, are we really going to make it? Is this thing going to hold up, or not? But you have to pinch yourself to think that, you know, here you are. And I think, yeah, once we got to Panama, was the realization that, hey, we're really going to make it, and everything's going to be OK."

Radio messages in Cristobal:

FROM ROBERT V. WHARTON

THE CALIFORNIA CHAPTER OF THE UNITED STATES LST ASSOCIATION AT OUR ANNUAL REUNION AT CONCORD CALIFORNIA APRIL 30, 1994 SALUTE THE SKIPPER, OFFICERS AND CREW OF THE *JEREMIAH O'BRIEN* ON THEIR GALLANT AND HISTORIC VOYAGE TO ENGLAND AND FRANCE COMMEMORATING THE 50TH ANNIVERSARY OF D-DAY. WE WISH YOU GOD SPEED AND A SAFE AND REWARDING TRIP. OH HOW WE ENVY YOU AS WE TOO ARE OLD SALTY SEA DOGS.

And:

TO: CAPTAIN AND CREW OF *SS JEREMIAH O'BRIEN*

NOSTALGICALLY THINKING OF THE *O'BRIEN* TODAY AS SHE TRANSITS THE CANAL. MY BIRTHPLACE CONGRATULATIONS AND GOOD LUCK ON REST OF VOYAGE.
ISABELLA Z LIVELY
BALBOA HIGH SCHOOL CLASS OF '43
NOW SONOMA CA.

Now we read in the *Chronicle* a response to the Morgans' letter:

Editor — I would like to respond to Harry and Joanie Morgan's letter, "A Risky Voyage" (Chronicle, April 23). As a personal witness to some of the hundreds of thousands of man/woman hours spent in refurbishing the *Jeremiah O'Brien* and also maintaining constant communications with the U.S. Coast Guard (USCG) and American Bureau of Shipping (ABS), NOTHING could be further from the fact on the alleged "bypass of repair procedures and test requirements." Besides USCG and ABS, we, as the owners of this fine vessel, ensured that the highest standards of safety were met prior to the vessel's sailing for Normandy. Countless extra hours were contributed by the USCG/ABS inspector(s) to make sure that the *Jeremiah* was fully capable of making this historic voyage without sacrificing one ounce of safety.

Only time will tell whether this historic voyage will place the national memorial in jeopardy. My bet is that next October when the *Jeremiah O'Brien* sails proudly under the Golden Gate Bridge, a lot of folks will be "eating sea gull."

Captain FRANK X. JOHNSTON
Western Region Director
Maritime Administration
U.S. Department of Transportation
San Francisco

By the end of the day the diesel fuel was on board and at 2000 the pilot, Capt. Mastin, arrived to take us out of the harbor. For some reason he seemed in a hurry. Normally the pilot takes a ship out of the harbor to the first buoy (called the Sea Buoy) beyond those marking the entrance to the harbor. But as soon as he backed us out of our berth and had us headed in the right direction, he pointed toward the breakwater and said, "red light, end of breakwater, green light, end of breakwater. Go between them. This is where I leave you." And he did. Disappearing quickly down the ladder, he left the captain, the admiral, the deck cadet and the chief mate standing there, blinking like owls caught in the sunshine.

6

A SMALL WORLD

Half ahead," said Capt. Jahn as we recovered our wits and the pilot boat pulled away from the ship's side.

"Half ahead," repeated Nate Taylor, deck cadet, swinging the engine room telegraph to that position.

Second Mate Ray Conrady had laid out a course paralleling the Panamanian Coast to our right, then toward Mona Passage between Puerto Rico and the Dominican Republic. As we turned onto our course of 045, the captain said, "Let's call that departure at . . . what time is it?"

"Nine oh eight."

"O.K. Make it nine twelve, that way it's easier to figure."

On most ships arrival and departure are taken in tenths of an hour to make mileage and distance reports easier to calculate.

At 2112 I told the cadet, "O.K. Ring it off." The cadet swung the telegraph from full ahead to full astern and back again, then called the engine room.

"That's departure at nine twelve."

"Nine twelve, departure," the engineer repeated.

The captain and the admiral left, the cadet was dismissed. Helmsman Jim Conwell and the chief mate settled in for the remainder of the watch.

There was no moon. The night was dark, the sea calm. To starboard was the Coast of Panama, darker than the night, with an occasional weak light on shore flickering through the jungle. From time to time a brightly-lit freighter was seen in the distance on our port side, coming down from the American Gulf Coast, its running lights showing it was headed for the Canal. Overhead, the constellations were clear, pinpricks of light on black velvet. The Milky Way was a powdery blur across the heavens; the Southern Cross was visible low over Panama. The only wind was that caused by the ship moving at 11 knots through the water. The wake coming off the bow hissed, glowing green with phosphorescence as it ran past on either side. The propeller was thump-thump-thumping through the water, like a healthy pulse. It was a good night to get back to sea.

Bosun Rich Reed and the chief mate started May 3 with the usual morning meeting on the flying bridge to talk over the work ahead. Now we began in earnest the task of preparing the ship for Portsmouth. We had twenty-one days in which to get the *Jeremiah O'Brien* shipshape. We agreed that in that time the sailors would slush all the cargo runners and rigging, chip any rust, paint all bare areas with rust-removing acid, apply primer, and give the entire ship a new coat of grey paint. Carpenter Bob Burnett would build a staircase from the ship's store in no. 3 'tween deck to the main deck.

The day started quietly with an overcast, grey sky and a short, choppy sea. Flying fish, bigger than those we saw in the Pacific, glided through the air in fan-shaped schools as they sensed our approach. Easing away from shore, the northeast trade winds, which were dead ahead, increased in strength and by the end of the day the deck log showed, "Wind NE [force] 5, Swell ENE 4. Vessel pitching to Mod NE'ly Sea & low short ENE'ly swell."*

---

*Wind force at sea is recorded according to the Beaufort scale rather than miles per hour. The "5" after "NE" refers to this scale.

The next day the winds were stronger, force six. The sea was a wild mix of color; frothy-white on the surface, but between the whitecaps, a sinister blue-grey, and, looking straight down close to the ship, bright blue. A swell coming from the same direction as the wind had built to a height of ten feet. From any other direction this wouldn't be bad but with both the wind and the swell head-on, the bow and stern pitched up and down. When the stern rose, the propeller came out of the water and, without the water to work against, raced in the air. Sometimes the swell changed direction and we rolled side to side about ten degrees, although once or twice the inclinometer showed twenty degrees. On these occasions people lurched across the decks like drunks. A few dishes, pots, pans and other loose items banged and shattered, a good reminder to everyone that we were on a ship at sea and things should be properly stowed. It was roughest for the crew who lived in the after deck house, directly over the steering engine and the propeller. The vibrations of the prop as it alternately raced and bit, and the grinding noise of the steering engine at odd intervals as the helmsman applied the rudder in one direction or another took getting used to. "It was tough," Otto Sommerauer, 76, said, "but we're tough, too."

Electronics were slow to catch on in the tradition-bound maritime industry. Until the 1970s sextants were used for navigation. In those days a star fix was considered accurate if it was within two miles, precise if within a mile. We could only get star fixes in the morning and at night. Positions during the rest of the day consisted of sunlines taken every hour or two which were run up by dead reckoning.

Our Global Positioning System (GPS) showed us making four to five knots. All the mates agreed that the GPS, provided by American President Lines, was a great gadget. It provided instant and total navigation. Working off a network of twenty-eight satellites, it constantly updated our position. We simply looked at the electronic screen which displayed our latitude and longitude to the nearest thousandth of a minute (*i.e.* 6.3 feet), and plotted the position on the chart. While in Cristobal I took our position and found the system not only showed us at the proper dock but at the correct position on the twelve hundred-foot face of the pier itself!

Pete Lyse: "The GPS was something that we would never even think of in the old days. Frankly, I must admit I asked about the method of navigation when I was asked to go. They told me GPS but there would also be a sextant aboard which I would probably have a great difficulty in handling at this time. But the whole thing is a unique experience, a lifetime experience."

Born in 1931, Pete Lyse first crossed the Atlantic at the age of 2½ as a passenger on the *SS Majestic*. After working on a small vessel in high school, he graduated and went to sea. Sailing from 1949 to 1954 he had worked as deck officer on eight merchant ships by the time he was a junior at Lehigh University in Pennsylvania. Graduating with a degree in civil engineering he worked in that profession for twenty-nine years before retiring to his present home in Menominee, Michigan with his wife, Shirley. He is in the Coast Guard Reserve, is a licensed pilot for the area bounded by Duluth, Geary and Buffalo and sails on the Great Lakes as third mate during the summer.

Once again, we fell into the easy routine of standing watches and whiling away the off-duty hours with b.s. sessions, card and chess games and books. A cult of sorts sprang up on the ship. Someone brought along the Patrick O'Brien novels about Capt. Aubrey and Dr. Maturin. Set in the era before and during the War of 1812, but better-written than Forester's Hornblower, they became popular reading among the crew and

Sam Wood takes advantage of a rain squall to scrub the main deck. Photo by Mike Emery.

with the long passage toward Portsmouth, many spent their off hours reading them. Each book takes up where the previous leaves off, so they must be read in sequence. Sam Wood and I traded back and forth, he sometimes finishing one before I finished the next. Then, every time he saw me, it was, "Finished that book yet?"

By May 5 the trade winds abated and we were once more at full speed, beating our way up the Caribbean toward Mona Passage. Carl Nolte's column subhead that day read: "[*O'Brien*] actually passes another vessel."

"It's a first," said Third Mate Pete Lyse. "We did pass a sailboat off Nicaragua, but there was no wind." He laughed.

Pete Lyse stood the 12-4 watch. He said that on his early morning watch a United Fruit ship contacted him, the *Chiquita Jean,* bound from New Zealand to Antwerp carrying a cargo of apples. They called because their GPS wasn't working and they wanted a position. We relished the idea of the *SS Jeremiah O'Brien*, the oldest American-flag ship on the ocean, giving a modern, new freighter an accurate position.

In a quiet moment on the bridge, Adm. Patterson, looking out over the wind dodger toward the ocean with a satisfied smile, said, "She's out here where she belongs."

In a reminiscent mood, he told how he got started in the maritime industry. He and a friend worked at a shipyard in Pennsylvania. They saw boats and ships constantly traveling up and down the adjacent river. His friend wrote away for applications to the Coast Guard Academy and the Merchant Marine Academy, and opted for the Coast Guard. Patterson said, "Well, give me the other application. I'll try that." He filled out the application, sent it in and was accepted. He graduated from Kings Point in 1944.

Just before 2100 the following day the chief engineer, Dick Brannon, called the bridge to tell us he was slowing the engine to 50 rpm due to a bearing problem. As the evening progressed, he slowed it again until we were turning 40 rpm and making 5.5 knots. He believed that somehow some diesel got in the lube oil making it thinner and causing the bearing to overheat.

The shipboard rumor mill, or scuttlebutt, ranged from ludicrous to illogical: the ship was too old, the engineers didn't know what they were doing, someone wasn't paying attention to business and forgot to oil the bearings, it wasn't the bearing but something far worse that "they" weren't telling anyone, somehow Harry Morgan had managed to sabotage the operation. Capt. Jahn was frequently in and out of the wheelhouse checking the rpms. The trade winds came up again and kept blowing. It was what some call a "nervous-making time."

But not for everyone. Cook Jimmy Farras took the opportunity to throw a line over the stern, trolling for anything that might care to bite.

Messman Ron Smith remarked that he could tell we were going slower because when he threw the garbage out the morning after we slowed down, it took longer to disappear. Phil Sinnott overheard the remark and said, "Hey, we could develop a new way of measuring speed from this, Ron. We'll call it 'Garbage gone through.'"

By now, the cooks had mastered the intricacies of the coal-fired galley stove. Each meal seemed better than the last. Al Martino, chief cook: "It was a learning process. Some things I knew and some things I didn't know. It became difficult but after awhile we worked through it and it seemed to work all right. Most important, make sure you keep it fired up. Don't let it die on you or else you have to start all over again. Get in there early in the morning. I get in there about ten to four. You have to take the ashes out, shovel in new coal, and then start the fire. As long as you have enough time it's OK. But if you get in there late, you're putting yourself under too much pressure."

Jimmy Farras: "That took a little while, to get used to the baking. There were different hot spots you had to rotate. A lot of pastries, sometimes cakes would be cooked on one side and raw on the other so you'd have to spin the cakes or pies. And you did a lot of the baking in the morning because when you baked, you couldn't fry on top of the stove because it was too cool. On a coal burner, it's not like you can leave it. You know, on an electric stove, you turn the thermostat on and you walk

Jimmy Farras removes fresh bread as Al Martino ladles out soup. Photo by George Bonawit.

away. Here you had to keep shoveling the coal for the next meal, to stack it so it would stay hot. There were no thermostats on there so you had to basically go by feel. Like, if you were deep-frying breaded prawns, you know if they're browning within two minutes it's too hot, so you'd put them [the frying pans] up on [inverted] pie tins to cool it down. Things like that you just got used to. That was a pretty big highlight in the character of the ship for me, being in the galley like that and that coal-burning stove."

Ray Conrady, second mate, sent periodic dispatches to the *San Francisco Examiner.* They billed him as the "Eagle," their spy on the ship. Why a spy or who he was spying on was never really made clear. It seemed to be a case of the *Examiner,* San Francisco's struggling afternoon paper, trying, belatedly and ineffectively, to counter the *Chronicle*'s popular Nolte series. One of Ray's dispatches provided an ironic contrast.

> Two warships were patrolling off Mona Passage — an American and a British — drug interdiction, I presume. They asked each passing ship lots of questions on the VHF radio-port of departure and destination, cargo carried, home port, flag, name of master, etc. The British ship knew all about us and our destination to Normandy and wished us good luck and smooth seas. The American ship didn't know anything about us and asked us to repeat and spell our name.

Problems in the engine room didn't stop the deck crew's major project for the next few weeks: painting the *O'Brien* from stern to stem. We didn't want any remarks about rusty old freighters turning up in the English press.

Bosun Rich Reed handed out paint brushes and buckets with the simple orders familiar to anyone who has ever served in the military or worked on a ship. "If it doesn't move, paint it," he said.

The paint job began on the fantail and moved slowly forward. While they worked, Bruce McMurty, Mike Emery, Carl Nolte, Joe Callahan, Jim Miller, Jean Yates and the others bantered about what the queen might say were she to come aboard while the ship is in England and how they would point out various places they had painted. Some, however, were holding out for Princess Diana, on the theory that she might be impressed, especially in the event her favorite color is cargo ship gray.

Meanwhile, back in the engine room, oiler Tom Alexander felt the engine problem was under control.

"Engines are like people," he said, "they have their moods and problems. Sometimes I think this engine is alive. But we'll make it. If any ship in the world deserves to get to Normandy, it's this one."

Bill Duncan: "We had a hot bearing on the way over that slowed the ship down for about eight hours or so. What we think was that because the ship had sat idle for so long, just going around the Bay [on the semiannual cruises] it wasn't in operation long enough to show any heat, but making the trip and operating twenty-four hours a day, the problem showed up. There was some blockage in the oil channels that keep the bearing cool. It eventually flushed itself out and we diluted it by forcing oil through and adding oil and so on."

The bearing was flushed out with diesel and re-lubed. The engine was slowly brought back up to speed and everything was fine again. We cleared Mona Passage and entered the Atlantic Ocean.

Otto Sommerauer, our gunners mate, was pleased to be going at full speed again. "There's no tow trucks out here," he said.

The increased speed produced mixed responses on deck. On one hand, it meant every turn of the screw put the ship closer to its goal. On the other, the *O'Brien* was now going too fast to fish. Along with Jimmy Farras, the chief mate put out a couple of trolling lines armed with feather jigs he got in Panama. Neither he nor the cook caught anything.

The halfway mark was passed on the 8-to-12 watch on May 7: 4,033 miles to San Francisco, 4,033 miles to Portsmouth.

Our first full day in the Atlantic came with squalls marching across the horizon.

It was Mother's Day. The radio shack was busy as the crew wired flowers and candy or made calls by radiotelephone. Crew's News for this day:

Good evening, San Francisco. Happy Mother's Day from the crew of the *Jeremiah O'Brien* — at sea today in the Atlantic Ocean surrounded by fathers, grandfathers, great grandfathers and fathers to be. Not a mother to be seen, but somewhere one to be cherished. A special person remembered with fond memories of a sweet smile, an encouraging word, and occasionally that special dessert at mealtimes thought to have been created just for you. Comments like: "Do your homework," "Clean your room", and "Time for bed" have been conveniently forgotten.

Please remember you are in our thoughts. At noon today, seaman Jean Yates sealed his daily message in a bottle and tossed it over the side at latitude 21 degrees 12 minutes North, longitude 65 degrees 45 minutes West. We hope Jean receives many replies. Today's course is 043 degrees true, 10.6 knots, distance covered from Colon, Panama, 1128 miles — 254 miles in the last 24 hours.

Jeremiah O'Brien — out."

Ordinary Seaman Jean Yates threw a message over every day the ship was at sea on the outbound passage. Placed in an empty Snapple bottle, the message gave the ship's name, position and a brief explanation of the voyage. He sent 27 messages in all. The last one, thrown over in the English Channel, was picked up by three people walking along a beach in Holland. Jean

After graduating from high school Jean Yates joined the Air Force where he flew as a radio operator during World War II. He flew in B-25's for the 14th Air Force under General Claire L. Chennault. A graduate of the Chicago Art Institute, he taught at a high school in Sonoma, California for 8 years and then at a junior college in Santa Rosa for 22 years. After retiring in 1984 he built his own house. He has been a volunteer with the *Jeremiah O'Brien* since 1986. He and his wife reside in Sebastopol, California.

found a letter from them waiting when he arrived home in July after leaving the ship in France.

The radio traffic went both ways. Gary North, KFS manager and "The Voice of the *Jeremiah O'Brien*" sent the following wire to Bennett.

I have been enjoying reading your bulletins aloud into voice mail each day. As you are probably aware, the number has been released to the press, so it is the general public as well as family and friends who are now calling in. Also, per request of the *O'Brien* Ops Ctr, I am adding info each day on how people can send donations to the *O'Brien*'s Normandy voyage fund. In addition, for those who like to track your position, we are adding Lat/Long from your noon report at end of each recording. With all of these additions, we are beginning to reach the two minute limit for each daily recording. I can just squeeze in a message of today's length.
Good luck with that painting job.
Best regards
Gary North
KFS Manager

The heat continued, day and night. Even the trade winds were warm. Beginning somewhere off the coast of Mexico, many of the crew slept in cots on the main deck and sometimes the area around no. 3 hatch looked like an infirmary. This was fine until it rained, which happened frequently in the early morning in the Atlantic. Then there was a rush of half-naked men, dragging bedding and pillows, to their assigned rooms in the midships house. There, porthole fans and wind scoops provided meager ventilation.

Dick Brannon: "One of the best things that Ernie Murdock did for the ship was to insist on these three hour watches. Three hours in that heat takes an awful lot out of you."

The pace of life in our little world was slow. Phil Sinnott had a slight infection and went to Dr. Haslam. "I went to the doctor for some aureomycin and you know, he doesn't have anything to do, so he spent the next half hour giving me the complete history of antibiotics."

Capt. Jahn recalled his early seagoing days as a cook's helper on tugboats. "When I first went to sea with my father, he would dip a bottle in the sea every day and fill a glass with it and make me drink it. It was a physic.

"I never got sick. I was always healthy."

Overall, the crew stayed healthy throughout the voyage, despite the seven-days-a-week schedule. The engine crew was even more remarkable, seventy-year-old men stood watches in 130° heat. But the enthusiasm, motivation and determination carried everyone through unscathed. In fact, some of the crew's health improved during the trip. Dick Brannon: "One guy I had strong doubts about was Gene Anderson, diabetic, eye problems, physical condition, and two days before we sailed he told me, I don't think I can make it. He wanted to desperately, but he says, 'Oh God, I just can't think of facing the heat.' I said, 'Gene, you have to do what you feel is right.' So he says, 'Well, I'm going to give it a try.' And he told the doctor his problems and, son-of-a-bitch, he was healthier when he got off of here than when he came on. His health problems, working in the heat down there, he sweated things out, he got a new interest in life."

From Carl Nolte's column on the subject of Fitness. "Joe Callahan used to be a telephone company executive; now he is a deckhand. He will be 75 next month. 'I had a friend who retired,' he said. 'The highlight of his day was taking his dog for a walk. He's dead now, but the dog is still alive.'"

The weather changed. On May 9, we had morning squalls but, rather than the isolated squalls of the tropics, they appeared to be part of a larger weather system. Large masses of grey clouds covered much of the distant sky. Now several hundred miles into the Atlantic, we would soon be leaving the northeast trades. For the first time in weeks the weather was comfortable, you could sit without sweating.

Today was Russ Mosholder's birthday, yesterday was Arnold Sears'. Beginning a tradition that would last the remainder of the voyage, Jimmy Farras baked a cake and decorated it with "Happy Birthday" written in icing. As Russ finished his dinner in the saloon, Jimmy carried the cake in, candles alight, followed by the rest of the crew. We sang "Happy Birthday" and Russ blew the candles out. He was pleasantly surprised, and somewhat embarrassed. The party was repeated in the crew mess for Arnold and the songs and laughter continued for almost an hour.

The *Jeremiah O'Brien* theater continued its WWII retrospective with "Casablanca," "Run Silent, Run Deep," "The Longest Day" and "Patton."

Meanwhile, back at the home office, planning for events yet to come continued. Marci Hooper radioed a message to Adm. Patterson, prepared in French, to send to the President of the French Senate and his Cabinet.

MISTER PRESIDENT

YOU HAD THE EXTREME AMIABILITY TO WRITE A LETTER TO MR. AL GORE, IN FAVOUR OF OUR VISIT TO FRANCE DURING THE CELEBRATION OF THE 50TH ANNIVERSARY OF D-DAY IN NORMANDY. WE WARMLY THANK YOU AGAIN FOR YOUR PRECIOUS HELP.

WE WOULD BE IMMENSELY PLEASED TO WELCOME YOU ABOARD *SS JEREMIAH OBRIEN* DURING THE CHERBOURG FESTIVITIES ON THE 25TH OF JUNE, FOR THE CELEBRATION OF THE CITY LIBERATION. THIS EVENT WILL BE ALSO FEATURING THE PRESENTATION OF DUKWS, THESE AMPHIBIOUS VEHICLES WHICH WERE VERY OFTEN COUPLED WITH THE LIBERTY SHIPS.

WITH OUR VERY RESPECTFUL REGARDS

RADM T. PATTERSON*

The northeasterly trade winds persisted. The sea was more on the beam now causing the ship to roll farther. The engine department, in addition to running the engine, continued with other repairs: washing machines, gangway stanchions, plumbing, electrical circuits.

---

*The translation from the French is literal. We did not actually send a message saying "your precious help."

In recent weeks we had become more and more concerned about our "sister" convoy ship, the *SS Lane Victory*. All the problems, difficulties and funding worries the *O'Brien* encountered as she prepared for the voyage were present on an equal scale at the *Lane*'s home base in San Pedro. With Herculean efforts, Joe Vernick, John Smith, Clint Johnson and other members of their Board of Directors overcame each new setback and the *Lane* finally began her voyage to Normandy later than planned but at her 16 knot speed, versus the *O'Brien*'s 10, we hoped she would catch us before our arrival in England. When we heard she had sailed, we all rejoiced. Mechanical and financial problems continued to beset her, however, and we anxiously sought news on her progress via radio.

Then, off Acapulco, the *Lane*'s boiler water became contaminated with oil. To her crew's bitter disappointment, the decision was made to return to San Pedro. Our crew was disappointed, too.

"A crying shame."

"Damn the luck."

Many of us were close friends and even those who weren't felt their frustration and anguish. So much planning, hard work, hope and effort, all for naught. We felt the steady thrust of our engines. The "Lucky *O'Brien*," as we've always been known. Her simple but steady engine, her homely yet durable design were dependable beyond compare.

This is the Voice of the *Jeremiah O'Brien*.
Good evening, San Francisco.
Jeremiah O'Brien sends her regrets to the Master and crew of the *SS Lane Victory* on their inability to continue the voyage to Europe. They, as we, have prepared for this voyage with many hours of labor and considerable expense in anticipation of participating in the ceremonies off the Normandy beaches. We realize this is a great disappointment for the crew and others concerned. With great respect and admiration for your efforts, the *Jeremiah O'Brien* will continue onward to Europe and proudly show the Stars and Stripes first flown from a US merchant vessel off the invasion beaches on June 6, 1944. *Jeremiah O'Brien* — out.

The Last Convoy was now down to one ship. In a somber mood we watched the evening movie, "Sink the Bismark."

The next day, the sea was even more on the beam increasing the period and travel of the roll. Still seldom more than ten degrees in each direction, it was beginning to get slightly uncomfortable. But the painting progressed with the crew putting grey on the after house and the midships house. The old ship was starting to look good.

Bosun Rich Reed applies a finish coat of grey paint to "Charley Noble," the galley smokestack. Photo by Bruce McMurtry.

Some days were more routine than others. May 12 found us wallowing along as we had the day before and the day before that. It was cloudy, overcast and dismal in the morning, but later burned off to bright sunshine and a cheerful blue in the late afternoon. The sea and swell slowly changed direction until it was coming aft of our beam. Late in the morning watch we passed a sail boat. Such are the highlights of a day at sea.

Carl Nolte: "It was quite a challenge, you know. You're in a place where your world was 441 feet long by 50 feet. What were you going to write six days a week about it? I ended up interviewing birds and stuff."

A ship at sea works on an around-the-clock routine. The deck watches change six times a day at 12, 4 and 8. Because the *Jeremiah O'Brien*'s engine department stood three-hour watches, they changed eight times daily at 12, 3, 6 and 9. Those who didn't stand watches, the cooks, the day workers, started their day at the same time, day in and day out — 8 a.m. for the day workers, 4 or 5 a.m. for the cooks. It was pleasant and low-key. The engines purred along. The black gang oiled bearings, watched fluid levels, checked steam gauges and changed oil burners. The deck crew continued painting grey. Inside no. 2 they painted the red deck, once again, red. Bob Burnett continued working on the stairway leading out of no. 3 hatch.

Tom Alexander, fireman/watertender: "I felt, particularly crossing the Atlantic, we were a little community. Everybody got to know everybody else, and we got into a routine."

Phil Sinnott: "One thing was the night lookouts and the swash of the water and the bow wave and that lift and fall of the bow. It's just great. And the porpoises, they're all silver in the phosphorescence, shooting off in all directions, and the stars are circling around overhead. It's a beautiful thing. It's very, very peaceful. The quietness of the ship, the ordered routine was a great pleasure."

On my 8-to-12 watch, I walked from one bridge wing to the other, sometimes pausing to look at the phosphorescence boiling along the ship's sides as it came off the bow wake. Little balls of green fire shimmered like luminescent watery fireflies, flashing for a teasing moment, then disappearing. Overhead, because there was no loom of city lights, were more stars than it was possible to count. Occasionally a shooting star sparkled across the heavens. As the helmsman rang the bell every half hour, reminding us of ships sailing through the centuries, it seemed like a very special place to be.

Some of the crew were practical jokers. Jack Carraher recalled one incident, "Rudy [Arellano] was a very light sleeper, had a lot of trouble sleeping. If there was a mouse walking down the passageway he'd hear it and jump out of bed screaming and yelling. Of course that made him very vulnerable. There was four of us in the forecastle, Pat McCafferty, Rudy, myself and Eduardo [Pubill]. Pat slept in an upper bunk and he could reach down with his hand and unlock the door. When the ship lurched, the door would open wide and then when the ship lurched back the other way it would slam. Out would come Rudy, screaming and yelling. It was a very clever deal because Pat would just reach down and nobody would see him. It would be dark, he'd just unlock it, pull back his arm and the door would be unlatched, then when the ship rolled one way, the door would swing wide. Of course, Eduardo got blamed for it."

Jack Carraher also noticed the *esprit de corps* that had developed: "The people in the first part of the voyage seemed to have a goal that was beyond them. They really wanted to do it, they had a real family feeling. I could see it in the mess 'cause we talked constantly. Their feeling about the ship and about our goals and things was really inspiring to me."

The enthusiasm of the crew was marked by their constant interest in where we were. Each watch would find Otto Sommerauer or Bob Nossieux or Pat McCafferty or Dennis Rodd or someone else in the wheelhouse or chartroom, watching the radar, asking about the weather forecast, looking at the charts. If land or a ship was in sight, five or six of the crew would be there asking questions, borrowing binoculars, watching the mate on watch as he navigated, talking to the helmsman, pointing things out to each other.

Unlike regular merchant ships, where rank and duties keep the various departments separate, on the *O'Brien,* no artificial barriers separated the crew. The traditional respect for officers was there; orders were never questioned. Otherwise, from captain and admiral, deck department and engine department, ABs, OSs, Oilers, wipers, messmen, we were a democracy — all volunteers without rank or station — bound together in the great adventure, "the trip of a lifetime."

Pete Lyse: "It was like we were youngsters again in many ways, like we were trying to relive something. Those of us who have lived it and others who were young enough were looking ahead, but it was an experience of a lifetime and you reflect on it. Just to sit up there on the boat deck on a sunny afternoon is something you'll never be able to do again. I saw it from the captain on down, it was something really unique. We were so diverse and individualistic. We came from such a wide country but yet we fit into the same routine and camaraderie. Fun takes over after awhile. No one is pegged at any social level. There was still that camaraderie and the lack of social levels. We were all in the same boat together."

In a quiet moment, Capt. Jahn revealed how determined he was to make this trip, to have the opportunity to return to Normandy, and to show "them" it could be done. He invited me into his cabin and showed me one entire drawer full of an old but healthy man's medicines; blood pressure pills, heart pills, maalox, milk of magnesia, aspirin, ace bandages, cotton balls, antiseptic and so on. He had a triple heart bypass years earlier and six months before sailing, also had his arthritic left knee replaced with stainless steel so he could be sure to make the trip. His determination was inspiring.

The Atlantic crossing seemed to put the crew in a reflective mood. Rich Reed: "I enjoy being at sea. So, for me, I thoroughly enjoyed the crossing. I don't even know how many days it was. I lost track of time. I really enjoy being at sea but, actually, it's kind of a copout 'cause you've got no responsibilities, no phones, you don't have to pay any bills. I get the guilts sometimes 'cause my wife's home raising the kids. Here I am out there with no responsibilities except my job at hand, keeping the ship on a straight course, yeah, making sure the jobs get done. But I like the serenity, I like the life-style. Like anything, like any other job, it's got its good points and bad points. You know, you get out there and you get pissed off and you say, I'm never going to do this again. This is my last trip. I'm never going back to sea, but, you know, you always go back."

Greg Williams: "I loved being at sea. It was close to nature, the changing scenery, it was never the same. You could always see something different, even in the water or the clouds or the wildlife. It can be quiet, especially on a steam ship. It was nice, seeing the water around the stern, very relaxing to watch and look at. I think you get a lot closer to nature. It seems like a funny thing to say since there was nothing around if you looked around, no trees or rocks or mountains or anything, but it was still very close to the earth. I like that."

Sam Wood, ordinary seaman: "When I first went to sea I felt that it was the first work in my life I'd ever found I truly enjoyed doing. I was content in it. I could see myself spending the next thirty, forty years going to sea. Didn't work out that way, but I still felt much that same kind of satisfaction on the *O'Brien,* that same completeness, if you will, in going to sea. My life was complete there. It was a kind of institutional life, it was regulated, hours, meals, work, time off and filled up my life very well. It gave me time to do the things that I enjoyed doing in my free time, reading, and playing chess and writing."

Mike Emery: "I felt that there wasn't going to be another commemoration of war, of American soldiers in my lifetime. My college roommate's father was a medic at D-Day and World War II had always interested me. Having the opportunity to ship out was one of my goals. It was something I always wanted to do and I lamented the fact that people in my generation didn't have the chance to ship out or ride the rails. The opportunity of going as a photographer and shipping out the way men did fifty years ago was very, very exciting to me."

And, on the lighter side, Phil Sinnott: "The most frustrating thing was this damn tradition of taking a cup of coffee up to the mate on watch. I had the damn chief mate's watch. He worried about that more than the ship. The condition of the coffee was more important than the condition of the ship."

The Training Ship *State of Maine* joined us on May 12. Operated by the Maine Maritime Academy, the ship is forty-two years old and carries 250 students and sixty-five officers and crew. She looks like a passenger ship, in fact she was built as a troop transport, and is much handsomer than the *O'Brien.*

Bob Burnett: "It was kind of a thrill when I knew that night we were to meet the *State of Maine.* I was standing lookout with somebody and I really wanted to spot that ship's light before I got off watch. I saw the loom and knew the light was there but never saw it for sure until just before the watch ended."

Phil Sinnott wasn't so thrilled to see the ship. "I liked it better when we had the ocean to ourselves."

The *State of Maine* was to be part of the gathering of ships in England. The Last Convoy would now be two ships — a converted troop ship and the last Liberty. She was a welcome diversion. Each watch there was talk back and forth on the VHF. She took up position on our port side. Some mornings she would be ahead of us, others, behind. Occasionally she would drop astern to conduct a boat drill or some other exercise. In the evening it was comforting to see the other ship's lights on our port beam as she kept pace with us.

The next day the weather was clear with blue skies, a very calm sea and the wind from astern. Adm. Patterson's comment for the day was, "This is the kind of weather we signed on for." For some reason, Capt. Jahn was in a dither over the distance to Portsmouth. He asked each of the three mates to work out the mileage independently. He was worried about giving an accurate ETA but with more than a thousand miles yet to go the ETA naturally would depend on our speed. If we made eleven knots we would arrive on Saturday morning, 10.5 Saturday noon, and 10 early Sunday morning.

Back home, Carl Nolte's articles had captured the public imagination. In contrast to the usual gloom, doom, violence and

Meanwhile, in the crow's nest . . . Bruce enjoys the sea and — room service. Courtesy Phil Frank and San Francisco Chronicle.

mayhem in the papers, what we were doing was exciting, interesting, upbeat and positive. A letter to the editor of the *Chronicle* succinctly captured this: "Editor — My nomination: Carl Nolte and his *Jeremiah O'Brien* series for a Pulitzer in Spellbinding Taleweaving and Least Depressing News. Tim Heaton. San Francisco."

Bill Bennett's Crew's News for May 13, read in a humorous tone by Gary North, revealed some of the goings-on aboard:

> Good evening, San Francisco. A solemn ceremony was held today aboard your ship. A change of command. Captain of the Head, Michael Emery, the ship's photographer, relinquished his duty as caretaker of seamans' toilets, wash basins, showers and foc'sles. He handed his tools — bowl brush, Sani Flush, Windex, broom and swab to Joe Callahan of Sacramento. Michael has done an excellent job maintaining our quarters. Sometime in his future, this unattached 31-year-old professional will make some lady a fine house husband.
>
> Joe, who has been married for 50 years to Kathleen, has many years of experience in household duties, we are sure, and should have no problem continuing to keep our quarters clean.
>
> *Jeremiah O'Brien* — out.

Mike Emery: "I made the voyage chipping and painting and scrubbing and captain of the heads and all that. I felt that as an outsider and a young guy on the voyage, I had something to prove. I felt that going as a volunteer and taking someone else's slot made it so that I better pull my own weight and then some. I wasn't going to just do the photography. I promised myself I would work harder than anyone else in the deck department."

Saturday, May 14, another balmy day with the wind astern and light tufts of clouds scattered throughout the sky. There was no swell and the seas were calm. The constant quiet throb of the engine was satisfying and reassuring.

At breakfast Capt. Jahn said, "The hell with the overtime, the crew is painting the ship today."

At mealtime every day, messman Jack Carraher went throughout the ship beating a cheerful tune on an old, hand-held xylophone. He paused at each open door to announce what was being served. "Tonight we have poached salmon, baked potatoes, rice pudding and a bunch of other stuff I've forgotten." Then, with a demonic cackling laugh, he would continue pounding his chimes until he got to the next room where he repeated the menu.

Jack Carraher: "Some of the tunes I had to make up. I just wish I'd taped some of that, but then some was so gross it would be unfit for human ear. But I just got a kick out of it because everybody seemed to enjoy me coming by. Now whether it was the thought of the food or what-have-you, I don't know. But I enjoyed it, because the crew seemed to respond and I, of course, in turn, responded to them. And it was a real working relationship. I'll always treasure that.

Jack Carraher first shipped out for a year in 1946 as wiper, fireman and ordinary seaman. When the post-war shipping slump put him on the beach he resumed his high school education and went on to a community college where he met his future wife, Joyce. He spent the next 27 years working for the Los Angeles County Road Department. After retirement, Jack began his second career, teaching English as a Second Language at California State University Los Angeles. He later returned to the Road Department where he worked as a construction consultant and project manager. Along the way he got a master's degree in history. Jack and his wife live in Monterey Park, California.

"I enjoyed my service as a messman immensely, especially the first part of the trip. My feet were killing me but I just enjoyed that crew. They were great. The camaraderie was simply great."

Bruce McMurtry: "Those guys in the galley were the hardest workers on the ship, bar none. The food was outstanding, it was just great. I was standing in line one Thursday and asked one

Jack Carraher, master of the dinner chime, in his element. Photo by Mike Emery.

of the cooks what kind of soup we had. He said 'everything soup.' It was great, all leftovers, but it was really tasty. I got where I looked forward to Thursdays because that's when we had 'everything soup.'"

Rich Reed: "My only concern was the crew. I tend to be overprotective. Sailing bosun I was really watching out for the guys and I thought all this time that's just asking too much of guys. I was really worried about 'em, but they're just to be commended. Everybody endured and held up and did their job. I didn't push guys as far as turning to and everything. You let guys come out and work at their own pace and schedule and every-thing. My hat's off to them. It was really a pleasure to work with all of them. And especially, like I say, the guys that never been to sea before, to see them take off and endure that much sea time, I think they're really to be commended."

Sunday was another pleasant day with the wind slightly abaft the starboard beam making the ship somewhat cooler. Jokes about overtime and painting aside, many of the crew took the day off. This was a time to relax, read a book, watch a movie, catch up on the journal, wash clothes, sew on a button or take a nap.

Idleness often leads to mischief. Jack Carraher was natu-rally mischievous: "Ed Lingenfield is slightly deaf. Actually pretty damn deaf. And to stir up the mess a little bit I used to hold conversations, very private conversations with him at the table. Nobody else could hear me, but I would talk to him and he wouldn't be hearing me at all. And then I'd straighten up and I'd yell out, 'I told you we don't have any chutney.' And I'd go through this whole damn routine, 'We don't have no chutney. You guys al-ways ask for something we don't have.' Of course, nobody would know what I was talking about, including Ed. Especially Ed. But everybody would have thought that he asked me for chutney. Who in the hell wants chutney. Nobody had asked for chutney. Finally it got so bad, I was raising hell every night with him about this chutney. Damned if Bill Duncan didn't bring some chutney aboard and I was in a real spot. So I explained that away by saying, 'We're not eating meat tonight so nobody wants any chut-ney.' So I put it in the refrigerator and, you know, somebody ate it. It was a grand thing to feed the crew with, cause they would start arguing with themselves. [laugh] 'I don't know which one of you ordered chutney but we don't have it.' It was a wonderful arguing point."

In the middle of the Atlantic, a ceremony was held on the flying bridge to commemorate the loss of Armed Guard sailors during World War II. Hundreds of Allied ships were sunk during the Battle of the Atlantic. In 1941 the U.S. embarked on an unprecedented program to build ships faster than they could be sunk. The Libertys, totaling 2,751 were, by far, the largest class of ships.

Carl Kreidler, gunner, organized the ceremony. He was the only crew member who actually served in the Navy Armed Guard during World War II. Jim Wade gave an eloquent eulogy and a wreath was thrown from the bridge wing. We carried the flowers all the way from San Francisco. They had resided since then in our refrigerated box, alongside salami, bacon and sausage. Everyone wanted to record the moment. There was a camera battle during the ceremony to

With Jim Wade steering, the ship was under "divine guidance."

see who could position himself for the best photo. Many of the pictures showed other people taking pictures.

Later in the day, Jim Wade took the wheel for a while. This was an opportunity for someone to remark that, when it came to steering the ship, we were certainly under divine guidance and, sure enough, someone did. Soon, other members of the crew came up for a turn at the wheel. It's something you don't see on a regular ship, the boyish delight of steering a big vessel through the ocean. "Hey, I steered the ship." Although in their sixties and seventies, the crew were still children at heart, with the same joy and exuberance.

The weather changed on May 16 giving a brief hint of what was to come. Night turned into a grey, overcast day. The equally grey ocean was calm. The air temperature was colder than before. Everyone switched to long pants, sweatshirts and jackets except the engine watch. They were always plenty warm. The deck crew continued painting, scrubbing, sanding, getting ready for Portsmouth.

There was a natural tendency for the crew to linger in the messrooms after dinner. At any time you might find Joe Callahan, Bill Concannon, Dirk Warren, Richard Hill, Bruce McMurtry or Mary Steinberg there. (Mary was the only woman on the crew on the voyage out. She worked as a wiper and occupied a room by herself in the old gunner's quarters in the aft deck house.) The day's work over, they could look forward to a gabfest, maybe a game of checkers or chess, perhaps write in their journal or read a book. But they forgot that because <u>their</u> work was done for the day, didn't mean that everyone else's work was done. The messmen couldn't clean up the messrooms until everyone had eaten and left. Rudy Arellano was outspoken and not the type of person to let this sort of thing go on for long. He finally had enough one night and made the following announcement: "There's too many people lingering in here. You come in here and eat, you get the ---- out." Brief, concise and right to the point.

Jack Carraher was more tolerant in the gunners' mess. "François [Le Pendu] would be mumbling there and pretty soon

Back in San Francisco, Farley is not only scooped by Carl Nolte, but by his raven, Bruce.   Courtesy Phil Frank and San Francisco Chronicle.

Dinner on the O'Brien. *Rudy Arellano pours Jim Conwell a glass of wine. Jim Miller, Phil Sinnott and Otto Sommerauer (partially hidden) chow down on the left. To the right are Carl Nolte and Joe Callahan. Photo by Bruce McMurtry.*

songs start coming from him. We never could figure out what they were. Or he would tell us stories of when he was a young man and sailing the South Seas. I don't know how true they were, but it didn't make any difference to us. And every once in a while he would do a French folk dance and whatnot which was always well applauded. And he'd dress for dinner. I tried to get the rest of them to dress, but the best I could do is get them to wear shoes. Which was something, when you look at it."

Ed Smith, deck engineer: "With Jack and François it was like a situation comedy every night. Every night, I mean. And it was not obnoxious, you know. You could say, François, give us your Alec Guinness and he'd jump up from his chair, and he'd give us this shot, like this, and all of a sudden he'd start walking out, the Alec Guinness walk. Or he'd imitate somebody, 'cause he was excellent, he could imitate the chief engineer, he could imitate Mary, he had a whole bunch of them that he could imitate. And Jack was a prince. I said to him, 'You know, you talk better standing up than sitting down.' And he says, 'You know, you're right.'"

Now we learned that the British press was heralding our arrival in England. The May issue of *Ships Monthly,* a British magazine devoted to maritime affairs, came out with a nice piece by Mike Simpson, on "The Last Atlantic Convoy."

Our only contact with the outside world was telegrams, faxes or radiotelephone conversations. These were all expensive — telephone time on the Inmarsat system costs $10 a minute —

and consequently limited conversations to emergency personal matters.

Karen Kamimoto: "The most difficult thing in the office was just trying to keep up and not be overwhelmed with what was happening, trying to keep track of the ship and match it with what we were doing. It was a real exciting time and the people that helped in the office felt they were part of the journey. We'd fill out proper papers for family coming on board the ship, especially for Portsmouth where security was so tight. Also some family emergencies came up and a lot of them didn't know how to get in touch with the ship, so we'd fax the ship and have them call home. The satellite phone was very expensive and they soon quit using that. I remember when François' wife got her first bill — $600 for one phone call. She sent a fax or letter saying 'Do not call from ship, call from land.'"

Many of the crew had portable radios. The BBC short-wave stations seemed to be the most popular because they gave broad news coverage. As each day brought us closer to England, the excitement mounted. It wasn't so much the adventure or the romance of arriving at a new country, although that was certainly part of it, but a growing undercurrent of pride and *esprit de corps*. We were doing what we set out to do. We were getting closer and closer to proving to the world that a fifty-year-old ship, manned by volunteers with an average age of seventy-something, carrying a cargo of American know-how, could do exactly what it said it would — return to Normandy for the 50th Anniversary of the D-Day landings.

We were now in the North Atlantic and it looked and felt like it — constant grey, dismal rain and drizzle. The wind, from the south, had a bitter edge. The northeast swell caused us to pitch uncomfortably. It was cold enough for the steam heat to be turned on. Being too wet to paint outside, the deck crew went to work painting the interior passageways and decks. This caused some confusion as only half of any passageway deck could be painted at a time. The dry half was marked in chalk with arrows and a notice to watch out for the wet paint. But the natural tendency was to avoid stepping on the chalk, causing some to step

Ever the opportunist, Bruce puts his brandy to good use. The crew appear to be spending all their time in the crow's nest. Courtesy Phil Frank and San Francisco Chronicle.

in the fresh paint, leading to the appearance of several red footprints in places they didn't belong.

May 18 broke sunny and relatively calm, as if the past two days were a dream. The ship looked like a leopard with red primer spotted everywhere on the foredeck. Rich Reed painted a large red arrow on the foredeck pointing toward the bow. Underneath it he wrote in big bold letters "Bishop Rock," our first expected landfall on the southwest tip of England. The sailors began "cutting in" the grey on the main deck. This is the process of painting with a brush all the angles, corners, edges, pipes and other places that couldn't be painted with a roller or spray gun. By the end of the day the entire foredeck was grey.

Now, Capt. Jahn received a call from the Coast Guard threatening to press charges, arrest him, go against his license, and other severe penalties for transgressions against the restrictions on the Certificate of Inspection that required he stay within twenty miles of the coast, not carry passengers and have an escort across the ocean. The restrictions were listed on a second page attached to the back of the certificate, and in the excitement of departure, no one on the ship noticed or read them. He was also criticized for carrying passengers in the Panama Canal. From 8,000 miles away, Capt. A. H. MacDonald had struck again. Capt. Jahn was livid. "These jackasses have never even been to sea. They don't know what they're talking about. That MacDonald is sick." He fumed and swore and sputtered.

Bill Vaughn, NLSM attorney, called the captain on the satellite phone from the office, assuring him that the Coast Guard

The Maytags did yeoman service. Here Tom Patterson measures out soap for his wash. Photo by Mike Emery.

had exceeded its authority on everything. "That made me feel better," said Capt. Jahn.

The satellite phone was in the captain's office which is just a few feet from the wheelhouse. Frequently the door was left open. I later overheard Adm. Patterson talking to someone in the Coast Guard about their shabby attitude toward *Jeremiah O'Brien*.

Rain, wind and choppy seas continued, but the crew worked on the after deck and put the finishing touches on the ladder coming out of no. 3. They painted a blue line on the main deck and throughout the midships house that would lead our visitors on a self-guided tour through the ship. Ron Smith jokingly [I think] said the blue line was so the mates could find the bow. I began working on a docent schedule for our European ports. It was the deck department's responsibility to provide guides or docents to keep people on track while going through the ship, explain things and answer questions. We needed to station sailors at the entrance and exit gangways to ensure a smooth flow of traffic. Others were necessary in strategic locations to keep people on the blue line, still others were needed in the wheelhouse and flying bridge to keep children from playing with the whistle, telegraph and navigation equipment and to answer questions. It was also important that everyone get a day off occasionally, that they get relieved for meals, or simply take a break once in a while. The logistics were complex, the list long. When it was handed out there was the usual grousing: "Why does so-and-so get the first day off?" "How come I have to be on the gangway at midnight?"

We were pleasantly surprised to learn our public was still following us. We still did not fully realize the tremendous interest in the voyage. People from all over the country were calling "the Voice of the *Jeremiah O'Brien*," (which logged a record 900 calls one week) news articles and TV reports on the progress were increasing, and on the rare day that Nolte's column did not appear, the *Chronicle* received numerous calls about the omission.

TO: CAPT, CREW, REAR ADMIRAL PATTERSON

CONGRATULATIONS WITH YOUR SUCCESSFUL VOYAGE. WE ARE FOLLOWING YOUR LOCATION EVERYDAY. KEEP UP THE WONDERFUL WORK. BEST REGARDS TO YOU ALL FROM MARIN SUPPORTERS AND DONORS AGGIE AND FRANK PAVIA, EX-LIBERTY MERCHANT ENGINEER TIBURON CALIFORNIA.

Crew's News for May 19:

Good evening, San Francisco. We are 540 miles from our destination of Portsmouth England and it is 0300 — it is time for the watch to change in *Jeremiah*'s engine room. As in a scene from Hollywood's movie "Grumpy Old Men," three engineers silently and sleepily enter and relieve the watch. Alex Hochstraser of Pacifica will operate the boilers; Dennis Rodd, a native of Canada now of Benicia, is the oiler. In charge of all of this is Bob Noiseux, at 21 the youngest licensed merchant marine engineer on U.S. vessels. A 1994 graduate of Kings Point Academy, Bob's home is in Brookline, Connecticut. Within minutes each person had checked his equipment, made minor adjustments where needed, greeted each other with genuine feeling, and settled in for a three hour watch. A great deal of responsibility rests on their shoulders and they will handle it well. We had travelled

248 miles at noon today at a speed of 10.8 knots. The temperature on deck is an invigorating 60 degrees.
Jeremiah O'Brien — out.

Carl Nolte's column for this date captured the mood of the ship:

Fair weather came to the Atlantic again yesterday after a stormy night on board this 50-year-old Liberty ship.

The *O'Brien* is on the last leg of its long trip from San Francisco. By evening yesterday, Land's End, the southern tip of England was only about 600 miles away, and there was a sense aboard the old ship of the beginning of the end of the Atlantic crossing.

The sun came out yesterday after two days of gloom and a rough night to show once again how lucky the *O'Brien* has been on its voyage so far.

The night before was no fun. The wind was cold, and the sea was choppy. The mist was in so close that the training ship *State of Maine*, which has been escorting the *O'Brien*, disappeared. The two ships pitched and rolled.

On the *O'Brien*, everything that could rattle around rattled around in the small hours of the morning. It was so cold, crew members turned on the steam heat in their rooms, only to discover that old steam radiators clank and bang in the middle of the night like rocks landing on a metal room. What with the pitching and rolling, crashing and banging, nobody got much sleep.

In its Atlantic voyages 50 years ago, the *O'Brien* had plenty of rough weather, but most of the time, this trip has been as smooth as a ride on the Larkspur ferry. There have been only two days of rough weather in a month of steaming toward England and Normandy.

Even the rough seas had moments of beauty. Seaman Marty Shields standing the midnight watch in the bow said that when the ship pitched, the phosphorescence of the ocean was stirred up so that the dark Atlantic glowed with a beautiful eerie light.

Everyone on the ship, including Bruce, reads that which appeals to them the most. Courtesy Phil Frank and San Francisco Chronicle.

The storm was the leading edge of a gale that swept to England yesterday, and now the seamen aboard can sense that land is close.

There is a feeling of pride in bringing the old ship so far. But there is a feeling of sadness, too, because once the ship reaches England and begins its European tour with calls at Portsmouth, three French ports and a side trip to London, the ship will no longer belong to the crew. The *O'Brien* will be open to visitors at every port, and crew members have all been assigned jobs as docents to answer questions and explain things. Already, the deck crew is painting blue lines to guide visitors through the deck house. Engine room personnel are cleaning the engine spaces and painting.

In port, crew members, who seldom carry keys, will have to lock up everything. The ship will be full of visitors — strangers — and you never know.

Crews are very possessive of their ship, and this seems like opening your home to visitors.

There is something else, too, in returning to land. There is an attraction to the sea that goes beyond the sea air and the ocean view. This is a happy ship, at least so far, and the routine is simple and easy to understand. "We are really going to miss being at sea," said Rich Reed, a professional seaman who is the bosun. He will be 47 the day the ship reaches England.

At sea, there are no phone calls, no traffic jams, no bills, no trees to trim, no dogs to feed, no office politics, three square meals a day and a clearly established set of duties. The engineers oil the engine at regular intervals, the firemen change burners, the boiler tubes are blown every afternoon at 4. The cooks cook, the deckhands are told what to paint and when, and even the helmsman is given a course to steer. The mates wear uniforms and look important, and the unlicensed personnel sit around on the No. 4 hatch every afternoon and tell tall tales of life at sea.

The highlight of the day is a single beer issued at 4:30 p.m.,

Afternoon beer call, a chance to relax after a hard day. Left to right, Mary Steinberg, Arnold Sears, Bob Noiseaux, Joe Callahan, Marty Wefald, Phil Sinnott and Tom Patterson. Photo by Bruce McMurtry.

followed by a bottle-throwing contest between three of the youngest members of the crew.

The ship's world is very small, and the real world is very far away."

Carl Nolte: "This was a 50-year-old vessel, a pretty old ship. And I think the sound and the feeling of the vessel were like something out of Victory at Sea. It was most unusual, the motion of the ship, the feel of it, and the constant feeling that it was alive. And these guys were brought back to life, you know.

"I always liked that sort of romantic stuff. She certainly wasn't a very pretty ship, not very romantic looking but had a lot of character, personality — character, mostly. If you looked up there at the house, boy was that homely. You couldn't beat that for homely. But I think the trip brought the ship back to life. The sound of the engine was actually like the sound of some heartbeat."

Mike Emery: "I think the highlight of the trip was the time spent at sea. Especially the last two weeks, that's when the nostalgia set in that I would never do this again. And once we dropped the hook and set the gangway down, it wouldn't be repeated. I think the best part of the voyage was the last week."

On the morning 8-to-12 a four-engine airplane buzzed us, appearing with a roar out of the mists astern and disappearing ahead almost before we knew what happened. A few minutes later the VHF came to life, "Jeremy O'Brien, Jeremy O'Brien, thees es the Channel patrol. Come een please."

"*Jeremiah O'Brien*. Go ahead."

'You are arriving for the D-Day commemoration, no?"

"That's correct."

"Welcome to Europe. We weel see you in Normandy on June the seexth. Channel patrol out."

"Thank you. *Jeremiah O'Brien*, out."

The threat from the Coast Guard continued. Bill Vaughn called and said we had to conform to Coast Guard demands. Vaughn had talked to Admiral Herberger at MARAD but was unable to get any relief. Capt. Jahn was frustrated and angry.

The morning of May 20 broke with overcast, wind, rough seas and patchy fog. We were less than one day from Bishop Rock and the Channel. Passing by several fishing boats in the morning, we noticed they seemed to be drifting, perhaps waiting for a change in the tide. That evening we passed about twenty miles south of Bishop Rock, a famous landmark from sailing ship days. Twenty years earlier we might have passed closer to be sure of our position after so many days at sea. But the GPS had us right on track, showing position, speed, distance to go, course to steer and even which satellites we were reading if we were so curious as to punch through enough electronic screens to get that information. Several of the crew came up to the wheelhouse to see the landmark, but at that distance it was a poor radar target and we saw only a few dim flashes of light.

It was Jack Carraher's birthday. Someone gave him a life-sized inflatable doll as a present. She was dubbed Rosie O'Brien and given a seat in the messroom. The laughter and singing went on for hours.

Jack also got a cake, one of Jimmy's culinary masterpieces. Photo by Bruce McMurtry.

Bruce McMurtry: "That broke me up. Jack's date with Rosie O'Brien. Everyone was singing songs and having such a good time. We all enjoyed that."

In the early morning of May 21 we passed the Lizard, another famous landmark on the southwesternmost tip of England. The day broke grey and drizzly and continued that way to nightfall. But we were in the English Channel. Without the long fetch of the Atlantic for waves to build up, the seas were flat, despite the weather. The *O'Brien* rode differently now than in the open ocean, if anything, more steadily. We encountered more fishing boats, which always seemed to be in the way. Frequent course changes were made to avoid them. As we skirted about ten miles off the south coast of England, the mists occasionally cleared and we saw brown bluffs and rich, green forests and meadows.

Our first contact with England, this helicopter hovered around the ship for half an hour, filming the deck department painting the primer-spotted decks during our approach to the Isle of Wight.   Photo by Bruce McMurtry.

Approaching the Bill of Portland, a British military helicopter joined us. Hovering in several locations around the ship, its loud roaring clatter brought everyone out on deck. We waved and the pilots waved back. A cameraman was strapped in the open bay on one side, filming us. As we watched the helicopter hovering first above the ship, then ahead of us at deck level, then off to one side, we began to feel somewhat like celebrities.

As the day progressed, the rain increased to the point where visibility was very low. We passed south of the Isle of Wight without seeing it, then turned north to enter the Solent and Portsmouth.

TO: CAPTAIN AND CREW OF JEREMIAH OBRIEN AND CARL NOLTE

REMEMBER D-DAY/AND APPLAUD YOUR SPECTACULAR RE-TURN VOYAGE MADE POSSIBLE BY EACH ONE OF YOU. WE WATCHED YOU SAIL OUT READ EVERY CHRONICLE DISPATCH AND CALLED ALMOST DAILY HIP HIP HOORAY FROM TWO MEMBERS OF YOUR HUGE FAN CLUB. WE SENT A LITTLE CONTRIBUTION SO HAVE AN EXTRA BEER.

ELLEN GREEN AND NANCY HALL

Tom Alexander: "When we were coming up the Channel, I was working the 12-to-3 watch and I go down in the shaft alley to check the bearings. And I said, 'OK, old girl, you've almost done it.' That was really something. I remember thinking, we're going to give her a pat when we get in."

Rich Reed: "One of the real highlights was when we actually arrived in Portsmouth. The first one was, Hey, we made it, we really got away, and the second was, Not only did we get away, but we got here. We made it."

Coming up the east coast of the Isle of Wight, the wind increased to gale force. Passing Nab Light, we saw the pilot boat approach. Soon Capt. Carnegie, a pleasant, cheerful pilot, was on board, skillfully guiding us into the harbor, at no cost to the ship.

"We weren't expecting you until Monday," he said. "We'll have to put you at anchor."

"I called in the arrival," said Capt. Jahn.

"Well, no matter. The Royal Navy doesn't work on weekends. They'll have a berth for you Monday."

 It was Saturday. We were two days ahead of schedule. We didn't know it then but this would be our *modus operandi* throughout the voyage.

Entering the Solent, we passed several rock forts set in the middle of the harbor. Each had a navigation light on it. "Built as a defense in one of our wars with the French," said Capt. Carnegie. "One of them is privately owned. You can buy it for about one-and-a-half million, if you like."

The gale diminished somewhat as we went farther into the Solent. The pilot located us in the Man Of War anchorage and we dropped the anchor.

Before departing, he pointed to a series of buoys a few hundred yards off our starboard side. "That's where the *Mary Rose* was brought up."

We had traveled a total distance of 7,894 miles from San Francisco since April 18, 4,600 miles from Panama in 18 days, 17 hours and 18 minutes. Our average speed for the run was 10.2 knots with 12.7 knots run from noon to our arrival at 1930.

We were so close and yet so far. Like children at the window of a candy store, we watched the lights of Portsmouth, knowing that just beyond it, all of England beckoned.

7

RULE, BRITANNIA

W ell, we're here. Where is everybody?"
We arrived in time to celebrate U.S. Maritime Day, this most fitting of all days for the culmination of an historic voyage. All of England, we heard, was awaiting our arrival. Where was everyone? We were anchored outside the harbor and all was quiet. We couldn't go ashore until we cleared customs and immigration and, of course, no one could come aboard until then, either. Since the harbor was closed on weekends, there was nothing to do but wait.

The day was cold and blustery. Stuck on our ship, we looked across the Man of War anchorage toward centuries-old Portsmouth. The crew were in and out of the wheelhouse all day, borrowing the binoculars for a look at objects on the surrounding land. Every inch of shoreline was laden with history, conjuring images of famous events. To starboard were the buoys marking the site of the *Mary Rose* excavation, Henry VIII's recently-ex-humed flagship. Swinging the glasses north, we saw Portsmouth and Gosport — Dickens, Nelson, the Spithead mutiny, Bligh,

Hornblower and the recently-read Capt. Aubrey. The Southsea Common area of Portsmouth was the most prominent, being the closest land to the ship, with sandy beaches, low modern buildings and the remains of a castle wall at the entrance to the harbor. It was here that the fictional Dr. Watson longed to be in one of the Sherlock Holmes stories. The views became more exciting. Clearly visible inside the harbor were the tall masts of *HMS Victory* and *HMS Warrior* and the sleek grey hulls of warships with wonderful names that brought to life historic images — Trafalgar, Queen Victoria, Lady Hamilton, the *Bounty.* A large, white semaphore tower bristling with yardarms, masts and brightly-colored flags crowned the low red brick buildings of the Portsmouth Naval Yard. Astern were Cowes and the Isle of Wight evoking images of hydroplanes, Sir Malcolm Campbell, Gar Wood, and their racing prowess.

Jim Conwell: "Being at the anchorage at the Spithead with all those hundreds of years of British history around us was exciting. We were anchored just a short distance from where they brought up the *Mary Rose.*"

Phil Sinnott: "In England I was captivated by the sense of tradition that exists there. We have such a short historic tradition in our country that it's terribly impressive to see a real tradition at work."

Most of the crew shared the enthusiasm, spending their off watch hours on deck looking and discovering new sights.

Ron Robson, who would join us in Portsmouth and manage the ship's store until we sailed from Le Havre, was on the beach at Southsea, watching us. "The first major impression was on the morning after the ship's arrival, to see it at anchor at Spithead with the cloudy skies and whitecaps on the bay, tugging on the anchor chain. Seeing it brought tears to my eyes."

Ferry boats began leaving Portsmouth, modern blue and white boats with "Wightlink" emblazoned on their sides, crossing to the Isle of Wight. They detoured to pass close to the *O'Brien* and give their passengers a better view. They waved, we waved, they waved back, we waved back, all of us cheerful and exuberant. Larger ships, cross-Channel ferries run by P&O with names like *Pride of Dover, Pride of Cherbourg, Pride of London,* sailed past, bound for ports on the Continent. Each was as large as a transatlantic liner with a large white house set on a dark blue hull, looking very ship-like and nautical. It was thrilling to see so much maritime traffic.

Customs came aboard in the form of a cheerful, helpful young man. His only concern seemed to be how to make our official entry into the port as easy as possible. It was our first experience with British courtesy, a national characteristic that became ever more impressive as our stay lengthened.

Although we weren't loading or discharging any cargo, the deck department spent the day raising the cargo gear. Part of our purpose in being there was to bring back the feeling of fifty years ago, when the "bridge of ships" from the U.S. brought help and hope to the people of England and we wanted to look like a working merchant ship when we arrived alongside the dock.

Just after lunch the mail was brought aboard. Suddenly the decks were deserted and the ship became silent as everyone adjourned to their room, the messrooms or the saloon with letters, bundles and parcels from home.

With the mail were some of the newspaper articles and Farley cartoons we missed en route. Carl Nolte's column dealt with our arrival:

> The crew members of the last seagoing Liberty ship from World War II drank many a toast to their ship and each other in this English harbor yesterday. It was a raw, cold, windy day — but also the end of a historic 7,894-miles voyage for a 50-year-old ship, the conclusion of the last and most difficult leg of a voyage to commemorate the 50th anniversary of D-Day.
>
> The crew members had every reason to be proud that they had sailed nearly halfway across the world on a ship that had not been to sea since before William Jefferson Clinton was born. They had promised to be in England in time for the celebration of D-Day — June 6, 1944. Fifty years ago, when the greatest armada in the history of the world was assembled, the *O'Brien* was in that armada, and it is the only ship that has returned.
>
> The old, gray ship dropped anchor at Portsmouth at 9:25 p.m. Saturday, 450 feet of chain dropping out of the hawsepipe with a great crash and rattling of the old steam winch. Ten minutes later,

chief mate Walter Jaffee, 50, rang down "finished with engines" to the *O'Brien*'s engine room and after 2,756,346 turns of the propeller, the engines stopped. It was a satisfying but odd moment for the ship. After 32 days at sea, the constant sound of engines, like the slow heartbeat of life, stopped.

The celebration on shore will come today, but yesterday the ship celebrated itself. The vessel had stopped sailing, but the crew raised the cargo booms from their seagoing position, painted the deck, dressed the ship — which means running up signal flags and breaking out the ship's best American ensign.

"We're here now," said Richard Hill, 68, an engine room oiler. "A lot of people said we'd never make it. You know what I heard? I heard, 'That old rust bucket, it's going to sink.' You heard that all over. You heard people say the steam pipes would break from the stress and strain of the sea, the engine would break down. But none of that ever happened."

The most experienced of the crew was Captain George Jahn, who at 78 is the oldest person on the ship. He never had a doubt, not at the dock in San Francisco, not getting ready for sea, not steaming out the Golden Gate, not ever. "I knew damn well we were going to make it, for crissake," he said at breakfast yesterday. "Did you have doubts? What the hell for? This is practically a new ship. I have a good crew. The engines are perfect. What's the problem?"

The lead editorial from the *San Francisco Chronicle* on May 21, 1994:

Jeremiah O'Brien: "San Francisco's Own"

Hearty congratulations are in order for the doughty geezer crew of the Liberty ship *Jeremiah O'Brien*, expected to drop anchor in British waters today after an adventurous and nostalgic 34 day voyage from San Francisco. Still to come are the nautical ceremonies commemorating the 50th anniversary of D-Day, when the *O'Brien* was one of 5,000 warships that attacked Nazi-occupied France on June 6, 1944, in the greatest seaborne assault in history.

But simply by getting safely to England, and setting Liberty ship speed records along the way, the 51-year-old *O'Brien* — the only survivor of the D-Day armada — has proved she's as good as she ever was, maybe even better. Of all the ships that have claimed to be "San Francisco's Own," none deserves the title more than this gallant old warrior.

And *Chronicle* staff writer Carl Nolte rates a special salute for his daily dispatches of life aboard ship and stories about the all-volunteer crew of 58, with an average age of 72. His sea yarns have been inspiring to many armchair sailors, World War II veterans and other old-timers who wish they could be aboard, too.

Nolte, who signed on as a utility man, introduced us to Captain George Jahn, the 78-year-old skipper, revered by his crew as the best seaman aboard. We met fireman water tender Dick Currie, 55, oiler Norm Burke, 69, and chief engineer Richard Brannon, 75, who spend six hours a day sweating in the engine room, where temperatures reached 120 degrees, and love it.

We got to know dozens of their shipmates who we admired for their gumption, and envied them their adventure.

We wish them continued good luck, fair winds and following seas."

All the news wasn't good. Capt. Jahn received word that the Coast Guard would board the ship on our arrival alongside to investigate the report that we had carried passengers in Panama. The crew was exasperated and angry. "Doesn't the Coast Guard have anything better to do?"

"Good God, we make this historic trip with all flags flying and that's all they care about."

"Thirty passengers for eight hours, for God's sake!"

Capt. Jahn's reaction is best left unreported. But, still, the *O'Brien* had made it. And in record time. Even the Coast Guard couldn't deny that.

A cocktail party was held in the saloon for everyone. The chief steward, Russ Mosholder, put out salami, cheeses and other *hors d'oeuvres*. Dick Brannon brought out a bottle of "Duggan's Dew o' Kirkintilloch" which he was saving for just such an occasion. Toasts were drunk to the *Jeremiah O'Brien*, the crew, Portsmouth and Normandy. Champagne was served with dinner. In the crew mess, songs broke out, "It's a Long Way to Tipperary," "Over There," "Loch Lomond," "Waltzing Mathilda." The singing and toasting went on well into the night.

Ed Smith: "The night we came into Portsmouth we had champagne for everybody. So Jack, he had this towel over his arm, and he was serving everybody like a fancy waiter. He sat down next to Rich Hill and I, and we all had our beer and I said,

'This isn't champagne.' So it was nonalcoholic champagne. We looked at the label and we started banging our cups on the table just like a bunch of prisoners of war. The next thing you know they had wine and beer in there to shut 'em up. I ate my dinner and later I came back. I'm not a wine drinker, so I couldn't sit and enjoy it. So I came back and the captain and the admiral was there and everybody was singing 'Red Sails in the Sunset.' I had a movie of the whole thing, you know, of 'Red Sails in the Sunset.' We sang that a few times and they're only little things, but I got it in the movie, that's the good part. Dick Currie was over in the corner and he's saying, 'What the heck are these guys doing here?' He's stone-cold sober and he don't know what's happening, well, he knew what was happening, they were having a good time. But, that was a bunch, I'll tell you."

Rich Reed: "I think that the real high point of the whole trip was that we made it. We proved to people that we could do it. You know, there was a faction said that the ship couldn't make it, and I think a lot of people even in the maritime industry thought it was kind of a lark, although everybody was behind us. I heard there they had pools going in the financial district of San Francisco about how many days it would be before we broke down. Yeahhh, save your money, suckers."

Bill Bennett: "As we left home I thought that it's gonna be one of two things. We're either gonna have a bunch of old men set in their ways or we're going to have a bunch of mature people who will get along. And it turned out to be mature people. Witness the end of five weeks at sea in the Solent where we stood around and sung songs for two hours on nonalcoholic champagne. That said it all right there."

Not all the celebrations were on the ship. Back home, Karen Kamimoto got word from Cory Brothers Shipping, our agent in England, which generously donated their services in all the English ports, that the *O'Brien* had arrived. "That made it official," she said. "now, we had to catch our breath and then gear up for Europe."

The following morning our English pilot, Capt. Bill Clark, who also donated his services, boarded us with representatives of BBC, ITC, Reuters and AP. Now, we began to get a good idea

Escorted by two tugs, the Jeremiah O'Brien *approaches the entrance to Portsmouth Harbor. Photo by Julian Herbert of* The Times [London].

of the *O'Brien*'s status as a celebrity. Cameras whirred, reporters were all over the ship talking into hand-held recorders, their English and European accents making us feel we really were in a foreign country. Weighing anchor, we started toward the harbor entrance. Jim Conwell was thrilled to steer us in: "It was especially exciting for me being at the wheel both when we came around the Isle of Wight and again when we went into Portsmouth harbor. I'll never forget it."

Crowds stood on the ramparts of Southsea castle at the entrance to Portsmouth, waving and cheering, some swinging American flags. Two people held a large banner, "W'come JOB. Well done."

The tugs *Powerful* and *Bolster* arrived and were made fast, tying to our stern and bow respectively. We couldn't help but admire the British way of naming ships and boats, expressive, almost noble names. As we slowly came alongside, the pilot told us we'd been given an honored berth, "This quay is usually reserved for the *Britannia*." The crew on the flying bridge exchanged glances. The *Britannia*'s royal berth. This <u>was</u> an honor, indeed.

Waiting on the pier we saw Bob Blake, Carl Otterberg, Nell Otterberg, and Marci Hooper from our San Francisco office, Ron Robson, Jo Lawrence to help him, Elizabeth Wade (Jim's daughter) and Coke Schneider who left the ship in Panama. It was good to see old friends after five weeks away from home. *Powerful* and *Bolster* skillfully and powerfully bolstered us into our berth and soon we were tied fast to the South Railroad Jetty, built for Queen Victoria before the turn of the century and still containing the wrought iron pavilion used to shelter her when she disembarked her railway coach to board the royal yacht.

Tom Patterson: "The Royal Navy had given us the most prestigious berth in Portsmouth, that is, the queen's yacht's own berth on South Jetty, big flags and a wonderful arrival in England. The whole world seemed to rejoice that the *Jeremiah* had made it all the way over."

Jimmy Farras: "Coming into Portsmouth, England, and seeing the reception, that really, that was breathtaking."

Left to right, Martin Shakespeare, R. S. Crighton and R. S. Riches. Martin was a great help to us during our stay. Photo by Jo Lawrence.

Among the first people on board were Cdr. R. J. Riches, Lt. Cdr. R.S. Crighton and CWO (Chief Warrant Officer) H. Y. Waters of the Royal Navy, assigned to orient us with Portsmouth, the Navy Yard and the 50th Anniversary Commemoration. Armed with packets of information for both the wardroom (saloon) and mess, they provided emergency telephone numbers, fire instructions, visitor passes, where and when to dump garbage, maps, brochures; in short, all the information we needed for our stay. We were pleased and impressed at how well organized they were. Included was the calendar of events for the days ahead:

D-Day 50th Anniversary 1994
Programme of Events

28-30 May   World War II Military Vehicle Rally, over 1,000 vehicles from all over the world will be assembled on Southsea Common

28-30 May   Navy Days, Portsmouth Naval Base

31 May   Propaganda Film Evening, at 8.00 pm D-Day Museum, Southsea. Women & Work in World War II and British Propaganda in World War II.

31 May-3 June   Portsmouth 800 Pageant which will include a section on the war years in Portsmouth. Starting at 8.00 pm each evening at Southsea Castle and Castle Field.

2nd June   Anniversary concert, Anglican Cathedral, Old Portsmouth (City of Caen Orchestra), 7.30 pm.

3 June   D-Day Concert at Portsmouth Guildhall, featuring the BBC Concert Orchestra and H.M. Royal Marines Band plus guest soloist and narrator starting at 7:30 pm.

4 June   Garden Party, *HMS Dryad*, 3.00 pm (invited guests only) Beat Retreat, *HMS Excellent*, 5 pm (invited guests only) D-Day 50 Dinner, for Heads of State, Guildhall (invited guests only) French Market, City Centre.

5 June   Unveiling of statue of Roosevelt & Churchill, 10.50 am, Southsea Veterans' Drumhead Service, Naval Memorial, Southsea Common, 11.00 am. Flypast by historic U.S., British and French aircraft. 1.00 pm (approx.), Southsea Common. A flotilla of historic vessels and ships from the Allied Forces will sail past Southsea Common.

6 June   Veterans Parade, D-Day Memorial, Southsea. John Dunn Show live from the D-Day Museum, Southsea.

Almost immediately behind the Royal Navy officers came the United States Coast Guard. They went directly to the captain's office. In an inspired maneuver, Tom Patterson got Carl Nolte to attend the meeting, sitting him in the very center of things, notebook in hand. Patterson made sure the Coast Guard understood that Carl was from a major metropolitan newspaper and was taking down everything that transpired. The Coast Guard had little choice. The combined effects of Patterson's earlier satellite call to Washington and Carl Nolte's presence had the desired results. As reported in the *Chronicle:*

> The *O'Brien* had two less conventional guests — U.S. Coast Guard investigators in civilian clothes, who went over the ship with a less sentimental eye. They had been sent to Portsmouth by the U.S. Coast Guard office in London to look into reports that the *O'Brien* had carried guests through the Panama Canal.

The officers brought a letter indicating that the *O'Brien* had violated the law by taking about 80 U.S. military personnel and their families through the canal earlier this month. They said the *O'Brien* is not supposed to carry passengers, even for a short jaunt.

Skipper George Jahn was clearly exasperated. After all, he said, he had brought the 51-year-old ship down the Central American coast, across the Caribbean and the Atlantic with no problems. He regaled the two investigators, who looked more and more uncomfortable, with stories of how he had sailed an identical Liberty ship on the highly dangerous Murmansk Run in wartime carrying a deckload of locomotives and PT boats. Where, he wondered, was the Coast Guard then?

"Well," said Lieutenant Brian Gove, the senior investigator, "We are here mostly to welcome you after your voyage, to see the vessel and to look into the occurrence in Panama."

"Hey," said his colleague, Chief Warrant Officer David Passman, "if they ask me, I'm going to tell them to leave this ship alone. That's what I'm going to say."

As one might expect, "our" berth, the Royal jetty, was ideally situated. It was a two-minute walk in one direction to the Portsmouth Naval Museum, adjacent to Lord Nelson's flagship, *HMS Victory*. Just beyond it was the *Mary Rose* exhibition. Three minutes' walk in another direction was the pier to which was tied *HMS Warrior*, Queen Victoria's sailing battleship. Just beyond it was Victory Gate, opening to Portsmouth itself with its restaurants, pubs, tattoo parlors and other historic points of interest.

Eric Brazil of the *San Francisco Examiner* described Portsmouth's D-Day preparations:

Bruce the Raven receives his own brand of welcome to England. Courtesy Phil Frank and San Francisco Chronicle.

Tickets to the nearby attractions Mary Rose *and* HMS Warrior.

Portsmouth has given itself over whole-heartedly to the D-day 50th anniversary celebration. The Portsmouth D-day Museum — featuring the world's longest tapestry, at 270 feet, stitched by the Royal School of Needlework and depicting the invasion in meticulous detail — was drawing big crowds. D-day memorabilia, including airport pins, baseball caps and the like, is a growth industry.

Public and private buildings bristle with armaments — the Hilton Hotel's entrance is flanked by a big naval cannon and its lawn ornament is a British Churchill tank, which participated in the D-day landing.

Everyone in the crew had a particular interest ashore. Some sampled pub fare and ales, others traveled to famous historic areas nearby — Stonehenge, Canterbury, Eisenhower and Churchill's wartime headquarters; to castles, churches and villages. For the author, it was a chance to visit some of the locales made famous in the Sherlock Holmes stories. A fellow Sherlockian, Michael Kean, from Carmel, California, had put me in touch with other Sherlockians in England and one evening I was taken on a private tour of Portsmouth by Group Captain and Mrs. Philip Weller. They showed me where Sir Arthur Conan Doyle was born and where he lived and wrote many of the Sherlock Holmes classics including *The Sign of the Four.* Here was a restaurant Conan Doyle was fond of, there, his home. One wall on an apartment building contained a plaque marking the spot where *A Study in Scarlet,* the first Holmes story, was written. After reading the stories since childhood, it was a thrill to actually walk (well, be driven on) the same streets.

The Wellers also described some of Portsmouth's seafaring traditions. When sailors went ashore drinking in days gone by, they often frequented "barrow houses." These were establishments where Jack Tar could pay the landlord 50 pence or so at the beginning of a night's revelry At the end of the evening the landlord put him in a wheel barrow and had someone take him back to the ship. Other pubs simply took drunken sailors into a room strung from one side to the other with small ropes at chest height. The seaman was "hung out to dry" by slinging his arms over the rope. In the morning the landlord simply cried out, "Back to the ship, lads," and cut the rope.

British hospitality knew no limits. Without fuss, fanfare or negotiating, as one might expect in the United States, the Royal Navy immediately installed a telephone and informed the crew that we could call our families in America free of charge providing we limited our calls to five minutes. The phone was busy into the small hours of the morning.

The manager of a local pub and restaurant decided to have his cooks and waiters prepare and serve a luxurious breakfast on board. Eggs Benedict were a welcome change from the usual Thursday morning fare of SOS and mush.

Our first item of business was the DUKW we carried. A portable crane drove alongside the ship just after breakfast. With loud hydraulic whining noises it extended a set of jacks to hold it firmly in place, then extended its boom over "Little Feather," Jean-Paul Caron's DUKW, our only piece of deck cargo, loaded so many weeks ago in Alameda. Jim Conwell and I watched as the amphibian was hoisted into the air. Some rainwater poured off the vehicle's canvas cover.

"What's that that just ran off the duck?" asked Jim.

"Probably sauce *l'orange*," I said.

He groaned.

The DUKW remained on the pier, alongside the ship, throughout our stay in Portsmouth. Jean-Paul used it as a camper.

A frequent sight in Portsmouth was Tom Patterson on the phone.

We broke sea watches when we arrived at the Man of War anchorage. This meant that the sailors now all worked days — 8 to 5 — the mates worked 24 hours on and 48 hours off and the engine room went on eight hour watches. Work on board consisted of cleaning and painting in preparation for Navy Days. Ron Robson and his crew, including his aunt, Ruth, Mrs. Patterson, Mrs. Otterberg, Mrs. Jahn, Jo Lawrence, Dottie Duncan and Ed and Saryl Von der Porten spent their time setting up the ship's store in no. 3 'tween deck. Items with the *Jeremiah O'Brien* logo on them proved to be very popular. In fact, we ran out of baseball caps several times during the trip. In addition, there were coins, medals, books, T-shirts, sweaters, sweat shirts, pencils, erasers, pins, badges and coffee mugs.

One of our first social events was an invitation for the officers and crew to have drinks and a buffet lunch at *HMS Nelson*. Known as a Stone Frigate, *HMS Nelson* carries the name of a ship, but is actually a base ashore. The concept dates from an early Royal Navy ship that was used as a supply depot. The ship never sailed and eventually the nearby shoreline worked its way around it. Soon the ship was landlocked but still retained its seagoing name. The tradition has held and now most smaller Royal Naval bases are named *HMS* even if they are office buildings.

A bus picked us up and we were soon driving through the streets of Portsmouth. Most of us wore our *Jeremiah O'Brien* crew jacket over our ship's blue or white polo shirt. We were deposited outside *HMS Nelson* in short order and our liaison officer, Lt. Andy Cropley, met us at the gate. Irish terrorism was a very real problem and the unsmiling guard at the gate, dressed in camouflage and carrying a very businesslike automatic rifle, checked each of our ID's before letting us in.

The building was large, extending several floors. Grand, museum-quality paintings of sailing ships hung on the wood-paneled walls, other art depicted the Battle of Trafalgar (of course) and there were several finely-crafted models of sailing ships in glass cases. In the wardroom the bartenders (actually, Royal Navy sailors) busily pulled drafts of the famed British beer and ale with both hands.

The buffet included several choices of salads, cold meats and cheeses and hot dishes with sauces and gravies, and a bountiful offering of desserts. One of the officers proudly told us that this was "the premier wardroom of the Royal Navy." It was easy to see why. The food and drink were excellent, our hosts were warm, friendly and very sociable.

On the way out we were shown the main messroom, a large banquet hall with high ceilings and long wooden tables for formal dining. At each end of the room hung paintings of Lord Nelson and Lady Hamilton. Our guide explained, "We cover Lady Hamilton on ladies' night so as not to embarrass anyone." It was a candid glimpse of British Naval life, so different from that in the United States.

Then it was back to the bus and a return to the decidedly Spartan accommodations of our fifty-year-old ship.

Tom Alexander: "The reception that we got was just so wonderful. People were just so friendly, so kind, and appreciative. I talked to several people who were just appreciative of our bringing the ship back and what these ships had done in the war, very rare."

That afternoon many of the crew went ashore to play tourist — visiting pubs, touring *HMS Victory* and *HMS Warrior*, shopping for souvenirs, visiting other ships, sampling English food, walking the cobblestone streets of Old Portsmouth, hopping the ferry to Gosport. Some stayed on board to continue preparing for Navy Days, the three-day period from May 28-31 when the Base and all the ships in it would be open to the public. Mostly this meant getting the ship's store ready. Ron Robson and his crew set up displays, tables, cash registers and merchandise. Ed Von der Porten, our museum director, was busy setting up a historic photo display of the ship's exploits during World War II in no. 2 'tween deck.

Bev Masterson: "Back home, I staffed the ship's store for the entire voyage and I started doing that back in February. I kept close contact with our office, and I would call people and try to recruit volunteers for different ports. It made me feel that I was part of the whole thing, even from California. I felt like I was part of the ship, helping to get it over there."

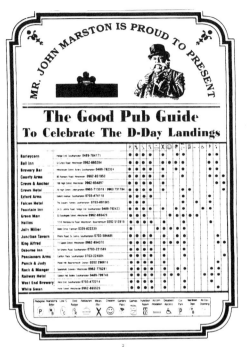

This advertisment from a local "giveaway" magazine was a good starting point when it came to pub-hopping.

Portsmouth Navy Yard wasn't open to the public, but the public wanted to visit the *O'Brien.* Visitors called from the various gates to the base wanting to visit the ship and the guard would have to phone to know if so-and-so was permitted to visit the ship. "Of course," we always replied. After several dozen visitors that day, we found our liaison, Andy Cropley, paying a concerned visit.

"The base is closed to the public, yet you are letting all these people come in. This is causing a lot of extra work for the guards at the gates."

"People want to visit the ship," I said. "We certainly aren't telling them the base is open, but the ship is."

"All right, let me work on it." And he did. Soon, somehow, the problem no longer existed. It was another refreshing example of British cooperation and hospitality.

Now, the *Jeremiah O'Brien*'s glorious time in the Royal berth was up. The queen would soon arrive for the anniversary ceremonies and the *Britannia* was due in her berth to take the queen aboard. Just after lunch on a cold, windy and rainy May 26 our Admiralty pilot, Capt. Wise, boarded and soon the large tug *Bolster,* and two smaller ones, *Foxhound* and *Setter,* were alongside. "We call these the 'dog' tugs," he said. There was also a *Dalmatian* moving around the harbor. We let go our lines and proceeded farther into the Portsmouth Naval Base to the Middle Slip Jetty. Our course took us past *HMS Victory*, Admiral Nelson's flagship. Although landlocked in a graving dock, she flew a large British ensign off her stern. As we sailed past, *HMS Victory* lowered her flag in the traditional maritime salute of one ship to another. We answered by lowering our flag, then raising it and watching as she raised hers. It was a singular honor, the flagship of England's greatest Naval hero saluting an old steel American freighter.

As we tied up and got our gangways out, a sleek sedan drove up and parked alongside the ship. Four men got out. Each had blow-dried hair and wore a carefully-buttoned suit and an equally carefully-unbuttoned trench coat. They boarded and soon disappeared behind the closed door of the captain's office with Adm. Patterson and Capt. Jahn. Soon word got out. They were the Secret Service and the White House staff.

Tom Patterson: "We were surprised and elated that the White House Secret Service advance team was there and said the president had decided to accept our invitation. So we had to really put in a lot of time with them to inspect the entire ship, determine his route and also to make arrangements for how the president would come aboard out in this open seaway called the Solent."

The "advance team" were aboard to analyze the potential dangers and arrange for President Clinton's visit. They were very, very serious. In the eleven days that we were in contact with them, I don't think any of them ever smiled.

We returned *HMS Nelson*'s courtesies of the past few days by throwing a party for them. No. 2 'tween deck was a severe contrast to the elegant surroundings of their wardroom. Where their halls were decorated with gold-framed masterpieces on wood-paneled walls, our steel bulkheads were adorned with steamship company flags, a board of seamen's knots and an engine room telegraph. But the British seemed to enjoy the ambiance. A catering company was hired to bring in food, beer and wine. Amidst trays of hot and cold canapes, French wine and good British ale, we mingled and talked, sharing the experiences and discoveries of the past few days. There was a general good feeling of Anglo-American camaraderie, a "special relationship."

The next day brought a welcome change in the weather. It was clear and sunny. A huge ship passed, bound for a berth to the north of us in the Navy Base. As big as any ocean liner, she dwarfed us, her machinery humming efficiently as she maneuvered carefully across the harbor. It was the *Pride of Portsmouth,* a *super* ferry, newly-launched, and it had been chartered to accommodate several heads of state, their personal staffs, VIPs and some 500 members of the press. The quay around her was to be cleared of all cars, motorcycles, equipment and stores and access to her would be strictly limited.

One chore that had to be attended to in Portsmouth was changing a burnt-out light bulb. Not just any light bulb, but the range light, at the top of the tallest mast on the ship. The bulb itself has two filaments so that if one burns out, you simply flip a switch in the wheelhouse and the other comes on. But when both are burned out you have to change the bulb and to change the bulb means somehow, someone has to get up to the light fixture at the top of the mast. Normally, a boatswain's chair is rigged and one of the sailors is hoisted up. But since we were in a Naval ship yard with cranes at every pier, it was thought the simplest thing would be to get the British Navy to lift a sailor up to the light fixture in a large bucket designed to carry people. Bosun Rich Reed explained how "simple" the process was: "So, first you go to the master rigger and he sends you to the crane department. So they've got this appointment book, yeah, and you schedule the crane and they write it in the book. Then you go to the bucket department to get a bucket. So they have a book, too, and you schedule it with them and they write it in their book, yeah. And now they've got to find the bucket. This is a big yard, see? And they have to look all over to find one. So then you've got the crane and the bucket but none of these people is allowed to hook anything up, so you have to go to the slingers and get them to make an appointment to hook up the bucket. So you get all these appointments in all these books and they all come together and that's how you change a light bulb at the Portsmouth Naval Shipyard."

The White House Secret Service was aboard again, deciding the route the president would take after he boarded the vessel. Not even the smallest step was left to chance. On our relatively circumscribed ship, crewed mostly by veterans, the Secret Service nevertheless plotted every movement, turn and view, and they took everyone's name and social security number to run a background check.

May 28, the first day of Navy Days, was bleak and grey with a cool wind blowing. The *Jeremiah O'Brien* was the only merchant ship on hand. Navies of other countries were represented by the *U-19* (Germany), *HNLMS Zwaardvis* (Netherlands), *BNS Wandelaar* (Belgium), *USS Normandy* (United States), *HMNorS Utsira* (Norway), *HMCS Toronto* (Canada) and *HMS Active, HMS Illustrious* and *HMS Liverpool* (Great Britain). Also on hand but not open to the public were the British vessels, *HMY Britannia, HMS Glasgow, HMS Birmingham, HMS Newcastle, HMS Fearless* and *HMS Ursula.*

The gates opened at 10 a.m. By 11:30 we counted 750 people on board and were pleased that the self-guided blue line tour seemed to be working. With a series of white arrows, it guided visitors to the aft house and guntub, then into the midships house, past the galley and crew messrooms, through the saloon, up two interior decks to the radio room and wheelhouse, up to the flying bridge, down the exterior of the midships house, forward to the bow guntub, back to no. 2, into no. 3 and the ship's store, then out the hatch to the main deck and off the ship. We were assisted by young Sea Cadets from Tunbridge Wells and Whitestable who, dressed in crisp blue Naval cadet uniforms, marched to the ship in formation each morning and helped manage the visitors by handing out brochures and keeping them on the blue line. Only in their early teens, the cadets were refreshingly earnest and sincere. We all admired their professionalism and the disciplined way in which they conducted themselves.

In the middle of the day we were treated to a flying display by several types of aircraft. British tradition has it that flying shows take place over the oldest ship in the harbor and that was the *Jeremiah O'Brien.* Harrier jets hovered above our masts, the

Red Arrows performed daring maneuvers as they trailed red, white and blue smoke from their gleaming red fuselages; helicopters flew sideways, backwards, and in almost every direction except forward; and large, low-flying cargo jets, Spitfires and Hurricanes passed overhead. The noise was deafening but it was a magnificent spectacle.

On board, our English visitors were enthusiastic and, as one would expect of the British, very well-behaved. They especially enjoyed seeing the galley, the crew rooms, the engine room and the wheelhouse. They pointed out the coal stove to each other, looked or climbed down to the engine room to marvel at the old steam reciprocating engine and filed through the wheelhouse with interest taking in the combination of old-fashioned brass, modern electronics and World War II functionality.

Dick Brannon: "The guys in England says how in the hell did you get to be chief engineer on this job. My God, any one of us would have given their eye teeth to go."

Everyone was impressed with the ship's state of preservation. And every day there were several old Liberty or "Sam" sailors (the British version of the Liberty carried the name Sam as a preface) with their discharge books and seaman's papers. Often

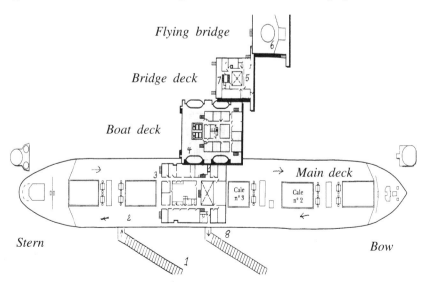

This exploded view of the ship shows the direction of the blue line tour. The numbers indicate key docent stations.

Bruce has his own reaction to the crowds boarding the O'Brien. *Ahh, patriotism. Courtesy Phil Frank and* San Francisco Chronicle.

they looked for "their room," the cabin they occupied on the Liberty ship they were on during or just after the war. Then it was, "Hasn't changed a bit. That's just where the sink was. I remember the bunk, exactly like that." They were all anxious to establish a sort of kinship, to share their experiences, to savor, once more, the thrill of being on a Liberty ship, and, for a few moments, like many of our crew, a chance to relive their youth.

Marching bands were everywhere on the dock. The TS Unity Nautical Training Corps started and ended the day with a concert at the bandstand. The Herb Miller Orchestra played 40's music throughout the day. The Combined Bands of Tunbridge Wells and Whitestable marched along, their orchestrations of the calypso ballad "Jamaica Farewell" and the rock-and-roll classic "Wanderer" as marches, surprising everyone in their crisp execution and sound. The cheerful tinkling of bell lyres gave their music an unsurpassed upbeat quality. At the end of the day, at 5:30 p.m., The Band of Her Majesty's Royal Marines Portsmouth beat retreat in precise formation, followed by the Tunbridge Wells and Whitestable Units of the Sea Cadet Corps' combined band.

May 29 presented a clear sky with a bright sun. Arrangements for President Clinton's visit went into higher gear. Meetings were held on everything from how he would get on the ship to where the crew was to stand. Lt. Martin Shakespeare (assistant to our liaison Andy Cropley) and I were on the jetty and about to get in his car to drive to a meeting with the Portsmouth Naval Base master rigger, when the White House staff and Secret Service drove up in separate sedans. Parking conspicuously in the middle of the pier, eight doors opened and eight ever-so-serious,

The Sea Cadets were a wonderful help in handling crowds. Here they (all but one) stand at attention, prior to turning to. Photo by Jo Lawrence.

blow-dried, button-suited, open-trenchcoated men got out. After a somber good morning, we explained where we were going. Suddenly we had an entourage of three people traveling with us in a separate car, "to be sure we understand all the arrangements."

"Serious, aren't they?" I said to Lt. Shakespeare as we drove to the master rigger's office.

"You'll forgive my candor," said Martin, "if I say they all sound and act like salesmen. I believe the queen has an advance team of one, on her state visits, to accomplish the same thing."

The master rigger seated us and our new escorts at a table in his conference room. He explained that after our ship was anchored in the Solent on June 5, they would tow a catamaran out. Our accommodation ladder could be lowered onto the "cat" and the president could board that.

"In America a catamaran is a twin-hulled sailboat," I said. "I gather it's something else here."

"Right," said the master rigger, with a smile, "it's a flat barge. Measures about thirty-five feet by fifty feet. We'll tow it alongside, provide the manpower and lashings to tie it up."

"Sounds fine to me," I said, half-rising from my seat to go.

"Let me be sure I understand this . . ." said one of the White House staff. I sat down again. First, he wanted to know if they could provide a rubber mat so the president wouldn't slip if the decking was wet. Then it was a question of whether the president would have to step up or down in getting onto the catamaran. Could a platform be built to prevent him stepping up or down? If he had to step up he might trip. Could anything be done so the president didn't get his feet wet? What boat traffic would be in the area? Could they lash two catamarans together to make a larger landing surface?

Driving back to the ship, Martin shook his head, "They want us to calm the seas and make it not wet for the president. Not even King Canute could do that."

Meanwhile, back at the ship, the second day of Navy Days was even better-attended than the first — 8,000 visited us that day. Again, bands marched to and from the bandstand and the arena behind the building adjacent to the *O'Brien,* playing cheerful marches. The bands of the day before were joined by The Combined Naval Volunteer Bands of *HMS Nelson, HMS Daedalus, HMS Collingwood* and *HMS Dryad.*

Just before the base closed for the day, the Red Arrows put on a stunning demonstration directly above the *O'Brien,* flying in wingtip-to-wingtip formation, forming geometric patterns, disappearing and reappearing where least expected, separating in all directions then racing toward each other and passing directly overhead in a deafening roar that left the crowd speechless.

The White House staff announced that the catamaran was being carpeted.

The crew was having a fine time ashore exploring Portsmouth's many attractions — and distractions.

Jimmy Farras: "One night I went aboard a submarine from Holland. That was great. I never thought I'd be on a sub. That was a highlight. That really stuck with me."

Alex Hochstraser returned from Gosport with a tattoo on his upper arm. In the best tradition of the sea it depicted a barebreasted mermaid resting on an anchor. The shank of the anchor displayed the name, "*S.S. Jeremiah O'Brien.*"

Alex Hochstraser's tattoo is a tribute to the ship and the voyage in true seafaring style.

Several of the crew had brought bicycles along with them. Every evening we'd see Bill Bennett, Bob Burnett or someone else pedal off for an evening on the town.

The crew usually wore *Jeremiah O'Brien* crew jackets or polo shirts with the ship's baseball cap when they went ashore. It was like an identification badge. We were frequently stopped on the street and asked about the ship, treated to ales in the pubs, and often told, "No charge, mate. We're 'appy you made it over," when entering places that normally charged admission.

Bob Burnett: "The pubs of England are great. They're very special. I just think that the English pubs have a type of charm that's challenging to find. They had a nice little folksy feeling to them."

Marty Shields, ordinary seaman: "The funniest thing that happened with me on this trip, I think, was an afternoon with Carl Nolte. I met this gal that lived in Gosport and Nolte and I were going to take the ferry over. I had been there once. When we got off the ferry Nolte decides he wants to walk. So, Nolte and I were walking around Gosport. I did have the address but I thought the phone number was the zip code, so we couldn't call. We stopped at a pub 'cause Nolte was thirsty. I asked him, tell me a little about Winston Churchill. Nolte went on for an hour about Churchill and Queen Victoria and everything that led back to everything in history. It was just classic Carl Nolte. Then we left and we're looking and we can't find the house. So after two hours of this, I suddenly realize that what I thought was the zip code was the phone number. That was one of the funniest moments on the trip."

One afternoon Jean Yates suddenly got dizzy. Fortunately Dr. Haslam was on hand. He put Jean in the second mate's bunk, then called an ambulance. In short order Jean was in a hospital ashore being examined for a possible heart attack.

Jean Yates: "When I went to the hospital, down in Portsmouth, I had been talking to an English couple there on the boat deck near the ladder, and chatting away and I got kind of faint. They saw it and I said, 'Please excuse me, I feel faint. I've got to sit down in the chair there.' The Doc came by just at that moment and these people said, 'Oh, your man is not feeling well. You should do something.' So he checked it right away. Well anyway I went to the hospital."

The final day of Navy Days, May 30, was perfect. The weather was clear and fine without a single cloud in the sunny, blue sky. The temperature was pleasantly warm. The White House staff was on and off all day, holding meetings with the captain and the admiral. In honor of Memorial Day in the United States, all the flags in the base were flown at half-mast from 0800 to 1200, a gracious gesture.

This was the busiest day so far with 10,082 visitors. The decks of the *Jeremiah O'Brien* are not very wide; the house, with its narrow passageways, and the hatches and equipment take up much of the space. There was not much space for anything like that number of people, but they squeezed by, good-humoredly, looking at everything with great interest, asking questions when they saw a docent or crew member. They were pleasant, orderly and appreciative; there was none of the noise or pushing or short tempers you would expect of such a crowd in the States.

But the interest of our visitors was not mere curiosity or coming to see a "celebrity." "It's an honor to be on board," people said. We must have heard the phrase a thousand times. The English observed the Commemoration very seriously, remembering the terrible days of half a century past. Many came very long distances to see the ship and shake our hands and thank us for coming. They remember the invasion vividly, and the ships that came to save England when all looked hopeless. They were very grateful to the U.S. then, and were vocal in expressing that gratitude to the crew, especially the veterans.

Carl Nolte's story described the prevailing sentiment:

"We have a special relationship with the U.S., and that's important to us. I hope it is important to you as well."

That may explain the tremendous reception the *Jeremiah O'Brien* has received. It is the last ship from that tremendous invasion armada that is still capable of steaming. It is as good as it ever was, and that is an important symbol.

The Liberty ships saved the country. To the general public, that matters, that's very important.

Bill Dickerson, who replaced Pete Lyse as third mate: "The British people were very kind and polite. I just can't envision 10,000 of our own countrymen stomping the decks of this thing. I think that would have been just out of control."

Our stay in Portsmouth was one delightful event after the other. We learned to keep our heads up and be ready for anything. The next bit of serendipity that popped up was engineered by our saloon messman, Pat McCafferty — and a humdinger it was. Pat is an enterprising man who pulled a real plum out of the pudding simply by asking. He called the *Royal Yacht Britannia* on the telephone and arranged a tour for a small group, fortunately including me.

As we walked up the *Britannia*'s gangway, we tried to keep an appreciative but cool, professional demeanor, but, inside, each of us felt somewhat like kids invited to visit Candyland. The *Britannia*! A fabled ship, so exclusive, so prestigious, so inaccessible. Only royalty and presidents and prime ministers go aboard. And here we were, a group of volunteers from the oldest, ugliest ship in the harbor, treading the Royal Yacht's decks. Lt. Kennedy

Bruce recalls his European roots and his grandfather's tales of World War II. Courtesy Phil Frank and San Francisco Chronicle.

of the Royal Navy, the officer on duty, and in charge of the ship's electrical systems, gave us a grand tour.

Launched at Clydebank in 1953, the ship has a length of 412 feet, a beam of 55 feet, draws 17 feet, measures 5769 gross tons, 5280 displacement tons, and is propelled by two geared steam turbines rated at 12,000 horsepower which produce a cruising speed of twenty-one knots.

Our tour started with the wheelhouse, surprisingly located away from the bridge and completely enclosed. There were no windows or portholes. Surrounded by highly polished brass and white bulkheads, the quartermaster receives orders from the bridge and steers with only a compass repeater to show where he is going. The bridge itself was equipped with the latest modern electronics, all neatly and unobtrusively arranged, giving the sense of being in a gentleman's study rather than on the bridge of a ship.

We went outside, walking along the neatly-scrubbed, white-colored, wood exterior decks where motor launches, painted the same deep, rich blue as the ship's hull, and trimmed tastefully in gold, hung in davits. We looked into the Royal public rooms. We weren't allowed to go in for all was in readiness for the heads of state arriving in the next few days. The rooms were simple, bright and cheerful but, at the same time, very elegant. A chalice from a foreign dignitary stood on a table, a ceremonial spear from a South Seas tribe was mounted on a wall. Fresh flowers and classic paintings added warmth to the rooms. We saw the crew's laundry (very different from our wringer Maytags) and the officers' wardroom. The officers dined at elegant tables or relaxed in

Bruce's ancestry goes back a long way, to both England and France, perhaps a form of Channel vision. Courtesy Phil Frank and San Francisco Chronicle.

easy chairs reading books or magazines. The bulkheads were hung with plaques and awards and portraits of the Royal family.

But the highlight of the tour was the engine room. It was absolutely spotless. All the machinery was tidily painted, most of it white, copper tubing and brass fixtures shone brightly, and the floor plates had not a mark on them. The engineering officer on watch wore a dress blue uniform with gold braid. Although the diesel generator was running too loudly for conversation, it, too, looked like a museum piece. This was a working engine room, yet there wasn't a trace of oil, a smudge of grease, or a bit of dirt to be found. It may be a cliche, but absolutely and literally true: one could have eaten off the engine room decks. We were utterly amazed.

With sincere thanks to Lt. Kennedy, we reluctantly took our leave and returned to the *Jeremiah O'Brien,* reevaluating our own standards of — everything.

From the sublime to . . .

While ashore in a nearby beer tent, Dick Brannon struck up a conversation with some sailors off a British submarine. This led to a tour of the *O'Brien.* The sailors and their Chief Petty Officer were several beers ahead of our chief and as the party moved into Dick's office they stayed ahead, getting louder and more boisterous. Finally the CPO loudly proclaimed how much he liked the chief, how well he thought of him, he was a fine engineer, etc. Then, paying Dick the ultimate compliment, in a loud voice that carried throughout the midships house, he said, "Chief, you're all right. 'Cause you've got all your shit in one sock."

Dick Brannon: "I was totally unprepared for the

Dick Brannon, chief engineer, explains some of the finer points of engineering to a rapt onlooker. Photo by Mike Emery.

enthusiasm of the elderly British engineers who remember the Liberty ship from day one. I couldn't believe their absolute fanatical interest in this ship, being in such good condition, just like original, 'Oh, my god, oh, hey, oh, my gosh.' They were just overwhelmed at the sterling condition the ship was in."

The genuine friendliness of the British was humbling. None of us expected the emotion and gratitude displayed by the "reserved" English people.

Tom Alexander: "I was in Gosport one day and we went into a restaurant for lunch. As I was leaving, I felt something tug on my jacket, I had my *O'Brien* jacket on. There was a little old lady sitting down there and she said, 'Thank you so much for coming back, I'll never forget you people.' That's beautiful. You know, it makes it all worth while."

Bill Bennett: "The feeling that I got from the people of England, dozens and dozens of people who'd come up to me, and they talked about what we did for them during the war. And it got to the point where I started to tell the people no, you know, it's not what we did for you during the war. We produced goods, sent them over here, but you people sacrificed, you had your homes bombed all the time, you took the heat of the battle. We stayed home and lived in safety . . . I'm thanking you for what you did."

Tom Patterson: "And so we entered into the spirit of their Navy Days which is kind of like our version of Fleet Week. The twenty-eighth, twenty-ninth and thirtieth we had a total of about twenty-four thousand visitors on board — one day nearly eleven thousand — all very happy English people from all generations, remembering what the ships like the *Jeremiah O'Brien* did for them in World War II."

Now, the Sea Cadet corps would be leaving us. It was surprising how attached we became to them in such a short time. Everyone in the crew admired the cadets' discipline, their politeness, and the courteous yet firm way in which they handled the crowds. From the first few hours on board, we found them a wonderful help in keeping people from wandering off the blue line tour and preventing bottlenecks where the line came back on itself.

The Sea Cadets in a more relaxed pose than earlier. They were fun to have on board and a great help. Photo by Jo Lawrence.

Being young, they were easy to semi-adopt, sneaking them Otis Spunkmeyer cookies from time to time, giving them breakfast, lunch and dinner if they were on board, making sure they had soft drinks or a place to sit if tired. The cadets were a particular bright spot even amidst the hoopla of the occasion and we knew we would miss them when they left. It was a surprisingly emotional farewell. Their leader, a lieutenant whom I only knew as Angela, shook hands and, as I thanked her, she stood on tiptoes and kissed me on the cheek.

The next day was bright, clear and warm. It was a Day of Rumors — all related to President Clinton's visit. The Secret Service and White House staff were with us all day and well into the evening, as were Martin Shakespeare and Andy Cropley. First, the White House staff said we would go to anchor at the Solent and take the president aboard there. This brought on a lengthy discussion about gangways, floats, the president getting his feet wet, whether or not Mrs. Clinton would get seasick. The next rumor was that we would stay at our present berth. The berth was scheduled for another ship but the White House staff said they would try to buy a berth for the other ship somewhere else so we could stay. Later, the rumor was that we would go to Southampton, then return to the berth we were at, then the president could visit in the morning of June 5 before boarding the royal yacht. At about this point, most of our people threw up their hands in disgust and began avoiding the presidential advance team.

Bill Dickerson: "That's the first time I was ever tangled up with their security arrangements, which I found just unbelievable."

In the late afternoon Martin Shakespeare came to say goodbye. Walking on the afterdeck to the gangway we talked over recent events and shook hands. Martin then came to attention, saluted, clicked his heels and in a very old and highly complimentary gesture, touched two fingers to his forelock. He was a real gentleman and had been a great help to the ship.

Later in the evening we were delighted to see Jean Yates back aboard. It wasn't a heart attack but merely a side effect of forgetting to take a medication.

One longtime volunteer who couldn't make the trip was Lou Switz, age 71, the ship's regularly-assigned second mate. Ten months before the trip to Normandy he fell from the 'tween deck in no. 1 hatch to the lower hold. His injuries were serious and his recovery lengthy. But now, he and his wife, Helen, joined us in Portsmouth, to be on board when the ship went to Normandy. He was assigned as night mate, relieving the regular mates in the evenings. It gave them a break from night watches and was a chance for Lou to help with the voyage.

June 1 was bright, clear and sunny but a little breezy and cooler than previous days. We departed Portsmouth for Southampton at 1045, leaving the harbor entrance behind, and proceeded farther up the Solent. Two pilots were on the bridge, one a student. To our left were the Isle of Wight, the city of Cowes and the Royal Yacht Club. From there we maneuvered in a broad sweeping "S" into the harbor of Southampton, tying up to the Commercial Dock in mid-afternoon. Capt. Denys Lomax, a former Liberty ship sailor in the British merchant marine, went along as a guest.   Another guest was Capt. Alan Swift of the *Shieldhall*, a historic sludge carrier.

     Southampton has a different maritime history than Portsmouth, but one perhaps closer to the heart of a merchant mariner. This was the port of the great trans-Atlantic liners.   Our berth once saw the *Queen Mary, Queen Elizabeth, Titanic, Mauretania, Aquitania* and other blue riband leviathans board and debark passengers bound to and from America. Across the slip was the quay used by the *SS United States* in her glory days.   Just a short distance farther into the port was the pier used by the *Jeremiah O'Brien* in 1944 when she made her eleven trips to Normandy.

     Bob Burnett: "When we were in Southampton, it was interesting docking right where the *Titanic* had been on its maiden voyage."

     As we tied up I heard Capt. Jahn mutter, "Oh, God, here they are again."   Looking down on the pier, we saw the shiny sedans with their doors open and the White House staff and Secret Service getting out.

     In a rare moment of quiet, before the visitors started and the White House people came aboard, Capt. Jahn talked about their briefings the day before. The White House staff asked that the coal be moved from the coal bin because the sight of it might distract the president which would make him divert from the planned route. The entire visit, step by step, was gone over again from beginning to end (and would change several times daily): the president would come aboard and walk into the officers' saloon for presentation of gifts and a few words with the captain and the admiral. Then he would exit the starboard aft door of the saloon, walk down the passageway and out the starboard aft door from the midships house, up the ladder to the boat deck, past the coal bin, and on up to the flying bridge where photos would be taken. A life ring would be hung from the stack to serve as background. After the photos it would be down to the main deck to shake hands with the crew and back to the admiral's barge* which would take him to the carrier *USS George Washington.*

---

*The small craft on board a carrier include an admiral's barge and a captain's gig, whether or not the ship has an admiral on board.

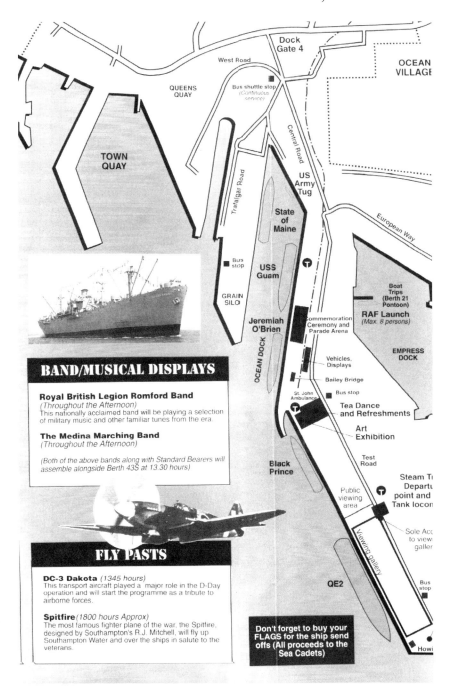

The official program shows the Jeremiah O'Brien's berth next to the parade arena and gives the locations of the other ships in Southampton. Courtesy Association of British Ports.

The *USS Guam* tied up to the berth ahead of us on the same pier. Some of our crew negotiated with the people installing the Navy ship's telephones. Eight lines were ordered for the *Guam*. A sympathetic lineman rerouted one of their lines to come to the *O'Brien*. The free calls home were a great boost to morale.

A very neat and trim-looking fuel barge came alongside and began discharging bunkers to the *O'Brien*. It was the first fuel we took since leaving San Francisco.

The *Shieldhall* hosted our crew to lunch on board their vessel. It was an attractive green-hulled ship with a white house and, similar to the *O'Brien*, preserved by volunteer effort.

We were especially pleased to receive a fax from our Congresswoman, Nancy Pelosi, telling us that we were in the Congressional Record:

House of Representatives

Statement of Rep. Nancy Pelosi
The S. S. Jeremiah O'Brien
May 26, 1994

MR. SPEAKER — As America prepares to honor its war dead this Memorial Day, and as we prepare to honor those brave Americans who gave the ultimate sacrifice on D-Day 50 years ago, let us pay tribute to those who survived to ensure that their sacrifices have not been forgotten.

This Monday last, the *S.S. Jeremiah O'Brien*, the last seaworthy Liberty ship of World War II, completed its 32 day, 7,894 mile voyage from its berth in San Francisco to Portsmouth, England. From Captain George Jahn, the 78-year old World War II Liberty Ship captain; to 75-year old Chief Engineer Richard Brannon; to Mary Steinberg, a former Navy Secretary who worked in the sweltering engine room; to Carl Nolte, a *San Francisco Chronicle* reporter by trade; and, last but not least, Retired Admiral Thomas Patterson, who rescued the *O'Brien* from mothballs in 1979 and led the efforts that restored its seaworthiness, the *O'Brien*'s 55-strong all-volunteer crew turned a labor of love into a voyage of history.

The *Jeremiah O'Brien* will be the only surviving ship of the 5000 vessel-strong D-Day armada to participate in the 50th

Anniversary commemorative ceremonies. If anyone doubts that the American spirit of adventure has subsided, or that American patriotism is a thing of the past, let them speak to the men and women who restored and sailed the *Jeremiah O'Brien*.

Mr. Speaker, let us offer the congratulations of the Congress to the sterling crew of the *S.S. Jeremiah O'Brien* and our thanks for their contributions to remembering our nation's heroes on this Memorial Day weekend.

More and more people began showing up from the States. Volunteers, former volunteers, people who weren't expected until later. We had no place to put them, but their attitude was, "Here I am, put me to work but also feed me and find a decent bunk for me to sleep in." Eventually we had people sleeping on cots in the steering gear room, the CO2 room and in no. 2 and no. 3 'tween decks. There was a great deal of crew discussion about all the people arriving and living on board. Capt. Jahn cut immediately to the heart of the issue: "Anyone who comes over [from the States] gets on board and rides to Normandy. It's the only chance for them to see it. This [event] will never happen again."

As in Portsmouth, hundreds of visitors came every day, including more former "Sam" ship sailors. Clutching their certification books and photos to "prove" it, they looked into the engine room, galley, wheelhouse and cabins, their eyes misting as they talked about memories of the war and their youth.

Ruth Robson: "I don't think any of us in America know what those people went through. The people in England, the bombings, and the people in France under the tyranny of occupation. I don't think we could fathom, we just don't realize what our being there did for those people. It's an experience you have to live through to know and none of us ever did. Oh, we had blackouts and rationing and things like that, but it wasn't like the real thing, really.

"It was a very emotional experience. Our ship seems to have touched a lot of people, it really did, and even young folks, not just the men and women that were connected with Liberty ships when they were young, but the children of people that sailed.

And mothers and fathers bringing their little children because grandpa sailed on one of these.

"Those are things that you can't put into words, you have to experience their happening to you and see it yourself. Because there's a lot of emotion there that's hard to express in words. You saw the expressions on their faces and the tears in their eyes and heard the sound of their voices. I was very much moved with that. There was a lot of it. I had no idea that we'd have that kind of experience. It was a growing experience for me to realize that there are people out there who remember what we did in '44 that meant so much to them and to their families that have followed after them."

Friday, June 3 began with blustery winds and fast-moving clouds. D-Day weather, everyone called it. The media coverage for the "Commemoration," as it was called in England, was almost overwhelming now. The newspapers were filled with pictures of D-Day 1944. The great leaders of the war were gone, but interviews with veterans, many of whom had been young soldiers, evoked the awful, yet exciting event. "The invasion" was how Europeans called D-Day, and on both sides of the Channel, historic ceremonies were marking the greatest maritime operation that ever was, that changed the course of history. TV crews and big-name news anchors from the U.S. broadcast via satellite, even as their European counterparts filled the local airwaves with news, interviews, old war movies and film clips.

Amidst the tidal wave of information and pictures, the *Jeremiah O'Brien* held its own. Outdone in every department by newer, bigger, faster, more beautiful ships, none could approach her unique historic presence and the "ugly duckling" basked in the special limelight.

The officers and crew of the *O'Brien* were treated with warm hospitality everywhere we went. Capt. Lomax brought aboard the June issue of *"Shipping Today and Yesterday,"* which was devoted entirely to Normandy, June 1944, and featured the *Jeremiah O'Brien* as its centerfold. The crew went out and bought up all the copies they could find.

After lunch and a tour of Southampton with author Mike Simpson, whose articles and reviews in *Ship's Monthly* had done so much to advertise the *Jeremiah O'Brien*, I returned to the ship to see the *QE2* coming alongside the berth adjacent to ours. The *O'Brien* was keeping fine company, indeed. The wind was howling at gale force and our ship was surging at her moorings but the large, majestic liner eased her way alongside so skillfully it looked easy.

Phil Sinnott: "It seemed like around every corner was another adventure on this trip. I came back from a car trip and here was the *QE2* and in the channel a couple of Whitbread around-the-world yacht racers coming in."

Now the real countdown to the Commemoration — D-Day plus 50 years — began. During the day there was a big to-do on the part of the White House staff to have the ship sail the following morning. But all ship movements in the harbor had been carefully calculated weeks earlier. Each vessel was to sail at an assigned time so that visitors could see them pass out of Southampton toward the Solent. Our scheduled departure time was 5:30 p.m. After lengthy discussion the White House staff insisted that Capt. Jahn order the sailing board set for 10 a.m. They wanted us to sail early so we could be at anchor and the catamaran or float positioned well before dark on June 4.

More strangers appeared on board that no one knew anything about, more people to staff the ship's store, unannounced crew replacements. A cadet from the Naval Academy, Tim Kinsella, arrived and reported for duty. No one knew he was coming, why he was there or what his purpose was. Others were expected, but we had short notice of their arrival. Mr. Griffiths, CEO from the Norton, Lilly Company, our agents in the United States, arrived. The Maritime Administrator, Adm. Albert J. Herberger, we expected. Lane Kirkland, the head of the AFL-CIO came aboard. The only room we had for these dignitaries was that used by our two Kings Point cadets, Dirk Warren and Nate Taylor, who were quickly reassigned to cots in the steering gear room. The bunks were remade for the distinguished guests. They were monastic accommodations, but all we had. The crew became increasingly frustrated. The ship was their home and all of a sudden here were all these strangers walking through their living room and sitting down to dinner and staying the night.

Bill Duncan: "There were some problems accepting that we were carrying so many outsiders on board, especially when we were so strongly set before the trip started, of carrying only people from San Francisco, volunteers. There were a number of people upset about that. Many people, old-time volunteers, wanted to be there. I had five meetings with the captain and the admiral and Otterberg over that. We had volunteers who couldn't make the trip for whatever reason, but would have gladly flown over to be aboard just for a few days. They were told they couldn't come, yet we had all these people we didn't know coming on board. The crew was upset about that but that's the way it was."

But there were no such ambivalent feelings between the crew and the English people who crowded the docks and the ship in the thousands from morning to night. The Anglo-American bonds grew stronger every day.

Carl Kreidler: "The English people, you know, they're fantastic. They're probably, except for our people, they're the best people in the world that I've met. I think they're really all right. Very helpful, want to do things for you, and they do it out of the goodness of their heart, not for money."

Jean Yates couldn't agree more: "About two days after I came back from the hospital those same two people [who tried to help him in Portsmouth] came to the ship to see if I was all right. They came back and they asked for that man who went to the hospital. They didn't know my name, and I thought, well that's pretty damn special. I had gone in town that afternoon and I missed them, then we moved to Southampton. So I was on the ship at Southampton and lo and behold these two people come walking on the deck. My God, she gives me a hug and a kiss, I shook his hand and he said, 'We just wanted to see that you were all right.' And they had been on the ship twice already, so I know they hadn't come all that way to see the ship again. They obviously came to see me and see if I was OK. That really touched me, it really did. And, you know, they got away and I don't even know their name. Don't even know their name and they don't know my name. It was just one of those . . . people being human. And I'm not going to forget that. You ask what I'm going to remember, I'm going to remember that."

June 4 broke ominously grey with drizzly skies and southerly breezes, cold, bleak, wet, dismal weather.

"It was a day exactly like this," said Lou Switz, who was chief mate on a Liberty ship that was off the Normandy beaches on D-Day. "Cold, windy, just like this."

The sailing board was changed back to 1730. The tugs and pilot were provided to us free by the harbor and they were not about to disrupt the ceremonies, carefully planned months ahead, simply to satisfy the insecurities of our White House entourage. We would sail when the pilot and tugs arrived and not a minute sooner.

In the afternoon the admiral and the chief mate went to *HMS Illustrious* on behalf of Capt. Jahn for a briefing of events. Capt. Lomax drove us in his Rover so we arrived in style, were piped aboard, and escorted to the wardroom where coffee and cookies were set out. In attendance were the commanding officers and staff of all the ships of the nations scheduled to attend the queen's review and the ceremonies at Normandy — Australia, Belgium, Canada, Czech State, France, Greece, Luxembourg, Netherlands, New Zealand, Norway, Poland, Slovakia, the United Kingdom and the U.S.A. The briefing was given by British Vice-Admiral Mike Royce. He told us that *HMS Edinburgh* would be the flag ship, discussed anticipated weather, the formation to use crossing the Channel, and even what VHF channel to communicate on. There was a reception after the briefing. It was a unique opportunity to meet our counterparts from many nations and we all made the most of it.

Returning to our pier in Southampton we found scuba divers in the water checking the *O'Brien*'s hull for bombs in anticipation of President Clinton's visit.

England was swarming with distinguished and other visitors now and events came one on the heels of the other — a D-Day

Concert at the Portsmouth Guildhall, featuring the BBC Concert Orchestra and H.M. Royal Marines Band, a Garden Party at Southwick House (the headquarters from which Eisenhower issued the final order to launch the invasion), attended by 1,000 veterans and the heads of state, Beating Retreat at *HMS Excellence.*

The Beating Retreat ceremony, now symbolic, stems from the time when soldiers were called back to their barracks from nearby towns to prepare for battle. It marked the end of peacetime activities and the beginning of war. In this case it symbolized the embarkation of the invasion force. Five thousand veterans, heads of state, the Queen Mother and Princess Anne were on hand for the occasion. Military bands from the U.K., U.S.A., Canada and France, and the Queen's Colour Squadron of the Royal Air Force marched in perfect step, each making a separate appearance on the grassy green field dressed in uniforms of red, blue and khaki. The music was inspiring and professional, military and precise. But the biggest round of applause went to the Band of the United States Air Force in Europe. As they played Glenn Miller's "In the Mood," two members broke ranks and jitterbugged, then chased each other through their fellow musicians who swung and swayed in time with the music. It was the hit of the Retreat. Even the Queen Mother was seen smiling delightedly and clapping her hands. All the bands came on the field for the finale which included the traditional "manning the mast," British sailors climbing in step to the top of the ship's mast and yardarms at the far end of the field.

The evening was capped by a banquet in the Portsmouth City Guildhall with the heads of state of Australia, Belgium, Czech State, Greece, New Zealand, Norway, Poland, Slovakia and the United States as invited guests.

Despite the persistent drizzle, the pier area alongside our ship had a festive air. Vintage steam trains chugged back and forth along the length of the quay. Veterans in uniform mingled with soldiers and sailors. Bands played and marched.

We sailed at 1730. It was cold and wet. We began casting off the lines, not knowing that this routine departure would be one of those transcendent moments, an epiphany, a memory to last a

lifetime. British Standard Bearers were gathered on the pier in
formation. As the lines fell, the band on the quay played "The
Star-Spangled Banner" and "God Save the Queen." Then the last
line was gone and the tugs backed us slowly out of the berth. The
final notes of the music faded. In the silence that fell, Paul Dunellon,
the head of security for Associated British Ports, came forward on
the dock and shouted, "Thank you for 1944." In that moment, the
events that had brought us here — beginning in 1944, throughout
the voyage, our recent experiences with the English people —
suddenly came together in an almost overwhelming wave. On the
bridge Adm. Patterson wiped away a tear. Capt. Jahn was misty-
eyed, my own vision was blurred. All over the ship, the crew
above decks stood silently in the rain, looking across the widening
water to the veterans standing in salute, the bands and the people
on the pier. It was a moment of grace, never to be forgotten.

Tom Alexander: "I remember there was a guy on the dock
at Southampton just as we were leaving and he said, 'Thank you
for 1944.' And that brought tears to my eyes."

*One of the bands at Southampton marches past shortly before we leave
the dock. Photo by Jo Lawrence.*

Bill Bennett: "Leaving Southampton, to see these people march, thinking about it I almost get kinda dewy-eyed. To see those old people who obviously were young people then, in the war, marching on that dock carrying the flag — the music, seeing them there in the rain, and they were crying and half of the people with me on deck, they were wiping their eyes, it was very emotional."

Tom Patterson: "We got underway at 1730 from Southampton in a pouring rainstorm with the whole Royal Marine Band, approximately a hundred-member band, playing their hearts out, the national anthem and 'God Save the Queen' and everything and one person yelling out 'Thank you for 1944,' as the bow of the *Jeremiah O'Brien* swung slowly past all these wonderful people and we proceeded out. It really brought home to us how much the British appreciated having a real American Liberty ship with a World War II crew over there to help celebrate this 50th that was so important to their survival. Many of them told us, 'You actually saved our lives. We were getting ready to be invaded and the Liberty Ships stopped that."

Greg Williams: "The highlight of the whole trip for me was when we left the dock at Southampton where all the old people were, when it was raining and they were playing the song. They were holding those banners and that was very, very touching. That was probably the highlight of the whole experience."

Jean Yates: "That voyage was the last great adventure of my life and I don't think I'll ever be the same again. The emotions we ran into and seeing the people in England and the way they responded to us and the way you turn kind of mushy when the band came along the dock there and started playing those marches and you saw those women standing there and oh, I tell you, it was kind of hard to find a dry eye."

Russ Mosholder: "In Southampton, when we left there, they had all the old timers, these old service people lined up. I went in and got my American Legion cap and put it on and come out at that rail. Every one of those people snapped to attention. And tears just ran down my cheeks. I think that was one of the highest highlights. I think that Southampton is the one that will really stick. Whenever I mention it, it brings tears to my eyes."

Pat McCafferty: "That was a very emotional time, that really set everybody back on the ship, including myself. Nobody talked for about an hour."

We backed into the channel and turned toward the Solent. As we got up speed and let go the tugs we passed the *QE2*. Her whistle sounded the three long blasts of the traditional maritime salute. We returned the honors, the *O'Brien's* steam whistle for some reason sounding especially mournful. As we continued down the channel, a single Spitfire came out of the clouds and rain, like a ghost of the past, and flew overhead, leading the way out of Southampton, then disappeared in the drizzle.

The route for the review by the queen's yacht was carefully planned, so it was important that each ship anchor exactly in its assigned position. A radar ashore was used to determine when we were in the right spot. Our pilot, used to more powerful and responsive ships, had trouble with the wind and our lack of horsepower. As we neared our anchorage he radioed the radar station for positions. They called out: 300 meters, 50 meters to the left, 200 meters, 60 meters to the left, and so on. We overshot it twice and had to steer a large circle and come back upwind each time. Finally, on the third try, we made it — almost. We were still a few meters short. After some discussion it was decided to leave us where we were.

There was a lot of talk of "D-Day weather" from those who were in the invasion but the following day looked more promising. Dawn came with a clear and fine sky. A slight breeze was on the water. During the night more ships came in to the anchorage. We were now in the company of the *USS George Washington*, the *QE2*, the *State of Maine*, the *Vistafjord,* the *USS Guam*, the *Canberra* and others, some 30 ships in all. It was probably the last time in history so many historic and famous ships would be gathered in one place.

Marci Hooper: "All the ships in the Solent, that was incredible, mind-boggling. You just don't see that today. And I don't know if we will ever see that again."

It was amazing how just leaving the pier brought a feeling of calm to the ship. With the attendant lack of unannounced visitors and intrusions, everyone relaxed and fell back into a sense of being at sea, even if only at anchor. For a short while, all was peaceful.

The admiral scheduled a crew meeting at 0830 to explain what to expect. We were to line the rail and salute the queen as the Royal Yacht passed. This procedure was carefully spelled out in a "Restricted" document the ship received earlier, "D Day Commemoration, Operation Order Part 2, Flotilla Programme, 4-7 June 1994." We would rehearse it before the queen's arrival. Then, before the president was due, the Secret Service would check everyone with a magnetic wand to be sure we weren't armed. Once this was done, no one would be allowed to leave the deck until the president departed. The crew that made the trip from San Francisco would be on the fore deck, everyone else would be on the after deck.

Tom Patterson: "On the morning of the fifth, a large tugboat brought out a floating platform that was approximately fifty feet long and thirty feet wide, and moored it on our starboard side and we let our forward gangway down on this floating platform. There were large fenders placed in between the float and the side of the *Jeremiah O'Brien* to protect the ship's hull. We were expecting heavy winds, gusts up to forty knots and seas up to six to eight feet."

Adm. Albert J. Herberger, the Maritime Administrator, came aboard. He presented us with the new Merchant Marine flag. We were honored to be the first ship to ever fly it. It was immediately raised at the halyard.

Ashore, the major event of the Commemoration was the Drumhead service. It was held in front of the Naval War Memorial on Southsea Common with 7,500 people attending. The Drumhead ceremony is one of the most solemn in the long tradition of the English military. It signifies "The Forces Committed," the point at which there is no turning back. Guards of Honor from the Royal Marines and the U.S. Marine Corps took part. The Archbishop of Canterbury presided, speaking over an altar which was an upturned drum covered by flags. "We gather here to remember with pride and thanksgiving and, yes, even with cheers, those who gave everything for freedom fifty years ago and who in our hearts we have never forgotten." Due to our own events, none of us could attend but later we viewed film of the ceremony.

The *Britannia* was scheduled to leave her berth at 1230 on June 5. To allow time for everyone to get in place and because no one could go back inside once they were checked by the Secret Service, lunch was canceled. It was the only time during the entire voyage a meal wasn't served. No one complained.

The captain, the admiral and the chief mate put on their dress blue uniforms. The rest of the crew wore blue *Jeremiah O'Brien* polo shirts and caps. Everyone was positioned, fore and aft, and we held our rehearsal for the queen's yacht's passage. At the cheer, "Hip, hip, hip, hooray," everyone was to take off their hats, hold them out and rotate them in a clockwise circle. We did

View of the anchorage in the Solent taken from the flying bridge of the Jeremiah O'Brien *on the morning of June 5.*

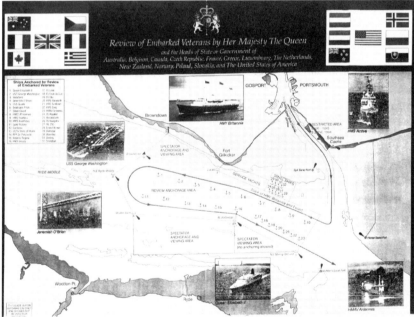

Front cover and center of the official program for the Queen's Review. The Jeremiah O'Brien was in good company; and probably the last time in history for such a gathering of ships. From The Queen's Harbor Master, Portsmouth.

Yachts, tour boats, ferries and small craft toured the Solent in the morning hours before the Queen's review. Here, the Waverly, *a famous British paddle wheeler, passes as the* O'Brien *crew waves. Photo by Marty Wefald.*

this three times. Then it was down past the Secret Service men, who by now were everywhere, and back out on deck to await the queen's arrival. One of them was asked when we should do the cheer, relative to the royal yacht's position. "Whatever," was the reply. Clearly, their only concern was our president. They had no interest in the queen, the *Britannia,* or anything that didn't relate to President Clinton. While we were on deck they went through every room on the ship, opening lockers and drawers, making sure there were no bombs hidden on board. You had to admire their thoroughness.

Ruth Robson: "I was a little frustrated with all the Secret Service that were rousing around into our stateroom and tearing it apart. The hour before he arrived, they did go in there and went into everything. They opened cupboards and our suitcases and didn't put anything back, which of course they don't have time to do. I suppose it had to be done, but I don't think we were a crew but that would be anything but honorable to our president."

D Day Commemoration

Operation Order Part 2

Flotilla Programme

4 - 7 June 1994

The cover of the restricted Op Order.
Courtesy the Royal Navy.

Shortly after 1230 we saw the Trinity House vessel *Patricia* come out of the entrance to Portsmouth Harbor. A medium-sized, modern ship, she has a tall house with large windows that give her a boxy, top-heavy appearance. Trinity House was once responsible for all maritime piloting and aids to navigation in England. The *Patricia* is the only vessel allowed to precede the Royal Yacht in review. Then came the *Britannia,* sleek and elegant with her white superstructure and deep blue hull. President Clinton was aboard as were other heads of state. As she rounded the outer Spit Buoy, turning west to begin the review of anchored ships, small boats of every size and description converged on her like drones to a queen bee. Motor boats, sailing yachts, steam boats — there were so many small boats around the royal yacht that they literally churned the Solent white. At the same moment planes appeared in the sky, passing down the Solent and over the fleet. First came historic planes, Royal Navy Swordfish and a Firefly, followed by a Lancaster bomber escorted by fighters — a Spitfire and a Hurricane. With them was a B-17 and a TBM Avenger. Then came a formation of more Spitfires with a Sea Fury, an F4U Corsair, a P-38 Lightning, a P-51 Mustang and a P-47 Thunderbolt. The fourth flight was a group of planes formed up to spell out the number "50." These were followed by sleek modern jet fighters and bombers from all the gathered nations. The entire air formation was twenty miles long and, at four miles a minute, took three minutes to pass.

The Britannia *passes, escorted and followed by so many boats that their wakes churned the Solent white.   Photo by Elizabeth Wade.*

As the Royal Yacht steamed past, true and steady, we shouted our three "Hip, hip, hip, hooray's," and swung our hats in the prescribed manner. The yacht continued on. As it neared the *USS George Washington*, we heard the cheers of her crew, some 5,000 strong, over the noise of planes, boats and the wind, although we were anchored a half mile away.

Amid the spectacular air and maritime cavalcade, one small boat stood out.

Bob Gisslow: "I was impressed that very day by the small vessel that sailed by with the occupants holding up a sign saying 'thanks for freedom.'" The picture was carried on one of the worldwide television broadcasts.

We waited over an hour as the *Britannia* finished her tour and disembarked the president, the first lady and their entourage. A tug arrived to push our stern into the wind creating a lee for the gangway and its platform.

First to arrive was the press corps. A boat came alongside the catamaran and unloaded more than two dozen reporters, photographers and cameramen. Soon the ship was swarming with newsmen asking questions, photographers looking for photo ops and video crews setting up tripods and cameras. Here, the White House staff came into their own. They gathered up the press corps and soon had them in a mob on top of no. 2 hatch, assuring

President and Mrs. Clinton with Capt. Jahn and Adm. Patterson. Note the excellent taste the president and first lady show in baseball caps and sweaters. Photo by Mike Emery.

them that the president would pass that way and it would be the best angle and lighting possible.

Then we saw a fleet of small white boats approaching. At first we weren't sure which one held the president. Then it became obvious. One boat was surrounded by eight rubber-hulled motorized boats full of frogmen or police, dressed in wet suits. "Police Escort" was written on each boat in luminous letters. Despite our best intentions of staying in our positions on the deck, everyone clamored to the railing. Mrs. Clinton stepped out to the float, and then the president, himself. At that moment the presidential flag was raised on our halyard, the first time in history a presidential flag was flown on a U.S. merchant ship. We watched with great interest as they came up the gangway.

Tom Patterson: "They were brought over in the captain's gig from the *George Washington* and with this perfect lee they were able to come right aboard and walk up the gangway. The captain and I met them at the head of the accommodation ladder,

The Daily Telegraph

NEWSPAPER OF THE YEAR

D-DAY
ANNIVERSARY
ISSUE
D-DAY POSTER OFFER
PAGE 18

NO. 43,219

MONDAY, JUNE 6, 1994   48p

A high-spirited armada displaying flag-fluttering, horn-honking pride

The Queen's Review made a splash in the next day's newspapers. Courtesy the Daily Telegraph.

saluted the president, welcomed them aboard and took them into the officers' saloon. There were Admiral Al Herberger, the Maritime Administrator, Vice-Admiral (retired); Lane Kirkland, the president of the AFL-CIO; Mrs. Jahn and my wife, Ann."

We had gifts for the presidential party: sweaters and baseball caps with the ship's logo on them, a numbered cloisonne pill box for Mrs. Clinton (No. 1 in the series, of course), a T-shirt for their daughter, Chelsea, and, most important as far as the writer was concerned, a copy of *The Last Liberty,* the history of the *Jeremiah O'Brien.*

The crew returned to their positions on the deck.   Soon Adm. Patterson and Capt. Jahn escorted President and Mrs. Clinton onto the main deck. The president was wearing one of our baseball caps and sweaters. Mrs. Clinton also had on one of the caps. As Patterson introduced the president to each crew member they shook hands, exchanged a few words and went on. "This is a

The president exiting the Jeremiah O'Brien'*s midships house. Photo by Jo Lawrence.*

great day for the merchant marine." "I'm proud to be on board." "You have a fine ship."

Capt. Jahn and Mrs. Clinton followed but the first lady began to lag farther and farther behind as each member of the crew seemed to want to talk with her more. Her smile was dazzling, her manner relaxed and friendly. Eduardo Pubill kissed her hand, as did one or two others. Adm. Patterson introduced the chief mate as the author of

The president and the first lady meet the crew of the Jeremiah O'Brien. *Note the press corps on top of the hatch (left) and in the guntub, upper right. Photo by Marty Wefald.*

The Last Liberty. He saluted. The president returned the salute, then said, "I got the book. Ah'm going to read it. Thank you very much."

They finished the foredeck, then went aft and shook hands with everyone there. Before leaving, president and Mrs. Clinton returned to the foredeck, he saluted, waved and said, "Thank you. Thank you for what you've done."

Someone shouted, "Three cheers for the president of the United States. Hip, hip, hip,"

"HOORAY," everyone shouted. We repeated it twice, by now well-practiced in giving cheers to heads of state.

They went down the gangway and, smiling, turned and waved, then got in the boat. Soon they were on their way to the *USS George Washington* where they would stay for the next few days.

As soon as they left, the tug that was holding the ship into the wind departed. The *O'Brien's* alignment to the wind changed and suddenly the catamaran was bouncing up and down in the choppy seas that had been building all day. Each time the float rose the bottom of the gangway rolled several feet across its surface and bounced and shuddered its entire length. When the platform dipped, the bottom of the gangway rolled several feet in the opposite direction. A boat came alongside the float to take off the press corps. They treated it as an adventure, each one timing his run down the gangway to reach the bottom when movement was at a minimum. Some of them had poor timing and had to stop and hold on tightly partway down. The Solent became more choppy. The last members of the press corps, the Secret Service and the White House staff got their feet wet but took it all in good humor, laughing (some of them for the first time since we'd known them) as they jumped aboard the waiting boat. When the boat pulled away, I was surprised to see Martin Shakespeare and Andy Cropley aboard it. I waved. Martin smiled and gave a thumbs up in salute and farewell.

Mike Emery later said the press corps told him it was one of the best events they had in the previous month.

Now, a continuous stream of ships sailed out of Portsmouth Harbor bound for Normandy. Heading this international flotilla were a force of eleven warships from the United Kingdom, the United States, the Netherlands, France, Canada, Poland, Greece, Belgium and Norway led by the flagship *HMS Edinburgh*. These were followed by the royal yacht, more Naval ships, passenger liners, small boats and vessels carrying the veterans of 50 years past. *Britannia* passed down the center as each ship threw a wreath in the Commemorative Act of International Maritime Forces. A Lancaster bomber flew over the *Canberra* releasing two million poppies. The flowers hung for a second, then fluttered downward to make a carpet of red on the waves before sinking into the choppy seas. After dark, the warships slipped in and anchored off the famous beaches and invasion sites — Arromanches, Ouistreham, Omaha, Utah, Sword, Juno, Gold and Pointe du Hoc, awaiting D-Day Plus 50 Years.

A dozen Hercules C130 aircraft from the U.S. Air Force dropped 560 paratroopers from the 101st and 82nd Airborne Divisions, along with 38 veterans aged 68 to 83, at St. Mère Église. Shortly afterward, twelve RAF, three French and three Royal Canadian Air Force C130s dropped 1,300 paratroopers at Pegasus Bridge near Caen. These were followed by historic and modern planes which were to take part in ceremonies at Arromanches and Omaha Beach.

At dinner, all the talk was of the president and Hillary. Everyone agreed they both had extraordinary presence, true charisma. The president and the first lady look you directly in the eye when they talk to you and they respond to what you say. You are their focus for that moment, as if nothing else mattered. Dr. Haslam said, "What a woman. I think I'm in love." After shaking hands with her, other members of the crew said they would never wash their hands again. That day there were no Democrats or Republicans, just Americans feeling proud and patriotic.

Phil Sinnott: "You can forget your partisan politics when you shake the hand of the president. And Mrs. Clinton is an utterly charming individual. In many ways, despite the grand reception we had had up to that point, it was President Clinton's presence on the *O'Brien* that made me genuinely aware of the importance of what we were doing."

Jim Conwell: "The visit of president and Mrs. Clinton almost made D-Day anticlimactic. I felt that was not only a personal highlight but also something for the ship and for the National Liberty Ship Memorial. Hillary certainly came across as a warmer, more friendly person than the president but, recognizing that he's the guy that has the job and not she, you can certainly appreciate how different they are."

Bob Gisslow: "It was special to the extent that it will be the only time that I have ever shaken the hand of a president. My impression of Hillary was that she never blinks and has very, very deep blue eyes."

Carl Kreidler: "I thought it was fantastic he could come aboard our ship. And Hillary, she was great. She was really a nice lady and asked a lot of good questions. And I thought the whole thing was really done with, you know, a touch of class."

Carl Nolte: "The president comes on the ship. Wow! That's amazing, that's great. And, hey, the president of the United States stood on the part of the deck I painted! I never thought I'd do that."

Ruth Robson: "I was much impressed with him. I had no idea he had the charisma about him he has. He is much more impressive in person than he is in a photograph or a newsreel. Hillary was a charming lady. I'm not one of these very high pressure persons and she comes across very powerful but of course she's the woman behind the man behind the big job, so you have to realize she has to be as powerful as he is, almost. She's a brilliant woman and charming, very charming. She shook hands with all of us in the line and when she was through she asked if she missed anybody. There are not many woman that would be that gracious. They were very personable people."

Tom Patterson: "It was the greatest day of my life; a wonderful event. First of all, for the *SS Jeremiah O'Brien* to have the president and first lady on board to recognize our Commemoration Voyage. It was a great tribute to the ship and to the crew. We were all genuinely thankful for that. And,

DECK LOG of the [S.S.] [M.V.] JEREMIAH O'BRIEN OWNED BY UNITED STATES OF AMERICA from the Solent Anchorage to

Date JUNE 5, 1994 SUNDAY

ZONE DESCRIPTION —1

VOYAGE NUMBER 8

DECK LOG—REMARKS

0001 — Vessel at Anchor with Zabot out in the Solent

0400 — Engine Ready. Checked Swing Ship Cabin in the Solent

0400 AT ANCHOR 50-43.8N 1-08.2W 12 Fath under Keel

0730 Standby Anchor to 5 5 Shots

0830 Vessel Secure

0845 Gen. Engines Motors Administration Aboard

1200 Vessel At Anchor. Bureaus Checking All Secure. Various White House, Secret Service and Civilian Personnel Aboard.

1140 — Pilot Aboard Capt Cmdr.

1410 (Approx) President Mrs. Wm Clinton Boarded This Vessel.

1835 (Approx) President (Party Away).

1535 — Commence Heaving Anchor 1530 S.B.Y Engine 1538 — Anchor Aweigh.

1629 — All Mn's Land Boat Aboard. 1652 — Southampton Pilot Relieving By Deep Sea Pilot Capt C.R. Lukehurst and Party. 1700 — Departing Southampton. Courses and Speeds As Per Pilot.

2000 VESSEL STEADY

2130 Approaching Point Di Effic. Anchorage. Engines At Best Cdt. Lukehurst Remaining Various Courses & Speeds

second, no president in anybody's knowledge had ever been aboard a United States-flag merchant ship. To have our Maritime Administrator and our president and the head of the AFL-CIO be there to witness this was a great day for the U.S. Merchant Marine."

Jean Yates: "The president coming on board, I never thought I'd ever live to see the day when I'd shake the hand of the president of the United States. I did. I did. And his wife, too. I regard her equally highly as I do him."

Capt. Jahn, a reticent man (except when it comes to the Coast Guard) didn't say much, but as he walked about his ship, he looked both pleased and proud.

The *Jeremiah O'Brien* sailed on in a southerly direction. Ahead and astern were other ships bound for the same destination. Overhead, planes flew on the same course. It was early evening, Sunday, June 5, 1994 and the *O'Brien* was bound for her appointment in Normandy.

8

Normandy — The Twelfth Landing

From the deck log, *SS Jeremiah O'Brien:*
"June 6, 1994.
0000 Approaching anchorage at Point Du Hoc — Arrival.
0118 Let go stbd. anchor — 4 shots on deck.
0130 FWE. Riding to moderate strain on 4 shots of chain in 14 meters of water. Point Du Hoc [bearing] 212°T, 0.8 miles."

The first American ceremony, to honor the memory of those lost in battle, took place at sunrise aboard the *USS George Washington.* The senior veteran crew members of the *O'Brien* who served during World War II were included: Carl Kreidler, Bill Duncan, François Le Pendu, George Jahn, Dick Brannon, Tom Patterson, Pat McCafferty substituting for Jack Carraher, Rudy Arellano, Ed Smith, Bill Rowlands, and by lottery, Jimmy Farras. At just after 0400 two boats arrived to pick them up.

It was wet, with a cold wind that whipped across the carrier's flight deck. American and Allied warships could hardly be seen through the fog.

DECK LOG of the S.S. / M.V. | JEREMIAH O'BRIEN | OWNED BY UNITED STATES OF AMERICA | from SOUTHAMPTON / SOLENT ANCHORAGE | to Point Du Hoc | Date JUNE 6, 1994 Monday

VOYAGE NUMBER 8 ZONE DESCRIPTION —1

DECK LOG—REMARKS

0000 – Approaching Anchorage at Point Du Hoc – Arrival
0118 – Let go Stbd Anchor – 4 Shots on Deck
0132 – Five – Riding to Moderate Strain on 4 Shots of Chain 15 14 Meters of Water. Point Du Hoc Ø212 T, Ø.1 Mile (Anchor)

0 4 — Boats Away with Crew Members R Conrad 74

0800 Vessel Secure at Anchor

12.00 Vessel at Anchor. Course by GPS 447.24854 Water T all Internal Good Order.

14.20 – Crew Returns From USS Dale
14.45 – Crew Mustered on Flying Bridge for Memorial Service
12.57 – Complete Memorial Service
13.50 – Commencement of Memorial Address
16.40 – Crew of Gangway Watches Light ...
18.00 – Vessel proceeding from Omaha Beach ...

1830 PC Ø4Ø PSC Ø24STD

2000 Vessel Steady R Conrad 74
2030 ¾ Ø33 Gyro TMG Ø42
2400 Pilot Capt. Lawrence Reserve Com
2400 Various Courses Per Pilot, Vessel Pulling Course To Shelly Sea, Small

LOOKOUTS & GANGWAY WATCHES | REFRIGERATION | DRAFT OF VESSEL

On the *O'Brien* many of the crew tuned their personal radios to the BBC which was full of reminiscences of the invasion and recordings of some of the original newscasts. The darkness slowly faded revealing several Naval vessels at anchor with us, giving some sense of what it was like fifty years before, when the *O'Brien*, carrying hundreds of American troops, rode at anchor in the Solent, awaiting orders to begin the first of her eleven landings on "Omaha" and "Utah" beachheads. Through binoculars we saw the shoreline, Pointe du Hoc itself, a low brown bluff capped with green. Set slightly back was a pavilion with a white roof and flag standards. To one side of the pavilion was a field with several helicopters at rest, their drooping blades making them look sad and reverent. People walked along the cliffs, heads bowed or gazing seaward.

Except for necessary watches, and the galley crew, of course, all work was suspended for that day. The *Jeremiah O'Brien* rested easily in the choppy seas. The mood aboard was quiet. Bob Burnett, Jim Conwell, Eduardo Pubill and others spent the morning studying the chart and coastline. Using binoculars, for we were anchored off away from the coast, they searched the shoreline until they found the historic beaches — Omaha, Utah, Gold, Sword. Others of the crew, Tom Alexander, Arnold Sears, Al Martino, Bill Williams, Jim Miller, Tim Kinsella, to mention a few, sat on the hatches or leaned on the rails, contemplating the history and serenity of the surroundings.

Tom Alexander was born in Edinburgh, Scotland in 1925 and served an apprenticeship as a machinist-fitter on the London-Northeastern Railway (eventually to become British Railways). He later worked in shipyards in Scotland, then migrated to Canada and eventually California. He lived in Great Britain during World War II and realizes "the importance of these ships in helping to keep Britain afloat." A volunteer for more than ten years with the *O'Brien*, he and his wife live in Santa Cruz, California.

Tom Alexander: "I felt quite emotional about it. Where we anchored at Pointe du Hoc was a very historical spot. I really felt that the quietness of that day was very appropriate. Several people said well why didn't we do more, or why didn't this happen. But I felt that that spot and that quiet day

— it was a grey day, the sea was grey and the land, of course, was green — for me, that was just right. It was the culmination of all that had gone before. I didn't think it was an appropriate place for brass bands and things like that. So I liked being able to sit on deck and just think, reflect on it."

Bill Dickerson: "I thought it was a very powerful, emotional experience. Frankly, I think only the people on this ship and maybe the Navy ships got a chance to see the same thing that those guys probably saw at Pointe du Hoc in similar weather conditions, on a grey miserable day. I'm just glad I didn't have to do it then.

"My wife was in France and she saw all the guys running down to Omaha Beach and getting little film canisters full of sand. One guy was at Juno, but the bus driver wouldn't stop so he could go down and get his little portion of sand. He was talking about it in some bar that night where the bus stopped. So he dropped out of the tour and went with a couple of Frenchmen and they drove him back to the beach and he got his sand. And then he came back and he said, 'You know, this is all I need, this is it. As far as I'm concerned, the trip is complete.'"

Pat McCafferty: "I lost a few relatives in the second World War. Actually I lost four uncles and that's all part of it. An awful lot of people in our country don't realize that it was quite a sacrifice for the generation ahead of us."

Marty Shields: "To be off the coast of Normandy, on June 6, at anchorage, it was a special time in history on a special ship. The only ship returning, the only one that was there on D-Day."

A few miles away Carl Nolte was aboard the *George Washington* with the *O'Brien* veterans. "On the *George Washington* there was not much talk about the ugly side of the war. Instead, they talked of a debt the living owe to the dead.

"The *O'Brien* people were honored guests, and they sat in the second row for the ceremony, next to four-star generals and cabinet officers."

Tom Patterson: "We met the new Chief of Naval Operations, Admiral Michael Borda. I was surprised at how young he was, how nice he was. I gave him a *Jeremiah O'Brien* cap, which he immediately put on and got his picture taken with us. Then he escorted our crew into their seats, the second row, in front of the president's dais. They had held me aside and said you're going to be escorted in separately and you're going to take part in the ceremony. That was when I learned that I had been selected to represent the United States Merchant Marine in laying the wreath with the president. I was escorted together with the U.S. ambassador for France, Mrs. Harriman, a very delightful, beautiful lady. We sat down together, she was on my right, on my left was the new Secretary of Defense, Bill Perry and then next to him was a legendary naval hero, Vice Admiral Buckley, "P.T." Buckley, who took MacArthur off of Corregidor, and winner of the Congressional Medal of Honor.

"Then the president came on the dais. He was seated about ten feet from us. He looked down, made eye contact with all of us from the *Jeremiah O'Brien*, as did Mrs. Clinton. We

One of the many programs printed for "D-Day plus 50 years."
The simplicity of the design underscores the stark reality of what
happened.

Courtesy Phil Frank and San Francisco Chronicle.

thought this was something, seeing the president two days in a row. Everyone was very, very solemn.

"Dean Stockwell, who was there at the invasion of Normandy, got up and recounted how it was that day fifty years earlier — similar conditions, very drizzly, high seas, almost the same situation we had that morning."

"We gather in the calm of sunrise today to remember that fateful morning, the pivot point of the war, perhaps of the 20th century," the president said.

All the U.S. sea services were represented — the Navy, the Marine Corps, the Coast Guard and the Merchant Marine. A prayer was offered by a colonel chaplain who had been at Normandy and a band played the traditional seaman's hymn, "Eternal Father, Strong to Save." A wreath was presented and put into the water.

Tom Patterson: "Following the ceremony we were escorted into the carrier hanger. There were about sixty-five hundred people on the carrier that day including the Clintons who were living on board. Then, to my amazement and delight, the Navy marine band struck out with 'Heave Ho, My Lads, Heave Ho.' I thought I had died and gone to heaven! I had sent the music ahead and, by golly, they did it. I noticed going around that everybody, from enlisted men and officers, to admirals and generals knew about the *Jeremiah O'Brien*. They came over to Captain Jahn, they came over to our crew and shook our hands and thanked everybody for bringing the ship there. That was really a recognition of the United States Merchant Marine that had never happened before on a capital ship."

Carl Kreidler: "That was kind of a tear jerker for me. Their ceremony on the *George Washington* was, well, you know, it was just kind of sad. But, number one, I got to go to Normandy with the Captain and the Admiral and other crew members and it was a great nostalgic thing to me. I got to meet other veterans and I got to hear about the *Curry* which was sunk right underneath us, and they're all still down there."

From Carl Nolte's column:

> The *O'Brien*'s people went back to the ship, with a detour to a destroyer. The skipper of the warship had each man come up the gangway alone — the chief engineer, two messmen, the captain, the admiral, the gunner's mate — one at a time, so each of them could be piped over the side, the boatswain blowing his shrill whistle, to honor them. It was the least he could do, he said.

At 1240 the captain, the admiral and our eight veterans returned. We were especially pleased to see Capt. Jahn briskly come up the vertical pilot ladder, knowing he was 78 years old with a triple by-pass, a stainless steel knee in one leg and a bad nerve in the other that made his foot drag, yet so determined and spirited. As they boarded, each person had a comment. "Powerful," said Adm. Patterson. "Great," said Capt. Jahn. "Terrific." "Unbelievable." "Moving," said the others.

The crew gathered on the flying bridge for a special ceremony to honor the merchant mariners who gave their lives at Normandy. Father Wade gave an invocation and a wreath was thrown into the choppy seas. At the end of ceremony Adm. Patterson took out a pocket knife and told a poignant story. It was given to him in Panama by Art Pine who works for the U.S. Military Sealift Command. "The knife, he told me, belonged to his father's brother, Art's uncle, a coxswain on an assault landing craft at Normandy. He said his father was always after his brother to carry a knife, he said a seaman needs a knife, but his brother wouldn't do it. He didn't like knives.

"On the sixth of June, 1944, his landing craft was hit by German shell fire and sank. His life jacket was made of kapok and was riddled with shrapnel. It was meant to save his life, but

The front page of the Stars and Stripes *commemorative edition carries a photo of the 1944 invasion.*

instead it dragged him down. He drowned. Art Pine told me his father always felt that if his brother had a knife, he could have cut the strap on the life jacket and lived.

The back page of the Stars and Stripes *commemorative edition was a reproduction of their issue fifty years earlier.*

"He asked me to take the knife to the beach and throw it in where he died. Well, here is the knife that would have saved a life." Patterson threw it far from the ship. Deeply moved, the crew watched it disappear into the gray water where the coxswain died fifty years ago.

NORMANDY VETERANS ASSOCIATION
50TH ANNIVERSARY
COMMEMORATIVE PLATE

This fine bone china (10 inch) plate edged with 22 carat gold, has been specially produced by Edwardian China, to commemorate the 50th anniversary of the Normandy Landings. A fine collectors item.

Price £15.99 + £3.50 Postage and Packaging

Cheques should be made payable to Edwards & Lockett

Send to :-

Tri Service Publications
62-63 Upper Street
London
N1 0NY

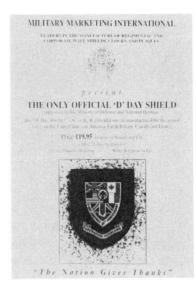

Among the many items available to the public were the commemorative plate and the official D-Day shield.

Ashore, tens of thousands of veterans fulfilled their pilgrimage to Normandy on the beaches and in the cemeteries. At the American Cemetery in Colleville, President Clinton, accompanied by other heads of state, paid homage to those who lay buried there. In one of his finest speeches, he said,

In these last days of ceremonies, we have heard wonderful words of tribute. Now we come to this hallowed place that speaks, more than anything else, in silence. Here on this quiet plateau, on this small piece of American soil, we honor those who gave their lives for us fifty crowded years ago.

Today, the beaches of Normandy are calm. If you walk these shores on a summer's day, all you might hear is the laughter of children playing on the sand, or the cry of sea gulls overhead, or perhaps the ringing of a distant church bell. The simple sounds of freedom barely breaking the silence. Peaceful sounds. Ordinary sounds. But June 6, 1944, was the least ordinary day of the 20th century. On that chill dawn, these beaches echoed with the sounds of staccato gunfire, the roar of aircraft, the thunder of bombardment. And through the wind and the waves came the soldiers, out of their landing craft and into the war, away from their youth and toward a savage place many of them would, sadly, never leave.

They had come to free a continent — the Americans, the British, the Canadians, the Poles, the French Resistance, the Norwegians and others. They had all come to stop one of the greatest forces of evil the world has ever known.

As news of the invasion broke, back home in America, people held their breath. In Boston, commuters stood reading the news on the electric sign at South Station; in New York, the Statue of Liberty, its torch blacked out since Pearl Harbor, was lit at sunset for fifteen minutes; and in Newcastle, Pennsylvania, a young mother named Polly Elliot wrote to her husband, Frank, a corporal in the Army, "D-Day had arrived. The first thought of all of us was a prayer."

Below us are the beaches where Corporal Elliot's battalion and so many other Americans landed — Omaha and Utah, proud names from America's heartland, part of the biggest gamble of the war, the greatest crusade, yes, the longest day.

During those first hours on bloody Omaha, nothing seemed to go right. Landing craft were ripped apart by mines and shells, tanks sent to protect them had sunk, drowning their crews; enemy fire raked the invaders as they stepped into chest-high water and waded past the floating bodies of their comrades. And as the stunned survivors of the first wave huddled behind the seawall, it seemed the invasion might fail.

Hitler and his followers had bet on it. They were sure the Allied soldiers were soft, weakened by liberty and leisure, by the mingling of races and religion. They were sure their totalitarian youth had more discipline and zeal. But then something happened.

Although many of the American troops found themselves without officers on unfamiliar ground next to soldiers they didn't know, one by one they got up. They inched forward and together, in groups of threes and fives and tens, the sons of democracy improvised and mounted their own attacks.

At that exact moment, on these beaches, the forces of freedom turned the tide of the 20th century. These soldiers knew that staying put meant certain death. But they were also driven by the voice of free will and responsibility nurtured in Sunday schools, town halls and sandlot ball games — the voice that told them to stand up and move forward, saying 'You can do it. And if you don't, no one else will.' And as Captain Joe Damson led his company up this bluff, and as others followed his lead, they secured a foothold for freedom.

Today, many of them are here among us. Oh, they may walk with a little less spring in their step and their ranks are growing thinner. But let us never forget — when they were young, these men saved the world. And so let us now ask them, all the veterans of the Normandy campaign, to stand if they can and be recognized. The freedom they fought for was no abstract concept. It was the stuff of their daily lives.

Well, millions of our GIs did return home from that war to build up our nations and enjoy life's sweet pleasures, but on this field there are 9,386 who did not — 33 pairs of brothers, a father and his son, 11 men from tiny Bedford, Virginia, and Corporal Frank Elliot, killed near these bluffs by a German shell on D-Day.

They were the fathers we never knew, the uncles we never met, the friends who never returned, the heroes we can never repay. They gave us our world. And those simple sounds of freedom we hear today are their voices speaking to us across the years.

At this place, let us honor all the Americans who lost their lives in World War II. Let us remember as well that over 40 million human beings from every side perished — soldiers on the field of battle, Jews in the ghettos and death camps, civilians ravaged by shell fire and famine. May God give rest to all their souls.

Fifty years later, what a different world we live in. Germany, Japan and Italy, liberated by our victory, now stand among our closest allies and the staunchest defenders of freedom. Russia, decimated during the war and frozen afterward in communism and Cold War, has been reborn in democracy. And as freedom rings from Prague to Kiev, the liberation of this continent is nearly complete.

Now the question falls to our generation. How will we build upon the sacrifice of D-Day's heroes? Like the soldiers of Omaha Beach, we cannot stand still. We cannot stay safe by doing so. Avoiding today's problems would be our own generation's appeasement, for just as freedom has a price, it also has a purpose, and its name is progress.

Today our mission is to expand freedom's reach farther, to tap the full potential of each of our own citizens, to strengthen our families, our faith and our communities, to fight indifference and intolerance, to keep our nation strong and to light the lives of those still dwelling in the darkness of undemocratic rule.

Our parents did that, and more. We must do nothing less. They struggled in war so that we might strive in peace. We know that progress is not inevitable, but neither was victory upon these beaches. Now, as then, the inner voice tells us to stand up and move forward. Now, as then, free people must choose.

Fifty years ago, the first Allied soldiers to land here in Normandy came not from the sea but from the sky. They were called pathfinders, the first paratroopers to make the jump. Deep in the darkness, they descended upon these fields to light beacons for the airborne assault that would soon follow. Now, near the dawn of a new century, the job of lighting those beacons falls to our hands. To you who brought us here, I promise we will be the new pathfinders, for we are the children of your sacrifice.

Thank you, and God bless you all.

At Bayeux, Queen Elizabeth II said, "The Europe which we know today could not exist had not the tide of war been turned here in Normandy fifty years ago." And at Omaha Beach, President Mitterand of France: "I thank you for the liberty of the world, which owes so much to you."

Carl Nolte's column:

In the afternoon, the *O'Brien* steamed slowly from Pointe du Hoc, where U.S. Army Rangers scaled an impossible cliff in the face of German gunfire, past Utah Beach, past Omaha Beach, past the anchored French and American warships. The French coast 50 years later looked very ordinary. There were small towns and church steeples and bluffs rising out of the channel. There were fields of yellow flowers.

'It looks so peaceful,' said Phil Sinnott, 73, a seaman on the *O'Brien*. 'You would think nothing ever happened here.'

At one place, not far from Omaha Beach, there appeared to be a field of white flowers, maybe a mile long. But through the binoculars, one could see what it really was: What looked like white flowers were headstones marking the graves of men who never lived long enough to be honored old veterans. They will never return to Normandy to relive their youth. They will stay there forever.

After a while, the ship turned away from France and headed back across the channel, back to England and later in the month to French ports and eventually to San Francisco. Nobody who was aboard yesterday will ever forget it.

Fifty years ago,
on a beach not far
from this ground, an
event took place that
changed the world
forever. It happened
during a great war.
It happened in a
place called...

NORMANDY

9

ON THE MEDWAY

The SS *Jeremiah O'Brien* raced at twelve knots on a north-easterly course toward the central traffic lanes of the English Channel. Wind and sea rolled in from the Atlantic, pushing on our port quarter, making the ship wallow. In the wheelhouse, the ghostly green image on the radar looked like a racecourse, with the speed-direction line on each target pointing northeast, as we entered the traffic lanes for Dover, as many as ten ships showing in a twelve-mile stretch. Fortunately, we were under the sure hand of our English Channel pilot, Capt. C. B. Lukehurst, who graciously donated his services. He eased us into the traffic pattern with consummate skill and soon we were but one of the many blips on the screen speeding toward the North Sea. We transited the Dover Straits at midnight and a few hours later took arrival at Margate, anchoring just after 0400.

Margate, on the southeast coast of England, lies just north of Dover and Ramsgate at the estuary of the Thames River. Although we were anchored well offshore, the sea was flat and peaceful with a slight breeze blowing off the water. We saw sandy-colored cliffs and a pleasant-looking village. The mood on board was one of quiet reflection, a chance to think about the events of the past few days. After all the hopes, dreams and hard work of the previous months, the volunteers and the *Jeremiah O'Brien* had accomplished their mission, making history again.

But we wondered — would the rest of the voyage "just be visits" to ports in France and the United States? Little did we know, at that moment, for many, the greatest event was still to come.

After breakfast on June 7, the crew gathered in no. 2 'tween deck to discuss their "Normandy Remembrances." Capt. Jahn recalled his experiences, fifty years earlier at Omaha and Utah, as master of the Liberty ship *William Matson*. Patterson described the memorial service on the *USS George Washington*. The *O'Brien* had finally been awarded an Operation and Engagement Star by the Department of Defense for its participation in the bombardment of the coast of France from June 8-25 in 1944. This was presented to the ship by Carl Kreidler of the Armed Guard and Coke Schneider, who had rejoined the ship for a few days. In a small recreation of part of the previous day's ceremonies, Adm. Patterson passed out copies of the merchant marine song, "Heave Ho, My Lads, Heave Ho." Then, he led, conducting with clenched fist, as we sang along. Following this, Father Wade led the group in the hymn, "Eternal Father, Strong to Save." As he finished the first chorus he asked, "Do you want to sing the other choruses?"

The crew answered a loud "NO."

The ship was still on a holiday schedule but Rich Reed busied himself with small miscellaneous jobs, straightening out the paint locker, tidying up the rigging and lines, checking the gangways. In the afternoon he attended to something that had been on his mind for several weeks — touching up the paint on the two drawings of Miss Jerry O'Brien on the forward guntub. Located so far forward on the ship, they were constantly exposed to the elements and hadn't been repainted for years. Setting to with artist brushes and several mixes of paint, he worked hard at achieving the right "flesh" color. Miss Jerry is a bare-breasted beauty and his efforts soon drew a goodly crowd of off-duty crew as onlookers. But when he began touching up the nipples on the pinups breasts, his audience's mild interest turned to enthusiasm. Soon there was a line six-deep in the forward guntub, each person waiting his turn to have a picture taken, brush in hand, as he painted the nipples. By late afternoon, the effect of so many coats of paint was quite three-dimensional. Several cases of beer were broken out at no. 4 hatch for an impromptu party. It was a good chance to relax after the emotion of the past two weeks, the

One of the highlights of a quiet day at anchor off Margate was touching up Miss Jerry O'Brien. Left to right, Phil Sinnott, Carl Nolte (with paint brush), Marty Wefald and Rich Reed. Photo by Mike Emery.

excitement of the queen's review, the president's visit, and the commemoration at Normandy. The crew was in high spirits.

The next day we took on a Thames Estuary pilot, Capt. Bordas, raised the anchor at 0800, and got underway for the confluence of the Thames and Medway Rivers. The grey sea was calm in a light drizzle. A twin-engine plane with the marking "Fotoflight" on its fuselage found us and made several passes. As we crossed the wide estuary we came to several large concrete towers standing on stilts in the middle of nowhere. They looked like a backdrop for "Star Wars." Capt. Bordas told us they were referred to as "The Forts" and were built on Tongue Sands Shoals as defenses during the First World War. At one time they were interconnected and housed several hundred soldiers but were now abandoned. A few years ago one was occupied and operated as a pirate radio station, broadcasting rock and roll to all of Europe. Now they were completely deserted.

Ships outbound for sea blew whistle salutes as they passed — three long blasts of their horn. We returned each salute and they responded with a single short toot, which we answered. Closer to the mouths of the Thames and Medway we passed one ship that didn't salute, one that couldn't blow her whistle, the Liberty ship *Richard Montgomery*. She had sailed from the U.S.A. to the U.K. in August 1944 with some 7,000 tons of bombs. On arrival, she anchored in the Thames Estuary, off Sheerness, at its confluence with the Medway. On almost the next tide, however, the ship's anchor dragged and it drifted onto a bank, grounding amidships on the crest of the bank, and shortly afterwards broke its back. The wreck now lies in some fifty feet of water, her masts and booms protruding above water at all stages of the tide. Intensive efforts were made after the grounding to unload the explosive cargo and about half was removed. The other holds were less accessible and when the wreck flooded, it had to be abandoned. Ironically, the *Richard Montgomery* continues to serve. For, although an obstruction to navigation, she marks for other shipping the bank on which she grounded and no vessel has ever come close to running into her. There is still a possibility that the explosives remaining on board could become dangerous, but experts believe that the best way to keep the risk to a minimum is to leave the wreck alone.

We passed our sister ship and blew the whistle in salute — three long, forlorn blasts to a fallen comrade. Jim Wade: "Going past the *Richard Montgomery*, the sunken Liberty Ship, was quite moving. Here was a vestige of World War II still with live bombs on board. It made 1944 not quite so far in the past."

Approaching Chatham, we pass a fallen comrade, the Richard Montgomery. *Photo by R. L. Ratcliffe.*

Bob Burnett: "One thing that I found very touching was when we went up the Medway and went by the *Richard Montgomery* and we tooted three times. That choked me up. That was really touching. I thought, oh, hello, sister."

As we entered the River Medway and worked our way toward Chatham the cloud cover began to lift. Nearing our destination the sun appeared, blotted out occasionally by a passing thunderhead. Several small boats and a paddle steamer, the *Kingswear Castle*, carrying Carl and Nell Otterberg and Bob Blake, came out to meet us, each blowing her whistle. We answered and answered until it sounded like "Dueling Whistles," with feeble toots, high-pitched, shrill horns, locomotive shrieks and, always, the *Jeremiah O'Brien*'s deep authoritative foghorn bellowing across the water in response.

We learned why we had to wait all day at Margate, why the timing of our arrival was so critical. We were to dock in a tidal basin. This meant going through a series of locks at high tide, the innermost of which would then be closed until we sailed, again, on a high tide. Capt. Bordas skillfully guided us into the first set of locks, positioning two tugs, *Pushette* and *Shovette*, ahead of us. It was a close fit between stone walls with little room on either side and just enough space ahead for the tugs to tuck in under our bow. We were early again and had to wait an hour for the tide to reach the correct height. Then the outer gates were closed and the inner ones opened. The tugs preceeded us and one made fast with a single line to our bow as we slowly worked our way into the large outer basin. As soon as we were clear, the second tug made up with a single line on our stern and we proceeded toward the far end of the basin where there was another set of tidal gates. The gates were open, but the notch in the stone wall ahead looked far too narrow for the *O'Brien*. As we drew closer and closer to the opening it looked smaller and smaller. How would we ever fit? Capt. Jahn and the bridge crew exchanged worried looks. The pilot quietly gave commands to the tugs and our helmsman. The bow tug entered the slot, pulling forcefully on the line leading off the ship's nose. What if the line broke? We seemed to be headed in at an angle. I could almost hear the horrid sound of stone rasping against metal. The pilot continued his commands. As we passed between the stone walls, the captain, the admiral and I anxiously walked from one bridge wing to the other and back. But we needn't have worried. Capt. Bordas had carefully calculated the maneuver, coming to us with years of experience. With perhaps two feet of clearance on each side we slid into the inner basin.

The tugs began pulling, the bow tug to the left, the stern tug to the right, turning us so we could tie up starboard side to. As we pivoted in the calm, quiet basin, a storm cloud rolled in from the west, obliterating the sun. Suddenly there was a loud crack as bright yellow lightning forked into the water directly ahead of us, followed immediately by a tremendous clap of thunder that made us cringe, sending chills up everyone's spine and making the hair stand on the backs of our necks. The air was literally filled with electricity. We continued turning and the lightning cracked again, even closer. As we straightened out and the tugs began to push us alongside, the storm passed over and the lightning and thunder moved slowly out into the Medway, leaving sheets of rain drenching us in its aftermath. Soon we were alongside and made fast. The tugs exited the basin, the gates closed, the sun returned and there we were, in a dreamscape.

To a seaman, the setting was bizarre, almost surreal. Our basin was about four ship lengths long and perhaps two wide. Beyond our berth was a large, modern industrial park with carefully trimmed lawns, neo-Victorian brick buildings and modern glass-faced edifices with parking garages underneath. There were no tides, no passing vessels, nothing to make our ship move. The gangway, which anywhere else would move back and forth on the dock with each change of tide and each passing ship, rested perfectly still. The mooring lines, which normally must be tended with each change of tide, would hang with the same tension day after day. To be on a large, ocean-going ship surrounded by land, looking out the portholes at buildings and parking garages, and not feel <u>anything</u> move is unique.

Tom Patterson: "We had the ship moored in what looked like a reflecting pond in a gorgeous new facility which was the old dockyard, all red brick and flowers and cupolas. The towns of Gillingham, Rochester and Chatham came out and just took us to their hearts. Our crew was made to feel so royal there, that we really couldn't get over it, just marvelous."

Chatham Dockyard started out as a safe harbor for British warships in the reign of Henry VIII. Here his vessels were protected from winter storms and could be refitted from a storehouse located just off Dock Road in an area later called Gun Wharf. In addition, the ships were conveniently situated near London, should the King take time from pursuing his successive wives to examine them.

When Elizabeth I took the throne in 1558, she decided the cozy, well-hidden location at Chatham was ideal for her new dockyard — a perfect place to build ships for the fighting fleet. In 1585 a huge chain was put

The basin at Chatham was a perfect reflecting pool.

across the Medway as a defense against a Spanish invasion. The first ship built at Chatham, the *Sunne,* was launched in 1586 and in 1588 she joined the "grand fleet" of the Medway which sailed out to assist Sir Francis Drake in defeating the Spanish Armada.

In 1765 Britain's most famous warship, *HMS Victory,* was launched at Chatham. Twelve years later, the twelve-year-old Horatio Nelson came through Chatham as a young midshipman on his way to his uncle's ship, *Raisonnable.* He got lost and in the course of his wanderings caught a glimpse of his brilliant future in the form of the *Victory* at anchor in the Medway.

Chatham was a busy dockyard during both World Wars, building submarines and sloops and refitting 1,360 other ships. But in 1984 the yard closed.

Rather than let the area languish, the yards became a museum complex with an adjacent real estate development and industrial park. *Jeremiah O'Brien* was the centerpiece at the grand opening of the industrial park, a living monument that evoked the yard's past while pointing toward its future.

The morning of June 9 hit us like a hammer — school kids all over the place playing with the telegraph, blowing the whistle, ringing the general alarm, opening closed doors, flipping switches, touching, feeling, prodding and pulling. Their harried teachers tried to keep them in order but, like kids everywhere, they had to try everything. Eventually we got the telegraph locked in position, the foghorn tied off, doors locked and our British and crew docents in place.

Once the children left, we settled down for another day as a tourist attraction. Our volunteer storekeepers, Jo Lawrence, Monica Conrady, Jean Hook, Ron Turner and Nell Otterberg, under Ron Robson's guidance, set up shop. Marci Hooper went to work coordinating upcoming events with Chatham, Gillingham and Rochester. Adm. and Mrs. Patterson and Capt. and Mrs. Jahn went off sight-seeing with Capt. Lukehurst, our English Channel pilot, as their guide.

Back at our office in San Francisco, Karen Kamimoto had her hands full. "It was hectic. A lot of it had to do with money coming in, including the response from the *Sea History* letter,

**D-Day 50th Anniversary
Commemoration 1944-1994**
at
CHATHAM
MARITIME

THE SOLE SURVIVING US LIBERTY SHIP
FROM THE D-DAY LANDINGS

**The SS Jeremiah O'Brien
berthed 9-14 June 1994**
Admission to the ship 9.30 a.m.- 5.30 p.m.

LIFE ON THE HOME FRONT 1944
an exhibition of civilian life 50 years ago

NOSTALGIC AND MARITIME MUSIC
THROUGHOUT THE WEEKEND

For further enquiries phone
Rochester Tourism Information Centre (0634) 843666
Gillingham Tourism Information Centre (0634) 380323

FREE ENTRY **FREE PARKING**

The Jeremiah O'Brien *was the center of attraction for Chatham Maritime as evidenced by this poster. It was a unique honor in an equally unique location. From Chatham Maritime.*

trying to catch up with the plaque program. Also, the ship was abroad and taking advantage of credit card sales but the charge slips were all sent here and we'd have to get authorization and process them. We also tried to fit in and keep track of all the people that were leaving and coming back, making sure they had the proper papers. Then we had to stay in touch with the ship, letting everyone know what was going on with government agencies, how we were doing in getting fuel oil and so on. A lot of our long distance calls to the ship were fax calls. The fax machine was burning with traffic. The time difference was a problem. In the morning I'd check the fax first for incoming messages and respond to them. Then I found out the fax on the ship was right in the captain's ears, so I had to be careful of what time I called. KFS' public service line was constantly busy with people following the voyage so we also spent a lot of time letting the families and the public know what was happening, answering their calls."

From Bill Bennett's Crew's News:

> Personal to Gary North:
> Several comments have been relayed to me that numerous ladies enjoy hearing my voice (yours) on the telephone message. So far none have been rich, so I have had to admit that I am only the writer. Thanks, Gary.
> Bill Bennett.

In the afternoon, Their Worships, the Lord Mayors of the three cities that shared the industrial park — Rochester, Gillingham and Chatham — visited the exhibit and the ship with their staffs. Resplendent with their chains of office draped about their shoulders, they toured the ship from bow to fantail and wheelhouse to engine room.

One of our visitors, a British veteran, gave me a brown paper bag to present to the captain when he returned. "He'll understand, when he sees it," he said. Later I brought it up to Capt. Jahn's office where he and Carl Otterberg were conferring. Carefully opening the bag, Capt. Jahn looked inside, then laughed heartily. He dumped out the contents on his desk — a can of Spam. "That's World War II, all right," said Carl.

Dick Brannon: "We took great pride in showing visitors around, had the engine room clean and neat and well swept down and everything looking beautiful. Showed them the engines, showed them the boilers and all that, and in one of the English ports, this person asked in absolute sincerity, 'Where are the boilers that you used to steam across the ocean, that you came across in, that you steamed the ship with? These are on display, yes, but where's the real boilers.' And I said, 'These are the boilers. This is the engine and these are the boilers.'"

Sleeping accommodations were a constant problem. In addition to our full crew of fifty-five, on board were volunteers — American and British — working in the store and serving as docents. More cots were set up in the 'tween decks. This was awkward because the cots had to be taken apart and stowed out of sight before we opened to the public each day. After closing, the cots went back up, in some cases surrounded by "privacy" blankets draped over ropes. People lived out of suitcases stowed under their cots at night and tucked in a dark corner under blankets during the day. Fortunately the public restrooms are located between no. 2 and no. 3 hatch.

The atmosphere amongst all the volunteers was collegial and good-humored. No one seemed to mind. Capt. Clifford Hook, a British master mariner serving as docent and later AB: "My impression after being on board for five minutes was as though you had never left a Liberty ship. Everything was authentic even down to the pattern of the cover on the beds and the chimes that the steward used at meal time. Even things like that still were identical. But the next impression, I think, was the crew. With one or two reservations, I was very welcome from the word "go." The age of the crew was something that staggered me. And their ability to do what they did. They may have been perhaps a little slower, but their ability amazed me."

The following day was windy with small tufts of white clouds scampering across a blue sky reflected in the calm, dark water of the reflecting pool surrounding the ship. After breakfast the deck department began the routine which served us well throughout the trip: Take the plastic bags of garbage, accumulated from the previous day, ashore for disposal, clean the main deck by washing and scrubbing with stiff brushes and brooms, load stewards' stores — coal for the galley stove, bread, milk, fresh produce. At ten o'clock docents on duty went to their stations and we took the rope off the bottom of the gangway, greeting our eager visitors who waited in queues along the pier.

From the moment we docked at Chatham, it was clear this visit would not be a weak anticlimax to the events of previous weeks.

A special D-Day display was housed in a large white tent just a few yards away from the ship. It was an evocative exhibit of life in Britain during the war. Inside the tent, the visitor walked through an Anderson Shelter. Made of corrugated metal it contained benches, an air raid shelter lamp and sandbags. There was a wartime kitchen complete with furniture, utensils, gas masks, utility

This photo of Bruce McMurtry wielding the hose depicts a typical washdown done each morning before letting visitors aboard. Photo courtesy of Bruce McMurtry.

radio, ration books, recipes and an actress playing a wartime mother. Nearby was a D-Day exhibition of newspaper headlines, maps of the landings, photos and letters to the forces from General Dwight D. Eisenhower. The favorite of the *O'Brien* crew was the display of Liberty ships featuring ship models, plans and photographs.

On June 10 a special D-Day 50th Anniversary Commemoration was held aboard the ship in No. 2. This was followed by a cabaret — a series of skits and songs provided by an amateur troop, the Phoenix Players, whose professionalism was astounding. Dressed in wartime uniforms, they sang World War II songs and kept everyone entertained. The next evening the cities of Rochester and Gillingham threw a party on the *O'Brien* and the entire crew was invited. A well-stocked bar and a well-set buffet were laid out, followed by another performance by the "Cabaret." In the finale, Adm. Patterson and Capt. Jahn were coerced up onto the stage and arm-in-arm with the cast they sang and did a little cancan kick to the music. Patterson was obviously enjoying himself; Jahn looked agonized. In one corner, some of the crew formed their own dance line with Marci Hooper, Carl Nolte, Mike Smith and others forming a chorus line. As the party broke up the refrain of one of the most-repeated songs, "We'll meet again, don't know where, don't know when . . ." seemed to linger in the night.

Carl Kreidler: "Our party that night was one of the best things I've seen for a long time. With all those people dressed up in the forties costumes and singing all the old-time songs. That was really great."

Tom Patterson: "We had a great cabaret for two nights running in no. 2 hold where we had about 40 professional entertainers that put on this marvelous World War II show for us. It was wonderful."

The hospitality extended to the weather — clear, sunny and warm.

The entertainments continued, as did commemorative services for those lost during the war. The two types of events were

The reception and cabaret were one of many highlights of our stay in Chatham. Courtesy Chatham Maritime.

never far apart, a paradox. We celebrated life while remembering the dead. A commemorative service was held under the pavilion adjacent to the ship for the seamen lost in World War II. The admiral and Father Wade both spoke. English prisoners-of-war joined us on that day.

The sponsors arranged a special shuttle to take the crew into Rochester. A replica of a historic bus, it operated daily from noon to early evening. Any of the crew could flag down the yellow and green vehicle puttering along the road and get a free ride.

Marci Hooper loved the bus: "Oh, what a cute thing, it was adorable. I wanted to take it on board and bring it home."

Nearest to the ship was the Chatham Historic Dockyard. Covering 80 acres, it is the most complete Georgian and early Victorian dockyard in the world. Most of the buildings and offices have been preserved, including the one in which Charles Dickens' father served as paymaster. There is a working rope walk, exhibits of shipbuilding (one titled "Wooden Walls" would put Disney to shame), an active flag and sail loft, model railroads, historic ships in various stages of preservation and sheds of boats and steam vehicles.

Tim Palange, first assistant engineer: "I think, from a standpoint of marine engineering, Chatham was a highlight, the historic dockyard, and there was a lot to see there."

Greg Williams: "My favorite port was Chatham, because I got involved in a volunteer project there and met some wonderful English people. It was a boat, a hundred-and-twelve-foot Norwegian trawler that was built in 1912. It was being converted to Great Britain's first oil pollution control and marine wildlife survey vessel. I did some carpentry work on it. I worked in their galley for a few days. Had fun doing that. I found out that the English from the South of England are not as reserved as we might be led to believe. [laugh] In fact, they were very unreserved."

I was fascinated by the ropewalk. Housed in a long shed, it was the source, in earlier days, for much of the rope and lines used on Royal Navy ships. Inside were unfinished wood beams, a flat, bare wooden floor and the peculiar dry, organic smell of rope. The small crew on hand demonstrated the machinery, fashioning a long coir, or coconut fiber rope, as we watched. Strands of fibers were fastened to timbers at one end of the shed and to hooks on a large black machine on wheels at the other end. At a signal the machine was started, hooks quickly twisting and turning as the device walked slowly toward the other end of the shed. In earlier times, workers actually "walked the rope." About halfway there it stopped, the rope complete. We were then guided to the testing room where a sample of "our rope" was put on a hydraulic device that pulled on it until it broke, testing that the rope was of the proper strength.

The nearby Royal Engineers Museum was a popular attraction, especially to our ship's engineers: Tim Palange, Bill Maus, Bill Duncan, George Hobbs, Fred Dewing, Dick Currie. The town of Rochester offered the Dickens museum, Guildhall museum, which presented a detailed and realistic display of the prison ships that were once kept on the Medway, Rochester Castle, which dated back to the time of the Norman conquest, the Rochester Cathedral, which also dates back to 1088, and, most importantly and delightfully, the Old Town with its pubs: the four-hundred-year-old King's Head Hotel, the Royal Victoria and Bull Hotel featuring the coat of arms of King George III and Queen Charlotte, the Rose, and on the route back to the ship, the Prince Albert, the Royal Oak and the North Foreland. The crew diligently visited all these attractions, and, being something of an attraction themselves, American-Anglo friendship prospered. As in Portsmouth, we always wore our *O'Brien* jackets wherever we went. It broke the ice instantly and led to many warm conversations, not to mention the odd pint of English ale.

There were other things to do, too, some not quite as popular with all of the crew. Jim Wade: "At the cathedral at Rochester, I became involved with the boys choir, and the people there at the cathedral. And I attended evensong and matins, beautiful, absolutely beautiful choral renditions of the psalms at those services."

Rochester Castle, one of the more popular attractions in the Chatham area. Photo by Marty Wefald.

Others of the crew went farther afield. Bosun Rich Reed did extensive research into the location of Lord Nelson's pub at Canterbury, the scene of a donnybrook when the *Jeremiah O'Brien* was in London in 1943. He eventually discovered it was razed in the 1950s to make way for the Ring, a redevelopment scheme to ease the flow of traffic into and around London. He also did lengthy and scholarly research at Will Adam's pub. Adams was the person on which the book *Shogun* is based. The real shogun was born in Gillingham. On his death he was buried in Yokosuka. Rich was proud of the fact that it brought the story full-circle for him. Now he had seen both Will Adams' birthplace and his grave and, in addition, the pub commemorating the man.

We were continually surprised and touched at the depth of gratitude the British felt toward America for helping them during World War II. Our ship seemed to symbolize all Liberty ships which in turn symbolized all that America did to help. We frequently heard remarks like, "You saved our bacon. America saved us. We would have lost the war without the Yanks." Even more amazing to us was that this history was taught in the schools and part of the education of even the youngest children. I sat at a table in the ship's store selling books when a cute little blond-headed boy, no more than five or six years old, came up to me and said, "During the war the Germans were bombing us and the *Jeremiah O'Brien* came over and brought us food when we were starving."

Karen Kamimoto: "People would call us in San Francisco and would just be excited about the voyage. From all over the country and England. There was a guy in Chatham called and told me when the ship came in and how it went up the Medway and so on. He was just like one of the family telling me what happened to dear old dad, a blow-by-blow account. A lot of the British people were great that way."

The following day brought clear skies, with a fine summery smell to the warm air. It was Monday and there were fewer visitors, although one couple came all the way from Wales to see us.

On quieter days such as this, the crew enjoyed the opportunity of visiting with the visitors. Swiss-born Otto Sommerauer, our gunner's mate, spent all his time in the forward gun tub demonstrating the cannon for the children that visited. He seemed to derive great pleasure from it — a gentle giant with big hands, anxious to please and so delighted to show off his guns. At the age of 76 he was probably the fittest man on the ship. Part of his off-duty time each day was spent working out in no. 2 'tween deck on an exercise bicycle. He had a flat, trim body and was very

Gunner's Mate Otto Sommerauer demonstrates the forward gun for a fascinated young admirer. Photo by Mike Emery.

strong.   In San Francisco, where he lives, when he isn't working on the *Jeremiah O'Brien*, Otto spends his spare time at St. Anthony's dining room helping feed the homeless.

The sailing board was posted for the following day, June 15, at 0730.   But, sitting in our landlocked little tub of calm waters, we had forgotten the reality of the world outside.   Hospitable and anxious to be helpful as our hosts were, and the *Jeremiah O'Brien*'s celebrity notwithstanding, the tides ebbed and flowed on their eternal schedule.   High tide was essential to transit the locks.   The sailing board was changed to 1130.

No one was disappointed by the change.   It just gave us all a few more hours in historic old Rochester.   The officers and crew were invited to have tea with the Lord Mayor of Rochester.   Her office was surprisingly sparse and simply decorated but she was a very gracious hostess serving cookies and tea to all who attended.

In the evening we were given a bus tour through the countryside with a special visit to the *Medway Queen,* a paddle steamer in the process of being restored.   Built in 1924 as a coastal pleasure steamer, the vessel was powered by a diagonal compound steam engine, an antique that much interested Rich Hill, Alex Hochstraser, François Le Pendu and others in the black gang. Originally powered by coal, she was converted to an oil burner in

The Lord Mayor of Rochester and the author at tea.   Photo by Rich Hill.

1938. At the outbreak of World War II, the ship was converted to a minesweeper and became *HMS Medway Queen* of the 10th Minesweeping Flotilla. During the evacuation of the British Expeditionary Force in 1940 the ship earned the title "Heroine of Dunkirk," saving 7000 troops from the beaches. By 1960 the ship was obsolete and was sold for scrap. But the public wouldn't have it. After many attempts and setbacks, the Medway Queen Preservation

Society was formed to rebuild and preserve her.

As veterans ourselves of the difficult process of bringing the *Jeremiah O'Brien* from scrapyard to restoration and back to full operation, our crew had an empathetic interest in the project. And what a task they had before them. In an industrial park with red dirt and gravel roads, the ship sat at low tide below a rise with only her funnel showing. We were welcomed aboard by a group of volunteers whose enthusiasm matched or even exceeded our own. Some areas were restored, others partially so, and others needed a great deal of work. In the engine room we saw mudlines on the bulkheads from the time she was sunk. What a job it must have been to clean that out. There were holes in the hull plating fore and aft. But the lounge was partially preserved, several areas on deck showed they knew what they were doing by the quality of restoration and one of the pumps in the engine room shined and hummed as it chugged away. We didn't envy them the job ahead, but couldn't help admiring their determination, feeling a kinship with them as volunteers and for the project before them.

The Medway Queen *in earlier days when she was an operating paddle-wheel steamer. Courtesy* Medway Queen *Preservation Society.*

On our way back to the ship we stopped at the Red Dog Inn for a pint. Set on a country crossroads, the inn seemed to be the focal point for those living nearby. The building was large, well kept, and neat looking. A sign depicting an Irish Setter hung outside. Families sat at tables eating dinner, a friendly dart game was going on in the bar, logs crackled in the fireplace. The decor was cheerful and bright, the people friendly. The atmosphere was relaxing and warm. This was true British pub life at its best.

We awoke the next day to a clear sky and a slight breeze ruffling the water in our pond. Last-minute visitors toured the ship. In all, more than 15,000 people came to see the *O'Brien* in Chatham. No longer looking over our shoulders for the Coast Guard, we invited several people to make the trip up the Thames with us, a special, rare opportunity seldom offered. One couple wanted desperately to go, but they had two golden retrievers and no place to kennel them. They were too polite to ask so the chief mate suggested they bring the dogs along if it could be cleared with the captain, who readily agreed.

Now, a Rochester Town Crier, resplendent in black hat and red costume, took up a position at the foot of the gangway. Ringing his bell, he periodically announced the departure of the ship. As we prepared to pull in the accommodation ladder, one of the crew suggested he come along. He hesitated a moment, looked around, and bounded up the gangway. Marci Hooper: "We departed Chatham on a sunny morning with the Sea Scouts, The Royal Marine Artillery veterans, our insurance brokers, some people from the Greenwich Maritime Museum and some extra pilots who went just for the ride."

The tugs were made fast, we let go our lines and with one hundred guests, two dogs, one Town Crier and our pilot, we slid across the harbor toward the tiny notch in the stone wall.

There was less anxiety this time as we went through, but we still felt some tension. It looked so small and with a two-foot clearance on either side, it was like threading a needle. But Capt. Milbourn, our pilot, skillfully brought us through, then it was across the outer basin and into the tidal locks. As the gates opened and we exited into the river, a lone Scottish piper, in full highland dress, marched in time-step across the face of the dock. The music from his bagpipes echoed against the hull of the *Jeremiah O'Brien*, mournful yet thrilling to all on board. We blew three long blasts of the whistle in farewell to Chatham and proceeded down the River Medway, the notes of "Scotland the Brave" fading behind us.

Bosun Rich Reed at the anchor windlass for departure. Photo by Jo Lawrence.

The Rochester town crier at the foot of our gangway announcing our departure. Photo by Jo Lawrence.

10

LONDON

On clearing the River Medway, Capt. Milbourn departed turning the con over to Capt. Thake, a Thames
River pilot. The ride up the Thames was spectacular. As
we snaked our way upriver the vista changed from flat, lush green
countryside to gritty industrial areas then to the magnificent urban
skyline of London, every ship and barge along the way saluting
with its whistle. Late in the afternoon we went through the Thames
River Barrier, truly a wonder of the modern world. Opened in
1984, it is a series of futuristic towers planted across the river
which raise a man-made barrier from the river bottom to prevent
flooding from the North Sea. Here we were handed over to Capt.
Griffiths who guided us past the Royal Naval College where we
were honored by the salute of a midshipman in full dress uniform
standing at the wrought iron riverside gate. We dipped our ensign
in answer. In the distance, jutting above the trees, we saw the
Royal Observatory at Greenwich and soon, much nearer, the *Cutty
Sark*, elegantly resting in its graving dock.

Changing pilots. We used three pilots going up the Thames. Photo by Marty Wefald.

On both sides of the river, people came out from their apartments, pubs and office buildings at the sound of our whistle, shouting and waving flags, toasting with pints of ale and cheering our passage. The air was charged with a holiday spirit. So many whistle salutes were going back and forth that at one point I got completely carried away and blew "Shave and a haircut, two bits." This brought a laugh from our passengers and soon all the barges and boats nearby were blowing the same beat, Dah-dah-de-dah-dah — Dah-Dah.

Passing the Royal Naval College at Greenwich, we returned their salute with our flag, raised caps and waves. Photo by Marty Wefald.

Tower Bridge opens, the first time in history, for a Liberty ship. Photo by Marty Wefald.

We approached central London and the great Tower Bridge. Traffic on both sides of the river stopped. The twin spans slowly opened. The old ship, proudly decorated with vividly colored signal flags from stem to stern, corporate flags aloft and our largest

Clear of the bridge, the Jeremiah O'Brien *approaches her berth alongside* HMS Belfast. *Photo courtesy Wes and Bev Masterson.*

Tom Patterson watches Tower Bridge close after our passage. Photo by Marty Wefald.

American flag on the steaming gaff at the mizzen mast, passed slowly through into the heart of London. The crowd on the bridge, above and below, waved and cheered. We waved and cheered back. Carl Nolte stood beside me on the flying bridge. "Now that," I said to him, "is what I call 'Making an Entrance.'"

Crew's News for June 15:

Good evening, San Francisco. This is the Voice of the *Jeremiah O'Brien*. *Jeremiah O'Brien* departed Chatham Dockyard today and proceeded up the Thames River to London. Returning the whistle blasts from several passing vessels with *O'Brien*'s steam whistle brought hundreds of citizens onto their shoreside sundecks. Upon seeing our ship arms waved and cheers were heard. We passed through the Tower Bridge at 1940 and moored alongside *HMS Belfast*. This well maintained ship served in the entire period of World War II. She acted as the Royal Navy's Naval Bombardment Command vessel for the three beaches assaulted by British and American Forces at Normandy. It is midnight now and the view of Tower Bridge and other buildings in the area is a sight to behold; and we have the honor of being right in the middle of it.

Jeremiah O'Brien — out.

Tom Patterson: "This was the first time in history that a Liberty ship had actually sailed under the Tower Bridge."

Pat McCafferty: "It was quite an honor to have Tower Bridge open up for us. We had such a good location, that was a real prestigious feeling."

Thursday, June 16, broke warm and clear. London was a designated change port for our crew. Many would be leaving and new faces would appear. The character, the persona of the ship changed slightly with each new member according to whether those coming aboard were more fun-loving, serious or adventurous than those they replaced. It was sad to see some of our British docents from Chatham leave us. One of them bid everyone

Capt. Jahn and Adm. Patterson spent most of their first days in London on courtesy calls. Here they enjoy a sherry with representatives of Trinity House. Photo by Mike Emery.

farewell, then went to the gangway and paused. Taking one last look at the ship, I heard him say, "Good-bye *Jeremiah*," softly under his breath. He walked across to the *Belfast*, turned, waved sadly, and was gone.

Capt. Jahn and Adm. Patterson were absent most of the day making courtesy calls on various English officials and representatives from France who were arranging matters for our next ports of call.

The ship opened to visitors at 1000. We had 698 people on board, many of them old "Sam" sailors looking for "my old room," and complimenting the engine crew on how good the engine room looked. Many others wanted to be part of the historic event and we hosted special groups and private tours. Even the famed shipping line, P&O, rented no. 2 'tween deck for a private catered party.

Pat McCafferty: "One of the things that did become a little hard was listening to the people who had a story to tell about a Liberty ship when they were young. You had people all the time. You'd listen to their story and they'd unfold their papers and say, I went to Long Beach at 16 years old and lived in a hotel for two weeks while they painted my ship to bring it back to the U.K. And they'd actually have tears in their eyes. You had to be very gentle. The first couple of times, it kinda grabs you, but after you've heard the story a half a dozen times or more, you start saying, un hunh, but then you think, no, no I can't do this. This is important to this fellow. And so you have to be very diplomatic about it."

> Born in 1944, Pat McCafferty first went to sea working in the slop chest on the passenger liner *SS President Wilson*. Later he went to work for Highlands Hospital as a building contractor, was a grocery clerk for several years and finished out his career as an independent contractor. "Semi-retired" from that profession, he made the entire voyage as a messman, serving in the saloon. He lives in San Francisco, California.

Phil Sinnott: "The total friendliness of the people in Europe was overwhelming. I certainly shall never forget their kindnesses, and I hate to admit it, but seldom did more than forty-eight hours go by that I didn't have tears in my eyes because of some kindness that was shown to me. People in Europe haven't forgotten us. I only wish I could have done more for some of the people I met."

The next day, the author had an opportunity to fulfill a life's ambition. To the mariner, Historic Maritime Greenwich is the equivalent of St. Peter's to Roman Catholics, Mecca to Muslims, Jerusalem to Christians and Jews, or

Pat McCafferty brings aboard, appropriately, a case of Liberty Ale. Photo by Mike Emery.

Disneyland to children. Greenwich is <u>the</u> center for navigation, history and the romance of the sea for all English-speaking cultures. The museum friends' group, headed by Penny Matheson and Miss D.A. Wayte, had been aboard the *O'Brien* for a tour while we were in Portsmouth and they kindly provided passes to Historic Maritime Greenwich for all our crew. First on my agenda was the museum itself. I spent hours looking at intricate ship models, grand paintings of historic sea battles and video presentations of modern ships at sea. Two things stood out: an exhibit on pirates that was both enchanting and realistic, and an excellent model of a Liberty ship. After a lunch of fish and chips at the museum cafeteria, I went to the Royal Observatory and finally stood astride the Greenwich Meridian, at zero degrees longitude, one foot in the Western hemisphere, the other in the Eastern.

Inside were the Harrison clocks (responsible for the establishment of longitude) a refracting telescope, and a well-documented history of the observatory building. Walking across the grounds I marveled at how well-kept and attractive everything was. The grass was thick and green and smelled like grass, the trees were in full foliage, birds fluttered, people strolled around. It was an oasis of beauty and serenity surrounded by the noise and hustle of small shops, traffic and greater London.

Then to the *Cutty Sark*. Approaching her, you get a sense of how near to perfection the design of clipper ships came. The rigging and hull seem to blend harmoniously in a sleek, graceful presence that captivates the imagination. Her lines are lovely, her presence majestic. Standing on the quarterdeck, one could almost relive her races from China and Australia through the Roaring Forties, around the Cape of Good Hope and up the Channel. Looking up from her main deck, the masts seem to touch the sky as if seeking "a star to steer her by." Thoroughly enchanted, I wrote a postcard home, "Spent the day at Greenwich. Straddled the prime meridian, boarded the *Cutty Sark*. All else is anticlimax."

To cap the day, the ticket taker at the boat landing returned my fare when he saw my crew jacket. *"Jeremiah O'Brien?*

Greenwich, the seat of maritime history for the English-speaking world. This scene was painted in 1750 and comes from their brochure. Compared to the photo on page 258, we see little change.

No charge, mate," he said, ushering me on board with a friendly wave.

Others had different agendas. Marty Wefald, AB and later bosun: "One of the highlights has to be when Carl Nolte and I went to Ascot Race Track, the Royal Ascot, which is somethin' I've never seen before and I'll probably never see again. I didn't win. Not that time, not that day. But I didn't do much betting. It was more of a show than anything else."

Mike Emery: "There was a morning in London I woke up and I realized that this 50-year-old ship had sailed halfway around the world and was in the Pool of London and I was part of it. That was rather remarkable moment for me."

That evening there was a private tour of the engine room on the *O'Brien* for the Foster-Wheeler company, manufacturer of our ship's boilers in 1943. Our engineers showed the boilers off, and the Foster-Wheeler people observed, both with justifiable pride. Then followed a party on *HMS Belfast*.

Many went to the usual tourist spots in London. Here Pat Jahn, left, and Nell Otterberg have their picture taken with a Beefeater at the Tower of London. Photo by Jo Lawrence.

Jean Yates poses with one of the Palace Guards. Photo courtesy Jean Yates.

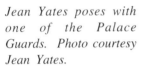

The weather on Saturday, June 18, was slightly cooler with an overcast sky that dissolved to scattered clouds toward evening.

There were more crew changes. Rudy Arellano left suddenly, due to a family emergency, leaving Russ Mosholder short-handed in the galley. Fortunately, Chuck Jennings arrived to work in the deck department and was reassigned to the messroom. Anna Falche, who was so helpful with the Normandy Committee, also arrived.

From the beginning there was the feeling that the ship should charge admission. We had incurred tremendous expenses to make the voyage and there would be more before the trip was over. Also, probably unique among the museum ships and training ships of the world, we were not sponsored by any government organization except for the onetime sale of the scrap ships. Although everyone was an unpaid volunteer, fuel, food, parts, supplies, insurance, postage and countless other items added to the costs of operating the ship. One faction argued that we couldn't charge admission because the port services — pilotage, tugs, berths, water, electricity, garbage — were provided free. Nevertheless, the ship still accumulated $3,000 a day in expenses whether at sea or in port. In London it was agreed with the authorities that any admissions to *HMS Belfast* that were over and above what that ship normally received would be shared with the *O'Brien* on a fifty-fifty basis. It wasn't much but it was a beginning.

Tom Patterson: "We had a very pleasant week in London. We were disappointed with the small number of people, only about 4,000 people that week, Our publicity apparently hadn't got through and the Londoners just didn't know where we were or that we were actually there. But our crew enjoyed London and we certainly enjoyed this prestigious mooring for our ship."

Marci Hooper added: "Coming and leaving during a rail strike was not helpful for press coverage. The media were more concerned with trains than ships at the time."

It was Saturday night. Walking through the passageways after dinner it was obvious what was on the crew's mind. Cheerful whistling and laughter were heard as steam billowed out of the showers and the crew shaved in the open bathrooms. The smell of cologne permeated the air. They padded to their rooms clad in towels and rubber go-aheads, clean, happy and ready to dress for a night on the town, a night out in London. Theaters, pubs, restaurants, Soho, Trafalgar Square, Picadilly all beckoned. We responded with alacrity and off we went, many not to return until much, much later.

Dottie Duncan and Ruth Robson shocked everyone by telling us they got tattoos. Dottie proudly showed hers on her shoulder, but Ruth's was in another place and she wouldn't show it to anyone. Later we learned the designs were appliques, not real tattoos.

The river traffic was a source of unending fascination. It was constant — workboats, tugs and barges chugged past, tour boats with two and three decks of people coasted by. We could hear the guides announcing on the public address system, ". . . the grey-hulled ship made fast to the *Belfast* is a Liberty ship, the *Jeremiah O'Brien*. She has come all the way from San Francisco and is operated by a crew made up entirely of World War II veterans. She has just returned from Normandy, where she was the center of attention and will be with us . . ." In the evenings sleek, modern dinner cruise boats slowly navigated the river as their patrons dined by candlelight. And at all hours harbor police, sailing yachts, motorboats and an occasional jet-ski passed by.

Sunday was the day that Jeremiah O'Brien came to see us. No, it wasn't the ghost of the ship's namesake, come back to haunt. The Jeremiah O'Brien that came aboard was a London cab driver. He was fascinated to read in the paper of a ship bearing the same name and had to see what it looked like. The crew welcomed him, giving him a seat of honor in the messroom. He explained he was born during the Blitz and spent most of his nights sleeping on the platform of the Warren Street underground station to avoid air raids. After school he was indentured as an apprentice compositor in the City of London and continued as a journeyman compositor in the printing trade. Made redundant (forced to retire) in 1982, he became a full time London taxi driver.

Mike Emery (doing the Stan Laurel imitation), Marty Wefald and Marci Hooper enjoy the hospitality of HMS Belfast. *Photo courtesy Marty Wefald.*

London cab driver Jeremiah O'Brien, next to his cab. He was the first Jeremiah O'Brien to visit the ship. There would be others later in the voyage. Photo courtesy NLSM.

Jeremiah was a long-standing family name, his father was also Jeremiah, but he wasn't aware of any connection to Jeremiah O'Brien of Machias, Maine.

That evening a 51st Anniversary party was held in No. 2 hold with canapes and cocktails for our 250 guests. The highlight of the evening was a poem composed by one of our British volunteers, Ron Turner:

Jeremiah, Jeremiah, Jeremiah O'Brien
Built in haste and energy of scrap steel and iron;
Prefabricated, welded, painted silver grey,
Given names of history and launched at one a day.

The need was dire and urgent, Britain we had to save,
Our men gave up their blood and bone and died in a
        watery grave;
Ships, ships, ships the cry went out, we want anything that
        floats;
Give us the tools, as Churchill said, we wanted, needed
        boats.

The cry was heard across the pond they would show what could
        be done,
The shipyards worked as though in hell from dawn to
        setting sun;
Under moonbeams, under cloudy skys the rhythm went apace,
To outpace sunken tonnage was a deadly knife-edge
        race.

But the Yanks they had the enterprise, they had the means, the
    will,
It was their mark in history, their destiny to fill;
Two thousand, seven hundred and another fifty one,
Were turned out from their shipyards, the war was to be won.

They served their time, the Liberties, they sailed on every sea,
Their silhouette synonymous in loving memory;
Their names will live for evermore as a goal that was achieved,
A class of ship that is no more, except for One reprieved.

It's *Jeremiah, Jeremiah, Jeremiah O'Brien,*
You've lasted all the others built of scrap steel and iron;
you've come across the Western at the age of fifty years,
And I call upon the lot of you for three good hearty cheers.

Hip, Hip, Hip, Hooorrraaayyy!

Probably the most memorable event of our stay in London
was a Beating Retreat ceremony held at the Tower of London on
June 20. The invitation was limited to the captain and three
officers. Capt. Jahn, Adm. Patterson, Capt. Otterberg and I donned
our dress blue uniforms. A car and driver were provided which
drove us across Tower Bridge to the Tower of London. The first
sight that caught our attention was the ravens. Sleek, black and
well-fed, they looked almost as big as turkeys. We were met at
the entrance and escorted into the White Tower where drinks and
a finger buffet of *hors d'oeuvres* were provided. A large group
of important guests was at the reception, friendly, courteous and
polite, as always. Surrounded by glass cases of medieval weapons
and suits of armor, we talked and sipped champagne. Then we
were seated around the square outside the White Tower with
Capt. Jahn in a position of honor on the dais. The resident Governor, Major General C. Tyler, CB, welcomed everyone:

It is my pleasure to welcome you to Her Majesty's Palace and
Fortress, The Tower of London, to mark the 50th anniversary of the
D-Day landings.

In a checkered and sometimes bloody history, The Tower has
been a fortress, prison, arsenal, treasure, Royal Observatory and,
above all, a Palace.

During World War II The Tower, like the rest of London, was subjected to constant enemy attacks. Despite suffering three severe bombing raids, it miraculously survived intact. Today it is the home of the Royal Armories, the Regimental Headquarters of the Royal Fusiliers, the Crown Jewels of the realm and the Yeoman Warders, whose role it is to bring 900 years of Royal history to life for the 2.3 million visitors who come to the Tower of London every year.

This evening, Bands from the Adjutant General's Corps and the London Regiment together with the Yeoman Warders pay tribute to those who took part in the Normandy landings. I am sure, like me, you will welcome the opportunity to remember the heroism and sacrifice of D-Day and want to give thanks for all that victory made possible.

He introduced Capt. Jahn as master of a Liberty ship at Normandy and master of the *Jeremiah O'Brien*. We were very proud of our distinguished master.

The Drums and Pipes of the London Regiment, a Territorial Army consisting of companies of the Princess of Wales Royal Regiment, the Royal Regiment of Fusiliers and the London Scottish and London Irish Rifles, gave a stunning marching exhibition, coming in at a diagonal from one corner of the square and marching across and back again to the sound of pipes and flutes. This was followed by a reenactment of the Ceremony of Constable's Dues. Based on an ancient custom dating back to the 14th century, the ceremony represents the paying of dues on the part of any ship moored in the Pool of London and coming under the protection of the Tower. Payment was in the form of a barrel of wine, strung beneath a spar and ceremoniously carried under escort to The Tower to be received by the Constable or his representative. A contingent from *HMS London* did the honors this evening with the recipients being the Resident Governor, the Chief Yeoman Warder, Yeoman Gaoler and Yeoman Warders. A group of sailors from *HMS London* marched across the square, a barrel of wine hanging on ropes swinging from side to side under the oars from which it was hung. On arriving at the Resident Governor's platform, the officer saluted with his sword. The general returned the salute, the sailors set down the keg, about-faced and marched off.

HER MAJESTY'S PALACE AND FORTRESS
THE TOWER OF LONDON

A MILITARY BAND
PERFORMANCE AND
BEATING RETREAT
TO COMMEMORATE
THE 50TH
ANNIVERSARY OF
D-DAY AT THE
TOWER OF LONDON

Monday 20th June, 1994

Next was the Ceremony of Beating Retreat, performed by the Band of the Adjutant General's Corps. Their instruments included bagpipes and they gave a stirring performance, marching in close formation.

The finale of the evening was presented by the combined bands which played several marches, "The Star Spangled Banner," and ended with "God Save the Queen."

On the way out we learned we were to return to our ship by boat and that everyone at the ceremony had been invited to the *O'Brien* for cocktails and a tour. A large, double-decked boat met us at the Tower landing and took us across to the boat landing on *HMS Belfast.* On the *O'Brien,* no one knew about the evening tour, but we muddled through and everyone seemed to enjoy themselves.

Up to this point, our stay in England had been one celebration after another of goodwill, helpfulness, warm hospitality and comrades-across-the-sea. Only one incident occurred to remind us that it wasn't a perfect world. A London newspaper, the *Evening Standard*, published an article based on an interview with one of the crew. In the article, it came out that the ship was short of money and many of the crew were concerned about whether the *O'Brien* would even have enough fuel to return to the United States. The tone of the article was favorable toward the ship and resulted in a few gladly-received donations. Early Tuesday morning, as Rich Reed was organizing the crew to wash down the decks, he was approached by an Englishman who had just come aboard. He said his name was Gary and he was sent by a group of friends from his favorite pub. After reading the article in the paper, his friends took up a collection for the ship — some £160. They were going to bring it to the ship but thought it would be more hospitable to have the crew come to the pub for drinks, dinner and the presentation of the money.

Rich told him it was a great idea and said the crew would be ready to go at three that afternoon. Gary went ashore to arrange transportation and the crew went back to work. Just after lunch Gary returned, saying he had a bus chartered to take the crew to the pub for dinner but the fee was 30 pounds and he was 15 pounds short of making it. Could the crew help out? Rich took up a collection and presented it to Gary. Thanking him, Gary told Rich to have everyone waiting on the curb outside the entrance to the *HMS Belfast* exhibition at 3 p.m. and he would arrive with the bus to pick them up.

The bosun and several of the crew were there at the appointed time. By 3:15 they were getting suspicious, by 3:30 angry. At 4:30 the last of them left, realizing they had fallen for an old trick. It was the only disappointment of the whole trip.

Wednesday, June 22, we would depart London.

Now, Carl Nolte would be leaving the ship. A willing worker with a good sense of humor, he was a favorite with everyone and we were all sad to see him go. His daily reports published in the *San Francisco Chronicle* had helped our families and friends at home share the voyage, and the whole San Francisco Bay Area, as well, was sorry when he had to return to his office. Rich Reed took

The author, right, and Carl Nolte enjoy a cocktail at a reception before Carl's departure. Photo by Elizabeth Wade.

Carl's paint-and-grease-encrusted work pants and hung them from the halyard on the mizzen mast as a tribute. The crew took up a collection and bought Carl a pipe which was presented to him as he left the ship. He snapped to attention, saluted the crew, then the ship, and left.

Carl posted a letter in the messrooms and saloon.

To the people of the *O'Brien:*

What passes for real life calls and I will be leaving the ship to go back to San Francisco on Wednesday, 22 June. My editors say they need me back to chip rust and paint the deck of the *SS San Francisco Chronicle*. They also say I have to stand all the cheap crime and misdemeanor watches I've missed.

Many of you were ashore yesterday visiting the British Museum or some such cultural institution and I haven't been able to shake each of your hands and wish you well. But I do want to thank you for helping me with my *Chronicle* stories, letting me be a part of the life of the ship and being great friends. Playing at sailor was always one of my boyhood fantasies, and, as you may have noticed, I never grew up.

I wish you fair seas and good times on the return voyage, and we'll be in San Francisco on your return. As the song goes, we'll meet again.

Sincerely, Carl Nolte.

Carl Nolte is a fourth generation San Franciscan. His education was in the local school system, including the University of San Francisco from which he received a degree in political science. Carl spent time in Korea, just after the Korean War, as a paralegal for the 51st Signal Battalion (Corps). Returning to San Francisco, he became Public Information Officer for his alma mater, and sports editor of their paper. Carl went to the San Francisco Chronicle in 1960 where he worked as an editor for 18 years, and has been a reporter since. He owns a Monterey fishing boat powered by a one-cylinder engine, and lives in San Francisco.

Karen Kamimoto: "His articles made you feel like you were on the voyage, too. I certainly did. So when Nolte's articles stopped, people all called asking for them back. The publisher of the *Chronicle* thought they would only appeal to a certain demographic. We got calls, our office was inundated, people calling us, the publisher, the editor. People missed those articles."

As with every movement of the ship, all the bridge equipment was tested an hour before sailing. At 1200 the engine room telegraph, whistle, navigation lights, general alarm, p.a. system, telephones and steering were tested and the bridge clock synchronized with that in the engine room. At 1220 the engine room was informed that the propeller was clear, they could test the engine by running it slowly ahead and astern. At 1225 two pilots, Capt. John Morton, who would take us to Gravesend, and Captain Lou Mann, who would take us to the mouth of the Thames, were aboard. At 1252 the engine room was given SBE, Stand By Engines. At the same time the tug *Sun Thomas* was made fast forward. The tug *Anglia* was made fast on the stern two minutes later. At 1302 the last line was thrown off *HMS Belfast*.

There was no room to turn around so Capt. Morton backed through Tower Bridge and down river. He seemed very nervous for some reason, whether it was the idea of being responsible for our museum ship or perhaps some sort of celebration the night before, we couldn't be sure. Unlike our other pilots on the voyage, he was irritable and on edge. With the tug *Anglia* pulling us stern first he gave the order for slow astern. The tide was with us and soon we were going backwards at a good clip down river. Most modern ships are diesel-powered causing them to vibrate and make a lot of noise. By comparison, a steam ship such as ours is deceptively quiet. Diesel ships are also very quick to respond. A steam ship takes time, especially in going from ahead to astern. Apparently Capt. Morton forgot these differences. Approaching the wide place in the river where he wanted to turn us, we were too far to one side and coming down on a buoy much too fast. He gave orders to the *Anglia*. The line between our stern and the tug tightened like a bowstring as the buoy disappeared beneath our counter. It soon appeared on the port side, a few feet away but we were already well into the turning area. Now the tug was rapidly pulling us toward some barges moored farther downstream on the opposite side of the channel. The pilot gave more commands to both tugs and finally ordered our engines stopped, then slow ahead and finally full ahead in rapid succession. Now we were swinging in the other direction again and quickly coming down on a yacht basin containing a floating pier with several cabin cruisers tied up to it. We watched the tachometer needle as it slowly, agonizingly, went from thirty revolutions astern to twenty to ten, then zero — and stayed there. The yacht basin drew closer and closer. Just as I was beginning to imagine the headlines in the next day's papers, the tachometer needle moved ahead, ten, twenty-five, sixty revolutions. The ship's entire hull shook and shimmied as the propeller took hold and the stack started vibrating, rattling in sympathy with the hull. The water astern churned and boiled, turning white with froth as the small boats bounced and strained against their lines. All the while Sven Keinanen, our third mate who replaced Bill Dickerson a few days earlier and was now stationed on the stern, called the distance over the walkie-talkie. "Forty feet. Thirty feet. Twenty feet. Fifteen feet. Twenty feet. Thirty feet."

We breathed a collective sigh of relief.

Tom Patterson: "We left there with rather an exciting trip stern first down the river at about 8 knots, towed by two London tugboats, one trying to pull the ship in half forward and the other trying to pull it in half astern. I think that the *Jeremiah O'Brien*'s crew began to realize what a lucky ship she was when we managed to avoid all the mooring buoys and ships and boats that were moored alongside the river. Captain Jahn, I know, as a master pilot, would not have done it the same way, but luckily we made it without any damage."

Capt. Morton turned the ship and without further mishap took us to Gravesend where he got off, turning the con over to Capt. Mann. By early evening we were out the Thames, past the concrete towers at Tongue Sands, and on our way to Margate. There, Capt. Mann left. We took departure at 2100 with an old friend, Capt. Lukehurst, once again guiding us toward the English Channel and our next port, Cherbourg.

In the messrooms the crew were busy practicing phrases they would need in France. *"Bonjour." "Bon appétit." "Parlez-vous anglais?" "Zoot [Zut] alors!"*

11

CHERBOURG AND THE BEACHES OF NORMANDY

Now, once again, the *Jeremiah O'Brien* sailed to the Normandy coast, heading for Cherbourg, a port at which she last called on September 23, 1944. The Channel was calm, sparkling under sunny skies. The cool air, damp with the sea, carried with it the earthy smell of land. Where warships and liners tossed and sailed on choppy seas in the historic event just two weeks past, today the white sails of private yachts dotted the bright blue waters. Here and there the distant silhouette of a passing freighter was seen on the horizon. In the early afternoon, the low hills of coastal France showed darkly in the distance. As we drew closer, the red rooftops and white buildings of the city itself materialized.

Nearing the harbor entrance, we saw the pilot boat approaching. Soon our harbor pilot, Capt. Pioteri, was aboard accompanied by the Cherbourg Harbormaster, Capt. Heaquat. As usual, we were early, so the pilot kept the engines at slow ahead as we glided through the western entrance to the breakwater. To our right it extended to shore and to our left it ran easterly for more than a mile to a second entrance to the harbor, thence to land. Three castle-like fortifications, now abandoned, were built into the ends and center of the rock wall. The pilot told us that the breakwater protecting the harbor was begun by Louis XVI in 1776 and was built over the years with the labor of British prisoners captured in the many wars between England and France. It was completed during the Second Empire of Napoleon III (1846), giving France a sheltered roadstead as large as the British Royal Navy's in the Solent. During World War II, Germany further fortified the breakwater with pillboxes containing gun emplacements. On this golden afternoon, however, it was not a forbidding fortress of war, but a welcoming haven into the harbor of Cherbourg.

We moored at the *Quai de France*, the terminal for the magnificent trans-Atlantic liners of years gone by. Ordering a tug made fast on the stern, the pilot turned the ship and backed us toward the berth. A large crowd was gathered on the pier and as the first lines went out they applauded. The ship drew alongside and a military band, in dark blue uniforms with can-shaped de Gaulle hats, struck up "The Star Spangled Banner." We secured the lines, rang off Finished With Engines and, suddenly, we were in France. It was 8 p.m. and we were on French double summer time. The sun was still high. It wouldn't get dark until after ten.

The *O'Brien*'s accommodation ladders are permanently rigged on the starboard side. Because we were port side to, we needed gangways from shore. These were lowered into place by a shore crane and the band came aboard, set up on the flying bridge and played marches.

Tom Patterson: "We arrived in Cherbourg on the twenty-third of June and started a two week period which none of us will ever, ever forget. Our arrival was timed to coincide with the fiftieth anniversary of their liberation from the Nazis, the twenty-sixth of June."

Friday, June 24, and daylight came well before six a.m., a clear, warm day with blue skies and a slight breeze. The first sights that greeted us were several fleets of sailboats scattered around the harbor. Each group consisted of seven or eight one-person boats propelled by a single sail. Within each group were several small boats manned by school children and a larger one, equipped with sail and motor, operated by their teacher. Several times each day during our stay we saw the larger boats towing their "flock" of smaller boats, tied bow to stern, to and from the center of the harbor — like mother ducks with their progeny. Sailing was a required course in the local school system.

From the ship, the crew surveyed this first French port, eagerly anticipating the chance to go ashore and practice the phrases they had studiously memorized. François Le Pendu, our French-born fireman/watertender, had given them some useful phrases including *"Un biere s'il vous plaît"* meaning "one beer please."

A large passenger terminal dominated the pier. Once bustling with travelers from the luxury liners such as the *Queen Mary*, the *France,* the *United States*, now the cavernous rooms with rows of dark kiosks, empty perfume counters, and dusty snack bars sat silent on dry, pale wood floors that had not seen a coat of wax for decades. In an adjacent room, equally large and dank, stretched two wooden tables, hundreds of feet long. One could envision the customs officials opening and examining the luggage of impatient travelers. Rail lines, rusty and weed-grown with disuse led to platforms under a vast barn-like steel-and-glass canopy, evoking images of shrilly-whistling black steam trains loading passengers for exotic, far away cities on the Continent.

Capt. Jahn and Adm. Patterson were soon off to make courtesy calls on the local French Naval commander, the Captain of the Port, the Mayor and others. Wearing dress blue uniforms they were chauffeured in a private car donated by our agent in France, Worms Services Maritime. Our dignitaries were followed in very short order by the off-duty crew going ashore for their courtesy calls on the shops, bars and restaurants of Cherbourg.

On the opposite side of the pier from the *Jeremiah O'Brien* was another waterway, the entrance to the inner harbor of Cherbourg. A yacht harbor colorfully marked its opposite shore leading past floating public piers through a small draw bridge to an inner harbor in the center of town. It was a short walk from the ship across this bridge directly into downtown Cherbourg's narrow, cobblestoned streets lined with shops, bistros, sidewalk cafes and creperies. Shopping in this old part of town meant walking through streets suffused with heavenly aromas — the scent of fresh-baked bread from the boulangeries, their windows piled high with loaves, round, long, seeded — coffee, chocolate, fresh fruits and flowers. Patés, sausages, cheeses, pastries and wines were gaily displayed in the windows of charcuteries, fromageries, pâtisseries and wine shops. Tables and chairs under colorful awnings lined the sidewalks of many restaurants, especially those fronting the harbor. Tuesday, Thursday and Saturday were market days with farmers' stands set up in the Place de Gaulle in and around the main theater and fountain — kaleidoscopes of fresh-cut flowers, fish, produce, sausages, fresh bread and rolls, cheeses, cakes and croissants. The crew was ecstatic and spent much of their free time wandering the streets, sampling the color — and the food. On any given day you might find Wes Masterson or Ron Robson coming out of a boulangerie with a loaf of bread, Tim Palange or Bill Rowlands or Ron Smith trying his luck in the casino, Eduardo Pubill or Chuck Jennings sampling a crepe at a restaurant or second engineer Bill Maus shopping at Printemps, the largest department store in the region. For those interested in history there was the statue of Napoleon overlooking the harbor and the nearby Trinity Basilica dating from the 11th century.

Cherbourg is a major ferry port and every day we saw several of these massive ships entering and leaving the harbor, each as large as an ocean liner. Their bow doors began opening even before the ship was alongside, great massive hinged mouths that yawned at the front of the ship to allow cars to drive off and on. In the evening, the blue and white P&O ferries arrived from England, nosing into a berth closer to town. After a few hours they departed, returning again the following evening. Less frequent was the boat from Ireland, green and white with a shamrock on its stack, tying up across the harbor. Occasionally, a grander P&O ship, but a ferry nonetheless, arrived from Bilbao.

Saturday was cooler with a somber overcast sky and a slight wind blowing. As it was a weekend we were inundated with visitors, with more than 5300 aboard. We still weren't charging admission but we had our donation barrel strategically placed at the gangway.

France definitely presented us with a different culture. The children were much more free-spirited than the British, running, shouting, nosing into everything. And their parents were far more curious, opening doors, looking in portholes and wandering off the blue line tour. One surprising discovery was how attached they are to their pets. Many French people brought dogs on board, as often as not carrying the animal the entire time they were on the ship. On several occasions we saw women carrying baskets and shopping bags with a small dog inside, its head sticking out as it viewed the surroundings.

We had a few French-speaking people on board — François Le Pendu from the engine room, Julie Arlinghaus, a National Park Service employee on loan to us, Clifford Hook, and Susannah Beckwith. Their talents were constantly needed to translate for the many French people who came on board to thank us. As in England, with tears in their eyes, our visitors told stories of the occupation, showed us old photographs and newspaper clippings, and expressed their gratitude to America for liberating them. This was another revelation to us. In England, the thanks were for our help and for saving them from the

NATIONAL LIBERTY SHIP MEMORIAL

JEREMIAH O'BRIEN

50ème ANNIVERSAIRE DU DEBARQUEMENT
DE NORMANDIE 1944-1994

ports d'escale

ANGLETERRE
Portsmouth
Southampton
Chatham
Londres

FRANCE
Cherbourg
Rouen
Le Havre

**Présentation du navire
&
plan de la visite**

The French version of the self-guided tour brochure. It was translated for us by Lee Curtis of The Wordmill in Healdsburg, California.

threat of Nazi domination. But the French had actually lived and suffered from the Nazi oppression and, even fifty years later, their gratitude to the United States for liberating them was heartfelt and sincere. The crew, unready for such an outpouring, was embarrassed. Such emotional displays were outside our experience. In time, we learned to accept them with understanding and empathy.

Bill Bennett: "In France I had not one single person mention any animosity toward the enemy, the Germans. All they did was talk about what we did for them. That had an effect on me I think I'll have the rest of my life. That's special."

Bob Gisslow: "What surprised me was the interest in the ship and in the past events by both the British and the French people. And especially the French who, in Normandy, remember so vividly their portion of the war. They had lost their freedom and are very thankful and expressed their thanks to us for being part of that [their liberation]."

Mike Emery: "I think one of the unexpected things was the response that we got from the British and the French, the old sailors who pointed out their fo'c'sle and their seat in the mess and where they slept. And to see the look of gratitude and the real feeling of nostalgia on the faces of the French and British sailors who had spent time on Liberty ships, and then taking them down to the ship's store and finding the history of their ship in one of our books."*

Sven Keinanen, our third mate from London through Le Havre, also found the French experience moving: "The highlight of this trip is that the people in France were most friendly, they were most thankful and they extended a warm welcome to the Americans. They treated us very, very gloriously and were interested in who was a veteran on the ship. They usually wanted to take a picture of that veteran or have him sign some of their pamphlets."

---

*After World War II, the United States sold hundreds of layed-up Libertys to foreign countries. These became the foundation of the burgeoning maritime industry of Russia, Greece, England, France and other countries.

Russ Mosholder: "I think in France one of the highlights was the younger generation coming up to me and talking and saying 'thank you.' And it happened more than once."

Someone came from shore looking for Sven Keinanen to return his crew identification, wallet and an envelope containing several hundred dollars' worth of francs. Sven lost them the night before, he knew not where. The Frenchman found them and made a special trip to the ship to be sure they were returned. Sven was touched at the gesture and thanked the man effusively. He wouldn't take a reward.

Sunday, June 26, was the 50th anniversary of the liberation of Cherbourg. To commemorate the event we began preparation for something planned many months earlier by Jean-Paul Caron, owner of the DUKW that came over as our deck cargo. In 1944 the normal port facilities for handling cargo were unusable after Allied bombing and German sabotage. Because Cherbourg was the only deep water port in Allied hands as the armies advanced, it was essential to find a way to get food, stores and ammunition off the ships and onto trucks. The answer was the DUKW, the amphibious version of the GMC 2½ ton truck. A "merry-go-round" was established, with DUKWs travelling out to Liberty ships anchored outside the harbor, accepting a cargo lowered by the ship's booms and travelling back to improvised ramps where they clambered out onto dry land and were unloaded by mobile cranes, or even other DUKWs fitted with A-frames. This final trans-shipment took place on the town foreshore near the statue of Napoleon and the area became known to irreverent American servicemen as "Nap and the Ducks."

One of the DUKW crew members, Dewane J. Englerth, was a veteran of the Cherbourg liberation. He recalled what it was like in 1944: "About two weeks later [after the landing at Omaha] we came back to the beach to run amphibious boats that we called 'ducks.' They could haul about five to seven tons of cargo. There were two twelve-hour shifts and I had the night shift. We were bombed and shot at by Germans about twice each night for three months. We ate 'K' rations and had little time to clean up or rest. We each dug a hole or a trench in the ground about a foot deep and that's where we slept.

"One morning when I got back to my trench, there was a hole through my blankets. I looked to see what had made the hole and found a piece of shrapnel about a foot long and an inch thick. It had gone all the way through my bedding and into the ground. I dug it out and carried it with me for a while, but finally threw it away. I was sure glad that I'd been working nights!

"About three months after the invasion the armed forces took over the boat docks from the Germans in Cherbourg. I think that this was the first dock opened, which meant that the big boats could come in and dock to unload. We didn't need to operate the 'ducks' anymore. By this time the Allied Forces were almost to Germany.

"We lost a lot of 'ducks' but we did our jobs well, keeping the front lines supplied with ammunition, gas, food, and bombs for the Air Force (some weighed a ton). All the while we were being bombed and fired upon by the Germans. After the opening of the docks, I became a truck mechanic and life became a little easier."

Tom Patterson: "*Jeremiah O'Brien* went out, dropped the anchor, and then our deck department manned no. 3 hatch and we off-loaded the specially made up dummy palletized cargo, 37 pallet loads, painted olive drab, all given to us by Stan Flowers through General Tripp."

As the crew began removing the crates from no. 3 hatch and setting them on deck, a BBC film crew came aboard. They were producing a film on the six types of transportation that were essential to winning the war. The Liberty ship, the DUKW and the 2½ ton truck were three of them, so in one fell swoop they would

The dummy cargo, suitably marked, for the DUKW operation. Bob Burnett, right, watches rigging off-camera.

cover half their subjects. (The others were the DC3, the landing craft and the jeep.)

In the city of Cherbourg, *Jeremiah O'Brien* veterans who served in World War II, including Art Taber, Bill Williams, Richard Hill and Wes Masterson, were marching as an honored contingent in a big civic parade. The streets were lined with enthusiastic citizens cheering and waving flags at each passing group.

Bill Rowlands: "Marching in the parade with the veterans at Cherbourg, with the different bands and what-have-you, walking down some of those medieval streets it seemed like the veterans of the *Jeremiah O'Brien* always got a louder ovation."

Jean Yates agreed: "When we were in the parade I had that same feeling, you know, these people were throwing flowers at you and clapping. As soon as we broke away from the grandstand, and got away from the officials and spectators along the

The Jeremiah O'Brien *veterans march past the statue of Napoleon in Cherbourg. Our crew drew the largest ovation. Photo by Mike Emery.*

The parade in Cherbourg was a moving experience. Note the difference in expressions between, left to right, Art Taber, Jean Yates and the French soldier. Photo by Mike Emery.

side, you heard the applause. Then the other veterans kind of followed behind us, a lot of French veterans. But, you know, it kinda gets to you. When we got near the buses, everything sort of broke up, people milled about shaking hands and everything and some little French woman came up to me and said, 'Where were you in Normandy?' And it broke my heart to tell her that I was in China, for God's sakes. My war was in China. I thought for a moment I should lie to her but there was no point in doing that. But, you know, I had the feeling that I had disappointed that woman, I let her down. She didn't speak that good English, I certainly don't speak any French but I tried to explain to her, I said, you know, it was a big war and we went where we were sent and we all did the best we could to win that war. It's part of the emotion that you have in this whole great big trip, you know. It all goes together."

Bill Duncan: "At the end of the parade, I got separated from the rest of the groups and people stopped and surrounded me, asking me for my autograph. An older woman was with a young girl, her granddaughter, who said, 'my grandmother said she washed your clothes in 1944.' I explained that I landed in Rouen, not Cherbourg, but the grandmother insisted, no, no I was that same person. I said, 'Well, madame, if you had washed my clothes in 1944, I probably would have married you.' They wanted to have some association, some contact, some kind of feeling. Even the young kids, even the youngsters, know all about how America came over and helped. I was very appreciative of that."

Around noon we left the pier and anchored out in the harbor. While we waited, the crew got busy with chalk, marking up the cargo with World War II slogans, "Kilroy was here." "Another bomb for Hitler." "Berlin or Bust." Then the DUKWs began assembling. Each was painted with authentic markings and the crew in each one was dressed in period uniforms, steel helmets, .45 automatics in leather holsters, khakis and combat boots.

One DUKW owner, who prefers to remain anonymous, described the scene: "There was a colorful and poignant parade in the morning by veterans, town dignitaries and bands — with the roads closed, as is taken for granted in France. By noon, the collection of GMC 2½ tonners was gathering, augmented by smaller Dodge ammo carriers and two larger articulated trucks, a Studebaker and an Autocar. We had six DUKWs available, less than hoped for, but which proved to be exactly the right number. As we came out from lunch — it was France, you can't rush that — we saw that the *Jeremiah O'Brien* had moved from her berth to the expected anchorage."

The first load went over the side of the *O'Brien* at 1430 with the BBC capturing the event on film, the crew photographing it from the decks of the ship, the DUKW drivers shooting it from their vehicles, and the public on the pier pointing their cameras.

The DUKW owner continues: "The transshipment area on the green was fenced off with efficiency, we stripped the canvas tilts and the hood hoops from the DUKWs, took our places for the show, and at 2.30 p.m. sharp, Bob James' DUKW splashed down the ramp. It had been agreed at the briefing that, as he would have a TV crew on board for his first trip, we, as second DUKW into the water, became the first to go alongside the ship for cargo.

This photo of our recreation of "Nap and the ducks," looks like it was taken in 1944 rather than 1994.

View from the DUKW toward the O'Brien. *That's Chuck Jennings on the left facing the camera. Photo by Jean Yates.*

"This was a stressful moment, as up until then we had not actually practiced receiving a load lowered to us by fifty-one-year-old steam winches, but the *Jeremiah O'Brien* has not been maintained by enthusiasts in vain. She performed perfectly. The control of each box was exact, and our two stevedores had no difficulty positioning them in the DUKW."

As the first DUKW was loaded and motored toward the beach, the second came alongside. Watching through the binoculars, we saw the first drive out of the water. "We took the cargo back to the ramp and drove ashore with 'the first load for the liberation of St. Lô,' blowing our airhorn and responding to the crowd's delight."

By the time the second rotation of unloadings was underway, some of our crew began climbing down the ladder for a ride on a DUKW. The last load went off at 1630 as planned. Then all the trucks and DUKWs made a triumphal circuit of downtown Cherbourg. "Even when moving, we were mobbed by cheering crowds in a way reminiscent of 1944."

Russ Mosholder: "One of the most memorable things of the trip happened to me when I was on the DUKW. I rode the DUKW through Cherbourg and I was standing up. I kind of backed off from it at first, when I seen what was happening, 'cause I had my American Legion cap on and everybody on the DUKW kept pointing towards me 'cause I was the older person. They said no, this is what they want to see. There was 30,000 plus and we went around that town twice. Hundreds of people run up to me and wanted me to sign papers, they wanted me to touch their children, and they would wave at me."

The streets were decorated with flags, bunting and large photographs taken during the actual liberation in 1944. It was the liberation all over again with crowds in the streets, people waving and cheering from windows and accompanying tears of joy. And it wasn't just the French. We, too, got caught up in the realization of what the liberation meant to France, even fifty years later, and understood a little more how important it was that we had come. The common bond of understanding linked us and the language barrier fell as we all wept and rejoiced together, just as we had in Southampton.

Ruth Robson: "They all wanted to touch Russ because he was a veteran. Anybody that was a veteran in any one of the DUKWs got the same treatment. We were a symbol of America to them. We weren't necessarily the *Jeremiah O'Brien,* we were Americans, we were America, and they were thanking us, thanking America. We were representing the United States. It was a great honor to be there and be in that position. I kind of think about it in that way, that some day I can say to my nieces and nephews, that I was there."

Jean-Paul Caron: "Cherbourg heavily advertised this unique performance . . . We were able to set up without any training, a super show attracting a crowd of 32,000 wonderful spectators viewing seven DUKWs unloading *SS Jeremiah O'Brien* and transferring the cargo to the legendary Red Ball Express Convoy reenacted for the occasion. The all affair has been total adventure and every participant made it with his guts, such as this Federal Truck driver of the Red Ball who had to rebuild his engine two time on the side of the road to participate. The reward was the incredible welcoming of the cheering crowd."

Tom Patterson: "The ducks and cargo rolled into town and the townspeople were just going absolutely ecstatic with this re-enactment. Everybody was hugging and kissing, it looked like a scene out of a World War II newsreel."

Marci Hooper: "People would come up and ask to have pictures taken with their children, ask to have their programs signed by our veterans. I hitched a ride on one of the vehicles and took the Red Ball Express through town. People were five and seven deep in some places waving flags and clapping and cheering, We'll never understand what it meant to them. The route was over a mile and it was amazing. And all these little kids, 'autograph please, autograph please.'"

We returned to the pier at 4:30 that Sunday to find a mob of people waiting on the dock. As soon as the gangways were in place, people swarmed on board, anxious to see the ship. Unfortunately, shortly after the first surge we had to cut them off — the

Lord Mayor was throwing a catered private party in no. 2 'tween deck (which no one on board knew about) to welcome the ship to Cherbourg. The people on the dock shouted their disappointment. Finally the Lord Mayor went down among them and after several minutes of shouting and hand waving the crowd calmed down and began to drift away.

Without the daily update in the *Chronicle*, KFS' *Jeremiah O'Brien* line, as the only direct source of information on the voyage, was busier than ever. Without their support and the grant from Pacific Telesis our friends and families would have starved for news.

> Crews News
> June 25, 1994
> This is the Voice of the *Jeremiah O'Brien*.
> Good evening, San Francisco.
> Almost 6,000 citizens of the Cherbourg area visited *Jeremiah O'Brien* today. Some of these good people were part of the hundreds that attempted to visit the ship as late as 10:30 PM last evening. We reluctantly explained that visiting hours ended at 9 PM and that in order to inspect the ship they must return today; and they did, in most satisfying numbers. Ron Robson reported that the ship's store had a very good day with purchases inclined towards the O'Brien coffee mugs and especially the "Back to the Beaches" tee shirts depicting the landing on the Normandy beaches fifty years ago.

Even Capt. Jim Nolan, former master of the *Jeremiah O'Brien*, called the "Voice" to find out what was happening on the ship. "Sometimes I called from home or, if I was in Virginia, teaching piloting, I'd call from Little Creek. That number was a good service, a good idea."

Ron Robson: "I had some very moving experiences in Cherbourg on the night of the fiftieth anniversary of their liberation. It was 11 p.m. and the church bells started ringing. Then people began coming out of their shuttered houses in twos and threes, walking down these narrow old cobblestoned streets to the common area where there was a fireworks display. To hear the church bells and to hear the sound system playing, mostly American music, it was phenomenal. The music was choreographed to

Gérald Guétat et Eric Ledru

LES CARGOS DE LA VICTOIRE
l'épopée des Liberty ship

le Jeremiah O'Brien
journal de guerre et renaissance

préface d'Etienne Taillemite

S.P.M.

The Jeremiah O'Brien *story in French. Gérald Guétat did a remarkable job of telling our story in this book, which was sold in the ship's store.*

the fireworks in a very professional manner and it was memorable."

While the people of Cherbourg were visiting the *O'Brien*, the *O'Brien*'s crew was visiting Cherbourg. Every day and night, the crew was out exploring and enjoying the attractions of the city. Starting just across the swing bridge at the tourist office they branched out into Old Town to window shop or enjoy the restaurants overlooking the harbor or the theater and town square. Others stopped for coffee, beer, pastries, cakes and croissants. Many brought back Normandy cheeses and Calvados, the apple brandy for which the region is famous.

While the crew was off on their excursions, one member had his own special destination. Jim Wade: "I became personally involved with the cathedral in Cherbourg. I was invited to attend mass at the cathedral and then was thrilled when I discovered that I was to be a co-celebrant. It was announced to the congregation that Sunday that I was from the *Jeremiah O'Brien* and the reception I got from the people administering the sacraments during the mass and then the smiles and warmth of the handshakes as they left the cathedral at the main exit was an honor."

Still others in the crew found unusual companions. Bob Burnett: "I remember the cat that came aboard and visited with me in Cherbourg when I had the midnight watch. She hopped up on my lap and she was company."

Monday was relatively quiet. Being a working day there were far fewer visitors. We were told the *QE2* would be arriving that evening and we would have to vacate our berth to make room for her.

The other DUKWs had departed but Jean-Paul Caron stayed to help, parking his "Little Feather" on the dock alongside the ship. He was valuable as a translator and for his knowledge of the ins and outs of French business. There were other new faces on board. Jean-Paul had a helper, a young Norwegian named Eric who helped maintain the DUKW. They both began eating in the messroom and using the ship's facilities. Marci Hooper had hired a French public relations specialist to work for the ship, Maud Paléologue. She helped in advance publicity, arranging for and inviting the right people to parties, and also served as translator, handling many difficult situations in the days to come. Gérald Guétat, an author, was also a volunteer translator. They were very valuable to us, and all contributed their services. But, from the crew perspective, all these French volunteers simply appeared one day, were eating the ship's food and using the ship's facilities and taking up space, and no one knew what their purpose was. It was the old problem of lack of communication. It had grown since our arrival and would continue to grow during our stay in France, the language barrier adding another level of complexity.

At the request of Ron Robson, a department head meeting was called, the first since our departure from San Francisco. Rich Reed started the discussion off and got right to the point. He said there was a need for better communication between the Board of Directors, management and the crew. For example, hardly anyone knew about the party in no. 2 hold the night before. The need to know was obvious. People who work these events have to be able to plan for them. We couldn't schedule people to act as waiters

The QE2 *arrives after we left our berth to make room for her.*

and bartenders, to clean up, to open the store if they didn't know when events were going to happen.

Also, as concerned volunteers, the crew needed to know and had a right to know who all the strangers were on board. What was their purpose? What was the impact on food planning and berthing? The steward and galley crew were swamped with unexpected guests and new volunteers. Underlying this was the crew's continued sense of possessiveness about the ship. It was their ship, their home. They had sailed it across the ocean, tended the engines in 130° heat, scraped and painted and guided visitors, giving up home and family for months. Now, strangers were appearing, and settling in without "paying their dues."

The rest of the meeting dealt with routine items but the overall effect was good because it let everyone voice what was on their minds. However, the communication problems weren't over.

We left the pier at 1800 and anchored near the breakwater, awaiting the arrival of the *QE2*. Perhaps the calm seas, the clear blue skies and the warm weather stimulated romance. Perhaps because it was France, and summer time — whatever the reason, love was in the air. The *Jeremiah O'Brien* has something of a reputation as a "love boat." Since leaving the Reserve Fleet, several permanent relationships have developed among the volunteers and this voyage was no exception. In London Russ Mosholder had invited Ruth Robson out to dinner. Now they were seen together more and more frequently. Hand-in-hand they watched from the main deck as the *QE2* appeared in the distance.

Russ Mosholder: "I think I'm a pretty lucky person. I met Ruth. I wasn't looking for anybody. Very positively wasn't looking for anybody, but that just kind of fell in and I don't know why.

I never really thought. I just wanted to go to dinner once in England and I didn't want to go alone. She happened to be the most logical one my age to ask. So it looks like we will be together for quite a while. I feel very lucky."

Tim Palange, our first engineer, had strong feelings for Maria Bosch, an English girl who came aboard in Chatham. She was now working as a volunteer in the engine room and living aboard with her mother, Beryl, who had also come to help. Now, Beryl and Ed Lingenfield, one of our firemen, sat side-by-side on a bench on the main deck, watching the great liner arrive. They, too, were an item.

Tim Palange: "I made a new girlfriend, Maria Bosch, and it may become a permanent thing." And, jumping ahead in the story a little, it was. Tim and Ed and the two ladies from Chatham were married, in England, Ed in December 1994 and Tim in January 1995.

Mike Emery: "Ed Lingenfield went and found a war bride in Chatham after finding one fifty years ago in Australia. Women came on board and fell in love with American men, and our crew went ashore and fell in love with the foreign women. Nothing had really changed in the last fifty years."

Tuesday, June 28 started with the crew washing down the deck after breakfast. The *QE2* sailed before dawn, so at 0930 we shifted back to our old berth. This was the day I discovered the *Alabama* museum. Set on the second floor at the back of the city's theater is a museum dedicated to the American Civil War raider, *CSS Alabama*. Commanded by Raphael Semmes, this ship was the most notorious of the Confederate raiders, plundering and burning Yankee shipping from Java to Madagascar and throughout the Atlantic Ocean. In 1864, after sinking and capturing 68 Northern vessels she came into Cherbourg for repairs. The French authorities allowed the ship in but her presence caused consternation among Union representatives in France. A telegram was sent to Capt. John A. Winslow aboard the *USS Kearsarge* in Flushing, New York. He sailed immediately for Cherbourg and set up a blockade outside the three mile limit. The *Alabama* was forced to leave to avoid internment. The citizenry of Cherbourg knew a battle was imminent and lined the breakwaters in anticipation. They were soon rewarded. Just outside the territorial waters, the ships began firing at a range of 2,000 yards from each other, sailing in ever-smaller circles around one another until at 600 yards the *Alabama*'s engines were hit. She soon sank with Capt. Semmes and his crew being rescued by the British yacht *Deerhound*. The museum displays include glass-encased models of both ships, paintings of the battle and re-

Wes Masterson goes over the side to touch up the ship's name on the stern. Courtesy Bev and Wes Masterson.

cently-salvaged artifacts from the sunken Rebel raider. It was a fascinating history of a little-known event in America's past.

The crew continued grumbling about the lack of communication and the "interlopers." It may be that with fewer visitors (600 to 800 on weekdays) and less to do the crew had more time on their hands. Perhaps there was an element of frustration at not understanding what most of the visitors to the ship were talking about. Then, too, for some reason, the two women from Chatham were a source of futility to the engine crew. Maria Bosch suffered less because she always wore coveralls and worked with the first assistant engineer. She was trying to carry her weight as a volunteer. Her mother had a more difficult time, trying to help in the ship's store, then the messroom and finally working as a wiper for the engine room. It was a problem and embarrassing for everyone. Then, to add to the angst, Jean-Paul Caron, set off by something, stormed across the afterdeck one day, threatening to quit working so hard for the ship.

The lighter crowds gave the deck department a chance to get back to the normal routine of washdown, garbage and stores, repairing and touching up. We were almost constantly in a state of "dress ship" with brightly-colored signal flags strung from bow to stern across the tops of the masts, our corporate sponsors' flags flying at the halyards and our largest American flag at the gaff. Winds changing direction and velocity shredded the older flags and blew others into gooey, slush-laden cargo runners, topping lifts and wire antennas. Quite a bit of time was spent cutting old or torn flags out of the strings, laundering them to get the grease marks out or replacing them with new. The job of repair fell to Phil Sinnott, our "flag AB," while Bill Bennett took on the chore of removing grease marks. The ship's name on the stern was scratched and marked by the wires from the tugs. This meant rigging a bosun's chair and sending someone (Sam Wood, Marty Wefald or Wes Masterson) over the side to repaint "*Jeremiah O'Brien*, Portland, Maine."*

When the anchor was weighed to come in from waiting for the *QE2* it was fouled with cables dredged up from the bottom of the harbor. These had to be cleared. The engine department used the time to open the bearings to the main engine for a visual inspection. Dick Brannon supervised Tim Palange, Bill Maus, Bill Duncan, the Mooney brothers and others in this work.

Everyone was looking forward to visiting the Normandy battle scenes. Our whole voyage was a "Return to Normandy" but, so far, all we had seen was a distant bluff from our offshore anchorage on June 6. Now the opportunity arrived.

A local bus company donated two sets of tours, complete with an English-speaking guide. Half the crew would go on one day, the other half the next day. Al Martino, Jimmy Farras and Eduardo Pubill made sandwiches and packed bag lunches for those making the trip.

We boarded the bus after breakfast, settling into the comfortable red and blue velvet seats. The vehicle was well-equipped with small television monitors suspended from the overhead, a restroom and large windows. Soon we were on our way through the streets of Cherbourg and out into the countryside of Nor-

---

*American ships are always registered in the port in which their owners reside. Technically, the *O'Brien*'s owner is the United States Government. Because so many ships were built by the government during World War II, they were registered in the port of construction rather than Washington, D.C.

mandy. Once we left the main highway the narrow roads delved through rich green pastureland, hedgerows and apple orchards. We frequently slowed as oncoming traffic pulled aside to let us pass. Occasionally there were herds of dairy cattle, at one point blocking the road itself. Our driver, through the guide, pointed out that these were French cattle known for the quality of their butter and cheese. We passed many small homes and hamlets of up to a dozen houses. Beneath each window was box of bright red geraniums and over each doorway were two, three and sometime four flagstaffs with the standards of France, America, the United Kingdom and Canada waving in the breeze.

Our first stop was Utah Beach. We were dropped at the entrance to the war museum, a modern, sandy-colored building with sloping roofs that fit well with the low sand hills fronting the beach. At the entrance were tanks and cannon left over from the war. Inside we saw that the foundation of the museum was the top of a former German gun emplacement. Photographs, displays and artifacts evoked that "longest day" fifty years earlier. Outside, several of the crew walked down to the beach, a long, gently-sloping expanse of hard-packed sand. It was low tide and in the distant surfline we saw tractors pulling in fishermens' nets. Closer to shore, a horse and sulky trotted, working out in the fresh sea air. It was difficult to imagine that this had been the scene of part of the greatest military landing in history.

Jim Wade's first trip to sea was in 1942 as a hospital corpsman bound for Britain. After the war ended he shipped out as a purser on a T-3 tanker. The responsibilities of raising a family then brought him ashore. He recently retired from a product development corporation and devotes himself to the *Jeremiah O'Brien* and his profession as unsalaried priest. Jim and his daughter, Elizabeth, also a ship's volunteer, live in San Leandro, California.

Jim Wade: "Thinking back to 50 years ago, thousands of young men went across that channel and they would never come back alive. Some of them are still there buried in the cemeteries. That was extremely moving. And also is reason to resolve that hopefully we will never see a conflagration like that again. I think remembrance of war is important if you remember it to avoid it again. I think this is what the celebration, especially in England and France, amounted to. A resolve that this should never happen again. Santayana said that those who don't remember their history are doomed to repeat it. And I think the French people in particular, because they had gone through occupation from 1939 until 1944 and some areas 1945, maybe this is why they were so more outspoken about their gratitude than the English. The English were very thankful that we had saved their country. The French were very grateful because we had liberated them."

The bus took us to

Left to right, Jim Conwell and Russ Mosholder, during one of our frequent excursions. Photo courtesy of Jim Conwell.

a nearby park where we ate our brown bag lunches and sipped short bottles of French wine. Then it was off to the village of St. Mère Église. A picturesque town, with narrow cobblestoned streets, its two and three story homes and shops are set around a large square. Our first stop was the church in the center of the square on whose steeple American paratrooper Private Steele hung by his parachute for two hours playing dead the night of the first Normandy landings. We were surprised to see a mannequin hanging by parachute from exactly the same spot. Inside, the church's stained glass windows depicted parachutists descending from the sky. St. Mère Église was the first French village liberated on June

L'équipage du Jeremiah O'Brien en visite à Utah et à Sainte-Mère

Le contre-amiral Thomas J. Patterson et son équipage sont en escale à Cherbourg, à bord du Liberty Ship, le Jeremiah O'Brien.

Ils sont venus et revenus en Normandie pour les cérémonies du cinquantenaire et le bateau-musée ouvert au public est reparti hier en direction de Rouen, puis Le Havre, et rentrera à San-Francisco, son quartier général.

Ce navire a été construit en 1943 à Portland dans le Maine (USA), en 56 jours (longueur 135 mètres, largeur 18 mètres). Le liberty-ship, le Jeremiah O'Brien a participé à de nombreux convois entre la côte Est des USA et la Grande-Bretagne avec des cargaisons de munitions, céréales et divers. En juin 1944, il effectua entre l'Angleterre et les plages d'Utha Beach, onze navettes avec des chargements de munitions, vivres et matériel.

Sur 2.710 liberty-ship construits entre 1941 et 1945, il n'y eut que deux « rescapés », le John W. Bron et le Jeremiah O'Brien, qui furent plus tard déclarés « monuments historiques » et exposés au musée de San Francisco. Il y a une douzaine d'années, le contre-amiral Thomas J. Patterson, président de la commis-

sion de marine marchande a décidé de remettre en état ce bateau-musée ouvert au public.

Ainsi, pour le cinquantenaire, l'équipage ayant navigué à bord du Jeremiah en 1944. Ce bateau a navigué seulement trois ans, jusqu'en 1946, puis il est resté 35 ans dans la baie de San Francisco.

A Sainte-Marie-du-Mont (Utah Beach), comme à Sainte-Mère-Église, l'équipage a été reçu par le maire de la commune. A Utah, comme à Sainte-Mère, ils ont eu le plaisir de découvrir une maquette du liberty-ship, confectionné par des maquettistes passionnés. A Utah, c'est Yves Osmont qui a offert la maquette au musée d'Utah, à l'occasion du cinquantenaire et à Sainte-Mère-Église, c'est M. Dupuis qui l'a offert, il est exposé à la mairie en s'appelle le « Sainte-Mère ».

L'équipage a été ému devant ces petits liberty-ship si bien reproduits. Après la réception à la mairie, ils ont visité le musée de Sainte-Mère-Église, ils font ainsi le tour des plages du débarquement.

L'équipage devant la borne 0.

RAVENOVILLE

Méchoui du comité des fêtes

Le comité des fêtes de Ravenoville que préside Michel Ber- dimanche 17 juillet à 12 h 30

The French newspapers carried an article with pictures of the crew at our visit to Omaha and St. Mère Église. From La Presse de la Manche.

6, 1944 and their gratitude to the 82nd Airborne has never dimmed. Nearby was a large museum filled with mementos of the war: a glider, a cargo plane, mannequins in uniform, clothing, munitions, weapons, posters, photographs and, outside, tanks, half-tracks and other vehicles. In the nearby shops and stores were postcards, books, wine, scarves, hats and countless other souvenirs depicting the liberation.

In the afternoon we drove to the Hotel De Ville, the city hall,* where Mayor Marc Lefevre invited us into the reception hall for a glass of wine. Surprisingly, after a few brief remarks in French, he left. Our guide explained that, as they were a small town, the mayor was also the veterinarian and he had a sick cow to attend. Finishing our wine, we returned to the bus and were soon once more driving along the narrow country roads. At one

---

*In the city hall was a model of the Liberty ship, *St. Mère Église*. Most French Liberty ships were named after cities and towns in Normandy where World War II battles took place.

intersection our guide had the driver pause at a pasture. Beside the road was a marker. "At one time," explained the guide, "there were 6,000 American soldiers buried in this field. They have all been moved to Colleville. During June 1944 each kilometer of countryside gained cost one life." It was a sobering thought. Fifty years earlier, American soldiers died on foreign soil so that others might enjoy the fruits of liberty and freedom. In that moment, our understanding of the gratitude of the French, so often expressed by visitors to our ship, so sincerely felt, deepened. Again, we were grateful for the privilege of making the voyage to Normandy, and very glad we had come to honor those who lived — and died — in the battle of Normandy. For all the plans and official ceremonies of the D-Day + 50 Years commemorations, it was these experiences with the ordinary people that really brought home to us just how important it was for the *Jeremiah O'Brien* to return to Normandy and share the memories and ceremonies with them.

Back at Cherbourg, a beautiful French three-masted bark, the *Belem,* arrived, giving us our first taste of what lay ahead at the tall ships gathering at Rouen. She gracefully slid across the harbor, tying up directly astern of us and became an instant attraction to our crew. She was black-hulled with white trim and her masts and spars glowed with varnish. Her brass was so highly polished and shined so brightly in the sun one couldn't look directly at it. The wooden decks were

The French training vessel Belem *was our first indication of what was to come in Rouen.*

buffed white. Built in 1896 by A. Dubigeon in Nantes, France as the *Giorgio Cini*, she was originally a cargo ship. After two name changes, several owners and many years, she became a museum ship. Her steel hull measures 173 feet overall with a breadth of 29 feet and a depth of 11 feet. In addition to sails she is powered by an auxiliary diesel engine. Although technically not a clipper, she rivaled many such a vessel in her trim lines, fine bow and the graceful way in which she sat in the water. We spent much time admiring her. Interestingly, our old steel ship seemed of equal interest to her crew and we looked across at our counterparts looking at us.

The next day we heard we would have an Independence Day celebration on board. In addition there would be bus tours of the cemetery at Colleville, the city of Bayeux and the beaches at Arromanches on July 6 and 7. In an effort at better communication, the information was immediately posted in the messrooms and saloon. This momentarily had a positive effect on crew morale, but soon the grousing set in again. Some of the engine department were still upset about the extra people living on board and getting in the way. The galley crew was tired of feeding so many extra mouths. Others complained about the lack of planning. Still others were upset that we still weren't charging admission and the donation barrel wasn't producing enough to make ends meet. The rumor went around that Capt. Jahn and Adm. Patterson were limiting their conversations with each other to necessary business only.

Even Capt. Jahn was frustrated. After dinner, I was sitting at my desk reading, when he appeared at the door.

"Come on up, I'll buy you a drink. I don't like to drink alone."

We went to his office and he poured out two glasses of scotch. The conversation wandered: what the deck department was doing, why the extra people were on board, and his relations with the admiral. He said that while in the Atlantic there was a call on the satellite phone from a San Francisco radio station. They wanted to interview Capt. Jahn but Patterson happened to pick up the phone and as the captain came from the wheelhouse to his office he heard the admiral say, "You can talk to me. I'm in charge here. This is my ship, I know what's going on." The captain was furious and, at the same time, hurt. It was a pivotal incident in their relationship, one which I would hear repeated several times in the months ahead.

We had a second drink and I excused myself and went back to my book. A few minutes later I heard a knock on the chief engineer's door on the opposite side of the ship. "Come on up, I'll buy you a drink." It was the captain's voice. "I don't like to drink alone." He was having a bad day.

The crew frustrations came to a head the following day. A "crew only" meeting (meaning no officers allowed) was called in no. 2 'tween deck. In general it seemed to concern the continuing problem of lack of communication about parties, tours and events. And there was a problem with Maud Paléologue. Although Adm. Patterson explained at the previous department head meeting that she was hired by, and working for, the NLSM, no one understood what her function was. She was frequently on board, working out of the purser's or captain's office, using the phone, asking favors. The crew wanted to be sure that no one took advantage of "their" ship.

July 4, 1994, American Independence Day broke with a high, thin cloud cover which cast a grey pall over everything. Just after breakfast a truck arrived alongside loaded with 55 gallon drums. We had ordered lube oil and diesel a few days earlier. The diesel was needed for the Caterpillar generator on no. 4 hatch which had served us well, providing all our electrical needs. The lube oil was for the main engine.

Bill Duncan: "We couldn't do major repair work although there were a couple of major things we could have done but didn't have materials and tools. One was our middle generator (there are three). The flywheel bushing and bearing that holds the flywheel on the shaft got worn and started to make a racket. We took it apart in France and just patched it up and put it back together. But we never really had to use it because we only needed them for emergencies. For power we used the Caterpillar 125 KW generator on no. 4 and converted the power to DC to operate the ship.

And when we had problems with that we shut it down and switched over. But all our main services were run off the 125 KW Caterpillar."

But the diesel fuel we loaded in Panama was dirty and clogged the fuel filters in the generator. Someone in the engine department had the task of changing the filter every day to keep the generator running. It had been decided to burn the Panamanian diesel in the ship's main engines and order clean diesel to eliminate the expense of putting a new fuel filter in the generator every day. Typically, we were told the diesel would arrive in the drums that were now in the truck alongside the ship. Accordingly, we swung a boom over the side to lift them on board. Then we saw the truck driver casually rolling the drums off the truck and setting them on the dock. They were empty. We then learned the drums were to be put on deck, a tank truck of diesel would come alongside and each drum would be pumped full from the dock.

The atmosphere of frustration was contagious. The crew, which had been so cohesive and flexible to this point, seemed to have run short on patience and tolerance. It may have been a reaction to the tremendous emotional and physical demands of recent weeks, but interesting as Cherbourg was, and much as we enjoyed our visit there, it was one of the more difficult times for everyone.

The department heads held a meeting in the saloon. It began, as usual, on the subject of communication. Other topics followed. Jim Wade wanted someone to man the purser's office when he wasn't there. The future schedule was announced: arrive Rouen July 8, depart Le Havre July 22, arrive South Portland August 6, Jacksonville August 23, San Francisco, Sept. 23. Ron Robson said the store would gross only $10,000 for the two weeks in Cherbourg, a disappointing figure, but the donation barrel had produced $14,000 since our arrival in Portsmouth. The meeting ended with a heated discussion about mail delivery. The crew was concerned that the purser didn't deliver the mail as soon as it came on board. Letters sometimes appeared hours after the mail was seen to come up the gangway. Again, something was accom-

Sandy Scott, wandering minstrel, provided entertainment at our Fourth of July celebration. Photo courtesy of Pat McCafferty.

plished, mostly in the sense that everyone had a chance to ventilate and express himself.

Another sailing ship arrived in the afternoon, the *Cuauhtémoc,* also bound for the tall ships gathering in Rouen. A beautiful white-hulled bark with green trim, it coasted across the harbor like a ghost from the past. At almost 300 feet overall it was much larger than the *Belem.*

The weather was fickle, turning cloudy and threatening, then clearing, then a strong wind came up. The July 4 barbecue was moved indoors. The crew spent the afternoon setting up tables and chairs, the steward's department turned to on salads, vegetables, steaks, French bread (of course) and cake. Our guests included all the people who helped us during our stay, the mayor, the owner of the bus company, port officials and officers from the local Naval base.

Sven Keinanen: "We had a party and the crew was included. We could all go dancing and have fun with the French people. Many had a good sense of humor and there was great happiness from that."

While exploring Cherbourg, Sven had discovered a wandering minstrel, a Scotsman named Sandy Scott. Armed with electric guitar and portable amplifier he became our entertainment for the evening. After cocktails and dinner and the standard thank you's and speeches, Sandy took over with a repertoire of American pop ballads and rock and roll that soon had everyone dancing and singing along. Later in the evening he segued into rhythm and blues, working up an impromptu *"Jeremiah O'Brien* Blues" that was an instant hit with the crew.

Well I was built at Portland back in 1943,
Well you know I was built down in Portland in 1943,
And when I left the harbor, they thought that's the last they
had seen of me.

'Cause I'm the *Jeremiah O'Brien*, and I sailed across the sea,
I'm the *Jeremiah O'Brien* and I've sailed across the sea,
You better stick around folks, 'cause you won't be seeing the
last of me.

Yeah, I was built in a little dockyard out in Portland, Maine.
You know I was built down in a little dockyard, way out in
Portland, Maine.
You stick around for another forty-nine years, boy, you going
to see me again.

We fought everybody, on the beaches in France,
Well, we brought stuff to everybody, on the beaches of
France,
And when they tried to get us, oh we led them on such a
merry dance.

So here's to the admiral, Admiral Patterson and all of his
crew,
From the guy who splits the cans, Jimmy and the kitchen too,
And when everybody's sleeping, there's always someone on
watch taking care of you.

Yeah, I'm the *Jeremiah O'Brien*, Yeah I was built down in
Portland Maine,
Yeah I'm the *Jeremiah O'Brien* and I was built in Portland,
Maine,
So stick around another forty-nine years, you're gonna see me
again.

We enjoyed the irony in a Scotsman playing American rock and roll for a French audience. The party lasted into the wee hours and went a long way toward relieving the frustration of recent weeks. The local paper carried a story about the festivities, and how honored the French felt at being invited to share in the celebration of our Independence Day.

The entrance to the memorial at Caen captures the grandeur of our experience at Colleville. Photo by Jean Yates.

July 5 was the first of the bus tours to Pointe du Hoc, the American Cemetery at Colleville, and the British landing site at Arromanches. We ordered wreaths to lay at Colleville honoring American merchant seamen who were buried there. To allow everyone to participate the ceremonies were held on two days, with the captain and the admiral presiding the first day and the chief mate the second. Each day half of the crew boarded the bus just after breakfast for the tour of the beaches. The days were perfect for sight-seeing with a bright blue sky spotted here and there with puffs of white clouds. The route took us through the picturesque French countryside, the dark green hedgerows alternating with lighter green pastures clipped short by grazing sheep and dairy cattle. Again, every village and country home we passed was brightly dressed with the flags of the liberating nations and cheerful window boxes and flower gardens. After about an hour's drive we arrived

One of the German gun emplacements near Pointe du Hoc. Photo by Marty Wefald.

at Pointe du Hoc. It was a short walk through a bomb-cratered landscape overgrown with grass to the cliff, marked by a stone monument, a granite pylon atop a concrete bunker with inscriptions in both French and English at its base. We looked out over the calm blue waters trying to envision the stormy Channel fifty years earlier when the 2nd Ranger Battalion attacked, scaled the one hundred-foot cliff under heavy fire and, after great losses, succeeded in capturing, then defending the area against German counterattacks. The sheer drop to the ocean looked impossible. A few feet back from the cliff were the remains of the German gun emplacements, fearsome-looking even in ruin. The remaining guns were twisted and rusty. The calm summer day, the butterflies fluttering about and birds singing made it difficult to imagine the great battles that took place on D-Day.

Our next stop was the Normandy Cemetery at Colleville-sur-Mer, overlooking Omaha Beach. One month earlier, President Clinton stood in this cemetery along with heads of the Allied Nations gathered to remember and honor the thousands of American soldiers who lie there. On this day we were met by Sgt. Hooker, retired from the U.S. Army and now an employee of the American Government in France. The Normandy Cemetery is actually American territory, given to us by the French government in gratitude for American sacrifices during the liberation of France. Sgt. Hooker escorted us along gravel paths through immaculately manicured lawns to the memorial. There was a natural reverence to the surroundings that caused us all to unconsciously speak softly. We brought a wreath from the ship. For the first time, a memorial wreath would be laid for the fourteen merchant mariners who lost their lives at Normandy and are buried in Colleville.

The memorial is a semicircle of colonnades, open to the sky, with shrines at each end depicting the D-Day landings engraved in stone and embellished with colored enamel. In the center is the bronze statue, "Spirit of American Youth," a tribute to those who gave their lives. Around its base is the inscription "MINE EYES HAVE SEEN THE GLORY OF THE COMING OF THE LORD." We gathered at the entrance to the memorial, then lined up on each side of the statue as three senior members

Left to right, Wes Masterson, Bill Rowlands and Ed Lingenfield place a wreath at Colleville honoring deceased merchant seamen. Photo courtesy of Bev and Wes Masterson.

of the crew, Bill Rowlands, Wes Masterson and Ed Lingenfield, veterans of World War II, carried the wreath and set it at the statue's base.

Bill Rowlands: "I was very impressed with Colleville, the cemetery. I was one of those chosen to present the wreath, at the memorial there to the merchant seamen and the armed guard that were killed in the D-Day landings. That was very touching,"

Wes Masterson: "That was a very emotional time. I helped put the wreath on the statue of youth at Colleville. Bill Rowlands and I were classmates at the merchant marine school in Catalina

The perfect rows of grave markers at Colleville inspire deep emotion and reflection. Photo by Marty Wefald.

during World War II, so I thought it was significant that we laid the wreath together."

Sgt. Hooker triggered a switch and an electric carillon played the National Anthem. This was followed by three electronic rifle shots, perfectly spaced, the saddest of all bugle calls, Taps and three bells. It was a moving ceremony. Tears trickled down many weathered cheeks.

We dispersed past the reflecting pool in front of the memorial and through the cemetery. Symmetrically arranged, row upon row of white markers indicated the resting places of our countrymen. At the edge of the cemetery was a parapet overlooking the landing beaches of Omaha. We stood there quietly, looking at "bloody Omaha," the site of the fiercest of all the D-Day battles, wave after wave of emotions flooding our thoughts.

For some the memories were more vivid. Sven Keinanen was there fifty years earlier: "I was on the *Henry S. Lane*, a Liberty ship, as an able-bodied seaman. We made the first run to Omaha on June 6th and arrived off the beach and we carried with us military equipment and also army personnel. And later on I found out on my second trip that quite a few of those first contingent of soldiers had been severely wounded and many had died. I made seven trips from Southampton to Omaha and Utah beachheads. I don't recall which other ships were there, but there were so many ships that you couldn't keep track. We had observers from the Royal Air Force on the ship and they would scan the skies and determine whether planes were friendly or unfriendly. We were shot at by the German eighty-eight millimeters. They missed the ship by about fifty feet, and the ship would just lift up just as if she was out at heavy seas. The weather was rough and it was dangerous discharging cargo because when we opened up down at the 'tween decks, we'd have to have a full force of people on each end of each of those beams 'cause they were swinging back and forth. It was dangerous, with those big heavy beams causing injuries to the sailors."

Rich Reed: "My dad was an infantry soldier, went in to Omaha Beach. I've been hearing about Omaha Beach since I was a little kid, all the little towns in Normandy that he went through for the liberation and everything. It was a big deal to him, I think, that fifty years later his son got there. Having a chance to see everything there, too, you know, the beach heads. It was just so peaceful and serene. But reading about it I learned a lot of history and I think I'll be able to share it with my kids, too. To actually see all this. And from the merchant mariner's standpoint, too, you start paying more attention to the convoys, the sea stories that the old timers told you about the convoys and the Liberty ships, about crossing the Atlantic. I was glad I made it."

A short bus ride took us to Bayeux, famous for its tapestry dating from the 11th century which depicts the Norman conquest of England by William the Conqueror. We had a bag lunch, thoughtfully packed by the steward's department, on a lawn outside the town church. Our guide handed out bottles of homemade Calvados (apple brandy) and soon corks were popping across the square as we poured his liquor into plastic cups to wash down our sandwiches. Some visited the museum to see the tapestry, others bought souvenirs and walked the narrow, cobblestoned streets. At 3:30 we met at the Hotel de Ville for drinks with the mayor. She was a gracious hostess, pouring Calvados and cider for everyone, passing out cookies and pastries and a book on the history of Bayeux for each person there. Then she signed all the books, taking the time to write a personal inscription to each crew member.

Ruth Robson: "A lot of the trip was very emotional. You almost have to cry to think about some of the things we saw, the little towns that we visited and the people who came up in these little villages. I think of the village of Bayeux and how they put that reception on for us and how grateful those folks were, particularly the older ones."

Our final stop was Arromanches, at the heart of Gold Beach during Operation Overlord. A small coastal village, it contains a museum dedicated to the British landings that freed the area of Nazi domination. Inside the museum we found glass-cased dioramas depicting the events surrounding D-Day, a theater showing a short film of the landings, and displays of artifacts, uniforms, weapons, ammunition, posters, letters, insignia and military equipment. We were all wearing our crew jackets and, as we entered the museum, the curator announced over the public address system that we were from the Liberty ship *Jeremiah O'Brien* and we had brought the ship from the United States to help commemorate the liberation of France. The room burst into thunderous applause. We were stunned. We simply didn't know what to do. The people shook hands with us, asked for autographs and even delivered a few hugs and the French custom of kisses on both cheeks. It was an overwhelming experience.

We returned to the ship in the evening, tired, yet uplifted, humbled, with a number of other indescribable emotions coursing through us, and, above all, deeply moved at the gratitude of the French people.

Jim Wade: "I remember several French people told me about some of the people who had just been youngsters during the war and grown up in France under the occupation. Then along came the allied armies and liberated them and they wanted to know what freedom was. They had never experienced it and they were confused about it, they didn't know what freedom was. That was something that I had never heard expressed before, until we were there in France. And to realize that youngsters growing up saw the Nazi uniforms and heard the boots and marching on the streets and what their parents considered as short rations they accepted as the norm."

Meanwhile, life on board continued. Mike Emery received word that his grandmother had a heart attack. Our photographer was on the next train to Paris to fly home, his voyage suddenly over. A Frenchman came aboard asking to take two of the crew home with him for lunch. Phil Sinnott and Art Tabor agreed to go. They returned hours later with tales of a wonderful meal — salad, fish, veal, cheese, dessert, each course accompanied by a different bottle of wine — that lasted the entire afternoon. An Italian warship, the destroyer *Minbelli* arrived. We exchanged flag salutes as she proceeded to a berth opposite the *Cuauhtémoc*.

El Comandante del Buque Escuela "Cuauhtémoc" de la Armada de México se complace en invitar a

AL *COMANDANTE DEL BUQUE DE ESTADOS UNIDOS "JEREMIAH OBRIEN" Y 3 OFICIALES*

A la Recepción que tendrá verificativo a bordo del Buque el DIA 5 DE JULIO DE 1994 *de las* 20:00 HRS *. a las* 22:00 HRS

R. S. V. P.

"The captain of the Mexican Navy schoolship Cuauhtémoc *is pleased to invite the captain of the United States' ship* Jeremiah O'Brien *and 3 officers to a reception he is holding aboard the ship on July 5, 1994 from 2000 to 2200."*

A funny incident occurred in Cherbourg. Two brothers, Charles and Gene Mooney, worked in the engine room. Gene is the younger of the two, in his early sixties. Charlie is tall and slim with white hair. He wears a black brimless cap to absorb the engine room sweat. Tired after his watch late one afternoon Charlie sat, dressed in faded, worn dungarees and black cap, on one of the benches facing the gangway, enjoying a cup of coffee as he watched the visitors come and go. Finishing his coffee, he held the white mug resting on his thigh as he stared ahead, his mind elsewhere. One of our visitors saw him, reached into his pocket and dropped a 10 franc coin into Charlie's coffee mug.

The ship's officers were invited to a party on the Mexican training ship. Tired from a full day of courtesy calls and ship's business, the captain and the admiral delegated the author to represent the *O'Brien*. Instructing our two Kings Point cadets, Nate Taylor and Dirk Warren, and our Annapolis cadet, Tim Kinsella, to put on their uniforms, I changed into dress blues and met them at the foot of our gangway. We walked to the *Cuauhtémoc* and were piped aboard, shrill boatswain's whistles piercing the air. Escorted to the main deck where the captain and the ship's officers formed a receiving line, we introduced ourselves. I presented the captain a copy of *The Last Liberty*, and in my best broken Spanish tried to convey Capt. Jahn's regrets at not being able to attend. We joined several local officials, whom we knew from parties aboard the *O'Brien,* on the quarterdeck. Arranged around the binnacle in the center was a massive buffet with hot and cold beef, chicken and pork, sausages, cheeses, bread, crackers — a cornucopia of food. Sailors in striped shirts circulated with trays of canapes, beer, wine and liquor. The lifeboats served as stationary bars with seamen cheerfully handing out bottles of Corona, snifters of brandy and soft drinks. But the most fascinating character was a sailor dressed as a *charro* wearing a sombrero, serape and black pants with silver medallions down the sides. A bandoleer was slung across one shoulder but instead of bullets it was loaded with shot glasses. In a holster on one hip he carried a bottle of Salza tequila and on the other hip several cans of 7-Up. On request he took a shot glass, half-filled it with tequila, topped it off with 7-Up, then put a napkin over the top and slammed the glass hard on the nearest table. You were then presented with the "shooter," now overflowing with fizz, and expected to drink it down in one swallow. I had four, just to watch him go through the process of preparing them.

We were given a tour of the *Cuauhtémoc* by the ship's doctor. Built in 1986, it was a magnificent vessel. The dark paneling in the officers' ward room was hung with awards and plaques from ports they had visited. The floor was varnished wood that reflected the polished brass and glass-fronted book and display cases that lined the bulkheads. The navigation bridge contained the latest equipment, including GPS, ARPA radar, as well as devices peculiar to sailing ships such as wind speed and direction indicators. In the galley we saw the cooks working at more platters of food for the party while on the back of one stove a large pot of menudo, a popular Mexican soup made of tripe, hominy, peppers and spices, simmered. Topside, the doctor pointed out the various masts, spars, shrouds, stays and other rigging. We talked about the differences between our ships and the terminology used on each one and agreed to exchange visits in the next few days or at Rouen, the next port for both of us.

Tom Patterson: "On the sixth of July I drove to Rouen with Maud Paléologue, the French communications expert assigned to us and paid for by the NLSM. Maud and Gérald Guétat took me in to Rouen, about a three hour ride, to meet with Mr. Patrick Herr who was the president of the organization that was putting on the *L'Armada de la Liberté*. We had a breakdown in communications. They thought for a while that the *John Brown* was coming and they didn't know what to do with two of us. They were going to cut the money down in half and nobody knew exactly what was going on. My purpose in going there was to bridge that gap but also because the way it was set up we wouldn't be able to charge any admission to the ship and we desperately needed money at that time. So we arrived, we went in and Mr. Herr was rather reserved and quiet at the beginning of the meeting. I carefully took two hours to explain our whole ship's program to him and what we had done and where we were and why we needed some money and the whole thing, and asked if we could charge ten francs [$2] per person admission to the ship. We knew that the other forty-six ships there were not charging admission as they were all government ships sent by their countries. I explained to him we were a museum and that we were operated by volunteers, not supported by our government, and we simply had to have this money. I said if he would allow us to do this we would make up the appropriate sign and explain to the French people why they're being asked to give us ten francs. At that point he said, 'I think you've made a very reasonable request. I agree with it. I will let you do it. Let us make up the sign and we'll post it for you.' And he said, 'Is there anything else?' And I said, 'Yes, we would also like to cruise down the river and we would like to take 500 guests and we would like to charge them 1,000 francs per person,' [the equivalent of about $200 per person]. We explained that to him and he agreed that was fair and reasonable and he would help us in any way he could. So then I met Mrs. Patrick Herr and she said, 'Oh, I just hope the weather's fair.' And I said, 'It's going to be fair. When I get back to the ship I'll ask our chaplain to make up a special weather prayer. It's going to be wonderful weather.'"

Thursday, July 7, was the day we sailed from Cherbourg. But first we had to say good-bye and thank several people. Adm. Patterson called the crew together for a dockside ceremony at 11 a.m. It was also to be a photo session so everyone wore their crew jacket or blue polo shirt and *O'Brien* baseball cap. We received several donations of 10,000 F each [$2,000] from French organizations for the ship and for fuel on our return voyage. Representatives from the French Rotary and Lions Clubs were thanked for their support as was the owner of the bus company for providing us with buses and guides and the tours of the beaches. Each organization was given a *Jeremiah O'Brien* plaque. The admiral is very skillful in public relations and always seemed to say just the right thing. After many expressions of gratitude to different organizations and individuals, he commented that there is always some sadness at parting. "But remember," he said, "we take you with us as we continue our journey and we leave part of ourselves here."

Tim Palange: "I remember the French volunteers like Daniele who used to sail Liberty ships after the war. He seemed to be one of the most enthusiastic people I ever saw volunteering on this ship. He was a big help and he was in tears when we left Cherbourg."

Group photos were taken of the entire ship's company, then of each department and finally we got someone to shoot the 8-12 deck watch. It was sad, Phil Sinnott and Jim Conwell, the two ABs on my watch, would be leaving at Le Havre. We had shared a lot of experiences in the previous three months and enjoyed each other's company. The crew and the ship would once again change character. I was surprised at how sad that made me feel. The earlier comings and goings hadn't had a direct impact on me, but although my own watchmates wouldn't actually leave until Le Havre, two weeks hence, I already mourned their departure.

Watchmates develop a special relationship; we saw each other at least twice a day, traded comments about the voyage, told jokes and probably got to the point where we were telling the same stories over again. But there was sincere affection. They would be missed. The same was true of the engine room watches, only there the element of danger from moving machinery required an additional layer of trust. Watchmates relied on one another for companionship and, sometimes, their safety.

There was another crew meeting, the captain and the admiral presiding. Capt. Jahn was in better spirits than he had been for some time and Adm. Patterson was quite eloquent on how well this trip was fulfilling his expectations. Again, the subject of communication came up. The crew still wasn't happy, feeling they were being left out of things. Patterson said that he told Capt. Jahn everything he knew as soon as he knew it. Capt. Jahn agreed this was correct and said that there were no secrets on the ship, his door was always open. Then, as an after thought, Patterson said something that underscored what the crew was complaining about. During our first week in Cherbourg, Gérald Guétat had an exhibit in town depicting the Liberty ship program, the development of the DUKW and the importance of supply in winning the war. The exhibit materials were stacked in no. 2 several days earlier but nobody knew why. Patterson told us now they were to be set up on one wall as part of the ship's exhibit in Rouen. This meant that we had one day to prepare. Had we known five days earlier, when the materials first came on board . . .

We tested the navigation gear at 2100. AT 2135 our deep sea pilot, Capt. François Pere, and our harbor pilot, Capt. Levavaseur, were aboard. Shortly before 2200 the dockside crane hooked on to the first gangway and took it ashore. Then the longshoremen hooked up the second gangway. They were just about to lift it off when, on the far side of the pier, a car was seen speeding toward the ship, lights flashing, horn blowing. With a squeal of tires it pulled up to the foot of the gangway. Both doors opened. From the driver's side came a beautiful, well-endowed blond woman dressed in tight-fitting sweater and skirt. From the passenger side came Pat McCafferty, saloon messman. They hugged and kissed passionately (definitely not on the cheeks), then Pat ran up the gangway to the applause of the crew and those who had come to see us off. It was a "pierhead jump" to beat all pierhead jumps.

The gangway went ashore. The weather, which early in the day was grey and overcast, turned to drizzle. As we began throwing the lines off fore and aft, the pilot asked for whistles. We blew a prolonged blast as the last line went ashore. Then, as we moved away from the dock, three long blasts. The small crowd remaining on the pier applauded. We blew three more long blasts in farewell to Cherbourg and, with the engines slow ahead, pointed our bow toward the breakwater.

Once outside the harbor, Capt. Pere left on the pilot boat. It blew three whistle blasts as it turned back toward the harbor. We returned the salute, rang off departure and headed into the night.

12

L'Armada
de la Liberté

It was a short run to Le Havre at the mouth of the Seine. At 0800 the next morning we circled the harbor buoy, waiting for the pilot to arrive. Suddenly, we were transported back a hundred and fifty years, to a busy harbor filled with beautiful, tall, graceful windjammers. To our starboard was a sleek, white-hulled sailing ship. Her seamen lined the foremast yardarms, clawing at billowing buff-colored canvas as they furled the sails. Farther aft we saw sailors climbing the ratlines on either side of the main and mizzen masts. On the quarterdeck stood the master, calmly giving orders to the mate who relayed them through a speaking trumpet. Aft of the brass and wood binnacle two seamen handled the spokes of the ship's wheel, their legs spread wide to hold the deck. A couple of miles astern another tall ship, a three-masted bark, black-hulled, under full sail, was heading our way with a bone in her teeth. Her sails were snow-white and swelled tightly as she sleekly knifed her way through the water toward us. Ahead were two other tall ships, their auxiliary engines pushing them toward the entrance to the Seine under bare masts. Even without sails they looked splendid, their lines hard and straight in a symmetry that was both aesthetically pleasing and spirit-lifting. Images of the great days of sail came to mind — the gathering of tea clippers on the coast of China, Donald McKay's ships rounding the Horn, each cutting the time of its predecessor, the homeward-bound ceremony of the last load on the nitrate clippers in Chile, the wool clippers from Australia; names such as *Cutty Sark, Rainbow, Sovereign of the Seas, Flying Cloud* and *Sea Witch;* images of bucko mates, King Neptune, hardtack and pirates. It was a thrilling beginning to the great event that awaited us sixty miles upriver.

We fell back to reality at the sight of the pilot boat in the distance, a billow of dirty grey smoke pouring from its exhausts. The sound of its diesel engines pierced the silence and grew louder. Then the orange and black-hulled craft with "PILOT" painted in large white letters was alongside. Capt. LeMalet climbed quickly to the *O'Brien*'s bridge and we began our voyage up the Seine to Rouen, sixty miles away and the closest port to Paris navigable by ocean-going vessels.

The weather was mild, the blue sky partly covered with white patches of clouds. The flying bridge, high on the ship, with open views, was an ideal navigation — and sight-seeing — platform. We passed under the Normandy Bridge (nearing completion), its suspension cables fanning out geometrically from two towers like the beginnings of a massive spider web. Now the delta of the river narrowed. On our starboard side were low hills covered with green grass and oak forests, pastures with brown cattle grazing and small houses with white stucco walls, red tile roofs and large flower gardens. To port was a wide, low, flat green marsh.

Capt. LeMalet, a tall slender man with brown hair and a walrus moustache, was full of boyish enthusiasm at being aboard the last active veteran of Normandy and the last Liberty ship and asked if he could steer it himself. Soon AB Jim Conwell was standing to one side as the pilot handled the wood spokes of the ship's wheel. A barge came down river and saluted us with its whistle. The deep answering bellow of the *O'Brien*'s foghorn echoed off the starboard bank and rolled across the flatlands to port. Capt. LeMalet was in ecstasy. He hadn't realized we had a real, bellowing, steam-powered fog horn and, once aware, he was at the whistle pull himself, saluting each ship, barge, boat, ferry crossing, town and chateau along the way. Between steering and blowing the whistle he had a grand time taking us up the river. His enthusiasm was infectious and we enjoyed his enjoyment.

The banks of the river drew closer and the terrain changed. Low-lying hills on each side were covered with green grass or vineyards. Occasionally a small castle was seen atop a nearby cliff or peak, its turrets and parapets commanding the surrounding countryside. We passed small villages with bustling shops, busy market places, town squares lined with open-air cafes and always a church, its spire the tallest structure in sight. Capt. LeMalet was still steering and whistling and at the sound of our foghorn people appeared in the windows of their homes, waving. They looked up from their gardening, their farming, their walks along the river banks, their shopping, to wave and cheer at the sight of the old Liberty ship steaming up the Seine.

Just after lunch and before the Brotonne Bridge and the town of Ville du Clare, about thirty miles up river, we changed pilots. Capt. Tilly took the con with Capt. LeMalet reluctantly going ashore. Now the river closed in. White chalk cliffs and white marble quarries punctuated long stretches of beautiful rolling green countryside. We saw old houses, half-timbered stucco with thatched or slate roofs, elegant chateaux and villas. Small boats, barges and an occasional freighter came downstream toward us. The people we passed on the banks of the river

One of the more distinctive small castles seen on the ride up the Seine. Photo by John Linderman.

waved and cheered. Capt. Tilly was equally enamored of our old steam whistle and blew it diligently and the people applauded each volley delightedly.

Jimmy Farras: "The steam whistle, the steam whistle was great. I loved that steam whistle."

Jim Conwell: "Sailing up the Seine River was something I was looking forward to. That part of the voyage was more rewarding than I expected. I wasn't aware of the extent of the beauty of the landscape, the limestone cliffs, but also the many chateaux and monasteries. And the houses with the thatched roofs and the grass growing on the roofs. I didn't realize that was as common in France. We saw things like that in England but I didn't realize it was in France, too."

In mid-afternoon we entered the river valley in which Rouen resides. Here the grasslands and forests of the country, the villages and chateaux, gave way to hard, flat industrial piers, grain elevators and faceless concrete warehouses and factories. Our berth was to be in the very heart of the city. At this point, the low *Pont Guillaume le Conquérant* (Bridge of William the Conqueror) prevents navigation farther up river by all but low-profile barges. This area of the river, which contained the berths for all the ships gathering for *L'Armada de la Liberté*, was lined on each side with a modern, concrete quay.

But before reaching the berthing area we had to be turned to face down river. Here the Seine branches off to a turning basin forming a "Y." The tug *Secours V* was made fast forward, the *Captaine Albert Ruault* tied up aft. Capt. Tilly ordered the helmsman to steer to the right to get us over to the side of the channel to begin the turn. A dredge was tied up to the wharf ahead to our right and behind it loomed the round silos of grain elevators. Overhead a helicopter clattered, filming our arrival for the evening news.

Capt. Tilly was used to the noise and vibration of diesel engines on ships, and their quick response. The *O'Brien*'s steam engine was quiet and lulled him into thinking it was moving slowly, so he ordered the bow tug to pull us to the left, beginning the process of turning us around. The line on the bow tightened as the tug walked across the water, trying to pull the bow away from the starboard bank. But our engines were still going ahead. The line grew tighter. As tension increased water began dripping off the line, squeezed out by the strong forces working at either end. Then, with a dull "pop" that shook the entire ship, it broke. We were heading toward the starboard bank and the dredge, while behind it, the grain elevators seemed to swell in size.

"Slow astern," ordered the pilot. The chief mate rang the order on the engine telegraph, recording the command in the bell book. We all looked at the tachometer. It was still going ahead. "Half astern," said the pilot, then, "Full astern." He shouted the orders and speed changes on top of each other. We careened toward the dock. The helicopter pilot saw what was happening and swooped down, circling the ship lower and lower until he was below the level of the navigation bridge, then below the bow, barely skimming the water, his rotors so noisy that we could hear only the loudest shout.

"Let go the anchor," screamed the pilot. "Let go both anchors," he roared. I relayed the commands on the walkie-talkie to Second Mate Ray Conrady at the bow and recorded the time in the bell book. The dredge crew frantically slacked their anchor lines to the river bed as we passed directly over them. A cloud of rust rose from the spill pipes on our forecastle, showing the anchor chain was paying out. The tachometer needle was on zero. We felt a slight shudder as the second anchor let go. We were almost on top of the dredge, so close it was no longer visible from the bridge. Its crew, however, was clearly visible running up the dock away from the scene of the impending disaster. The entire ship began to shake and shudder, the stack shimmied and clattered. The tachometer needle climbed from twenty to forty to sixty revolutions astern, still our momentum carried us forward. Finally, the propeller dug, grabbed hold and we came to a stop — our stem ten feet from the dredge.

The ship began backing away. The pilot was in a frenzy. "Raise the starboard anchor," he said. "Raise the port anchor. Raise both anchors. Stop engines. Slow ahead. Slow astern. Make the tug fast on the bow again." The commands came on top of each other. It was impossible to relay them to the engine room and to Ray Conrady and get an answer before the next contradictory command came. Recording it in the bell book was out of the question. God only knows what the engine crew thought. In frustration I threw the bell book on the deck at the pilot's feet. "We can't do it that fast," I said. "No, of course," he said, and started again. "Raise the starboard anchor. Make the tug fast."

Capt. Jahn quietly intervened. "Just stop the engines. Then heave the anchors up slowly. We want to be sure we haven't fouled the lines coming off that dredge."

The pilot took a deep breath. "Very well," he said, more calmly. On raising the anchors we found that neither of them had snagged the dredge's lines, the dredge crew had slacked them to the bottom just in time. The tug was made fast to the bow, the ship turned and we backed into our berth.

Tom Patterson: "We had one little excitement coming into Rouen. The tug parted the bow line and our bow was being set down on a moored dredging barge. The mate on the bow, Ray Conrady, and the bosun immediately dropped both anchors and saved the ship from swinging her bow into this barge. That prevented a lot of damage."

We were starboard side to on the face of a long concrete wharf or quay, the *Rive Droite* (right bank), that stretched downstream more than a mile from the bridge of William the Conqueror. On the opposite side was the *Rive Gauche* (left bank), not quite so long but equally well-laid-out. The area adjacent to where the Armada ships would moor was a broad esplanade about 100 feet wide. Brick buildings and white tents of various sizes housed the Armada's souvenir stands, snack bars, bistros, wine bars, exhibits, a post office, first aid tents and a bank branch. The official souvenir stands featured every item imaginable with the logo of *L'Armada* on it: post cards, posters, insignia, umbrellas, baseball caps, T-shirts, jumpers, blouses, jackets, and the favorite novelty item of the crew, *L'Armada* condom in a small white box with red and blue logo.

Larger tents were set up as open-air restaurants with a stage for evening entertainment and a kitchen in back. The smaller

The logo of L'Armada *was everywhere. Here a large banner dresses the top of a nearby building. Photo by Bob Black*

ones offered such treats as American-style fast foods — hot dogs

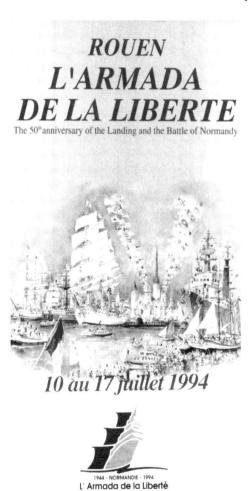

One of the many attractive brochures advertising L'Armada.

and hamburgers with *pommes frites* (french fries), sandwiches, crepes, Haagen Dazs ice cream, pastries, cakes, soft drinks, beer and wine. There were also tent-shops offering paintings, ship models, brassware, prints, clothing, jewelry and the opportunity to join the French Navy. Just beyond the tents, adjacent to the ship, the crew quickly discovered a bar that immediately became a popular hangout. For the duration of *L'Armada* it featured a nightly wet T-shirt contest.

Tom Patterson: "You have to understand that Rouen is probably the only port in the world that has a river with berths on both sides and a bridge at the end of it and you can display all these beautiful, wonderful ships. And you can see them all together. Any angle you look at it you're seeing beautiful ships and over 2,000 sailors from these ships. It was an unbelievable spectacle, and *Jeremiah* was right in the middle of it as the guest of honor, being the only original ship from World War II."

Just on the other side of the William the Conqueror bridge on our side of the river was the center of Rouen with its Old Town, university, cathedral, shops and restaurants. Here, narrow, cobblestoned streets wound through blocks of half-timbered houses,

1944·NORMANDIE·1994
L' Armada de la Liberté
ROUEN July 10-17 1994

Another of the advertising brochures, this with a photo from the previous Armada.

many dating back hundreds of years. The centerpiece of the Old Town is the Great Clock, or Gros-Horloge, on the street of the same name. The Great Clock itself is housed in a Renaissance structure which spans the street, open to pedestrian traffic only, like a gate. The clock's large gilt face can be seen from either side, its single hand showing the hour. In the many squares, the crew found restaurants and shops offering everything imaginable. The cathedral, dating from the 1100s, is delicately-spired and sits tall and majestic in a large square in the center of town. There was always musical entertainment of some type going on in the square: a brass band from one of the Russian ships, a bagpipe band from the Omani ship, folk-singers, blues musicians. In another part of town, a cross marks the spot where the English burned Joan of Arc, France's greatest national heroine, at the stake in 1431. Next to it was a modern, futuristic church, its architecture evoking the feel of waves and the sea. Inside are stained glass windows dating from the early 1500s that were saved from St. Vincent's church and sheltered from bombing during World War II by hiding them in nearby cellars. This church is set incongruously next to a fish market, providing its worshipers with an odd assortment of sights and smells.

Because the Armada wouldn't start for two days (we were early again), most of the berths were empty although some of the ships were already there — across the way the *Lobelia,* a Belgian minesweeper; the *Kaskelot,* a British three-masted bark; the *Möen,* a Danish minesweeper, the *Sagres II,* a Portuguese three-masted bark. On our side of the river were the *Gloria,* a Colombian three-masted bark; the *A. Von Humboldt*, a German three-masted bark; the *Jeanne d'Arc*, a French helicopter carrier and flagship of

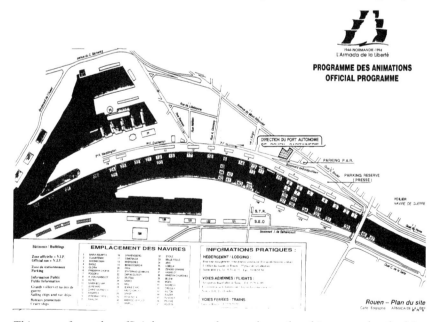

This map from the official program shows where the ships were berthed in Rouen. The Jeremiah O'Brien *is at no. 14.*

the French Navy; and the *Dar Mlodziezy*, a Polish three-masted ship.

As soon as we were tied up, a meeting was called in the captain's office with Jean-Paul Caron, Maud Paléologue, Gérald Guétat, the admiral, the captain and the chief mate. Maud had scheduled several events for the crew — *L'Armada* organization was offering a trip to Paris for four of the crew, the nearby town of D'Isneauville was inviting the entire crew to dinner later in the week, a parade at which *O'Brien* veterans would be expected to participate, a Jazz concert each night featuring B.B. King, Mambo Mania, Mingus Big Band and others.

Maud had also arranged for volunteer docents to help us with crowd control. Gérald, Maud and Jean-Paul said literally millions of people were expected. Plans were made for the cruise down the Seine at the end of *L'Armada*, a wonderful opportunity to raise funds. We would need lunch and dinner for everyone, portable toilets, 500 lifejackets, permission from the French Coast Guard, transportation back from Le Havre for the passengers. As he closed the meeting, Adm. Patterson reminded us, "Remember, we carry only good will, no cargo."

On Saturday, two other people came aboard who would be our translators, guides and organizers, helping us immeasurably during the remainder of our stay in France: Darwin Curtis and Pierre Cole. Darwin is a retired State Department official who speaks fluent French. It was his daughter, Lee, who translated our brochure into French. Pierre is a retired French ship captain who speaks excellent English. They volunteered to help in any way they could during our stay in Rouen. I asked them to accompany me to the meeting of our French volunteers at the nearby Maritime Museum. As we walked along the esplanade talking about the things we needed to do, it became apparent that Pierre was a natural leader and organizer. Entering the museum, Darwin pulled me aside. "This guy has a flair for leadership. Why don't you let him organize these French volunteers. They can report to him and he and I will coordinate your needs with them." Following Darwin's good advice, I gave Pierre his battlefield commission. "It would be a great help if you could organize all these people, assign them duties and have them work for you." He hesitated for half a second, then jumped to it. Quickly gathering the group of enthusiastic, eager young people in their teens and twenties around him, he began explaining what was expected, laying out assignments and writing up work lists.

"He's got this well in hand," said Darwin. "We can go back to the ship and he'll catch up later." Darwin was not in the diplomatic service for nothing.

Returning to the *O'Brien,* we went over the blue line tour, analyzing bottlenecks and problem areas. When Capt. Cole arrived he had everyone scheduled for the days ahead, with feelers out for yet more docents. He was a superb organizer, as was Darwin. We really couldn't have handled the people we did in Rouen without the assistance of both men. The crowds on the quays and the visitors on the ships far surpassed even the best turnouts in England. Never had we seen so many people. We were to learn that more than five million people came to see *L'Armada* in the nine days it was open.

In a quiet moment, Darwin Curtis mentioned that he laid the wreath for the merchant marine at Colleville on June 6 and he had been on the *USS George Washington* with our crew that same morning. He also mentioned how often he had heard the French express their gratitude and admiration for us for bringing the ship to France, something we were beginning to understand.

The constant contact with the French people continued to touch us emotionally. Each day brought new stories of white-haired veterans, former seamen and civilians coming aboard and, with heartfelt emotion, saying again and again, *"Merci,* thank you." We now knew how the French and English felt about the United States and the ships symbolized by the *Jeremiah O'Brien*, yet we were constantly surprised and moved at the depth of emotion and feeling.

More beautiful, tall-masted sailing ships arrived. Our friend from Cherbourg, the Mexican *Cuauhtémoc* motored past, a huge red, white and green flag flying from the stern. Her cadets manned the yardarms in traditional style, standing atop them, their bright uniform jerseys standing out against the clear blue sky. Then came

Our old friend from Cherbourg, the Cuauhtémoc *arrived shortly after us. This photo is from the official program. Courtesy* L'Armada de la Liberté.

The USCG training vessel Eagle *arrived shortly after the* O'Brien. *Here she is pictured tied to the quay with the Rouen cathedral in the background. Photo by* Paris Normandie.

the U.S. Coast Guard training ship, *Eagle,* white-hulled with a broad diagonal orange stripe across the bow, her crew likewise aloft. By far the most colorful — and, to the author's eye, the most dramatic-looking — ship to arrive was the *Amerigo Vespucci,* the three-masted full-rigged ship from Italy. She was massive with an extreme length of 331 feet, breadth of 50 feet and a draft of 21 feet. Built in 1931, her black steel hull with horizontal white stripes displaces 3,550 tons. Her cadets, too, stood on the yard-arms amidst flags and bunting, making a truly grand entrance.

The Italian Amerigo Vespucci *with cadets lined up the ratlines and at the yardarms. Photo by Marty Shields.*

Although *L'Armada* hadn't officially opened, people thronged the walkway next to the ships. As the day progressed, more and more people came and soon the whole esplanade was a mass of colorfully-dressed humanity, ebbing and flowing past the ship.

One of the most popular items for sale was a full-color program. Inside were listings of events and historical descriptions.

The German training vessel Alexander Von Humboldt *arrives with crew manning the yards. Photo by Bob Black.*

Each ship in the Armada was given a page of its own with a color photograph of the ship and a place for the "ship's stamp." Someone on the dock gestured up at one of our crew leaning on the rail watching the crowd. He went down and learned she wanted her program stamped. Bringing the program up, he then heard other people asking the same thing. We quickly realized this was going to be a very popular memento of the Armada and set up a card table and chair at the foot of the gangway. Suddenly there was a long line of people waiting to have their programs stamped. Then they began asking for autographs. We brought out another chair and another crewman to autograph while the first stamped. This went on nonstop from mid-afternoon, through the supper hour and into the night with Rich Reed, Sam Wood, Jim Wade, Bill Rowlands, Jim Conwell and others relieving each other. At midnight they were still signing autographs.

Bill Bennett's Crew's News for this evening:

This is the Voice of the *Jeremiah O'Brien.* Good Evening, San Francisco.

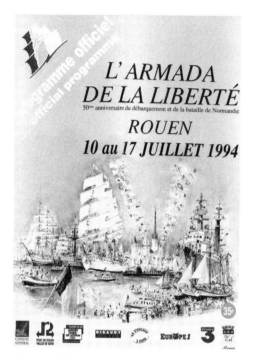

Cover of L'Armada *program, probably the most popular item for sale.*

From *Jeremiah O'Brien*, the centerpiece of the Armada de la Liberte at Rouen, France:

All day today magnificent three and four masted training ships from nations such as Portugal, Chile, Mexico, Italy, Russia, and some 12 other nations have been arriving. To my personal delight no ship received as much interest as did the three masted bark *"Eagle,"* training ship for the United States Coast Guard. Our young Coast Guard cadets, both male and female, manned the rigging two to each yardarm. Captain George Jahn, when notified of the *Eagle*'s approach, participated in the dipping of our colors. This was in turn promptly returned by *Eagle*. This celebration, held every five years in Rouen, promises to be one of the highlights of our trip back to the beaches of Normandy.

Jeremiah O'Brien — out.

Sunday, July 10, the first day of *L'Armada*, broke fine, clear and calm. The quays were lined with large and small tall-masted sailing ships, in some cases moored two and three abreast. In the crowds on the pier we saw the uniformed officers, midshipmen and sailors of a dozen countries, enjoying a meal at one of the open-air cafes or walking arm-in-arm with beautiful young French girls. Excitement was in the air. This was a gathering of ships to end all gatherings of ships and the *O'Brien* was right in the middle of it. We brought our ticket booth with us from San Francisco and now set it on the dock at the foot of the entrance gangway. The sign explaining in French why we charged admission was hung from the ship directly over the ticket booth in plain view. The card table and chairs were still on the dock. We were scheduled to open at 10 a.m. but the line started forming well before that. Darwin Curtis and Pierre Cole had French-speaking docent-volunteers in the ticket booth, at the top of the gangway, in the engine room, on all three levels of the midships house, at the forward guntub and in the ship's store. In

This sign explained to our visitors why we were the only ship at L'Armada *to charge admission.*

addition, Clifford Hook was stationed at the card table, Bob Black, a cadet from California Maritime Academy who arrived two days earlier as ordinary seaman, was in the wheelhouse, Bob Gisslow was in the radio shack, Bill Rowlands was at the exit gangway, Phil Sinnott was on the flying bridge, and Carl Kreidler was in the guntubs. The engine department had Tim Palange, Bill Duncan, the Mooney brothers and Dick Currie ready for engine room tours.

At ten o'clock we opened the gangway and immediately lost any sense of "our" ship. It became like a ride at an amusement park and we were suddenly in the business of moving people. The crowd swarmed aboard and lines formed outside the after main deck house, at the aft entrance to the midships house on the port side, throughout the interior passageways inside the ship and at the staging area for the engine room tours, starboard side, main deck, aft of the midships house. The card table partially blocked the foot of the gangway so that after visitors bought their tickets they had to work their way around the mob getting their programs stamped and autographed. This caused a bottleneck. Someone decided to move the card table and alleviate the bottleneck. Now the bottleneck formed on the main deck where everyone followed the blue line to go through the after house with its gunners' quarters and steering engine.

We moved the table back to its original position; better a bottleneck there than on deck. French-speaking docents were repositioned at the ladder coming down from the boat deck to the main deck and at the aft end of the bridge deck, two places where the blue line crossed back on itself. The docents acted as traffic cops, holding the line up to let a few dozen pass in one direction, then the other.

People also came aboard to see the captain or the admiral on business. It took half an hour to work our way against traffic up to the captain's office. The warm day turned hot, then blistering. Tempers ran short. Our valiant volunteers did their best but needed brief breaks or water to drink. When a crew member assigned to the exit gangway left to eat lunch, some of the mob on the dock made a rush up to the main deck. Someone else noticed the bottleneck at the gangway and moved the table again. The after deck became packed with the unmoving line running back down to the quay. We moved the table back to the original position again. Some of the docents had to leave early. It was a crazy, hectic day with lots of confusion, misunderstandings and interference by well-meaning crew members.

By now we were all worn out with the heat, the unending crowds, and the strain of trying to be friendly and hospitable,

The crowds were unrelenting. This scene was repeated every day from 10 am to midnight. Photo by Bob Black

answer questions, and yet keep the line moving. The narrow interior corridors were jammed and every inch of the ship was packed with people. We closed off ticket sales at five but soon realized that was a mistake. There was a line of people four wide extending from midships to the bow on the dock. Many had waited more than an hour in the heat, so we put someone at the end of the line with a "closed" sign and stayed open. When we finally did close we tallied 4960 visitors aboard and had taken in a total of $7825 for the day. Not bad for our first day, and although we had several weeks of no income to make up for, it was a good start toward getting us home.

Darwin Curtis: "That first day of visits seemed pretty wild to me. People went through the ship, only some of whom followed the arrows. Soon, people were struggling through the narrow passageways against the flow, causing what the French like to call *embottlements*. Wherever constraints were not in place, and often where they were, the orderly parade would fragment, much like cockroaches when the lights go on. The resolution of a traffic jam in one companionway would quickly contribute to another somewhere else. Pierre Cole and I charged fore to aft and bridge to engine room, trying to cope. When the scrimmage was over, we met in the middle with our tongues hanging out. It was still over ninety degrees and we hadn't even gotten a supply of water arranged for the volunteers. Half of them, including Pierre and me, missed lunch because the cook closes the galley at 1230 hours, not 1231, just like the National Maritime Union told him to do fifty years ago, so as not to be exploited by management. The volunteers had winged it all day, too. We were learning by doing."

Ron Robson: "In Rouen, the huge crowds were unbelievable. We were warned of them, but I didn't expect anything like what happened. I was so taken with the sheer mass of people that were there that week."

Tom Patterson: "When we got to Rouen the ship was just besieged with French people trying to get on board, and this became our single biggest challenge. The weather that week was gorgeous. It was so gorgeous but it was up in the high 90's most of the time. In France people take vacations in July so the quay by the side of the ship, which was about a hundred feet wide, was completely jammed with people. There were six million people reported to be in Rouen to see this *L'Armada*, which is fantastic."

Bob Black: "I joined the ship at Rouen. It was a remarkable experience — the crowds, the enthusiasm, the ships. I've never seen anything like it. I think one of the highlights of the trip was seeing that huge crowd of people visiting the various ships of the nations, walking up and down the pier where the ships were moored and having five thousand tourists on board a day."

A French company had the ship booked for a private party that night. Fortunately it was catered and required little effort from the crew.

It didn't get dark until after ten and the nightly fireworks displays started just before midnight. Looking across the river we saw the first colorful balls of yellow sparkle shooting off in all directions somewhere behind the ships. Then came puffs of red, green, blue and white climbing higher and higher and coming more and more frequently. Some of the fireworks exploded with a cannon roar, delayed by the distance from the harbor, others fizzled and crackled, like water on a hot stove. The display ended with a crescendo of multicolored sparkling balls of light and thunderous explosions. When it was over everyone in the harbor cheered and applauded, their ovations echoing across the water from ship to ship. The parade on the dock continued with revelers stopping at one or another of the tent-cafes for a late night snack and live entertainment. Slowly, then, the crowd thinned, until by two a.m. the quay was empty, the ghostly yellow light of the tall lamps shining dispiritedly on scraps of paper and empty soda cans.

The following morning we awoke to the shrill piping of boatswain's whistles as the various Navy ships piped morning colors for their crews. Then came the morning announcements over ships' public address systems in a polyglot of languages, one on top of the other through the still, smoky air in the harbor. Thirty-four tall ships were part of *L'Armada*, plus eighteen Naval ships of various nations and twenty-five assorted brigs, pinnaces, yawls and catches.

Our crowd control problems this day were less severe. We had learned from the previous day's mistakes.

Darwin Curtis recalled: "Pierre and I decided there would be merit in a bit more structure to our doing things. Over the course of the next several days, we developed more efficient ways

The French press gave us good coverage. This article is from Paris Normandie.

of deploying the volunteers and cooked up other tactics to facilitate the movement of the torrent of visitors through the ship. Most of the volunteers were French kids in their late teens and twenties, bright and eager to work. Some developed such loyalty to the *O'Brien* that they followed her to Le Havre and worked there, too. A number of retired French merchant mariners, some who had served on Liberty ships, volunteered, as well. One day, there were eight retired ship captains on duty, and taking a nostalgia trip the while."

Two or three times a day, Darwin walked through the blue line tour to see where the problems were. In this way we located difficulties as they developed and quickly dealt with them.

As in Cherbourg, we saw many former Liberty ship sailors, back again to relive their youth, just as we were reliving ours.

Dick Brannon: "The French got seventy-six of these after they were built. And the last one that I personally knew of was trading to Rouen in the middle of 1972. We had relatively young Liberty ship engineers coming aboard there in Cherbourg, Rouen, Le Havre. We had one guy who had been on the *Horace Lurkin*, which became the *Royanne,* and he came aboard twice. And thousands of people, many guys who had been on the same French Liberty ship. They didn't know each other, but they came at different times. I looked it up and I could give every guy the history of his French Liberty, from its birth in the States to its change of name and everything. So I had a lot of fun and it was really wonderful being able to help these guys, both the Brits and the French tracing the history of their ships. I got the three basic Liberty ship books, the Naval Institute book on Liberty ships, and Sawyer and Mitchell [*The Liberty Ships*], of course, and I.J. Steward [*Liberty Ships in Peace Time*]."

Darwin Curtis: "My most indelible memories of this experience will be the visitors to the ship. No one associated with the *O'Brien* had any idea of the emotions she would evoke in France. She had revived the memories of older Normans about that cataclysmic time of their liberation so long ago. Liberty ships, hundreds of them, had suddenly appeared off the battered coast of France with all the means necessary to rid the country of its plague and begin its reconstruction. To their minds she was a symbol of deliverance.

"Countless times, I looked down into the moist eyes of old faces and heard a whispered, '*merci.*' Most would then turn away, overcome. Some would dig in a pocket or purse for old, dog-eared photos of Liberty ships moored at rubble-strewn quays, or produce some other memento they wanted to share with a veteran."

Almost every crew member had similar experiences, repeated dozens of times over the nine days we were there. The gratitude of the French people was overwhelming, so different from the unfriendly image we had previously, it was sometimes difficult to assimilate. Again and again, as through the whole trip, we were made to feel that all the effort to bring the ship over was worth more to the people than we could ever understand.

Throughout the days and well into the early hours of each following morning, the walkway alongside the ships was a river of people, ebbing and flowing in a colorful mass. At the foot of the gangway to each ship a logjam formed as visitors waited to board or grouped around the sailors stamping and autographing programs. During our open hours the line waiting to come aboard was four, six and even eight wide and as long as the ship itself. It was a carnival atmosphere with white tents strewn from one end of the quay to the other. Everything was open until ten or eleven at night with those bistros and brasseries that featured entertainment not closing until one or two in the morning. You could sit down to a full dinner or snack your way from one end of the esplanade to the other. Everything was priced for the event. A serving of *pommes frites* cost the equivalent of $3. A Haagen-Dazs ice cream cone was $3, if you bought it at a tent. Otherwise, if you purchased it from one of the portable carts, you paid $4 for chocolate-covered vanilla ice cream on a stick, similar to an Eskimo pie. But here the ice cream was presented in a most unusual fashion. The vendor, always a young woman, opened the cardboard container and paper wrapper, then held the package in her hands, presenting the stick end to the customer. The purchaser then grasped the stick and slowly withdrew the ice cream from the wrappings. It was a sensuous and provocative presentation.

With most people dressed in casual summer clothes, uniforms stood out. We quickly learned to recognize many of them. The crew from the Mexican *Cuauhtémoc* always wore high-pressure white officers' hats, a thigh-length dark coat with epaulets, brass buttons and swords. Their appearance was elegant and formal. The French Navy sailors wore a blue uniform similar to the United States Navy, but their caps were distinctive; round, white, flat tops with a vivid red pom-pom in the center. Supposedly, if a girl squeezed the pom-pom, the sailor was entitled to a kiss. By contrast, the crew from the Coast Guard *Eagle* were easy to spot in their bland pale blue dress. Probably the most unusual uniform was that worn by the Russians. Their high-pressure hats were much larger than any other nation's, as big as pie plates. Their jackets were pale yellow with short sleeves and looked like a cross between a sport shirt and a pullover.

The crew were interested to hear that a force of 500 . . . er, "ship followers" were expected from Paris to supplement those already on hand for the Armada. It became something of a game to try to recognize visitors from those who were there on "business."

Inevitably, some of the crew did manage to "recognize" some of the "ladies." A minor problem about allowing one crew member to bring his new-found friend aboard was avoided early one morning when he thought better of it. We watched from the railing as they kissed good-bye and she walked up the dock, hips swinging seductively.

Some of our crew reported visiting the *Kershones,* the handsome white square-rigger from the Ukraine berthed ahead of us. Their sailors were so hard-pressed for currency they were selling pieces of uniform and insignia to get dollars. It wasn't surprising, then, when a delegation of four officers from the Russian ship *Natoychivvy* came aboard. They had a briefcase full of hundred dollar bills that no one seemed to want. Ron Robson agreed to change a few of them into smaller denominations.

Daily, various volunteers staffed the ship's store: Monica Conrady, Jean Hook (Capt. Hook's wife), Ron Robson, Art Taber, Ruth Robson, Mrs. Cole and some of our French helpers. Located in no. 3 'tween deck, the store was crowded, hot, stiffling and busy. As always, the most popular items were those with the ship's logo: baseball caps, coffee mugs and T-shirts. The store

was a good money-maker for the ship.

Daily, various members of the crew manned the card table at the foot of the gangway, signing autographs and stamping programs until well after midnight. The notoriety had a good effect on morale. "Got writer's cramp yet?" was frequently shouted from the deck down to whoever was at the table.

The party atmosphere on the esplanade hardly let up. Around 3 a.m. one night we heard the sound of drums coming through

The entrance to our ship's store with appropriate signs.

the open portholes facing the pier. The noise grew louder and now came the added clanging sounds of metal. The din came from a mob moving along the esplanade from town in our direction. At that distance, all we could see was a ball of people beating on conga drums, pots, pans, garbage can lids, sticks and anything else that made noise. The drums set an underlying samba beat but it was all but drowned out by the accompaniment. The mob moved to the *Simon Bolivar*, two ships away, then stopped although the noise continued. Three or

SS JEREMIAH O'BRIEN
(États-Unis)

Our page from the official program kept the crew busy signing autographs night and day.

four sailors separated themselves, dropped their "instruments" and staggered aboard. The mass of people moved again, toward the *Christian Radich* tied up behind us. Now individuals took shape. There were sailors from the *Jeanne d'Arc*, their pom-pommed hats askew, sailors in white T-shirts from the *Inhauma*, a Brazilian frigate tied farther up the dock, crew from the Ukrainian ship ahead of us — in other words, about fifty "drunken sailors" returning from a night on the town, having the time of their lives and making as much noise as possible. A couple of sailors weaved their way aboard the Norwegian square-rigger and the mob continued toward the *Jeremiah O'Brien,* drums pounding, pans and tin cans clattering, sticks beating. As they neared our gangway a police car appeared in the distance behind them and sped up the dock, blue lights flashing, its claxon all but drowned by the noise. A police van came into view following the car. The mob finally became aware of them and the "music" stopped. The car and van slowed, detoured around the sailors and continued on to the gangway of a ship farther down river. The band struck up again and continued on its way. The music slowly faded as the sailors got farther away and their numbers diminished at each stop.

Bill Duncan: "These guys had drums and would beat a rhythm in the morning after the bars closed. And the crowd would move down the quay back and forth, everyone doing his own dance out there. They stopped in front of our ship and stayed awhile and then the garbage trucks came along and they had to stop until the band went on. The quay was loaded from seven till three the next morning."

The Armada officials were as good as their word, given to Adm. Patterson at the meeting the previous week, providing free charcoal for our galley stove, diesel fuel and food. In the morning we loaded real French bread (which the cooks ruined by freezing and serving later), fresh fruit and pastries. The pastries were wonderful, crisp, flaky, cream, custard or chocolate-filled gooey delights covered with slices of strawberry, blueberries, and chocolate, vanilla or strawberry frosting. They didn't last long.

We were officially open to the public from 10 a.m. to 5 p.m. Marty Shields suggested to Adm. Patterson that we stay open later because of the money we were making on admissions. But the deck department, which would have to act as docents and crowd control specialists, was dead-set against it. By five o'clock most of them had already put in a nine-hour day washing down the decks, loading stores, off-loading garbage, standing night gangway watches and then acting as docents. It was hard work and they

Even Bruce the Raven got into the act, inspired, no doubt by the enthusiasm on the part of the French for all things American. Courtesy Phil Frank and San Francisco Chronicle.

weren't willing to work longer hours. Neither were the French volunteers. They had families and homes to go to. One of our AB's said, "You tell the admiral that as long as he stands there at that gangway I'll be right there with him. But as soon as he leaves, I'm gone."

Tom Patterson: "So we did the best we could that week and we opened the ship in the morning at ten and we shut it down at 4:30 in the afternoon and even that exhausted the crew, doing that much. We had to keep men down at the bottom of the gangway just to sign souvenir programs. And when we'd leave the ship it would take an hour to get through these people, they'd all want autographs. It was hard to be impolite, and our crew tried their best but it was like being locked up in a bank vault with a mountain of gold in front of you. If we could have taken all the money from the people that wanted to come on the ship that week, we would have had enough money to last this ship 'till the year 2000 but we simply could not do it."

Jim Wade: "I remember the families that opened up their hearts to us in Rouen and the way that people were just so enthusiastic about our being there. You could hardly walk away from the ship. If you wore anything that indicated that you were from the *O'Brien,* you could hardly walk away without being mobbed by admirers, people who wanted to express their thanks and also wanted a remembrance of our visit by having us autograph their booklets."

By 10 a.m. the pier was a seething mass of people. The line from our ticket booth extended beyond the bow. It was hot again this day, hotter than it had been since our arrival. As we let the people on board it became clear the heat would be a problem. We had many requests for water or something to drink. In the early afternoon we had our first case of heat stroke. An elderly woman collapsed under the forward guntub. Fortunately, Nils Anderson, a professional fireman and trained paramedic, was on hand and tended to her while an ambulance was called. It arrived within a few minutes and the woman was escorted down the gangway and taken to the hospital. We called the ambulance twice more that day, each time for an elderly woman with a case of heat stroke. The temperature was 100° F. at 4 p.m. The newspaper the next day would report more than 1,000 cases of heat stroke at *L'Armada* that day. Nonetheless, it was our best day in Rouen with more than 5,200 people coming aboard.

Ron Robson: "I cannot imagine anybody going through what the galley crew went through in the tropics and the intolerable heat in Rouen. These guys, it was relentless, seven days a week, twelve hours a day, every day. I really salute them for their persistence."

That night the fireworks were even better than before. From the chief mate's journal: "Tonight's fireworks were so good that all the ships and boats in the harbor blew their whistles."

The following day was overcast which had a welcome cooling effect. We had ordered diesel fuel which was supposed to come during the night so as not to interfere with visiting hours. Of course, the fuel barge came alongside just after we opened. This meant we had to prevent smoking on board and rope off a portion of the offshore main deck where the fueling was taking place, to prevent the public from interfering or being injured. The roped-off area was an integral part of the blue line tour. To make it work we decided to run part of the tour backwards. In theory, a strategically-placed French volunteer would instruct everyone to walk against the white arrows on the blue line instead of with them. Later in the tour another docent would tell them to resume following the white arrows. The end result was everyone going every which way. Confusion reigned. Just about the time we got things sorted out, the fueling was complete, the barge left and the normal route was open again. As we learned to say, "*c'est la vie.*"

Phil Sinnott: "The passageway by the deck department fo'c'sles was cordoned off to visitors. After taking a shower one afternoon, I figured nobody was around and leaped naked from the shower across to my room. There were six women standing there watching me. The thing that bothered me most of all was that they laughed."

Greg Williams: "The crushing crowds really got to me for a while, especially in Rouen. Just facing this constant crush, trying to make my way to the pantry to work and get out of my fo'c'sle,

I had to psyche myself up sometimes just to try to make my way through the crowd. And people poking their heads through my porthole, saying the same things all the time, like what's for lunch and *bon appétit* and giggling. If I hear that one more time I'm going to scream or do something. That got real old. But I would never tell that to anyone, never. I would never say anything or do anything because when it's open house, it's open house. You can't hurt peoples' feelings or offend anyone. That's part of the game. It doesn't mean I have to like it or not get tired of it and I was."

They might complain amongst themselves, but the crew was always sensitive to the fact that, in the eyes of the French and British, we represented the United States, the merchant marine, and the veterans of World War II. Under very difficult circumstances they came through as the best possible examples of American good will.

Rich Reed: "All the port time I think was really tough on everybody. You know, you get five or six thousand people a day in your home, with the heat and everything that we went through, guys get frazzled, they get tired. There was noise all night long, and we had been in port for a long time. I think a lot of guys were antsy to get back to sea, get back to where they got their ship, their home, back to themselves. But, on the other hand, that was why we were there. We knew we'd be exposed to that stuff. We were there to show the ship to people."

Darwin Curtis: "And there were surprises: a sudden freeze of the tour while the ship loaded portable toilets with its antique steam winches, the arrival up the 'down' accommodation ladder of bottle-laden caterers for the evening Kiwanis party, the heatstroke of a dear lady who hallucinated about having a husband who must be summoned over the loud speaker."

There wasn't much time for sight-seeing in Rouen, but occasionally we did get away. The favorite sights were the cathedral in town and the shops and restaurants along Gros-Horloge Street and surrounding the marketplace.

One crew member discovered a small restaurant in Rouen serving the *Jeremiah O'Brien* pizza. Many of us detoured past the cafe when ashore, just to see our pizza on the menu. Made of ham and mushrooms, it was tasty and popular with all hands. Off-duty time was mostly spent visiting other ships or hosting their crews. Of the other ships the most popular were the *Drakesburg* from South Africa, the *Jeanne d'Arc*, the *Christian Radich* from Norway and the *Amerigo Vespucci* from Italy, although she was difficult to see because visiting hours were short and the lines long. The *Jeremiah O'Brien* and the *Jeanne d'Arc* vied for first place in popularity with the visitors to *L'Armada*.

Each night almost every ship in the harbor had a private party on board. The *Jeremiah O'Brien* was no exception. Caterers began preparations even before we closed to the public for the day. One evening, the Kiwanis were hosting and round tables were set up on the foredeck with chairs for ten circling each one. Linen tablecloths followed, then elegant white china, gleaming silverware and thin, tapered candlesticks. Meanwhile, a band set up their amplifiers and music stands on top of no. 2 hatch. Food arrived — smoked salmon, mussels, smoked fish, oysters, crab, paté, veal, chicken, petit fours, cookies, pastries, champagne, wine and mineral water. It was the most lavish banquet to date aboard our ship. The crew got the leftovers, the ship got a $2,000 rental fee for the evening, and everyone was happy.

The *O'Brien* received an invitation to a party on the Colombian training ship, *Gloria*. The captain and the admiral were busy with the Kiwanis, so the chief mate was designated to represent the *O'Brien*. In white uniform, I gently pushed through the sea of humanity toward the *Gloria*. Passing the *Christian Radich*, the sounds of "Begin the Beguine" poured over the dock as their party got underway with well-dressed people dancing on the decks, champagne glasses tinkling. A similar party was taking place on the *Simon Bolivar*. Finally arriving at the Colombian ship, I was piped aboard, explained Capt. Jahn's absence to the captain and was soon ensconced on the quarterdeck with a glass of champagne trying to understand a conversation in broken English between a Polish captain and a Belgian chief mate. An awning was spread overhead to keep out the sun. The wood decks were spotless, the railings varnished and the brass highly polished. Looking forward

I could see the wheelhouse, masts, yardarms, furled sails, ratlines and all the accoutrements that make up a great sailing ship. Later, three officers from the *Eagle* arrived and we munched canapes and talked. After a short while I wandered around, looking at the ship's wheelhouse and interior. The wheelhouse was small but elegantly furnished with modern electronic equipment. The visibility was surprisingly poor with all the masts and rigging blocking the view forward. I struck up a conversation with an Englishman who was boatswain and mate aboard the Omani ship, the *Shebab Oman.* He

The Shebab Oman, *under sail, taken from the official program.*

mentioned that his ship was affectionately referred to as the "Shish-Kebab." We soon abandoned the Colombian ship for the Omani, where, in the manner of seaman everywhere, he showed me the wheelhouse equipped with the latest in electronics, quarters finished in refined elegance, the galley and public rooms. A three-masted schooner, the ship was small, modern and trim. The crew were all from the Sultanate of Oman except for my guide and the master, who were British. The crew wore native garb, long robes and pillbox hats and were extremely gentle and kind to the visitors. After a small buffet of egg sandwiches I left, promising to have him as a guest aboard the *O'Brien.*

Tom Patterson: "Our week went very fast, it was just running constantly. As representatives of the ship, the captain and I had a busy social program. A French captain was assigned to us, Stanislaus Bienville, and he was excellent. He got us through all the crowds, to every place we had to go, told us what uniform to wear, when we had to take a plaque to give, told us everything. Everybody on the ship was working hard and we hardly ever saw each other that whole week."

As part of the festivities, the Pernod Corporation gave us a donation of $10,000. One of their aperitif products is "Pastis 51," the tie-in to a 51-year-old ship seemed natural and it was a great help with our cash shortage.

Darwin Curtis filled us in on the French press' reaction to our efforts at making money: "All this fund raising inspired one French journalist to write that Yankee shrewdness was alive and well and the *O'Brien* would sail from France with 'her holds full of dollars.' That provoked an irate response from a knowledgeable Frenchman, citing the facts and shaming the big French oil companies for not bunkering the *O'Brien*. 'It would take no more fuel than you mop up when cleaning a storage tank,' he wrote. The next day, the paper printed a very helpful piece to atone for the damage, if any. Contributions kept coming, including free tugboat service and two pallets of charcoal for the galley's stove."

Thursday, July 14, was Bastille Day, the French equivalent to our Independence Day. Morning began with the usual sound of boatswains' whistles skirling through the harbor, then the announcements over the various shipboard public address systems. But today, the *Jeanne d'Arc* fired her deck cannons. We counted as each report sent a cloud of grey-white smoke wafting across the river — twenty-one volleys in honor of French independence.

Darwin Curtis: "The other ships of the Armada were mostly stately. The great square-riggers were naval training ships from Chile and Italy and Brazil and Germany and other countries. They were alive with scrubbed midshipmen springing into the rigging to balance on spars and sing lusty sea chanteys. There were also modern warships, notably the brand-new French helicopter carrier, the *Jeanne d'Arc*. One day there was a big parade of all ships crews. The vets of the *O'Brien* formed up and marched, too. According to the local press, they received by far the greatest ovation from the huge crowds that lined the way."

En ce 50e anniversaire de la Libération, les vétérans du Jeremiah O'Brien - le Liberty Ship - étaient émus, ils ont été très applaudis

Our crew of veteran mariners received the strongest ovation from the crowd in the Bastille Day parade.   From Paris Normandie.

Bill Duncan: "While we were waiting for the parade to start we saw this bagpipe band from the *Shebab Oman* and they had been instructed by British and Scottish teachers.   Anyhow, while we were there I went up to them and asked them to play "Flowers of the Forest," one of my personal favorites, and they played it."

As they passed the reviewing stand, the *O'Brien* veterans were given a standing ovation.

Wes Masterson: "In the parade, we saw the older people with tears in their eyes, reliving the liberation.   They threw flowers and rose petals at us and whenever we stopped people came over and asked us for our autographs."

The high level of excitement was constant.   Day or night there was always *something* going on.   The instant one stepped out on deck one was in the middle of, and part of, one of the greatest maritime spectacles of all time.   The great majestic ships with their tall masts, the warships' monumental masses, the uni-formed sailors, the crowds, it was all one great, big, colorful ka-leidoscope of shapes, color, movement and enthusiasm.

Early each morning, many of us got up on deck, steaming mugs of coffee in our hands, trying to take in our surroundings. Forward of our bow a line of tall ships and Naval vessels led in a gentle arc against the bank down river.   First was the Ukrainian square-rigger *Kershones,* white hulled with gold trim. Ahead of her, the *Esmeralda,* the Chilean four-masted schooner, then the *Dar Mlodziezy*, a Polish three-masted tall ship, then a mix of warships and tall ships from all over the world — South Africa, Brazil, Denmark, Italy and Russia — a forest of masts cutting through the smoky morning air. Astern of the *Jeremiah O'Brien* was the *Christian Radich*, the three-masted Norwegian square-rigger, next to her the *Asgard II,* an Irish brig, then the *Simon Bolivar*, the *Astrid,* the *A. Von Humboldt*, the *Pogoria,* the *Frederyk Chopin*, the *Gloria,* the *Eagle,* the *Shebab Oman*, the *Cuauhtémoc* and the *Maria Asumpta*, tall ships all. On the opposite bank of the river lay the *Amerigo Vespucci, Belem, Winston Churchill,* and a grand mix of warships and sailing ships. "There will never be a gathering of ships like this again," said Capt. Jahn.

Bastille Day was our best day yet with almost 5,300 visitors on board. There were complaints when we sent a volunteer down to the ticket booth an hour before closing with a sign advising of the closing time. In addition to our status as the only Liberty and the last veteran of D-Day, we were also the only ship in the harbor that opened her interior to the public. This added to our attraction. Someone commented that we were the equivalent of an "E" ride at Disneyland.

Brian Goldman, fireman-watertender: "I came aboard on Bastille Day. That was something for me, arriving in Rouen and walking down the streets with my fifty-five-pound backpack. Then coming on the ship and just seeing the masses of people and shops. And everyone wanting you to stamp their books and sign them. And then the

Jean Yates commemorates our stay with a work of O'Brien art. Photo courtesy of Jean Yates.

French people coming with discharge papers from Libertys, shaking your hand, telling you 'Thank you, Thank you.' I never got a respect for history to that degree in school and now I have a

This magnificent photo from the official program shows the crew of the Ukrainian ship Kershones *at work.*

The view down river from the O'Brien. Tall ships into infinity.

And the view back toward town and William the Conqueror Bridge. Photo by Bob Black.

whole different view of history, a whole different idea of World War II."

The gratitude of the French people seemed inexhaustible, often as touching as it was surprising. Darwin Curtis: "One day, a tiny old lady, beautifully dressed, came up the accommodation ladder, saw the collection box and put in twenty francs. Then she came over and handed me a plastic envelope. Inside was the 8 June 1944 edition of a Rouen newspaper. The front page was covered with stories of the allied invasion, the devastating German counterattack and the confidence expressed by the German General Staff in Berlin that the invaders would soon be hurled back into the sea. At the top, in pencil, she had written in English, 'For the Liberty ship *Jeremiah O'Brien* for whole veterans crew with gratitude Armada Liberte Rouen — 10 July 1994.' She had treasured it for fifty years but now she wanted the captain to have it. I asked for her name and she demurred, she preferred to remain anonymous."

Jim Wade: "It's really the gratitude of the people which I will remember for the rest of my life. Especially a sixteen year old girl who came on board with her mother and father and then later sent a couple of little gifts for me with a note that said, 'Thank you for the visit of *SS Jeremiah O'Brien*, thank you to liberate France, June, 1944.' That says it all."

Jean Yates: "I was on the bridge and a couple and their daughter were there. I chatted with them and they were speaking French and, of course, I was having trouble trying to explain. They both were the last people on the bridge that day. And they pulled out a bottle of red wine and it had a ribbon on the top and little things and they handed it to me and it said something about, 'for an American friend, who brought this ship in.' I looked at it, it was written in French, but I got that much of it. I wasn't sure that they were going to give it to me. I said, 'Is it for me?' Yeah, it was for me. I had a little moisture in my eye. You know, you're a big old tough strong hairy man and you shouldn't do that, but that kind of gets to me."

Our World War II veterans were very much in the forefront of peoples' interest. Capt. Jahn, Adm. Patterson, Ed Lingenfield, Bill Duncan, Russ Mosholder, Jim Wade, Phil Sinnott, Dick Brannon, Jean Yates, Bill Rowlands, Bob Gisslow, Carl Kreidler, Ed Smith, François Le Pendu, Jim Miller, Rich Hill and Wes Masterson were constantly in demand because of their status as World War II veterans.

In the evening some sailors from the Russian ship, *Natoychivvy,* came aboard with gifts and souvenirs. We treated them to a late snack and traded curios and stories. The language problem was eased by the fact that one of them spoke excellent English, but no one understood why. We later learned that in the old regime he had been the political commissar on board the *Natoychivvy* and was fluent in many languages. They brought several bottles of vodka and introduced us to the Russian custom that requires once a bottle of vodka is opened, it must be finished. The party, with Ron Robson, Phil Sinnott, Jim Conwell and the chief mate, went from saloon to messroom and settled into a contest of who could propose the best toast and drink his shot of vodka down in one gulp without wincing. First it was "To Russia," followed by, "To America," and "To *L'Armada,*" to "The Russian-American friendship, may it last forever." "The *Jeremiah O'Brien.*" "The *Natoychivvy.*" "Vasily." "Ron." "Gregoravich." "Jimmy." "The girls we left behind." and ended with "the future," "Hope," "apple pie" and "borscht."

The following day started before the previous one even ended. At 1:15 a.m. the conga band went past, pounding drums,

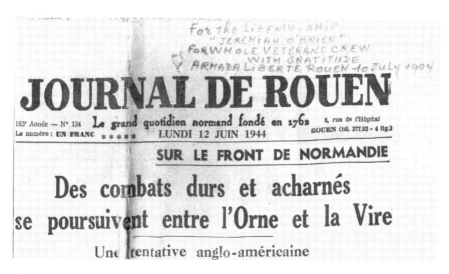

This is the front page of the newspaper presented to Darwin Curtis by an anonymous French woman.

beating pans, blowing trumpets. On board the *O'Brien,* we pulled pillows over our heads and tried to get some sleep before the morning's onslaught. Even at daybreak, we could tell that the heat would be upon us again.

In the early morning the esplanade was empty of tourists. The fronts of all the tents were rolled down, moisture condensed on their white surfaces. Here and there artists sat or stood, their easels holding canvas or paper as they sketched, watercolored and painted. The *O'Brien* became a popular subject, surprisingly, because she was one of the few vessels that <u>wasn't</u> a tall ship. Mechanized street-sweepers ran the length of the wharf, their round brushes whirring away dirt and debris from the previous day. Then delivery trucks began to appear, loaded with produce, milk, bread, fruits, vegetables and meats to carry the ships through another day. These were followed by the professional caterers, taking down the detritus of the previous evening's party and setting up for the one to come. Around 8 a.m. people began appearing on the quay, families, women, children, teenagers, seniors, mothers with strollers, men with dogs on leashes, small groups. Crowds began gathering at some point of interest, growing larger, until, once again, the esplanade was covered with a gaily-colored river of people. On the *O'Brien,* the crew turned to, washing down the main deck, carrying garbage to dumpsters ashore, renewing flags, cleaning the hand rails in the engine room, making bag lunches for the crew and volunteers (because of the crowds we quit serving lunch after the second day). Our French volunteers, lead by Darwin Curtis and Capt. Cole, began coming aboard about nine. There were discussions of the problems from the day before, suggestions as to how to resolve them, and then it was ten o'clock. Time to get everyone in place, open the ticket booth and take the rope off the gangway, ready for another intense seven hours of people-moving. As usual, the crew spelled each other at the card table at the foot of the gangway, signing autographs and stamping programs.

During the day one of our French-speaking docents asked me where to find Mrs. Hook. She and Capt. Hook were still with us, he helping on deck and she in the ship's store. I told the docent where she was and, surprisingly, a few minutes later, saw the same girl making her way toward the store with four uniformed ambulance men behind her. It seemed perfectly obvious that Mrs. Hook, like many others, had fainted from the heat. Concernedly working my way to the store, I was astonished to see her in position, happily ringing up sales as if nothing was wrong. "Are you all right?" I asked. "I'm fine, how are you?" was her puzzled reply. I told her the conclusion I arrived at. She laughed. She had tripped and hurt her hand while ashore five days earlier and was taken to the hospital in an ambulance. Her hand was sore but not broken. The ambulance men now aboard were those that took her to the hospital and they were simply stopping by to see how she was. It was a reminder of the incident with Jean Yates in Southampton; the compassion of the ordinary people in England, now reenacted in France.

The store had its own set of difficulties, among them what to do with all the cash that was coming in. Ron Robson: "We had tremendous problems making deposits. In England and France they use coins for £1 and 10 francs and 20 francs. We had so much coin, we had thousands and thousands of dollars worth of coins to deposit. And neither country has coin sleeves like we do. In England we put them in color-coded plastic bags, but in France they had flat paper that the coins had to be rolled in. It took hour upon hour to make up a deposit. Bob Burnett and Art Taber took backpacks, loaded with forty and fifty pounds of coins, to make our bank deposit. This was frequent."

An embarrassing mix-up occurred when the town of D'Isneauville invited the crew to dinner and sent a bus to pick them up. Under the impression that we were a Navy ship with hundreds of crew, they expected at least fifty to sixty guests and had arranged for thirty families to host them. On a Navy ship, this wouldn't have been a problem — simply order fifty to sixty sailors to get on the bus. Our small crew were volunteers, and even if they had all been willing to go, we couldn't have all left the ship to go to dinner. Also, everyone was simply so tired from the demanding difficulties of handling 5,000 people a day that they just didn't want to go anywhere. So they didn't. The few that went were treated royally, made guests of honor, had a fine dinner and saw the dedication of the town's maritime museum to the *Jeremiah O'Brien.*

Wes Masterson: "Eight or ten of us went. A bus took us to that town and the French people met us at the town hall. The mayor met us there and a different French family took each one of us to their houses for lunch. We came back to the town hall at six, had a ceremony, they played 'The Star Spangled Banner,' the mayor presented us each with a medallion. Then they served appetizers and cocktails and followed that with a barbecue. That was an exciting day."

And something to write home about, Our agents in Rouen, CGM Le Havre, were our "post office." They handled all the mail coming in and going out and were our link with home.

In California, Bev Masterson checked the mail daily for letters from her husband, Wes. "We've been married forty-seven years and this was the first time we've been separated, It seemed like he was gone forever. We wrote quite often, but we wouldn't get the mail, and sometimes packages and mail came all at once, some didn't arrive until after he returned home."

On board, another candlelight dinner was held on the main deck, sponsored this time by Eurest. The fireworks display that night was so grand that again every ship, including the *Jeremiah O'Brien*, applauded with its whistle. All over the harbor we heard toots, bellows, claxons, bells and horns. But our 51-year-old steam whistle with its deep-throated authoritative booming roar outdid them all.

On July 16, one of our replacement crew, John Linderman, joined us from San Francisco bringing several copies of the previous day's *San Francisco Chronicle.* Everyone was eager for news of home, and, really, not so much the news but the simple familiarity of the hometown newspaper. We also heard that the ship was being asked to go to Washington, D.C. It was felt that the presence of the *Jeremiah O'Brien* in the nation's capital would have a favorable effect on pending maritime legislation. This was exciting news, similar to being asked to give a command performance.

Liberty-ship : un morceau d'histoire industrielle et militaire

Des navires témoins d'une aventure militaire, industrielle et humaine

Présent cet après-midi en rade du Havre, demain sur les quais, le "Jeremiah O'Brien" est un cargo vieillot de 134 mètres. Lancé en 1943, ses lignes n'ont en effet rien d'époustouflant. Pourtant il ne faut pas s'y tromper, c'est bien un vestige d'histoire militaire et industrielle.

Le "Jeremiah O'Brien" est l'un des deux seuls rescapés de l'armada de 2710 "Liberty ships" construit par les Américains entre 1941 et 1945.

Rustique

Le problème qui se posait alors aux alliés était tout simple : la base arrière étant de l'autre côté de l'océan, l'armée allemande occasionnant de gros dégâts à la flotte, il fallait construire très rapidement une immense armada capable d'encaisser de lourdes

pertes et de transporter une gigantesque armée des Etats-unis vers l'Europe.

Pour cela, il a fallu construire en série un bateau simple, rustique et fiable.

Dix-sept chantiers furent construits sur les côtes est et ouest du USA. Ne restait plus qu'à produire, vite, très vite, excessivement vite, en profitant d'une technique révolutionnaire pour l'époque : la soudure qui venait remplacer les rivets.

Moins de cinq jours

Aux Etats-unis, les chantiers étaient de véritables ruches, et l'aventure humaine es resté gravée dans la mémoire des ouvriers américains.

Les entreprises fonctionnaient souvent 24 heures sur 24 et un chantier comme l'Oregon Shipbuilding qui employait 35.000 salariés

réussit le tour de force de construire 322 bateaux entre 42 et 44.

Durée moyenne de construction : 47 jours. Mais les chantiers se lançaient de véritables défis. Ainsi l'un de ces Liberty ship fut assemblé en moins de cinq jours, ce qui ne favorisait pas toujours la qualité des navires.

200 au fond

Malgré cela ces navires remplirent parfaitement leur mission, s'acquittant d'un lourd tribut à la victoire. Plus de 200 coulèrent, victimes de leur lenteur et des attaques de l'armée adverse.

Après guerre, ces navires ne furent pas abandonnés. Nombre d'entre eux convoyèrent les aides matérielles du plan Marshall, d'autres furent vendus un peu partout dans le monde. La France en récupéra notamment près de 80.

Our coverage in the press continued. This article is from Liberté Le Havre Dimanche.

The boatswain-mate from the *Shebab Oman* came aboard and we were delighted to reciprocate the tour he so courteously provided on his ship. We also had visitors aboard from other ships. The receptions and gala events went on non-stop, from luncheon to midnight, and we all visited as many ships in the Armada as we could manage. It was another once-in-a-lifetime opportunity, this chance to go aboard and receive guided tours of so many famous vessels. We would meet someone at a reception, be invited back for a tour during off-hours, and return the favor. Everyone was curious about the *O'Brien* and its history, just as we were curious about their ships. We enjoyed the different cultures, cuisines and wines, and the language "barriers" were not barriers at all. It was the brotherhood of the sea, in spades.

Darwin Curtis: "Officers and crew from other ships came aboard frequently. Some acted as though it was a shrine. 'You are welcome aboard,' I said to a smart French Navy commander from the *Jeanne d'Arc*. 'It is an honor to be here,' he answered."

Almost everyone had a little slice-of-life story about our visitors. Phil Sinnott is an animated person who talks with lots of gestures: "I was on the flying bridge explaining in fractured French how things work and the group had the blankest look. I asked them if they understood — they said "No." I said, 'Where are you from?' They said 'London.'"

Darwin Curtis: "There was a loud argument on the after deck between two French people. A woman standing in line was complaining out loud about everything — it was too hot, the line was too long, the ship was a mess, the admission was too high and so on. A Frenchman behind her finally got fed up and handed her ten francs and told her to get off the ship, to applause from the onlookers."

In all, about 35,000 people visited the *O'Brien* at Rouen. The gate receipts and store sales gave us enough to continue the voyage.

Jean-Paul Caron and Maud Paléologue had converted our ship's hospital, located in the after house, to an office. From there they coordinated parties, acted as liaison with our ship's agent, arranged press interviews and dealt with the giant task of selling tickets and coordinating logistics for our trip down the Seine. It had already been decided that to reward our French volunteers for all their help, we would let them ride down the Seine with us. It would be small enough thanks for all they had done. We borrowed 500 lifejackets from the *Jeanne d'Arc* for the cruise, limiting ourselves, in theory, to that many people. Both the French and American Coast Guard would not let us carry more people than we had lifejackets. As Jean-Paul Caron realized the ship would earn $180 per person from the cruise and carrying the volunteers would mean reducing the number of paying passengers, he began lobbying not to let the French volunteers go along. Jean-Paul

> Born in San Francisco in 1920, Phil Sinnott shipped out as an ordinary seaman in the Army Transport Service (ATS). Later he joined the Army and saw action in Ardennes, Belgium and through Germany. After the war he returned to the University of Oregon, then went to work as a reporter for the *San Francisco Chronicle*, got a teaching credential and taught first in elementary school then at the University of California, Berkeley. While there, he was loaned to the Department of Education for Samoa and spent two years in American Samoa. Retiring in 1978 he has worked as docent at Point Bonita lighthouse and been involved with the *Jeremiah O'Brien* since she came out of the Reserve Fleet. He served as AB on the Normandy voyage from San Francisco to Le Havre on the 8 to 12 watch. He and his wife live in Lafayette, California.

went to Capt. Cole and told him the volunteers couldn't go. This was unacceptable to me. We had a list of fifty people who had helped us from the very beginning, giving up their time, working in scorching weather with difficult crowds of people, who were promised the trip. I spoke to Adm. Patterson, to tell him that we could only carry 450 paying passengers because of the volunteers. He listened patiently as I reminded him of our promise to the volunteers, then said "Is four hundred fifty your recommendation? Then tell him that's the number."

Tom Patterson: "This wonderful French carrier, *Jeanne d'Arc*, which was the largest ship there, and her young French captain, Captain du Monte, became a very good friend of ours. He did everything possible to help us, even to loaning us five hundred lifejackets, all brand-new, for our French passengers. We were inspected by the U.S. Coast Guard Representative and also by the French Coast Guard representative and given an excursion permit which made it legal for us to carry these. We actually carried four hundred eighty-five people although we could have taken five hundred."

July 17 came, our last day in Rouen and the day scheduled for *L'Armada de la Liberté* to sail down the Seine to Le Havre. We woke to an overcast and — finally — cool day with very mixed feelings. It had been a hectic, frantic, nerve-frazzling nine days; we were worn out, tired of coping in a foreign language with thousands of people, exhausted from days that began at 6 a.m. and ended with noise, fireworks and samba bands at 2 a.m. And yet it had been the most exciting, most remarkable nine days of all our lives. In a trip filled with highlights, memorable events, emotional upwellings and nostalgia, *L'Armada de la Liberté* would probably stand out as the highest highlight, the most memorable event, the pinnacle of our once-in-a-lifetime voyage. "Never again will there be a gathering of ships like this," we told ourselves, and each other, over and over. With great regret we prepared to bid farewell to Rouen.

We boarded our passengers and volunteers at 0730. It was a day of celebration, with cannon fire from the Naval vessels and the sound of ships' whistles echoing back and forth across the harbor. At 0820, the *Maria Asumpta*, a British brig, departed followed every five minutes by another ship for the 60-mile run down the Seine to Le Havre. The *Jeremiah O'Brien* was scheduled to leave at 0930. The last ship, the *Iskra*, would depart at 1135. Helicopters hovered above the harbor as the procession got underway. Crowds were gathered on the pier cheering each ship as she sailed slowly by. As our turn came, we singled up, then threw off the last line. The people applauded as we slowly moved out to midstream. Ahead of us was the *USS Grasp*, a U.S. Navy underwater recovery ship. The *Minbelli*, an Italian destroyer, soon pulled up astern. As the *Jeremiah O'Brien* passed ships that were still tied up awaiting their turn, we received flag and whistle salutes. On some ships the officers and sailors, in formation at their ship's rail, hand-saluted.

Both banks of the Seine were lined with people, from Rouen sixty miles to its mouth at Le Havre. The French newspapers the following day would report an estimate of six to eight million. They were waving and cheering and hollering that European duophone sound uhhhh-ohhhhh, uhhh-ohhhhh. People, millions of people, waved American and French flags and blew whistles and horns. As we returned their salutes with our ship's whistle they shouted and applauded even louder. It was an unforgettable experience — an unsurpassable cap to the whole glorious Armada.

Sailing down river, we recognized the chateaux, thatched roof cottages, castles on hills, towns and villages we had seen just two weeks before. Looking beyond the people, the view was peaceful and serene, like a Monet painting, fields or hills, small towns and villages. The sky was hazy with an occasional grey plume of smoke listlessly rising from a chimney. From time to time we even smelled the wood fires burning. But these sights were overshadowed by the unbelievable crowd gathered to see *L'Armada de la Liberté* pass into history. Up and down the river were the great sailing ships, their masts probing the sky, in a tableau from centuries past. The whole scene was mind-boggling — the *Jeremiah O'Brien* sailing down the Seine in the midst of a fleet of tall ships, millions of people clustered on the banks, behind them chateaux-covered hills or small French villages. Bands in some of the towns we passed played "The Star-Spangled Banner" or "Battle Hymn of the Republic."

Not all the bands were good, but that was part of the fun. Bob Black: "We were listening to some of the bands on the shore try to play 'The Star-Spangled Banner.' There was one band which had a saxophonist that I suspect may not have known his instrument very well and certainly didn't know 'The Star-Spangled Banner' very well. It sounded like somebody was trying to kill a sea otter."

Bob Burnett: "As we were going down the Seine from Rouen to Le Havre, there were probably millions of people that lined the banks to watch all the ships. Every now and then we saw American flags and heard our national anthem. But in one place on the bank of the river, on the port side, was written in English in large letters 'THANK YOU.' It was absolutely meant for us. I was moved to tears. It was a very special moment."

There was something about our steam whistle that captivated everyone. After one particularly long whistle blast to roaring applause, our pilot laughingly commented about the quiet of the ship's engines and the loudness of the whistle. The crowds continued, a festive, happy, holiday spirit prevailing. Parasols and umbrellas twirled happily at our approach. On one bank a trumpeter blew reveille. On another the crowd stood at one end, then sat creating "the wave," as others stood and sat again, the effect rippling down the bank beyond us, like fans at a football game. The river banks were alive with people, six deep, and each village we passed was packed to overflowing. We heard three cheers from one river bank. It was answered by our passengers, then by the ship's whistle, which brought more cheers and applause.

Ed Smith: "Coming down the Seine was overwhelming. You say, six million people? You know, nobody can really envision six million people. But sixty miles of people. That was overwhelming!"

The spirit from shore was contagious. Everyone waved and hollered and shouted and gave three cheers, hour after hour.

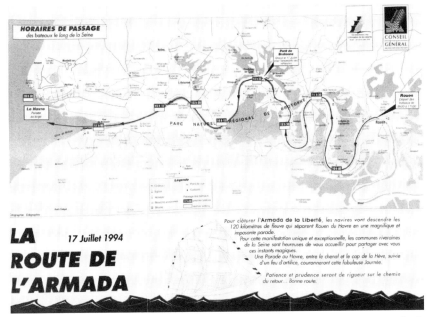

The official parade route down the Seine as provided by L'Armada de la Liberté.

Sam Wood: "I think we will all remember coming down the Seine River. The intensity of that, the visual sights, the bands, the banners, the messages in various languages, the people. The cheering was an infectious thing and even 300 feet out in the middle of the river you could still feel it. To experience that is, it's electrifying to be part of that. For the ship and the crew, you can't help but share in that. That will always be a highlight."

In the excitement, Tom Patterson armed himself with a battery-operated megaphone and went from one side of the flying bridge to the other, shouting to the people lining the banks, "*Merci, merci beaucoup. Viva la France.* From Jeremy O'Brien. *Merci Beaucoup.*" He did this for hours and when his voice gave out he handed the megaphone to Jim Wade who took up the chant.

Tom Patterson: "We went down the river and I would say this is another highlight of our voyage, from Rouen down to the English Channel there at Le Havre. According to the French newspapers the next day there were over 6,000,000 people lining both banks of the Seine to watch these forty-six ships or forty-seven ships go down. And the one they seemed to be the most

Crowds lined the river and villages were packed with people. Photo by John Linderman.

The Jeremiah O'Brien cruising down the Seine looks almost like it's traveling across land. Photo by Jean-Yves Brouard.

This was a typical scene as more than 6,000,000 lined the banks of the river. Photo by Jean Yates.

interested in was the *Jeremiah O'Brien*, because we saw so many American flags being waved back and forth and bands playing 'The Star-Spangled Banner.' It was so heartwarming to see these people and huge gatherings where the towns were, waving and cheering and all the people on our ship were waving and cheering. I had a sound-powered bull horn that I was shouting, '*Viva la France, Merci Beaucoup.*' People would yell back at us, 'Vive America.' It was a great spectacle to see."

Ed Smith: "Even the admiral was in the spirit, up there *merci beaucoup*-ing all over the place with that bullhorn."

On board, Sandy, our Scots musician, held sway on the after deck with ballads, blues and hillbilly music, while on the fore deck a band hired for the event played swing music. A caterer provided the meals — ham, roast beef, salad, potatoes, bread, dessert.

The crew reminisced about recent events. Bob Burnett: "The last night in Rouen there was a gal that I met at the museum party and she took me around town and showed me some of the city she was proud of. The following day her mother rode the ship down the river. I told the mother I'd met her daughter and the mother said, 'Well, I see she's learned some of the habits of her mother, picking up American sailors.'"

Bill Bennett remembered another incident: "One thing that comes to mind is how Marty Shields handled two women on the ship at the same time down the Seine. He put one on the bow and one on the stern and he kept going between them. He'd tell one, 'Darling I gotta go do some work on the other end of the ship' and he'd disappear for awhile. I could learn something from that guy."

As we neared the Normandy bridge and the wider mouth of the river, fishing boats, motor yachts and small, privately-owned sailing yachts came out to greet us, their passengers shouting, waving and cheering. And even there, in the widest part of the river, the banks were lined with people happily watching the passing of the ships.

As we cleared the bridge, Le Havre came into view. Some of the ships, the *Jeremiah O'Brien* included, were scheduled to

Bélem, drapeau
tricolore au vent :
centenaire dans
deux ans.

Kershones, trois-mâts
ukrainien : la voile
traditionnelle sur
coque d'acier.

Basé à Saint-Malo, le côtre-
hunier Le Renard appartient à
un certain Robert Surcouf : ça
ne s'invente pas !

Jeremiah O'Brien :
comme à Rouen, le
liberty-ship rivalisera,
au Havre, en nombre de
visiteurs, avec la Jeanne.

Press coverage was phenomenal. This article is from Paris Normandie.

LE BORD DE MER PRIS D'ASSAUT PAR DES DIZAINES DE MILLIERS DE SPECTATEURS

The cover and headline speak for themselves.

complete *L'Armada de la Liberté* in Le Havre. The plan was for those ships to make a pass under that part of the city which was on a bluff facing the water, then come around and anchor for a fireworks display that evening. We peeled off from the parade route toward our destination. A strong wind was blowing and some of the sailing ships unfurled their sails, sailors and midshipmen climbing the rigging to unfasten lines, as they passed in front of the city, beautiful majestic ships with acres of white canvas. They sped gracefully past, some continuing out to sea, others joining us at the anchorage. We let go the anchor, the *Jeremiah O'Brien* fetched up on her chain, and we settled in to wait for darkness and the fireworks.

13

LE HAVRE

The fireworks display was at its grand finale when Capt. Jahn ordered the anchor raised. As we approached the harbor entrance the last explosions burst in the air shooting multicolored dandelion-shaped balls of flaming sparkles over the city. Inside the harbor we saw several of our Armada compatriots — French, Russian and Brazilian Naval ships — moored to the piers between tall-masted barks and square-riggers, all palely illuminated in the ghostly yellow flood lights of the harbor docks.

Just after midnight, we entered the breakwater and by 0100 we were approaching our berth, gliding past the *Jeanne d'Arc*. Late as it was, her band was assembled on the flight deck and as we passed she dipped her flag while the band played the theme from "The Longest Day." It was a singular honor to be saluted by the flagship of France. We were all deeply moved. It was a special ending to this remarkable day.

But it wasn't over, yet. We tied up close to the main gate to the harbor. The port authorities put two gangways aboard and our passengers filed ashore into waiting buses for the trip back to Rouen. Watching the buses disappear between the warehouses, we heard a loud commotion from one of the ships at the far end of the pier. Soon a ragtag mob of Brazilian sailors dressed in undershirts, shorts and odd pieces of uniform, came samba-ing up the dock. All through July the World Soccer finals were played in the United States and now word came that Brazil had won the World Cup. The sailors were ecstatic. They

L'Armada de la Liberté

Parade et Escale au Havre
17.18 Juillet 1994

The program announcing the parade to Le Havre, the official termination of L'Armada.

danced past, chanting and singing, drums beating out a rhythm punctuated by spoons clanging on galley pots and pans. Shouting and cheering lustily, they danced to the end of the dock, then back again. When they finally returned to their ship, we wearily turned in.

Monday, July 18, started with thick clouds and overcast which turned to drizzle by mid-morning. At breakfast Maud presented us with an exhausting program laid out by *L'Armada* officials: 1015 ten sailors from each ship attend a War Memorial ceremony at the General de Gaulle Square, 1115 ten sailors from each ship attend a Peace Ceremony aboard the *Jeremiah O'Brien*; 1200 to 1400 lunch for invited crews, 1400 to 1700 ships open to visitors, 1500 to 1730 musical entertainment at the Frissard Quay, 1700 to 1830 cocktail party at the local officers' club, 1900 cocktail party for ship captains aboard the *Jeanne d'Arc*, 2200 to 2300 an awards ceremony, from 2200 to 0200 a farewell party to the Armada at the maritime terminal.

Our communication difficulties were running true to form. What Peace Ceremony? This was the first we heard of it. We had two hours to clear the litter of the previous day's trip down the Seine — garbage, overflowing port-a-potties and chairs — return the life-jackets to the *Jeanne d'Arc* <u>and</u> wash the ship down <u>and</u> set up some kind of public address system on top of no. 2 hatch for the ceremony. But at this point everyone was too tired to complain. We simply turned to and tried to do the best we could in the time allowed.

Tom Patterson: "The next morning we were up-and-at-'em again because we had a big memorial service to go to, the captain and I. They had selected *Jeremiah O'Brien* for a Peace Ceremony. This involved about 500 people, the masters of all the other ships, commanding officers, members of the clergy, members of the state government, the city government."

JÉRÉMIAH O'BRIEN

Un bateau de guerre porteur de paix

« *Il est important de se recueillir avec vous pour se souvenir de votre arrivée en 1944*», a déclaré aux vétérans du Jérémiah O'Brien Jean-Yves Besselat, vice-président du conseil général chargé de l'arrondissement du Havre. « *Vous avez défendu notre liberté avec votre coeur et votre foi.* »

La foule était venue nombreuse assister à la cérémonie de la paix sur le Liberty ship américain. Mais pour avoir le privilège de monter à bord, il fallait montrer patte blanche. La plupart des badauds est donc restée sur le quai, où l'orchestre de la Jeanne d'Arc saluait en musique les vétérans américains venus participer à l'armada. Les choeurs André Caplet ont aussi participé à la cérémonie oecuménique en entonnant des chants religieux. Pour fêter la paix, une cérémonie religieuse mais pluri-confessionnelle, organisée pour rendre hommage aux marins disparus lors de la bataille de l'Atlantique, et à la liberté qu'ils ont défendue au prix de leur vie.

Un rabbin, un prêtre, un pasteur, ont successivement commenté le passage biblique de la tempête apaisée. Pendant la guerre, la tempête fit rage, et les hommes ont commencé à désespérer. Mais la foi soulève des montagnes, et a poussé une armée à défendre sa liberté. Avec la paix, la tempête s'est apaisée, et l'espoir a commencé à renaître.

Un jeune Havrais qui fêtait ce jour-là ses 18 ans a exprimé sa reconnaissance au nom de tous les jeunes de la ville : « *Nous n'avons pas vécu ces événements, mais nous désirons en conserver la mémoire* » , a-t-il déclaré aux anciens combattants français et américains. Le contre-amiral Patterson, fondateur de l'association qui a remis à flot le Jérémiah O'Brien, a remercié avec émotion les Normands pour leur accueil. « *Je suis heureux d'avoir découvert toute l'affection qu'ont les Français pour les soldats américains* » , a-t-il déclaré. « *Nos cargos ne transportent plus du matériel de guerre, mais sont devenus désormais des porteurs de paix, de mémoire, et d'espoir.* »

A.L.M.

The Peace Ceremony made the local paper, Le Havre-Presse.

As it was, some of the early arrivals for the Peace Ceremony had to dodge the deck department still washing down as they came aboard. The *O'Brien*'s officers put on their dress blues, the commanding officers from each ship came aboard, their contingents of ten sailors each formed up on the dock facing the ship. There was a light mist in the air as the band played the theme from "The Longest Day," followed by the French and American national anthems. Several speeches followed in French (with English translations) and Adm. Patterson's (in English with a French translation). Speaking without notes, he gave an eloquent speech telling how proud we were to be there, how honored we were by the reception the French had given us and the importance of commemorating D-Day as a call for peace. It was one of his best and we were quite proud of our admiral.

The remainder of the day was spent resting and straightening up the ship for the first visitors. It was a short but welcome relief from the intensity of our long week in Rouen.

That evening some of us went to a party aboard the Russian ship, *Natoychivvy*. We were given a tour of the vessel including crew quarters, missile launching turrets, guns, navigation bridge and officers' messroom. We were treated to what our guide referred to as a typical Russian sailor's dish: cabbage, ham, black bread and noodles. The refreshment, of course, was vodka. And, as we now knew, once the bottle is open . . . After dinner the party moved aboard the *Jeremiah O'Brien* with the Russians again providing the liquid refreshment. As the evening progressed, we made lengthy inroads toward cementing the friendship between our new ally, Russia, and the United States.

July 19 began with a steady rain that kept up all day. Surprisingly, despite the bad weather, by opening time, 1000, people were lined up at the ticket booth holding umbrellas, waiting to come aboard.

It may be an indication of how tired we were that we reverted to labeling each new problem the "crisis *du jour*," as we did before sailing from San Francisco when everybody was so exhausted. In any event, the "crisis" of this "*jour*" was that several French families had asked members of the crew to lunch and dinner every day during our stay in Le Havre. We didn't learn of it until 1000, and found out the cars would be showing up at noon. As in earlier ports, the French thought they were dealing with a Navy ship with a crew of hundreds that could be ordered to accept their kind hospitality. Hardly anyone wanted to go. Tom Patterson, ever sensitive to the feelings of people not attached to the ship, got quite excited and went from person to person trying to talk people into going to lunch with the French families. Capt. Jahn's reaction was, "Hell no. I'm not going anywhere." Eventually the admiral rounded up eight people to go to lunch; thirty were expected.

Nils Anderson, wiper: "The hospitality of the French people was just great, their graciousness, taking us into their homes, their businesses, like we were visiting some long-lost relatives."

Bill Bennett: "People opened their homes to us, we had receptions. This was amazing, the reception we got. It was a lot more than I thought we'd ever have on this trip."

The Armada ships began leaving in the late morning. As each ship passed, we dipped our flag and blew and returned whistle salutes. Several of our new friends on the Russian ship waved their hats. By late afternoon we had the entire pier to ourselves.

A new schedule was issued by the home office for the remainder of the trip: Portland, Maine August 6-15; Mid-Atlantic "Port to be determined" August 18-23; Jacksonville, Florida, August 26-29; Miami, Florida August 31; San Francisco, September 23. The port to be determined was a source of scuttlebutt although most of us were pretty sure it would be Washington, D.C. Miami was a surprise, but we were told that would be a fueling port. Fuel was reportedly several dollars a barrel cheaper in Miami than in other ports.

Le Havre was flattened during the war. As a result the city architecture dates from the late 1940s and early '50s. Compared to Rouen it was completely devoid of any points of interest or character. Those that went ashore exploring the town soon came back shrugging their shoulders.

That evening another party was thrown in no. 2 'tween deck to thank all the French people who had helped us in Rouen and Le Havre. Al Martino, Jimmy Farras and Eduardo Pubill outdid themselves with a roast beef dinner with all the trimmings — salad, bread, potatoes, vegetables, cake and wine. The speeches went on and on. They seemed longer than usual because Patterson had Gérald Guétat translate everything he said into French, but everyone seemed to enjoy themselves. The feelings of gratitude and sadness were genuine. We were in France for almost a month and in that time saw many of the beautiful French cities and much of the countryside, made many new friends and developed a fresh understanding of and appreciation for the French attitude toward the liberation of their country.

The following day brought a welcome change in the weather with a fine, clear day, blue skies and not a cloud in the sky. This was our last day to be open to the public in Europe. Jean Yates had painted a red, white and blue emblem on the pier at Rouen, similar to that which we left in Panama, giving the date and the ship's name. Now he did the same in Le Havre. Former French Liberty ship sailors continued to visit us and there was a steady stream of visitors but nothing like the crowds we had in Rouen.

Jim Conwell: "Hearing from French merchant mariners who sailed on these ships before, it certainly makes you part of a unique fraternity. For many of them, like myself, it was very early in their careers in the merchant marine and they have very fond memories of that."

Bob Gisslow: "I think the highlights have been the actual meetings with the people who came into the radio shack and the visits we made to the French homes and the English homes. And the friends that I've made, people that I'd probably never have met had we not made this voyage. But I'm impressed by that and will continue to correspond with them in future years."

There was still some grousing by a few of the crew about people from the "outside" coming aboard and eating their food and using their ship. And some of the old-line volunteers still resented the newer crew. Another problem was the idea of women being on board. It's an old superstition that women are bad luck on a ship. Of course, in modern times there's no place for such an attitude, but it existed. Mary Steinberg was a wiper from San

Jean Yates left his final calling card on the pier at Le Havre.

Francisco to Chatham. Saryl Von der Porten, Dottie Duncan, Jo Lawrence, Ruth Robson and Marci Hooper lived aboard for much of our European stay as did Julie Arlinghaus and Susannah Beckwith. Now that we were returning to sea, most of them were leaving. Russ was short a person in the steward's department and no one was available on short notice. We decided to have Ruth take the position, giving her the cabin that Mary used in the first part of the trip. This brought some grumbling. "She has to have her papers and work at a job every day. Unless she's at her job, she should stay out of the midships house as much as possible. She better not cause any trouble." Ruth always acted like a lady and was a willing and capable worker. There was no reason to complain. It was another case of people simply having a need to grumble and voice their opinions.

There seemed to be a strange sense of emotionalism in the crew throughout the day, a mix of sadness underlaid with a current of excitement. This was another crew change port. We would be losing Phil Sinnott, Jean Yates, Jim Conwell, Sven Keinanen, our third mate, and several others from the engine room. Many of those leaving had been with us since San Francisco. We would miss them. There was also a sense of excitement at preparing for sea again. Most of the crew were tired of dealing with so many crowds of people. They wanted their home, their ship, returned to them. They wanted to be at sea where everything was routine, predictable and there were no telephones or unexpected intrusions from shore.

Born in Brooklyn, New York in 1936, Jim Conwell lived there for twenty-two years, graduating from Polytechnic Institute with a degree in Civil Engineering. As a result of college R.O.T.C. he spent four years in the Army, three of them in the Normandy region of France. He worked in water resources planning for the U.S. Bureau of Reclamation from which he retired in 1992. An O'Brien volunteer since 1985, he and his wife, Jeannette, live in Sacramento, California.

The French continued to express their gratitude in many ways. Two French people came aboard and presented us with 500 franc notes ($100) to help us on our way. A French woman who had worked for Foster-Wheeler came aboard to buy a copy of *The Last Liberty*. She didn't have her check book, drove all the way back to Paris to get it and returned the next day for the autographed book. She said how grateful France was to America for liberating their country. While Clifford Hook was selling tickets one morning a woman gave him an envelope with 500 francs in it. Also in the envelope was a note which said, "Thank you very much. This is written on paper as old as your ship." There was no signature on the note and she disappeared in the crowd without identifying herself.

Phil Sinnott: "We were wrestling with the gangway in Le Havre one afternoon. It was threatening to fall off the pier be-

The paper Havre Libre *did a full page on the* Jeremiah O'Brien *while we were in port.*

cause of the monstrous tides, and the crowd was waiting to go on the ship. A woman ran out and said, 'I want to thank you for what you did in World War II and for bringing the ship back to France.' Then she gave me a bottle of Calvados."

Wes Masterson: "This one particular lady came up to me on the ship and was talking about when she was a young girl. The Germans came in and took their home for a headquarters, and they had to fend for themselves. And she remembered the *Jeremiah O'Brien* very well, that it was one of the first ships to bring supplies after the liberation. She remembered the ship and was so touched that it returned fifty years later."

Tom Patterson: "I think Le Havre was different than any other port. If there ever was a love affair between a ship and a port it had to be that. What took place there with Le Havre and our crew, not only did these people come down aboard our ship, but they took our crew members to their homes, they took them out to the country, they took them everyplace. And they just were marvelous. We made so many good friends there."

Thursday, July 21, we were closed to the public. We were scheduled to sail the following day and needed the time to take on fuel, boiler water, food stores and stow everything for sea. We would be in the North Atlantic, the most unforgiving of oceans, and wanted to be ready for it. This meant lowering all the cargo gear, lashing everything in place, making up all the loose gear, cleaning the decks, checking that everything was in its place, tied down and ready for sea. Marty Wefald, promoted to bosun with the departure of Rich Reed, took over, skillfully instructing Jim Miller, Bill Rowlands, Marty Shields, Sam Wood, Bob Burnett, John Linderman, Cliff Hook, Bill Bennett, Bob Black, Bill Fairfield, Jack Carraher and Ron Smith in their duties. Jack and Ron had become gunners for the remainder of the voyage. In the engine department Tim Palange, first assistant engineer (who once referred to himself as the Norman Swartzkopf of the engine room) was assisted by Jeff Speight, second assistant engineer, Kevin Kilduff, third assistant, and Bill Duncan, now third assistant. Together they supervised Ralph Ahlgren, Nils Anderson, David Aris, Bill Cannady, Brian Goldman, Lawrence Goldwaithe, Alex

Hochstraser, Ed Lingenfield, Ed Smith and Frank Vincenzo in preparing the engine room for sea. In the steward's department the routine of three meals a day continued with Russ Mosholder ably assisted by Al Martino, Jimmy Farras and Eduardo Pubill in the galley and Richard Allen, Lou Casaletto, Chuck Jennings, Pat McCafferty, Ruth Robson and Greg Williams in the messrooms.

The Mertz Company donated boiler water to the ship. This eliminated the need to distill our own water, saving wear and tear on the ship's evaporators. All day long and into the night, large, modern tank trucks came alongside, pumping water into the ship. Each truck was divided into compartments. The water was pumped under pressure so that as a compartment was emptied, the compressed air escaped and a loud "Swoooosh!" was heard all over the ship. This continued until late in the evening.

July 22 was our last day in France and Europe. The *San Francisco Chronicle* had us departing a day early. In an article that appeared on July 21, they reported:

> The San Francisco-based Liberty Ship *Jeremiah O'Brien* leaves Le Havre, France, today for its return voyage to the United States after a triumphant tour of England and France for the 50th anniversary of D-Day.
>
> On Sunday, the *O'Brien* was among 47 ships that sailed down the Seine River from Rouen to Le Havre as 3 million spectators lined the route. The ship is due to arrive August 6 in Portland, Maine, near its birthplace in South Portland, said Marci Hooper, business manager for the ship. On August 15, the ship is scheduled to leave Portland for a three-day call in Washington, D.C., and then on to Jacksonville, Fla., before returning to San Francisco via the Panama Canal.
>
> Portland is a diversion for the ship on its route to her home port of San Francisco, and the crew hopes it is a profitable stop. Portland is proud of the work of its shipyard, even though it no longer exists and a condominium project was built on the site.
>
> "They believe Portland ships are good ships, and that we have one still afloat proves it," Hooper said. The local shipyard society is holding a fund-raiser that will include two-hour cruises for $50 aboard the *O'Brien* and a $50-per-plate dinner. Hooper said it is hoped that the events will bring $100,000 to help maintain the ship at its Fort Mason berth.

About half the crew that took the *O'Brien* to England and France
will be on the ship on the trip home, Hooper said.

Departure day was surprisingly sad. Many of our French
volunteers had been with us since we arrived in Rouen. They
were quite attached to the ship. We saw tears in their eyes as they
walked around the *O'Brien* for the last time, then milled on the
dock waiting for our departure.

Jean-Paul Caron and a few others, including Maud
Paléologue's husband, arranged for a small convoy of World War
II vehicles to be on the dock for our departure: motorcycles,
jeeps, trucks and, of course, Jean-Paul's DUKW. Parked at the
foot of the gangway, they were a constant source of attention
during that final morning.

One task remained before departure from our last foreign
port. From the deck log: "0945 Completed search of all accessible areas for stowaways. None found. [signed] W. Jaffee, c/m."

Five pilots came on board, one to guide the ship out, four
to take a last ride on what would probably be the last Liberty ship
in French waters in history. The tugs *Abielle No. 7* and *Abielle
Le Havre* were made fast fore and aft. The gangways were taken
ashore and we started singling up the mooring lines. As the last
line came off and the ship moved away from the dock, Jack Carraher
threw a heaving line ashore. One of our French friends quickly
slipped a bottle of wine into a plastic bag, tying the bag to the end
of the line. By then we were thirty feet off the dock with the
distance widening. The Frenchman dropped the bottle as Jack
pulled sharply on the line. It went under and the crowd on the pier
gasped as it hit the side of the ship with a loud clunk. But Jack
heaved the bag up and pulled out the bottle, unbroken. This
brought a round of applause.

We blew our traditional three whistle blasts to the crowd.
They applauded and cheered, waving. Some dabbed at their eyes
with handkerchiefs. Offshore, a large tug-fireboat spouted water
in white, frothy, arcing spumes as the other tugs spun us around
and pointed us toward the harbor entrance.

This is almost the entire crew, including French volunteers, just before departing Le Havre. Photo by Marty Wefald.

Tom Patterson: "Finally the day came when we had to sail, July 22, and there were a lot of teary eyes both on the dock as well as on the ship. Our young French volunteers were so sad to see their ship go. Some of our wives were leaving to fly back to the United States."

As we sailed away from the pier, the World War II convoy on the dock fired up their engines and came chasing after us, sirens and horns blowing. They ran the length of the pier, faster and faster. Capt. Jahn said, "I hope their brakes all work." They did, bringing the vehicles skidding to a stop a few feet from the end of the pier. Then the drivers got out and waved after us.

A number of motorboats and yachts escorted us out the harbor, horns and whistles blowing. When we reached the sea buoy, the five pilots got off, climbing down the Jacob's ladder. The deck crew pulled the ladder on deck, rolled it up and tied it behind a mast house. The pilot boat blew three blasts, we returned the salute. Capt. Jahn ordered full ahead and we were on our way home.

Bill Bennett waxed poetic in the Crew's News for this evening:

Fore 'n aft the bos'n shouted
The deckies ran to their mooring station
We're homeward bound now, shipmates —
We're made this trip for our great nation

Our ship did sail some time ago
For Normandy beachhead and lands so strange
The Brits were great, the French so gay
We sail at noon, we need a change.

A long, long trip to west we'll travel
With volunteer crew, and none with pay
Jeremiah O'Brien's coming home, San Francisco
Please meet with us and celebrate that day.

Jeremiah O'Brien, the only World War II ship to return to the beaches of Normandy, departed Le Havre, France at noon today. Final destination, San Francisco.

14

SUMMER, NORTH ATLANTIC

We sailed into an absolutely flat calm English Channel. One had to look out the porthole to be sure we were at sea, so steady and solid did the *Jeremiah O'Brien* ride. After almost two months in seven ports, more than a hundred thousand visitors and innumerable bus tours, parties, dinners, cathedrals, ruins, foreign languages, strange customs and cultures, it felt good to be at sea again.

Everyone immediately settled into the seagoing routine — watch-standers stood their six or eight hours in two shifts, day-workers worked from 8 to 5, breakfast at 0730, lunch at 1130, dinner at 1700. When not working there was sleep (especially in the first few days), books (Patrick O'Brien was still making the rounds), letters to write, Sam Wood got a chess tournament going, others played backgammon, the 1600 beer call at no. 4 hatch (now supplemented with several kegs of Kronenberg left over from the run down the Seine), clothes to wash, movies after din-

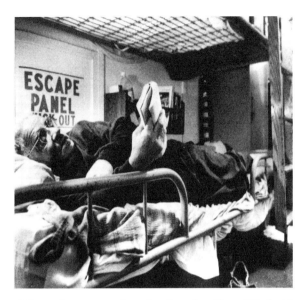

Off-watch we rested and relaxed. Here Ed Smith catches up on his reading in the comfort of his bunk. Photo by Mike Emery

ner, and, from time to time, just the "lonely sea and sky," with more stars in the heavens than could be counted or steered by.

Capt. Jahn gave Second Mate Ray Conrady instructions to lay out a course in a southwesterly direction passing near the Azores. Once abeam of them we would steer due west, then, as we approached the North American Continent, we would steer northwest into Portland. His reasoning was that we would be able to stay south of most of the storm tracks and find better weather. Time would prove him right.

In the evening we passed a drilling rig being towed out the Channel. It stood straight up out of the water, tall, thick metal tubes supporting a steel framework with buildings on top. It looked ungainly and out of its element in the middle of the ocean. Even at a distance of a mile away it was gigantic with bright lights showing in every direction, like a small city at sea. The tug struggled ahead of it, laboriously churning the ocean and making about four knots. Word quickly went through the ship that we passed something, a truly noteworthy occurrence for an old Liberty ship doing eleven knots. The engine department was especially proud of the fact that their engine constantly produced more speed than anyone expected.

July 23 broke fine and clear with high overcast. We started feeling the effects of a low swell on the starboard bow which made the ship pitch slightly. As we were almost out of the Channel, traffic was thin. We only had to dodge one coastal tanker and one trawler on the 8-12 morning watch.

The rift that developed between the captain and the admiral widened. We were so busy in England and France that their coolness to each other was not too apparent, but now, back at sea, it was obvious to everyone. On the voyage out from San Francisco they spent the hour before dinner having cocktails in either the admiral's room or the captain's office. As our deck cadet said once, "I have to bring them a bucket of ice every afternoon. Then they sit around having drinks and eating peanuts and talking about whatever it is that admirals and captains talk about." This practice continued even in port if there were no social demands on their schedule. Now their cocktail hour ceased to exist and whenever they met in the chartroom the conversation was limited to business matters.

It rained during the night and the weather continued to threaten all the following day, with the wind from the north-northwest. The chief mate and the newly-appointed bosun, Marty Wefald, discussed getting the ship ready for Portland. As always, the deck department's main concern was the *O'Brien*'s appearance. We would do some painting in the days ahead, then work on repainting the entire ship for our arrival in San Francisco. One thing that had to be done was renew the self-guided tour path, the blue line with the white arrows. We had so many people on in Europe that it was worn down to the underlying grey paint in places. As a beginning, the crew spent the day washing down the ship, getting the "land" off it. The threatened rain didn't materialize and we were able to start the painting process with chipping hammers, wire brushes and primer.

Capt. Jahn was in a nostalgic mood, reminiscing about his experiences as a tugboat captain. He was in command of one tug that had a peculiar configuration, with the towing engine located in the engine room, rather than on the after deck as on most tugs. The towing lead went up and out on the boat deck. This put the towing force and fulcrum much higher above the water than normal. The captain said he towed the passenger liner *Lurline* or *Mariposa,* he couldn't remember which, with the tug but was always leery of it, feeling it had a strong tendency to capsize. He said that after he left the boat, it was towing another ship somewhere else and did capsize, sinking immediately with the loss of all hands.

Although Mrs. Jahn had been with us in most of the British ports, the captain sent her a bouquet of flowers this day, "Just because she let me make the trip."

There was a quietness and stillness to the atmosphere aboard ship that was different from that outbound. It seemed to be made up of complex series of emotions and attitudes. Partly, those who made the whole voyage were tired. Partly, there was a sense that the most exciting part of the voyage was over. We only had a few remaining obligations and we'd be done, home; the end of the voyage was in sight. Another factor was that some of the crew that recently joined were active in the modern merchant marine. Where, earlier in the trip we relived "our" youth of break-bulk ships, World War II era and even Vietnam, with long stays in small ports in South America and the Far East and slow passages at sea of 10 to 15 knots, now conversations in the saloon and messrooms settled around topics such as the high-technology of the Persian Gulf War, today's Olongopo, Diego Garcia, modern Singapore, modern shipping — container ships or "box boats," roll-on, roll-off car carriers, six months on a ship without setting foot on shore and fast passages at 25 and 30 knots. The sense of anticipation seemed to have been replaced with one of just getting the job done. Was it the inevitable "letdown" after so much

Meanwhile, in the crow's nest . . . Courtesy Phil Frank and San Francisco Chronicle.

excitement and ceremony? Or was it merely the after effects of all those days in port? Time would tell.

Jack Carraher: "The first crew, on the way over, seemed to be full of life. I believe they were more elderly than the following crew but they seemed to have jumped right in with both feet. It was a big, big adventure and that's what I thought of it, too."

The next day, the North Atlantic lived up to its reputation. Dawn came cloudy with rain squalls and head winds, the ship pitching and rolling. We spent a dismal day in grey, choppy seas with long, high-rolling swells and whitecaps from one horizon to another.

Brian Goldman: "The night we got into those heavy rolls in the North Atlantic was something. We had ice-skating in the engine room, because of oil on the floorplates, where I was sliding back in front of the boiler fronts watching the water levels. That was kind of comical."

And, suddenly, irony of ironies, we got tired of being at sea. In only four days, boredom set in. People began asking about the next port. From the chief mate's journal: "A morbid day. Off watch at midnight, sleep till 7, get up, dress, breakfast, watch 8-12, lunch, nap 'til 2 p.m., check on deck gang and ship, read, cocktail, dinner, read, watch 8-12." Perhaps it was the weather.

Jim Wade: "What's interesting is when we are out at sea and everyone is looking forward to getting into port. After you've been in port for maybe five days, six days or maybe even 10 or 12, everybody is relieved to get back to sea. And it's a cycle, looking forward, getting to sea, and then getting back into port and then after you've spent your time there, getting back to sea."

On Tuesday, July 26 the weather kept changing all day long. Beginning with dark clouds and rain squalls, it turned to patchy fog and overcast then broke into scattered clouds and sunshine. And, suddenly, with a little sunshine, it wasn't so boring after all. The sea was alive with movement, the sun sparkled off wave tops, the *O'Brien* seemed to dance through the water.

After a ship is delivered to its owners it operates in a "guarantee" period, during which the crew makes up a list of repair items that need attention. This period usually runs six months or a year. Our chief engineer, Dick Brannon, wasn't going to let a minor technicality, such as the fact that the guarantee period for the *Jeremiah O'Brien* expired fifty years earlier, deter him. He faxed a letter to the Portland Shipyard Society asking them to make good on a guarantee item. The main spring on the engine room clock had failed after 51 years.

To: Mr. Ed Langlois — Liaison, Visit of *S.S. Jeremiah O'Brien*
From: Richard Brannon — Chief Engineer *S.S. Jeremiah O'Brien*
Subject: GUARANTEE/WARRANTY REPAIRS -- Hull 806 USMC Hull 230 NESBC

Dear Mr. Langlois:

The above subject pertains to a matter of some importance to the continued successful operation of the above captioned vessel. In as much as you are listed as the source of Inquiries regarding the current visit to the building site of the vessel, we would very much appreciate your directing our problem to the proper Contract follow-up personnel of the New England Shipbuilding Corporation.

The vessel in general has performed quite well in its assigned duties to many parts of the world since being accepted on June 30, 1943 by Mr. R. Peaslee Dumont for the United States Maritime Commission. However, in the port of Cherbourg, France on July 6, 1994, the Engine Room clock failed — apparently due to a broken main spring. We realize that the vessel is out of the original Guarantee Period after 51 years; however, it might be that the manufacturer's Warranty covering original parts could still be in effect. The name plate data of the clock in question is:

U.S. Maritime Commission
17533
Made by Seth Thomas Co. U.S.A.

In the event that the GUARANTEE/WARRANTY periods have indeed expired, it could conceivably be quite newsworthy should an article appear in the local Press stating that "Locally built Liberty Ship, *S.S. JEREMIAH O'BRIEN* after travelling over 75,000 miles to England, France, South America, Australia, India, China and the

Philippine Islands over a period of 51 years without any reports of machinery malfunction, returns to Builder's Yard to have main spring of ship's Engine Room clock replaced. This will enable the vessel to operate successfully well into the next century. According to its crew and the Regulatory Bodies, the ship is in perfect operating condition otherwise."

> Thank you for your assistance in this matter,
> [signed] Richard Brannon — Chief Engineer

It wasn't long before Dick received a reply.

A SPECIAL MESSAGE

To: Richard Brannon — Chief Engineer aboard the *Jeremiah O'Brien*
From: Ed Langlois — Hard working, loyal president of the S.P. Shipyard Society
Subj: GUARANTY/WARRANTY REPAIRS — Hull 806 USMS — Hull 230 NESBC

1. I received your message loud and clear.
2. I note, with some regret (some, but not much) that you have an Engine Room Clock failure.
3. I have this to report:

I spent seven hours last night (while someone was waiting patiently for me — I will introduce you) looking over my vast supply of GUARANTY/WARRANTY papers on the *S.S. JEREMIAH O'BRIEN*. If you had not delayed in reporting this incident of the broken main spring you would have come under the GUARANTY/WARRANTY. Unfortunately it expired at high noon June 30, 1994.

I contacted the Seth Thomas clock company, to talk to Seth. Unfortunately (once again) he died early this month. He was 119 years old. I did talk to his assistant, Ezra Snodgrass, and he told me that the main spring for this engine room clock was made in Sweden, and he gave me the name of a person to call.

I called Olaf Clockenstein in Sweden. Unfortunately he died in mid-June of this year, so they asked me to talk to his granddaughter Griselda Foodlesquink. We had a nice talk and by coincidence she said she visited the *S.S. Jeremiah O'Brien* while you folks were in France on this particular trip. She said no one told her the damn clock was busted. She said she could have fixed it right on the spot if someone had only told her the damn thing was busted.

I asked her if she had met the Chief Engineer while she was on board, and she said, "you mean Dickie Brannon?" I gulped. She

said she would fly over to Portland and meet you on the dock with
a new main spring for the Engine Room Clock. Isn't that nice?
4. I took your story to the local newspaper.
5. When I stood engine room watches on the Maine Maritime
   Academy training ship after the war, I would ask the Cadet Engineer, "Tell me the only instrument in the engine room that you
   can't control." No one knew the answer.

The following day was partly cloudy with a slight northwesterly sea and swell, ideal for painting. The deck department
turned to on the flying bridge, bridge deck and the boat deck.
These areas had the greatest number of curious visitors during our
stay in Europe and were badly in need of fresh paint. Fortunately,
over the years the *Jeremiah O'Brien* had scrounged enough grey
paint to cover two or three aircraft carriers, so quantity wasn't a
problem. Shelf-life and color were another matter. Most of the
five-gallon pails that Marty the bosun opened had a thick skin on
top. Once the skin was removed, the upper part of the can was
watery and most of the pigment was congealed in the bottom.
This meant stirring each can for up to an hour just to get enough

usable paint. Marty
often started mixing
paint several hours
before starting a
project, sometimes
the day before. And
even then several
inches of thick
"mud" remained on
the bottom of each
can and had to be
thrown away. Be-
cause the paint
came from different
manufacturers
Marty then had to
use his "judicious
seaman's eye" to

Shipboard housekeeping includes cleaning the flags.
Bill Bennett applies soap and brush to grease and
dirt.

get the right color. It was easy enough on any given day, but to come up with a hue of grey on Friday to match what was applied the previous Wednesday was a challenge. There were times when the *O'Brien* looked like a mottled pinto in various shades of grey.

Other housekeeping chores were attended to. A fire and boat drill was held, the first since before our arrival in Europe. Many of the crew were new and went to the wrong stations. Others, although on board the whole trip, simply forgot

Bob Burnett, ship's carpenter, repairing a drawer.

where they belonged. In a short while we had everyone sorted out, briefly explained their duties and cautioned them to wear hats, pants and shoes to abandon ship, to prevent suffering from exposure.

Jack Carraher and Ron Smith worked in the steward's department on the way over. But with the departure of Carl Kreidler and Otto Sommerauer, they asked to move into those positions. Jack was one of the most popular people on board and it came as a shock when some of the crew complained that he and Ron were, in reality, trying to get out of working. Nothing could be further from the truth. Jack's feet had bothered him all trip. Being in the gunnery crew would give him a chance to sit down more often when he painted or greased and oiled the guns. Ron was a retired Air Force captain with experience in gunnery. Jack and Ron had worked hard through the trip and Jack was astounded that anyone would even care, much less resent the fact that he and Ron chose to go into the gunnery department. But the attitude stemmed from the notion on the part of the tenured volunteers that no one should be a freeloader, everyone should carry his weight and, for some reason, they looked on the gunnery department as an unneeded frill.

Now, Jack took charge of the evening movies for what he labeled the "*Jeremiah O'Brien* Twin-plex Cinema." Each day he posted the names of the two movies to be shown that night in the officers' mess and in no. 2 'tween deck, with a listing of the stars. That someone new was running the theater was obvious in his first selections: "10" with Bo Derek and "Heaven Can Wait," with Warren Beatty. No more war movies.

Although it was summer, the North Atlantic had a reputation to uphold, and benign summer weather was not on the list of attractions. The next day began cloudy and drizzly with a wind of force 4-5 blowing from north by west. Before noon, the wind diminished, the clouds turned to patchy fog, then to thick fog.

Our tentative routing called for us to go from Portland, Maine to Washington, D. C., then to Jacksonville, Florida. If we could get the pilotage donated, this would mean going through the Cape Cod Canal and the Chesapeake and Delaware Canal. This was something we all hoped for. We could save several hundred miles in our journey. For some of the crew, it would also be a unique, first-time, experience. Otherwise, after leaving Portland, we'd have to sail around Cape Cod and Maryland and up into the Chesapeake Bay to get to the Potomac River and Washington. Capt. Jahn reminisced about going through those waterways early in his career. He was a sailor with Dollar Line before World War II and had transited both canals in that company's around-the-world service but he was concerned about the pilotage costs.

Friday, July 29 was a sad day. We learned of Janet Doyle's death. A long-time volunteer with the ship, everyone knew her as "Wendy the Welder." As a teenager she went to work at Kaiser's shipyards in Richmond, California and became an accomplished welder involved in the construction of several Liberty ships. She had a picture taken in her welding leathers, her head tilted at a jaunty angle, holding her welder's helmet, looking beautiful and just slightly saucy. In later years the picture was made into

postcards and posters. She graced a full page in *The Last Liberty*.
A talented artist, she repainted the pinups on the forward guntub
when the ship came out of the Reserve Fleet. She was cheerful
and enthusiastic and would be sorely missed by everyone.

Now Capt. Jahn wanted to take the ship straight home.
His attitude was that our purpose in leaving San Francisco was to
go to Normandy. We did that, now let's go home. The captain
and the chief mate got into a heated discussion, the mate arguing
that we owed it to the country and the ship to visit as many ports
as possible. This was the *Jeremiah O'Brien*'s one chance to make
the rest of the nation aware of her existence and, for the sake of
history, we should do it. And charging admission would be a
good way to subsidize our voyage. Opinions from the home office
and the crew weighed in. Adm. Patterson had a different concern.
Hurricane season in the Caribbean-East Coast begins in September
and he wanted the *O'Brien* out of harm's way. In the end, we
kept the Portland-Washington-Jacksonville-then-home route, by-
passing Philadelphia, Houston, Galveston, New Orleans and other
ports that were part of the ship's history. It was frustrating to
miss these opportunities, but the realities of our long voyage were
wearing on the captain.

One indication of how close to land you are is the radio
stations you hear on your personal set. In mid-Atlantic we got
Voice of America and BBC on shortwave. Late at night we might
hear an AM station but usually these broadcast bible-thumping
evangelism or hard rock, each in its own way unpopular with the
crew. It was interesting that these two, so different, had the most
powerful transmitters.

On July 30 the engine room called to report the revolution
counter had just turned its six millionth revolution since the ship
was built. Reflecting on the history of the *Jeremiah O'Brien,* it
was remarkable that after fifty-one-plus years, six million revolutions of the propeller, World War II and travel across most of the
major oceans of the world, the engines had not had any major
problems. One could picture Dick Brannon patting the ship on the

boiler and saying, "Good girl, keep it up." Like most of the crew, he thought of the ship as a person.

Dick Brannon: "The ship absolutely, definitely has a personality. It seems eager to go. It wants to do its thing. Yeah, the whole ship has a personality, very definitely. And the engine, you have to approach it, I told you the story, like making love to a woman, with finesse. You're free to quote me on that. In fact I wish you would, cause the ship does have a personality but you can word it anyway you want."

Brian Goldman: "It's just like the [California Maritime Academy] training ship, like the Energizer Bunny, it just keeps going and going and going. She's a good old girl. Knows what she needs to do to get from point A to point B and does it. We just kind of help it along."

Tim Palange: "She does have a character all her own. Even the engine has its own certain character. Sometimes it was cantankerous and I was usually the one who wound up warming it up. Sometimes it just didn't want to cooperate and sometimes it was just smooth as silk and did everything you wanted it to. The same goes for the ship, I think. Sometimes you just ran into mysterious problems, they cleared themselves up and you just had to baby it and talk nicely to it, [laugh] that seemed to be all it took."

Bob Black: "I tend to think of all ships as animate creatures. I would say *Jeremiah O'Brien* does have a personality, she's almost like a farm girl. She's a steady workhorse and she gets the job done and yet she's no nonsense. Not really super pretty and no frills but she's somebody you'd like to know and somebody you'd like to work with."

Jack Carraher: "Oh, yeah, definitely. She is alive. She talks to us. She moans and groans, especially back in the after end, we hear a lot of talking back there, and occasionally almost music. You know, I've been trying to track that down but I haven't been able to; especially in the forward gun tub I can hear music every once in a while. It's not my kind of music, this is just a single tone. As the ship goes on she develops more and more of a personality. I can't put my finger on it but she's very much alive. Of course, the crew's the lifeblood of her but she responds to them."

Bob Gisslow: "I think of it that way, as having a personality. The ship is very easygoing, she adjusts herself to the sea. It seems like she knows that the determining factor ultimately is the sea itself and it's just part of it to make herself comfortable. It's a lot like a living being in that respect."

Pat McCafferty: "The ship definitely has a personality. It's just like going back in a time machine, it really is. When you walk the decks at night or early in the morning you can actually imagine yourself fifty years ago, very easily, and you take a step back in history."

Ruth Robson: "She's just a grand old lady. Everything about her is, I wouldn't say antique, but it's old and we're living with old fixtures, old radiators, old curtains. She's held up beautifully. She's aged well, let's put it that way, a grand matron of the sea."

Sam Wood: "This ship has a spirit about it. All things have spirits about them, and I'm not talking about ghosts. There are no ghosts on this ship. But there is a spirit in this ship and it exists and in our daily activities, when we do something, we promote the well-being of the ship. We maintain it. Let me put it this way, any number of times I found a rust blister, bigger than a silver dollar. Each time, I took my hammer and chipped away the painted coating of rust, I had to chip away almost a quarter inch of steel but I got down to the good metal and I couldn't help but feel that I am renewing something. I am preserving the metal, beautifully. I wire-brushed it, primed and then I painted it. I am maintaining life in a great animated thing that is bobbing along through the ocean.

"If you don't see a spirit on this ship, or on any ship for that matter, you don't have a heart within your breast. It's all around us. And it's our job to protect it, if you will, to maintain it. Go crawl down into the bottom of no. 2, change a light bulb. It's all around you down there. It's a good spirit. It's something that is a part of me because I'm giving something to it. I like that sort of thing. I'm comfortable around that. I can shinny up that mast and lie on my stomach up there perfectly at ease because I am doing something that I am supposed to do and I am contributing to the ongoing life of this. Everybody on this ship is doing the same thing. You're doing the same thing, the engine people are doing the same, the steward's people . . . in various ways and the ship lives. There it is. By sight, and movement through the water. We are it. It's a living thing." Sam's words could be called the credo of the volunteer.

That day we reduced our speed from 65 to 60 revolutions. A welcoming ceremony was planned requiring us to pass the Portland Head Light at 0800 on August 6. At the speed we were making we would be early again and might get there before all the dignitaries, bands and well-wishers.

Ed Langlois: "After forming the Society, I began to correspond with members of the NLSM staff, visited the ship twice and was kidded about stealing the ship. I got word that the *Jeremiah O'Brien* was going to Normandy and I held my first meeting to plan for her coming to Portland. I rallied some thirty local friends and associates to join me and the society in bringing the ship to

Off-duty, Sam Wood uses the after guntub to get his thoughts down on paper. It would be difficult to find a better atmosphere. Photo by Mike Emery.

Portland. At that meeting the pilots, the towboats, the docking master, the agents and all other services, including berthing, linehandlers, etcetera, all said they would contribute their time at no expense to the Society or the ship.

"But one of my major problems was to pin down the date that the ship would arrive and depart. I had to get publicity out, rally the press behind me, I had thousands of names of merchant marine veterans and armed guard people to write to, but couldn't do anything until I could get the date when the ship arrived. I actually reserved eight Saturday evenings at the Sonesta Hotel, in order to make sure. We had people coming from all over the east coast."

The next day brought some welcome excitement. In the late afternoon a message was received in Morse Code from the Canadian Coast Guard at St. John's, New Brunswick:

A white sailing vessel reported adrift in position 42.18N, 048.07W It is unclear whether vessel is abandoned or in distress. Mariners transitting through the area are requested to attempt to establish communication with the vessel. Investigate further and make reports to RCC New York.

Ray Conrady laid the position out on the chart and found we would pass within a few miles of the last location. This captured the imagination of the crew. Talk immediately went to rescue at sea, how to treat the survivors for hypothermia, where they would sleep, how to get the boat on board and the notoriety from the press when it was discovered that we had saved the occupants of a sinking sailboat. We made a slight course change which would bring us to the last reported position of the boat the next day.

Crew's News for July 30:

Good evening, San Francisco.
Dinner time. Bon Appetit. *Jeremiah*'s meal tonight needed only one call for the crew to come running to the mess hall. Cooks Al Martino, Jimmy Farras and Eduardo Pubill are serving up one of the meals this ship is famous for. Starting with a fresh shrimp cocktail, followed by the entree (grilled New York steak, sauteed mushrooms,

potatoes au gratin), it is topped with peach pie a la mode for dessert. Prior to this trip the crew had visions of food at sea being hardtack, beef jerky and moldy potatoes. We have been pleasantly surprised and pleased with our seagoing fare. Home cooking it is not, but nonetheless it has been one of the highlights of our trip.

Today's position in the middle of the Atlantic Ocean is latitude 47.07 North, longitude 43.36 west; 265 miles travelled in the past 25 hours* at 10.6 knots. We are in the warm Gulf Stream current with sea water temperature of 75 degrees and air of 80, very humid, but very pleasant.

Jeremiah O'Brien — out.

Sunday, July 31 and the weather was predictable only in its unpredictability. After days of fog and low overcast, day came with blustery winds from the west northwest. A message was received: "Regarding white sailing vessel. Canceled." Apparently the boat reported in safely.

John Linderman, AB: "You should see all the guys down below. The medals were just dropping off their shirts. They were all going to be heroes."

After checking our speed made good, Capt. Jahn ordered another reduction, 48 revolutions per minute. The old girl just didn't know how to slow down.

We received a telegram from Capt. Denys Lomax, who had been so helpful in Southampton:

THANKS FOR ALL YOUR EFFORTS IN GETTING THE SHIP OVER. MANY OLD SAMBOAT VETERANS WERE DELIGHTED TO SEE YOU. I APPRECIATED JOINING YOU PORTSMOUTH TO SOUTHAMPTON
BEST WISHES

One of the rituals on a steamship is blowing tubes. The burnoff from the crude oil used to make steam collects as a residue of soot and ash in the exhaust pipes leading up through the stack. If allowed to accumulate, the efficiency of the engine is

---

*Crossing through time zones in a westerly direction ships retard their clocks periodically to stay on local time. This often results in a day being 25 hours long.

reduced, so, once a day, at sea, the engine room blows tubes, shooting compressed air up through the tubes or pipes and blowing all the soot and ash out to the atmosphere. Unless the wind happens to be blowing strongly from the beam, the entire after part of the ship from the stack to the stern gets covered with a black snowfall of sooty flakes, gritty ash and sulfuric residue. To prevent this, the engine room calls the mate on watch who turns the ship away from the wind for the ten or fifteen minutes it takes to blow tubes, and everything blows over the side rather than aft.

Today the crew gathered at no. 4 hatch at 1600 for their regular beer break. Just about the time everyone was settled in with their first glass, can or bottle, the engine room blew tubes without calling the mate on watch. We were treated to a black blizzard that settled in everyone's hair, on their clothes, and, worst of all, in their beer. The party broke up early.

August 1 was the day we ran out of coffee. Seafarers and their coffee are inseparable. Tradition calls for coffee at all meals and, of course, during coffee time at 1000 and 1500. In addition, many mates have a cup brought up when the sailors relieve the wheel during their watch. The *Jeremiah O'Brien* was nothing if not traditional and I always had a cup brought up at each change of steering, 0800, 0920 and 1040. Today at 1020 Capt. Cliff Hook (who had signed on as AB when we departed Le Havre) sheepishly came up to steer empty-handed. He said there was no coffee. No coffee! This was impossible on our well-run ship. I told Capt. Hook I would call the union hall, get my union delegate, we'd tie the ship up, it was unthinkable . . . Of course we had coffee, but whoever made it in the large urn in the pantry forgot. Word got back to the chief steward and he apologized. It was all in good fun.

That evening we started getting "good" AM stations on the radio, from New York, Canada and Nova Scotia.

August 2 started out as a beautiful day with blue skies overhead but in the distance we saw the large dark anvil heads of thunderclouds lined up across the horizon. Sure enough, by noon we were being drenched with heavy squalls which turned to drizzle in the afternoon. It set our painting schedule back a day. We had spent the past few days painting the nooks and crannies on the foredeck, "cutting in," so that we could later come along with rollers and a spray gun.

The following day was rainy and drizzly, again ruining our painting plans. We were still going too fast and reduced speed to 40 rpms.

Our meals had developed a continental flavor. Several evenings since our departure we had wine with dinner. And, in addition to dessert, Pat McCafferty passed around a platter of Camembert and Brie with crackers, offering the "formage" (instead of the French *fromage*). Pat had a way with foreign words. Whenever we were served the New Zealand fish known as orange roughy, he called it "orange roughage."

Two things on our menu got monotonous. Breakfast was always either eggs, pancakes or French toast with bacon or sausage and oatmeal or some other type of mush. The eggs, which were fresh, not powdered, were invariably scrambled. We were now more than four months into the trip and every time we had eggs they were scrambled. I asked Jimmy Farras if he couldn't cook them some other way for a change. He exploded, "I ain't cooking no over-easy for no fifty-six people." That was the end of that subject. The other thing was the sandwiches at noon. For some reason Russ was enamored of bologna. We seemed to have bologna and cheese sandwiches every other day. Any processed meat is high on the list of cholesterol-rich foods, to say nothing of sodium. For a group of people whose average age was seventy-something, it seemed a poor choice. As the voyage progressed, peanut butter became more and more popular at lunch time. Someone tried taking the bologna out of the sandwich and smearing the peanut butter over the cheese. He said it wasn't too bad but the mayonnaise didn't set too well.

Our British crew found our eating habits a bit odd. Clifford Hook: "I found the food a little strange. Very different, in fact, the way that you ate aboard this ship. The order in which you put things in your mouth I think was odd. For instance, if we are having breakfast we always kick off with cereal, not with the hash browns and the sausages and followed by the cereal. It's a little bit, ah, backwards. And also the lunch, just a sandwich. That's not quite the way we do it."

Other than that, however, the crew gave the galley good marks all the way through for their food. David Aris, fireman-watertender: "A high point of the ship was the food. I think if I had to stand back and look at this ship, I think the people who really get the top marks are in fact the galley. I don't know how they did what they did in that little galley. The temperatures in that galley, as far as I understand, are just about as high as the temperatures that we're going on about in the engine room. But they served all these meals absolutely spot on time, first class food, and they stuck it all the way from San Francisco back to San Francisco and it was always there and it was always served well and cheerfully. And I think that's much to their credit."

The minimum required food on a merchant ship is specified by law and listed on the Forecastle Card, an extension of the shipping articles. Each seaman is to receive, "in addition to the daily issue of lime and lemon juice and sugar, or other antiscorbutics," the following: "5 quarts water daily, ½ pound biscuit daily, 1¼ pounds salt beef 3 times per week, 1 pound salt pork 3 times per week, ½ pound flour 3 times per week, 1 pound canned meat twice per week, 1½ pounds fresh bread daily, 1 pound dry, preserved or fresh fish weekly, 1 pound potatoes or yams daily, ½ pound canned tomatoes twice per week, ½ pint peas twice per week, 1/3 pint beans 3 times per week, ½ pound rice twice per week, 3/4 ounce coffee daily, 1/8 ounce tea daily, 3 ounces sugar daily, ½ pint molasses 3 times per week, 3 ounces dried fruit 3 times per week, ¼ pint pickles 3 times per week, ½ pint vinegar twice per week, 4 ounces cornmeal twice per week, 4 ounces onions 3 times per week, 1 ounce lard per week, 2 ounces butter per week, and mustard, pepper and salt sufficient for seasoning." The *O'Brien* provided better than the "minimum."

Brian Goldman: " I felt like I was in a five-star restaurant. My first few meals were salmon and lasagna and veal, [laugh] you can't complain. Jimmy should open up his own restaurant. He was something. He had the food down pat. Any man who can cook that well on a coal-fired stove. I tried an experiment, scrambling eggs on top of the main engine. I wanted to see if you could really cook eggs on top of the main engine and I found out that you can. I did that myself. My next experiment's going to be for French Toast [laugh]."

Tim Palange: "The food was outstanding. I mean it really was. As far as the food goes, this was the best feeding ship I've ever been on. Including the *Constitution.* [Tim is second assistant engineer on the *SS Constitution.*] Oh, this by far surpasses the *Constitution,* even though the officers get passenger-quality food."

Bill Rowlands: "Oh, the food was excellent. Yeah, this was what you call 'a good feeder.' Orange roughy, we've had I don't know how many times. You go to a restaurant and that's a thirty dollar meal, you know. We were very fortunate that way. Jimmy and the crew were to be complimented. That makes a difference. Naw, it was a good trip."

By Thursday, August 4, we were clearly getting closer to land, even at our new speed of 36 rpms. We were near the Grand Banks and, especially at night, there were large numbers of trawlers in sight. It was disconcerting because they didn't turn their lights on until we got close to them. We'd see targets on the radar but no lights. Then, all of a sudden, a light would flash brightly, close on the bow. As we maneuvered past, the light would be extinguished.

The captain and the admiral were still nursing their grievances. Capt. Jahn called a department head meeting and deliberately didn't tell Patterson about it. We discussed the upcoming stay in Portland, where we were going next, and a few other items. But the main thrust of the meeting seemed to be for the captain to hold it without the admiral knowing about it or being there. Capt. Jahn laughed about it later in the day. "I was hoping no one would tell him."

We received a fax transmission from General Kicklighter:

The 50th Anniversary of D-Day Commemorations are now behind us and by all accounts were a tremendous success in thanking and honoring our veterans of World War II. Nowhere more so than with the participation of the *S. S. Jeremiah O'Brien.* The presence of your vessel ensured that World War II Merchant Marine veterans were also thanked and honored. The visit by President Clinton was a special tribute to you and your crew.

We are extremely proud of all you have accomplished in restoring the 50-year old *S.S. Jeremiah O'Brien* to a safe operating condition, crewing her and taking her back to Normandy. Best of all, the *O'Brien* will remain as a continuing educational exhibit so that new generations will be told of the immense value of the United States Merchant Marine.

Please pass my personal thanks to all who were involved with this great project.

Very respectfully,

Claude M. Kicklighter
Lieutenant General,
United States Army Retired
Executive Director

We reduced speed to 30 rpms. Our last day at sea before arriving in Portland was spent frantically painting. The previous days had been foggy and/or drizzly making painting all but impossible. It looked like more of the same at daybreak with a thick, wet fog surrounding the ship but it cleared by noon to distant haze and cold wind. Marty Wefald, Bill Bennett, Bill Rowlands, Sam Wood, Jim Miller, John Linderman and Bob Black turned to with rollers, brushes and spray guns. Marty Shields, who was one of our best painters and our "blue line" expert, worked until almost midnight, painting in the line with a four-inch roller, then going over it with a spray can of white paint and an arrow stencil to put in the white directional markers. We all wanted the *O'Brien* to look good when she came home to visit her folks in Portland, Maine.

15

PORTLAND, MAINE

This is the Voice of the *Jeremiah O'Brien.*
"At precisely 0800, August 6, 1994, *Jeremiah O'Brien*
passed abeam Portland Head Light."
After 51 years, the *Jeremiah O'Brien* came home. Maine
is where she was born. Maine is also the home state of Jeremiah
O'Brien, the Revolutionary War hero for whom she was named.
His hometown, Machias, is just a short distance up the coast from
Portland. It was there, in 1775, that Jeremiah O'Brien led a group
of patriots armed only with shotguns, a few muskets, and several
pitchforks and captured the British man-of-war *Margaretta* in the
first naval engagement of the War for Independence. We were
doubly proud to be returning.

The sky was clear, the sun was out and a brisk breeze blew
from shore carrying with it the land smells of evergreens and New
England vegetation. Grey and white seagulls glided astern of the
ship, looking for scraps. The rugged Maine shoreline, a mosaic of
green, blue and brown, grew larger and larger, then her rocky

JEREMIAH O'BRIEN'S MAINE EVENT

AP / SCOTT PERRY

The Liberty Ship *SS Jeremiah O'Brien steams past the Portland Head Light in Cape Elizabeth, Maine, Saturday, its first U.S. stop after par-* *ticipating in the 50th anniversary of D-day commemoration. The ship, now based in San Francisco, was launched in Portland on Dec. 26, 1940.*

With a play on words, the San Francisco Examiner *captured the spirit of our arrival off the Portland Head Light.*

coves and inlets became distinctive, each one begging exploration, promising adventure. Within each inlet and cove solid New England brick, masonry and wood houses, many surrounded by thick, green trees, faced the ocean, the morning sun reflecting off their windows. Of course, we actually arrived an hour early, but after boarding at 0700, our pilot, Capt. Earl Walker, simply directed us to cruise in circles around the sea buoy until word came that the reception committee was ready for us.

We approached the Portland Head Light, the oldest light house in the United States, built on the orders of George Washington and first lighted on Jan. 10, 1791. We were in our finery, the deck officers in dress blues, the ship with signal flags from bow to stern, corporate sponsors' flags on the triatic stay, our large American ensign on the steaming gaff. We were astounded to see a great mass of people lining the

More than 1,500 people were on hand for our arrival off the Portland Head Light. Photo courtesy Ed Langlois.

shore around the light, waiting to view us.

Tom Patterson: "Portland has a man dedicated to the building of the Liberty Ships. Ed Langlois is the instigator and founder of the South Portland Historical Society honoring the old New England Ship Building yard there and that started a whole week of reestablishing a living history of the *Jeremiah O'Brien*'s roots in the New England Shipyard. And it couldn't have worked out finer. We were due to pass Portland Head Light at 0800 and right on the second our bridge passed the Light. There were fifteen hundred people waving and cheering. Ed Langlois was on VHF channel sixteen welcoming us officially to Portland. Our pilot was a Kings Point graduate, which made Captain Jaffee and I very happy, and everything went well from there on in."

Ed Langlois: "One of the most memorable moments of the entire visit was when I drove into Fort Williams Park on Saturday morning and found over fifteen hundred people who had come, through our invitations in the press.

"I'll never forget a man over ninety years old with tears rolling down his eyes who said, 'I never dreamed I'd see a Liberty ship again.' When the ship went by at eight o'clock there wasn't a dry eye at Fort Williams Park."

As we passed the light, the pilot asked us to blow the whistle. Three times the *Jeremiah O'Brien*'s foghorn bellowed out into the crisp morning air. The crowd waved and cheered. In addition to those at Fort Williams Park, other welcomers lined the shores of Cape Elizabeth, South Portland and Portland. The American Legion Militia honored the *O'Brien* with a twenty-one cannon salute* and the Civil War re-enactors fired their twenty-one gun salute at Spring Point Light at nearby Fort Preble. Bob Crocker, who was in the ship's original Armed Guard gun crew on voyages 5 and 6, came up from Florida for our arrival and, from the shore near Portland Head Light, watched the ship come in. "To see my old ship come in after all these years was one of the most moving

---

*We later learned it was actually a twenty-<u>three</u> gun salute. The Militia had some black powder left over and rather than take it home they fired twice more.

A view from the water, the Jeremiah O'Brien *with "a bone in her teeth," approaching Portland harbor.   Photo courtesy of Ed Langlois.*

experiences of my life.   There were a couple of minutes there I couldn't say anything."

Passing the Head Light we were joined by yachts, motorboats, excursion boats and a fire boat, her nozzles sending glistening arcs of water into the blue sky, creating misty rainbows in the morning sun.   They all formed up in a water parade toward the harbor.   One excursion boat, the *Odyssey,* of Casco Bay Lines, charged $5 a head to meet the *O'Brien* and follow her in, then generously donated the proceeds to the National Liberty Ship Memorial.

Ed Langlois: "I'm sure if you ask any one of the people in those two hundred boats that escorted the *O'Brien* in, you'd find the same deep sense of sentiment that was expressed by those at the Head Light."

Portland is situated on two peninsulas jutting into Casco Bay giving it a large deepwater harbor.   As we entered the port we saw a refinery and residential areas on our left, and modern office buildings ascending a low hilly area on our right.   Closer to the water, at the harbor itself, were modern glass and steel ferry terminals, picturesque wooden fish buyers' shacks, restaurants and ferries, lobster boats and excursion boats.

Every cove, lagoon, fairway, both sides of the ship channel and the channel itself was peppered with lobster pot markers — red, green, blue, white, yellow, orange, day-glo colors, stripes, spots, bands and diagonals. The floats are attached to lobster pots sitting on the ocean bed and painted in distinctive colors so each owner can recognize his pots from a distance. As someone in the crew said, "I don't see how a poor lobster has a chance."

We tied up at the Maine State Pier next to the Bath Iron Works. It was a unique arrangement with us going port side to across the end of the pier forming, if viewed from the air, the letter "T" with the pier being the upright and the *O'Brien* forming the crosspiece on top. The pier was about eighty feet wide so our stern hung over on one side while the bow projected into the entrance to the Bath Iron Works on the other. Two gangways from shore were rigged to the main deck at no. 4 hatch and, after quickly going through the customs and immigration formalities, we were ready to receive visitors.

Well, almost. There was one immigration problem. We had two British citizens on board: Clifford Hook and David Aris. David had a visa, but Capt. Hook was shipped at the last moment in Le Havre on a pierhead jump. Not having a visa he was technically an alien and entering the country illegally. He argued that he could quite easily come into the country as a tourist without any problem. The official countered that may be true but he wasn't entering as a tourist now, but as a working crew member of foreign nationality on an American-flag ship. The end result was the ship had to pay a small fine (less than $100) for bringing him into the country.

Ed Langlois, a former shipyard worker, is president of the South Portland Shipyard Society that commemorates Portland's wartime yard. "In 1980 I founded the Society for three reasons: one, to preserve the historic contribution of the men and women in Maine who built Liberty ships and to honor the men who sailed on these ships as officers and crew and to recognize the contribution of the U.S. Armed Guard who served on these ships; two, to create a museum and a memorial tribute to the Liberty ships, the men and women who built them and those who sailed them, and; three, To bring the *Jeremiah O'Brien* back to Portland. "We had people on hand who helped build this ship and who sailed on board during the war. We are very grateful to the folks out there in Frisco who saved the *O'Brien* and keep it sailing, but we think it's our ship and we were all very excited to have it return."

Herbert Adams, a member of the Maine House of Representatives, is a historian and journalist. He captured the feeling of the people of Portland toward the *O'Brien* in an article in the *Maine Telegram*. Quoting Ed Langlois, he wrote:

> Ed Langlois started working in the shipyards in 1941. In 1943 he entered Maine Maritime Academy and after graduation went into the Navy and served one and a half years in the Pacific on an AKA [troopship]. Returning to the Academy in 1946 he was on the staff for ten years as executive director and founder of the alumni association, doing public relations and promotion and marketing for the school, and served as public relations director, engineering officer and instructor. In 1956 Ed became general manager of the Maine Port Authority in Portland and was the first person in the federal American Association of Port Authorities to be named chairman of the Environmental Affairs Standing Committee. He retired in 1982 and is now executive director of the Maine Innkeepers Association. He lives in South Portland, Maine.

"For the younger generation, it will be their first chance to see her under sail," he says. "For my generation, it may well be the last."

The *O'Brien* is docked on this visit at the Maine State Pier in Portland. Her long-ago birthplace, the basins of the West Yard, now are home to the Portland Pipeline Corp. and a public ramp where families now launch pleasure boats into Casco Bay.

She returns to a very different Portland than the one she left, a living reminder of a war and an era gracefully fading from memory into history. As with all World War II veterans, the years and miles have taken their toll, but the *Jeremiah O'Brien* remains the symbol of the days when Mainers willingly sailed out to do the world's work.

"More than any other emissary," *Sea History* [magazine] said, the *O'Brien*, "represents all the Americans, from shipyard workers to assault troops, that helped the Allies breach Hitler's Atlantic wall."

For Ed Langlois' generation, the meaning may be more personal. "We built them when we were young, and part of a great cause," he says. "When I see a Liberty ship, my eyes and my heart fill up."

The people of Portland were hospitable in the extreme. They couldn't do enough for us and their enthusiasm was equal to any we encountered during the trip. Many of them took time off from work or donated their vacation time to come aboard and help out.

Herb Adams, whose district the ship was in, volunteered his services. He was a wonderful help, standing at the gangway on the main deck most of our stay and handing out *O'Brien* brochures to all who came on board. He pointed out where the *Jeremiah O'Brien* was launched, just across the channel from our berth. The New England Shipbuilding Corporation went out of business after the war and the old launching ways are now filled in, part of a tank farm belonging to an oil refinery.

Two of our first visitors were Tom McGeehan and Bob Crocker. Tom was the deck cadet on the *O'Brien* when it made its eleven Normandy landings in 1944. He had hoped to sail on the first leg of the voyage as third mate, but couldn't get away. Driving up from Mountain Top, Pennsylvania, for our arrival, Tom spent the day looking at his old room and the rest of the ship. Bob, another World War II crew member, was thrilled. "It was just great. The ship hadn't changed whatsoever, the smells were the same, and the guns on the bridge and the signal light I used to use were all the same. It was a thrill that is hard to explain or describe, everything looked great and they kept it in excellent condition." He showed us the doorway they broke into to get at the beer in no. 5 hold when he was on board during the *O'Brien*'s South Pacific run. The door was locked and protected

Left to right, Gary Dow and Herb Adams, volunteer Mainers who were a great help during our stay.

with a wax seal, but the enterprising crew got in late one night by removing the hinges. They took out several cases of beer, then replaced the hinges and repainted them. "By morning it looked like new and no one ever caught on," said Bob.

Sunday, August 7, was a lovely, warm day. A Big Band concert was held on top of our no. 2 hatch by the Music Makers, directed by Jack Kazenski, featuring World War II songs by the Feeley Sisters (Martha, Elizabeth and Amy) of Auburn, Maine. The singers were dressed in World War II Army WAC uniforms and did a fine job with hits from the forties, evoking old memories and a time long past.

This was the day for *Jeremiah O'Brien* namesakes. We were pleasantly surprised when a young man came to the ship's store and announced that his name was Jeremiah O'Brien. He was 16 years old and no relation to Jeremiah O'Brien of Machias, but his enthusiasm was real and we welcomed him with a T-shirt and a hat. He brought along an album he had collected of news clippings about our ship and the original Jeremiah. The crew gathered around to look at his album. Asking him to wait, one went to get a camera. Then an older man introduced himself as Jeremiah O'Brien. He was a doctor and the sixth generation offspring of Morris O'Brien, Jeremiah's brother. They both showed identification so we knew they weren't pulling a stunt. We introduced the two Jeremiahs to each other and took their

Happy homecoming for Liberty ship

The Feeley Sisters of Auburn belt out a World War II-era big band song during a concert Sunday aboard the S.S. Jeremiah O'Brien. Visitors got their first chance to board the Liberty ship on Sunday; tours continue through Aug. 15 while the vessel is berthed at the Maine State Pier. Story, 1B

Press coverage was excellent. Here the Feeley sisters entertain "the troops." From the Portland Press Herald.

J.O.B.³ Left to right, Jeremiah O'Brien and Jeremiah O'Brien, taken in the ship's store of the Jeremiah O'Brien. Photo by Bill Fairfield.

picture together. Later, we met people who drove from Machias, Maine, the original Jeremiah O'Brien's home town. They were very well-acquainted with the history of the Revolutionary War hero. We gave them all special tours of the ship and told them how pleased we were to have our ship named after someone so illustrious.

The next day brought more perfect weather, clear skies and light breezes. We were charging $3 a head for visitors and were delighted to see about 2,000 people per day coming on board. That evening, Ed Langlois had arranged a private tour of the vessel by employees and retirees of Bath Iron Works and the Gibbs and Cox Company, famous naval architects who adapted the early British design to create the Liberty ship. Bath Iron Works is one of the oldest shipbuilding companies in the United States and has an excellent reputation for craftsmanship. In its early days it built freighters, passenger ships, ferries and Navy ships. In recent years it has built ships exclusively for the Navy.

Meanwhile, the crew was getting acquainted with downtown Portland. In fact, they began making their first sorties into town as soon as the ship was tied up. We were berthed in the older part of the city, known as the "Old Port Exchange." Consisting of an area about nine blocks square, its architecture, although relatively new, was designed to evoke historic Portland. Most of the buildings are red brick and some streets and alleys are cobblestoned. The Old Port is a tourist area filled with bookstores, dress shops, souvenir shops, coffee stores, ice cream parlors and candy stores. The most popular spot with the crew was the proverbial "first bar outside the gate," the Drydock Tavern. Walking past the Tavern's plate glass windows any afternoon or evening it was common to see inside a row of blue and green jackets with "*SS Jeremiah O'Brien*, Crew" emblazoned on the back, lining the barstools. Farther along the waterfront were Boone's Restaurant and DeMillo's floating restaurant, a former ferry boat. Each offered lobster prepared in its own way and added to the atmosphere of a busy, tourist-friendly fishing port. DeMillo's had a display of 45 shipyard photographs in their Port Lounge taken during 1941 and 1945.

Several other restaurants, bars and cafes popular with the crew offered the ubiquitous Maine lobster in the cuisines of Mexico, China, Italy and, of course, Down East Maine. By the end of our stay it became a contest to see who could sample lobster in the greatest number of ways. One crew member claimed to have had baked lobster, steamed lobster, lobster stuffed with crabmeat, lobster roll (a sandwich), lobster in black bean sauce, broiled lobster, lobster benedict and lobster stew. One shudders to think what his cholesterol count was after that.

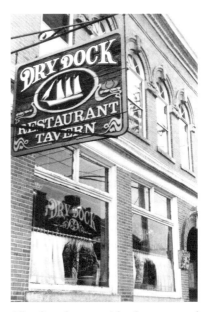

Other sights included the Portland Observatory located in an old signal tower bristling with masts and halyards, the University of Southern Maine, the birthplace of Henry Wadsworth Longfellow and the Portland Head Light.

Bob Burnett: "I was able to satisfy one of my own pet goals and go to the remains of the shipyard and find way no. 1. There I found some pieces of the original pilings. I took a couple of trips and spent time rummaging around the area."

The first bar outside the gate and a favorite crew hangout.

On August 9 Ross Bertran, a professional film producer, was aboard early in the morning to begin filming for a tape he was preparing of our visit to Portland. He spent the next several days interviewing crew and visitor alike, filming the interior and exterior of the ship and developing the history of the *Jeremiah O'Brien* for his film.*

The DiMILLO FAMILY RESTAURANT is pleased to present an exhibit of photographs of the building of LIBERTY SHIPS in South Portland, Maine in World War II.

The exhibit is the property of the SOUTH PORTLAND SHIPYARD SOCIETY, representing over 35,000 men and women who built 236 LIBERTY SHIPS for the United States Merchant Marine and 30 OCEAN VESSELS for Great Britain, during World War II.

The exhibit is in celebration of the return visit of the LIBERTY SHIP, S.S. *JEREMIAH O'BRIEN* to Portland Harbor from August 6 to August 15, 1994. The S.S. *JEREMIAH O'BRIEN* was built in South Portland and launched on June 19, 1943. Over 2700 LIBERTY SHIPS were built in 18 shipyards around the country during World War II. The S.S. *JEREMIAH O'BRIEN* is the only LIBERTY SHIP in its original condition still afloat.

YOU ARE INVITED TO VIEW THE EXHIBIT IN OUR PORT SIDE LOUNGE

The steel hull LIBERTY SHIP is 441'6" in length with a beam of 57

FOR INFORMATION ABOUT
VISITING HOURS – HARBOR CRUISE – DINNER/DANCE
during the visit of the S.S. *JEREMIAH O'BRIEN*
please pick up a flyer at our reception desk in the Main Foyer
or call the SHIPYARD SOCIETY at 207-773-7670

YOU MAY KEEP THIS ANNOUNCEMENT

DeMillo's was popular for dining and for its photo exhibit.

The diesel fuel that we loaded in France was just about used up. We ordered more and had to pump it from a truck into the empty drums on deck. This brings to mind probably the most ironic aspect of the voyage — our fifty-one-year-old ship ran perfectly without the least problem. But the diesel generator on no. 4 hatch, kindly donated by the Caterpillar Corporation, was so finely tuned and of such high technology that it caused more problems than anything else. When we had dirty fuel, the engine department had to change fuel filters every day. Because the clean fuel was in drums on deck it had to be pumped each day into the reservoir on the generator itself. The thing required constant daily attention of one kind or another. We couldn't help comparing it to the old, unsophisticated equipment on the ship which ran with a minimum of fuss and a goodly bit of Dick Brannon's "Tender Loving Care."

During our tour of England and France, we were surprised and moved by the deep emotions the sight of our old ship, and her old crew, stirred in so many people. We came to understand the feelings expressed by so many and treasured the experiences as among the most memorable in our lives. But we didn't expect the deep emotional response that our ship would evoke in our own country. The difference this time was, in Portland, the ship brought

*The final product was outstanding and can be ordered by calling 207-642-3417.

back memories of youth and a sense of important contribution to the country.

Thousands of people who worked in the New England Shipbuilding Corporation's yard during the war, including several of the *O'Brien*'s old crew members, visited the ship. There was always somebody pointing out the weld they laid in, or the wiring they installed or explaining the difficulties of connecting piping in the bowels of the ship or pointing out the bunk they slept in or explaining what it was like living aboard the ship.

Most of them claimed to have worked on the *Jeremiah O'Brien* herself, but in reality they only worked in the yard at the time the ship was built. New England Shipbuilding constructed more than 200 Liberty ships and most of the workers wouldn't have been aware of the name of any particular ship they worked on. Each one was just another of those ships "built by the mile and cut off by the yard." The Libertys were designed to be simple, uncomplicated ships that could be "built faster than they were sunk," and in yards around the country, 2751 were stamped out of the same giant ship cutter and sent across the oceans.

As The Last Liberty, the *O'Brien* embodies all those that went before her or came after. She is the living symbol of all Liberty ships. Maybe, in a sense, those thousands <u>did</u> work on the *O'Brien* and could now come to see her one more time with tears in their eyes and nostalgia in their souls as they touched a welding seam with shaking fingers or ran their wrinkled hands over a rail.

In Portland, we came to understand one universal human desire that transcends culture and language — the need to share important memories of events that are bigger than day-to-day life. Just as they had in Europe, visitors came up to crew members, showing long-kept badges, treasured papers and keepsakes of their youth. We were learning that it wasn't just people who suffered in a great war who were forever marked by it. Here in Portland, it was people who worked in a great cause, and who, too, were forever changed by it. In Rouen, we talked about the brotherhood of the sea. Now, we were realizing the brotherhood of humanity.

Nils Anderson: "I was really impressed with Portland, Maine, and what the ship meant to them. That was pretty special.

People came on board and I remember one gentleman, he had worked in both shipyards and he still had his picture ID badges. I remember my father wearing one of them. And he had both those badges. The guy was so proud of it and the fact that he had worked on these ships and probably worked on this very ship.

"Women came on board, little old ladies. This one lady had a letter from her superintendent of how she had progressed from an apprentice tack welder on up to a finished overhead welder. Here's an eighty-five-year-old woman who was a welder and worked on this ship and it was really special. There has been more than one occasion on this trip that tears come to your eyes listening to people."

An eighty-seven-year-old woman, accompanied by two nuns and her younger brother came into the captain's office to present a $10 donation and some mementos. She came back twice more in the ensuing days just to look at the ship again.

From an article in the *Maine Sunday Telegram,* August 7.

Many were forever changed by the *O'Brien* or other look-alike Liberty ships — men who sailed to Normandy on them, women who built them using skills they would never have otherwise learned, couples whose lives together began in welding shacks in the yard.

Marion Senechal, one of 3,700 women workers in South Portland, met her husband, Bob while both were "burners" on the *O'Brien.* The war was on, the need was great. In the yard, she recalled, there was a "singleness of purpose" and great pride. "There was a job that had to be done," she said, "and we did it." Shipyard workers around the country built 2,751 Liberty ships from 1941 to 1945 — a feat Ed Langlois calls "a miracle."

"People simply worked 24 hours a day," he said. "There was a war effort that said, if we're going to get the equipment, and carry troops, and get food and medicine into the war zones, we've gotta have the ships to do it."

Langlois worked on Liberty ships as a teen-ager. Like most of his co-workers, he was untrained: "What did I know about building ships? Nothing, except I liked ships and I had worked on my bicycle." He remembers the sense that "there were men fighting overseas, and you had to do your part. The men in the yard, and all these salty women — you just knew you had to do what you had to do.

"We had a mission. You never even thought about working seven days a week. At break you ate your peanut butter and jelly sandwich, and went back to work."

Marion Senechal, now 78, was 25 when she began building ships. "I started at 50 cents an hour and thought I was in heaven," she said.

After two weeks of training she began work as a burner. "I used an oxygen and acetylene torch to create a very hot flame that cut through the steel. There were women welders, chippers (who trimmed welds), riveters, pipe fitters. The women were matter-of-fact about their work: "There was nobody else to do it, so here we were." She still feels the pride of her work. "I was contributing to the war. I had a meaningful job — I could measure its meaning," she said. "When we heard of ships being sunk, it felt like a personal insult. It just made you more determined."

It was a workplace where hot metal, rivets and sparks flew. She wore a leather jacket and steel-toed boots and covered her hair from the sparks. She worked seven days a week, and often double eight-hour shifts. "On the bus going home, I invariably fell asleep," she remembers.

Helen Goodine of South Portland, now 93 with 62 great-grand-children, worked as a welder. She was a young widow with six children and remembers a time when "everybody worked together. My heart is filled with the memories of when we women went to work in South Portland." Others shared memories of landing at Normandy on a Liberty ship, of an uncle who went down on a Liberty ship, or a father who shipped out on a Liberty.

Clarence Adams, 85, was a welder and lead man on the *O'Brien.* He bought his West Falmouth house with his earnings. It cost $3,500. Adams excitedly pointed out the *O'Brien*'s life rafts, air vents, machine guns.

"He read about it in the paper a few months ago and has been talking about it ever since," explained his daughter. "It's a sentimental thing." She drove him up to see the ship, to be sure he got there.

Joseph Katusa was misty-eyed when he first saw the *O'Brien.* He sailed on Liberty ships to Normandy and the South Pacific. "It feels like I'm 17 again, when we were a bunch of high school kids and we learned how to make that thing work."

Ed Langlois echoed the day's cyclical theme. "She's home," he said. "We have to remember Dorothy in 'The Wizard of Oz.' There's no place like home."

Brian Goldman: "I was impressed with the people coming down to the engine room showing you where they were responsible for welding, talking for an hour and a half about how to lag the piping. It added character to the ship. It added faces behind the scenes — the people who put the ships together."

Ed Langlois explains some of the finer points of organizing our visit to, left to right, Capt. Jahn, Adm. Patterson and the author. Photo courtesy of Ed Langlois.

Bob Black: "If you want to know the best liberty port, I'd have to say Portland, Maine. For two reasons: it was our first United States port after the Atlantic crossing and it was the birthplace of the ship. Hearing the stories of the people, the shipwrights that actually worked on this vessel and her sisters made it very interesting."

Bob Crocker, left, gunner's mate in the ship's original crew, joined Norm Robinson, his former gunnery officer, on one of our cruises. From the Maine Sunday Telegram.

Tim Palange: "I think in some ways the visit to Portland Maine was the highlight of the trip as far as visits go, 'cause having a lot of people on board who actually worked on this ship and helped build it really stands out in my mind. We had a lot of them down in the engine room, not to mention relatives of Jeremiah O'Brien."

Radio Operator Bob Gisslow's domain was a popular spot during our two cruises in Portland. Photo courtesy of Ed Langlois.

Many visitors came down to see Dick Brannon at his engines. *From the* Portland Press Herald.

First Assistant Engineer Tim Palange checks the engine room gauges during the cruises. From the Portland Press Herald.

Ed Langlois: "One of the most traumatic moments of the visit was when the crew volunteered to carry the wheelchair with one of the women workers up the gangway. I watched them carry that wheelchair up to the main deck and it was precarious, the pressure each man was under. It was even worse on the way off. I

Sam Wood, left, and John Linderman during a quiet moment. Photo courtesy of John Linderman.

thought sure if they slipped, that lady was going right down the gangway, but they made it. They were exhausted and they just smiled and shook hands with the husband and they went back to work."

This is the Voice of the *Jeremiah O'Brien.*

Good evening, San Francisco.

Another very satisfactory day of open ship in Portland, Maine. The crew is all smiles as citizens of this New England city board our vessel to witness first hand the results of their skill as shipbuilders. Many men and women point out their areas of handiwork in the building of Liberty ships many years ago. Statements such as "I was a machinist and I had the job of installing propeller shaft bearings." "I was a burner." "I was a welder," etc.

All of them were proud to see the results of their talents still in first class condition 51 years later. We in turn thank them for their devotion in constructing such a sturdy vessel. Most off duty crew are ashore tonight enjoying a dinner of genuine New England sea food, baked clams and lobster. Yum, yum.

Jeremiah O'Brien — out.

One problem that never went away was the financial burden of operating the ship. From Day One back in 1993, and every day of the voyage, finances were a major concern. Wherever we were, messages went back and forth between the home office and the ship about money.

Karen Kamimoto: "While the ship was gone we ran an ad in the paper and it was touching. People would send in all these little $5, $10 and $20 donations. They were so proud of our crew and their ship. The people of San Francisco and the Bay Area really rallied. It was very heart warming."

Ed Langlois, who organized our stay, said he would do what he could and he did a remarkable job, arranging free pilotage, tug service, berthing and water. He advertised the ship in local newspapers and got regional businesses involved. Among other things, he arranged for fund raising in the form of gangway admissions, private evening tours, a fund-raising departure dinner at the Sonesta Hotel, and two cruises.

Tom Patterson: "We brought in over a hundred and twenty thousand dollars there through their generosity — through the gate, the paid admissions."

The ship's store did a thriving business in baseball caps, coffee mugs, books about the ship and anything that had "*Jeremiah O'Brien*" on it. Ruth Robson did a wonderful job of managing the store with the cheerful help of Dottie Duncan, Barbara Speight (wife of Jeff, second assistant engineer), Mrs. Jahn, Mrs. Patterson and Mrs. Otterberg.

Each of the half-day cruises was profitable — we carried more than 800 people which helped our financial situation. The cruises were filled with old friends and acquaintances. Norm Robinson, who was the officer in charge of the Armed Guard on voyages 5 and 6, was aboard, driving up from Florida for the occasion. He and Bob Crocker, who was now in our steward's department, had a nostalgic reunion. Bob Crocker: "Robby and I live near each other in Florida, so we kept in touch through the years. But I saw Swan on board. He was in the original gun crew and I hadn't seen him in fifty-one years.

"I was glad to sit in my old seat in the messroom. Bob Burnett showed me my name in the room I used to have. I saw my name on the bulkhead. They painted right around it. Everything looked fine. Nothing had changed. I waited on tables and met a lot of good people and they were a great crew. I wouldn't have missed that for anything. Everyone was so excited to talk to an original crew member. They were really a good crew, everyone of them was just great."

Paul Krinsky, former superintendent of the Merchant Marine Academy at Kings Point, was also on board. The ship's first radio operator, Robert C. Morgan, joined us. H.O. Runkle, who in *The Last Liberty* provided a great narrative about the cracking of his Liberty ship, made the trip. Hundreds of enthusiastic former shipbuilders from Portland were there. From the younger generation we heard: Dad was a welder - burner - cutter - lead foreman. Mom was a drafter - riveter - welder - burner - painter. Again, everyone was so grateful we had come. "That you think enough of us to come back," was a sentiment often heard.

Tom Patterson: "We had two wonderful cruises in Portland. It seemed like everybody in the State of Maine had worked on the *Jeremiah O'Brien*'s building. We had very young-looking ninety-year-old people coming back aboard to look at the work that had survived for fifty-one years. And it was a thrill to them, there's no doubt about it. This five-year building program will never be forgotten in South Portland, and the fact that one of their ships is still operating and looks like it's brand-new was a great thing for them. They responded, generously."

The next day was another warm sunny day with the waters of Casco Bay sparkling blue all around us. The deck department spent the morning washing down the decks, loading stores and preparing for our visitors. And, as always, we had problems with visitors not following the blue line. Here, it was because so many had been so involved with Liberty ships they didn't want to miss anything. They feared that by simply following the blue line, they might miss a view of the engine room or not get an opportunity to see the sacks of potatoes on the boat deck, or bypass the interior of the galley. We tried to keep them pointed in the right direction, but understood if they lingered or deviated from the line. It was their ship, too. They built it.

Lou Geronimo, a retired Honolulu harbor pilot, had joined us as third mate in Le Havre, bringing the ship across the Atlantic to Portland. Now returning to his family in Tahiti, he was replaced by Otis Phelps. Our new third mate was from San Francisco. He

The Portland Press Telegram *did a fine job of creating interest in our visit in this piece on our homecoming.*

had recently retired from Matson Lines where he sailed as a deck officer on some of their newer container ships. Now he wanted to sail on a "real" ship. Like many of the crew, he liked being back on a ship where <u>people</u> made the difference — people stoked the galley stove and oiled the engine and steered the ship rather than sitting at consoles doing things by pushing buttons.

David Aris: "The watch-keeping on a ship like this is real old-fashioned watch-keeping for the simple reason that there's virtually nothing in that engine room automated. On a modern ship you can press buttons and things happen when they're supposed to happen. In this engine room if you want something to happen you've got to make it happen. You've got to open a valve or shut the valve or pull a lever or do something like that. So when you're on watch you actually have got to be on watch. In fact, it's true to say, my job in the boiler room, the physical content of the job is quite small. All the work that you got to do like cleaning burners, now you can do it in about twenty minutes, but you spend a lot of time adjusting a little bit here, watching temperature mix, small adjustments, because the ship does not have automation. As a matter of fact, I've been asked to comment on that when I go back to England, the difference between being a watch-keeper here and on a modern ship. And that's the fundamental difference, it's hand-operated. The whole engine room is hand-operated. The lubrication is a very good case in point. Every drop of oil the engine needs is put on by a guy with an oil can, no lubricators and that sort of thing. I think that's what is rather interesting and medieval about it, you might say."

David Aris joined the ship in Le Havre. He was one of our volunteer docents in Portsmouth, England and was asked to return with us to San Francisco in the engineering department as a fireman-watertender. Born in Great Britain, David has been a marine engineer all his life, serving first as an apprentice building engines. He went to college and took a degree in marine engineering. He then went to sea with Caltex company serving on T-2 tankers. After getting his first class British certificates for steam and diesel ships (chief engineer's license) he came ashore into ship building, ship management and finally ship repairing, from which he retired in 1983. He and his wife live in Sunderland County, England.

As enthusiastic as they were, and much as we enjoyed meeting them, sometimes the crowds began to wear on some of the crew. Pat McCafferty: "Sometimes what got me was the hardship of the people walking around on the ship. We kind of had the ship back in our possession again, and then all of a sudden there were people walking through our ship again. There in Portland we didn't spring back so quick. But it was all right. People in Portland were very proud that we showed up. They were very ecstatic about us being there."

Jack Carraher: "Our popularity kind of worked on me. I grew very tired of the large crowds that we had. They tired me out. I'm 71 and I do tire, I guess, pretty easily. Although they were very fine people, I mean courteous, and civil in all respects but it was just dealing with them that tired me out."

But the people of Portland were very hospitable, buying the crew drinks in bars, inviting them to their homes, including them in activities. The chief mate was invited to an evening lobster bake on a beach at the fishing camp of Wayne Duffet, a city employee, on the coast at Cape Elizabeth overlooking a small, rocky inlet. When we arrived, we saw his brother, Neil, out in a small boat picking up lobster pots for the evening's dinner. The "camp" was a lovely wooden-sided house with a large living-dining room, a kitchen, a loft and several platforms for laying out bedding. What made it a camp rather than a house was that there was no electricity. All the lighting was by kerosene lantern. Among the guests were two Russians from Archangel, Alexander Pashkovin and Captain Valery Kokovin. The Archangel Committee (The Russian Sister City Committee of Greater Portland), arranged and financed their visit to Portland to take part in the celebrations surrounding the *O'Brien*'s arrival. Capt. Kokovin was a World War II veteran and a former Liberty ship sailor.

The dinner was a magnificent spread of freshly steamed lobster, baked potatoes, corn-on-the-cob, hard-boiled eggs and cake. Everything but the cake was cooked at the same time in a single large kettle over an open fire on the beach and served on a large rectangular table, set with a red-checked tablecloth that dominated the living-dining room. We hungrily sat around it enjoying the dark shadows thrown on the wood walls and floor by the old-fashioned lighting. The Russians provided ample quantities of Stolichnaya. And, again, as we know, once the bottle is open . . .

David Aris: "Of all the ports that we visited, I think I enjoyed Portland the most. Probably because it wasn't too hot, but also there was this nice relationship with the people who built the ship. I think that was rather special. The other ports were just nice places to go to, but there was something special about Portland and it seemed to rub off."

One minor problem happened which could never occur anywhere else. Someone wanted to mail a letter and asked one of the locals where the main post office was.

"Any one you want," was the reply.

He scratched his head. "What? No, I mean the <u>main</u> post office. I want to buy some stamps, mail some letters."

"They're all Maine post offices," said the local.

"How can that be? You must have one that's bigger than the others, a central post office?"

"Sure. That's a Maine post office, too."

The crew member borrowed some stamps from a friend and used a mailbox.

Saturday, August 13 brought a change in the weather. The sky was overcast and hazy. Visibility was down to just a couple of miles. The deck department took advantage of being alongside the dock to paint the hull, something we couldn't do at sea. Of course, we could only reach one side of the ship and our access there was limited by our being tied across the end of the pier, but we went ahead and did what we could. From the dock Marty Shields and Clifford Hook used paint rollers with manhelpers (an eight-foot handle) to reach and roll the side of the ship. Taping a second manhelper to the first extended their "reach" by an additional eight feet.

Jeremiah O'Brien's great, great-grandniece from Tucson, Arizona, was aboard the ship, having flown in just for the occasion. We asked her why she didn't come to see the ship in San Francisco since it was closer. But she didn't know of its existence until we arrived in Portland. She was given a special tour and had pictures taken with several of the crew.

Ed Langlois graciously invited the crew to the fund-raising dinner at the Sonesta Hotel in downtown Portland. "I reserved the main ballroom of the Sonesta for what I thought was one of the most important parts of the visit on Saturday evening August 13. One week before the date, I only had fifteen people signed up at a $50 contribution per person to go to the dance. The Sonesta called me on Wednesday, August 3, and said, 'Tomorrow you must come up with $4,500, Ed, and we think you should cancel and save the prospect of going into debt.'

"I said, 'Give me one more day. We'll fill the ballroom with two hundred people.' I went to see my friends on the waterfront and inside of four days we had a hundred eighty people signed up. That pleased me because it gave me the opportunity to invite the officers and crew of *Jeremiah O'Brien* to the event as our guests."

Capt. and Mrs. Jahn on the flying bridge of the Jeremiah O'Brien. *Photo courtesy of Ed Langlois.*

We arrived in the early evening to find ourselves in an elegantly-restored old-fashioned hotel with a grand entrance, large public rooms and high ceilings. The dinner was held in a ballroom with round tables seating ten, set around the edge of a large wooden dance floor. The tables themselves were luxuriously laid out with white linen, heavy silverware and tall-stemmed glasses. In the center of each table, on a small stand, was a yellow card with a number on it. Before sitting down to dinner there were cocktails. To keep some control over the situation, Ed had given each crew member two small yellow slips of heavy paper to use as drink chits. We talked with several of the people we had met in the past few weeks, including Wayne and Neil Duffet, our pilots on the ship, representatives of local industry and some former shipyard workers. When we sat down to dinner, someone noticed that the numbered placards in the centers of the tables were made of the same stock as the drink chits. It was quick work with a pair of fingernail scissors to produce all the yellow chits anyone could want. The crew had a <u>very</u> good time at the dinner.

Ed Langlois: "We knew they were doing that and endorsed it." [laughs]

Bob Burnett: "At the Sonesta, Marty Shields showed up with yet another girl."

Among the those who spoke at the dinner were Frank Emery, charter member of the Shipyard Society*; Richard Mallett, of the American Merchant Marine Veterans; Jerry Graves, of the U.S. Navy Armed Guard and Ann Noyes, of the Greater Portland Archangel Committee. Ann introduced Alexander Pashkovin and Capt. Valery Kokovin of Portland's sister city, Archangel.

State Representative Herbert Adams presented the captain and the admiral with proclamations and flags from the State Legislature.

Ed Langlois: "One of my honored guests was Bill Hultgren of Pennsylvania. Bill is the foremost authority on photographs of Liberty ships in the world. He has photos of almost every Liberty ship ever built. He was there as our guest, at the head table, to salute his major contribution to Liberty ships world wide."

Music was provided by the Ted Manduca Big Band and the Feeley Sisters, again dressed as WACs, sang songs of the '40s.

Ed continues: "Two members of the orchestra approached me after the affair was over, professional musicians, and they told me they never heard the band play so well. There was something mystical about the entire evening, they didn't want to stop. That was a tremendous tribute to the whole evening. The drummer said. 'We never played better than tonight and we haven't practiced together since January.'"

Sunday, August 14, was our last day to be open to the public. We had a good turnout with 2279 people on board, including shipyard workers and D-Day veterans of the Marine 4th Division who received a special tour. They shook our hands and said over and over how wonderful it was that we brought the ship there. It was impossible not to be affected by the sincerity of our visitors. Yardworkers from the shipyard where the *O'Brien* was built were also on board, making a last visit, many with tears in their eyes.

---

*The Shipyard Society is working now to establish its own museum on the grounds where the ships were built and to erect a memorial monument on the site which people from generations to come will be able to share what took place in World War II.

Virginia Taylor, 80 years old, one of the ladies who welded Liberty ships at South Portland, came to visit. She described what it was like working in the shipyard during the war. "I started work in the East Yard on January 10, 1943, worked in the basins for three years, then went to the outfitting piers. I worked the inner bottoms and drain wells, which were very confining spaces. The engine room, shaft alley, afterpeak and forepeak, and deckhouse were better jobs.

"I'll tell you how confining the inner bottoms were. I would go down and come up, go down and come up, time after time, because I'd get claustrophobic. I had nightmares the whole time I worked there. The drain wells, where the ship picks up the extra water, were so narrow that your back almost touched it." One inspector went below to check the inner bottoms and the welder, not knowing he was there, welded the hatch into place. "He went out with the ship and they never knew.

"Every time I went down there, I was filled with fear that they could put the cover on. I used to have to climb down four or five holes through decks on just a ladder, carrying everything I needed. Those were the days before OSHA."

"The winters were very cold right off the waterfront. One day we were all sent home. It was thirty-five below zero." All winter, workers wore long underwear, two pairs of wool pants, wool shirts over flannel shirts, coveralls, boots, wool mittens under leather gloves, and hats. "I think my clothes must have weighed fifty pounds."

"In the morning, the girls looked good," said Taylor's husband, Carlton. "They had their makeup on, and you'd want to ask them out. But the end of the day, no one dared ask them."

"It was welders' smoke," continues Virginia. "My face would be so black. You'd go to town on the bus, and you could almost see the other passengers raise themselves up — they didn't want to sit alongside us."

Katherine Robischaud said she got angry when male workers called her "Rosie the Riveter." "It was the beginning of women wearing slacks and doing men's work. There was a lot of teasing at first, but then they found the women could do the work and it stopped."

One of the welders who visited us said the first ship they welded on needed a beam and they didn't know how long to cut it. So they went down to a Liberty farther along in construction and measured the same beam on it. It had been accidently made 3 ft. short and had a stub added on to it. Not knowing any better, they did the same thing.

In the evening, a merchant marine veteran, Mr. Forty, arrived to visit the ship. He drove all the way from New Hampshire to see the ship after learning at 3 p.m. that we were there. Although the gangway was closed, we let him on board and gave him a private tour.

The day of our departure, Monday, August 15, opened with blue skies behind thick, fast-moving clouds. After a few good-byes we took a quick departure. Our pilot, Capt. Granville Smith, shook hands with everyone on the flying bridge and said, "God bless you for bringing the ship to Portland."

Ed Langlois: "Taking part in the visit of the *Jeremiah O'Brien* was a wonderful, wonderful experience and there was never a moment that I felt this would not be accomplished."

Bob Burnett: "Portland Maine was beautifully organized. Ed Langlois deserves a huge amount of credit for all that he did."

At 0830 we departed buoy "P" into a moderate head sea. It was a "straight shot" to the Cape Cod Canal with no course changes. We could see the New England coast to our right, and an occasional fishing boat, pulling its lobster pots.

Although gone from Maine, we had part of the state with us. Gary Dow, a merchant seaman and assistant to Ed Langlois, came along as an engine room wiper. We had the state flag, given to us by Herb Adams, and, also supplied by Herb, several hundred plastic pins in the shape of lobsters.

Ross Bertran, who made the video of the *Jeremiah O'Brien* in Portland, wrote a touching letter to the ship, describing what its visit meant to him.

It's Sunday evening. Tomorrow the *Jeremiah* will be steaming out of Portland harbor, bound for San Francisco. I'm not much for writing letters, but I had to take the opportunity to attempt to tell you what this past week has meant to me.

Up until a week ago Saturday, the term "Liberty Ship" conjured up vague memories from my childhood of playing around in an old, abandoned shipyard, and short references by family and friends. Tonight, as I write you this letter, I have a much better understanding of what this class of ship has meant to us and to a free world, and, more importantly, the role that merchant mariners have played in our country's defense and commerce.

I'd like to thank Captain Jahn and the crew of the *Jeremiah* for bringing her home to Portland. As I'm sure you're all aware, it has meant so, so much to so many people. I have seen the gratitude in the eyes and smiles of many former shipyard workers. I have heard the "thank you's" from the lips of many former sailors and gunners. I have sensed the pride children have had in the work and dedication of their parents; those who helped build and sail these fine ships. You all have brought the D-Day celebration, and the recognition of a job well done, home to the World War II veterans of New England.

Personally, the *Jeremiah* and what it represents has helped me focus on values which are being neglected in today's America: duty, responsibility, love of country and the cost of freedom and liberty. As I interviewed crew and visitors this week, a phrase from the third stanza of <u>America The Beautiful</u> kept coming to mind: "Who more than self their country loved, and mercy more than life." Your visit to Portland this week helped me to focus on the sacrifice that so many made so that I might live in a free and prosperous land. It helped point to the fact that there are indeed causes and values which subordinate individual wants and needs to the greater good of society and mankind. My generation's parents didn't want to go . . . they <u>had</u> to go. It was the price of freedom. The miracle of the Liberty Ship was possible because it <u>had</u> to be done to secure the freedom of our country and our allies. There certainly could have been no more appropriate name for this class of ship than that of Liberty.

This documentary I have the privilege of working on has grown from being "just an interesting project" to a labor of love and gratitude. I am grateful for the sacrifice that this ship represents. I am truly grateful for your allowing the *Jeremiah O'Brien* to again touch the shores of her birth port. I am eternally grateful for the kindness and assistance which the crew of the *Jeremiah* has shown me. Neither Portland nor I will be the same for it. Thank you.

16

SOUTH,
TO CHESAPEAKE BAY

Two thousand seven hundred and fifty-one Liberty ships were built in the 1940s during America's greatest ship-building era. Of them, only two remain operational. The *Jeremiah O'Brien* and the *John W. Brown*. The *O'Brien* is the only unaltered Liberty in the world, looking exactly as she did fifty years ago, inside and out, including guns. The *Brown* is modified from her original configuration, but she is still an active ship. The *Brown* was to have been part of "The Last Convoy" to Normandy (together with the *SS Lane Victory* and the *Jeremiah O'Brien*), but the high cost of replacing too many rivets prevented the trip, to the disappointment of her crew. Instead, she observed the 50th Anniversary by sailing from her home port of Baltimore to visit ports on the East Coast.

A few days before leaving Portland we received word that the *Brown* was sailing from Baltimore, bound for Halifax. As we departed Portland, "Sparks" (Bob Gisslow) received word that the

The John W. Brown *approaches . . .*

Brown was scheduled to transit the Cape Cod Canal at noon.* The last two Libertys set a rendezvous for 1530.

As the time approached the crew gathered on deck, their cameras at the ready. The sky was clear, the ocean a calm blue, a picture-book setting for the meeting of the last two Liberty ships in the world. Just after 1500 hours the *Brown* was sighted on the horizon, slightly on the port bow. John Borowiec, who joined as a messman in Portland, came up to the bridge to borrow the binoculars. Soon, every pair of binoculars on the bridge was in use, as we watched the ship grow larger. Steaming closer, we saw a freshly-painted grey hull and superstructure and the familiar Liberty silhouette. The differences were minor — her boot-topping was red where ours was black and her after machine guns were on raised platforms while ours were on the same level as our after gun. Otherwise, it was almost like seeing a reflection of ourselves. Capt. Jahn brought our ship to the left to give us a better view while the *Brown*'s master, Capt. Esbensen, did the same. We both kept turning left, left, to get closer and closer.

At exactly 1532 Eastern Daylight Time (1932 Universal Coordinate Time)+, on August 15, 1994, the Liberty ship *Jeremiah O'Brien* and the Liberty ship *John W. Brown* passed port side to port side one-quarter of a mile apart. The traditional three-whistle salute and short answer were exchanged and flags were dipped.

---

*By tradition all radio operators in the merchant marine are called Sparks because the early marine wireless sets were prone to throwing off electrical sparks, just as all ship's carpenters are called "Chips" because that is the by-product of their labors.

+Formerly known as Greenwich Mean Time.

A historic meeting. The John W. Brown *and the* Jeremiah O'Brien *pass at sea. Photo courtesy of Denys Lomax.*

Tom Patterson: "Just north of the Cape Cod Canal we had the great pleasure to meet *SS John W. Brown* on her northbound leg to Halifax. The two ships saluted each other. It was a great thing; I wish we had longer to heave to and have a gam with them, but we couldn't spare the time. We were rushing to make our schedule and they were rushing to make theirs. But the two Liberty ships did meet and pass."

Ruth Robson: "I think probably one of the most impressive things was the passing of the two Liberty ships. It had lot of significance — just two ships passing in the sea, but when you think about it, what those two ships are and what they mean, it was quite a thing. It would be a once-in-a-forever experience. That was a very special moment."

Capt. Denys Lomax, who had been so helpful to us in Portsmouth and Southampton, was aboard the *Brown*: "In July Capt. Brian Hope, Chairman of Project Liberty Ship, asked if I'd like to be a member of the crew of the *John W. Brown* on her forthcoming trip from Baltimore to Halifax, Nova Scotia, then Boston was added. As you can imagine, I jumped at the chance having sailed out of both ports, Boston and Halifax, during the war on the *SS Samfoyle*.

"On this trip, Brian Hope and I shared the cadet's cabin, the counterpart of the one Admiral Patterson occupied on the

O'Brien. So there was I in the same cabin and lower bunk that I'd spent nearly two years in towards the end of the war. A strange feeling, one wondered if the intervening 50 years had actually happened. Here I was signed on as a seaman, my first voyage under the Stars and Stripes!!

"It was great to meet up with the *O'Brien* after we had passed through the Cape Cod Canal. I was hoping that the two ships would meet, after the *Brown* had been delayed sailing from Baltimore with boiler problems. I'd had my binoculars trained on the horizon ahead, straining my eyes to spot the masts and upperworks of the *O'Brien* and I think most of the people on the *Brown* were very excited at the prospect of an historic meeting at sea of two Liberty ships unlikely to ever happen again, though Captain Esbensen seemed relatively unmoved.

"I thought we should have made a bit more of the occasion, exchanging signals, get our whistle going earlier, etc. but then it wasn't up to me!! although I was on the monkey island (flying bridge) close to the whistle control."

On both ships everybody cheerfully waved, then each vessel continued on its way, the crews watching one another grow smaller and smaller. It was an occasion of mixed feelings. We were delighted to see each other. But it was sad because it was probably the last time in history that two Liberty ships would meet and pass on the open ocean. *Sic transit gloria mundi.*

The idea of building a canal across Cape Cod was first envisioned by Miles Standish of the Plymouth Colony in 1623 as a way of facilitating trade with Dutch merchants in New York. Unfortunately, the technology didn't exist to actually build the canal. The first formal survey for this purpose came in 1776 at the behest of General George Washington, but again the means to build it weren't available. It fell to wealthy financier August Perry Belmont over a century later to actually get the job done. Begun in June 1909, the Canal was completed in 1914, just seventeen days before the opening of the Panama Canal.

The Cape Cod Canal is slightly over seventeen miles long with a width of 480 feet and a depth of 32 feet. There are no locks but three bridges connect Cape Cod to the mainland. Transiting the Canal rather than going around Cape Cod saves many hours and hundreds of miles on the voyage south along the Atlantic seaboard.

Washington, D.C. as a port of call was dropped because the Potomac River wasn't deep enough for the *O'Brien* (one of the crew suggested the president get the Corps of Engineers out and have them dredge the river deeper. After all, we were the *Jeremiah O'Brien* and this was a command performance, but, no such luck). Baltimore was substituted as a port close enough to the nation's capital to allow visits by interested congresspersons, our primary purpose for going to Washington. "Coke" Schneider, who served in our steward's department on this voyage from San Francisco to Panama, arranged for pilotage and berthing for the ship's cruise down the East Coast. A Kings Point alumnus, he knew several King Pointers on board, and arranged for the ship to layover at our *alma mater* on the way to Baltimore.*

At 1742 we took Capt. John Neary aboard and started through the Cape Cod Canal. The surrounding countryside slopes gently up from the grass-covered banks of the Canal. Bicycle paths and hiking trails parallel the water with an occasional fishing camp or yacht basin nearby. Set farther back were elegant homes, roads and, behind, thick, green forests of maple. Hundreds of people, not wanting to miss the chance to see two Libertys in one day, lined the banks on both sides. They cheered at our passage and waved when we blew the whistle. We saw Bob Crocker's friends and relatives in two locations with a large sign proclaiming "BOB" in huge letters.

Bob Crocker: "When we went through the Cape Cod Canal my two daughters and six grandchildren (they're between seven and twelve years old) were all there. They were all stretched out under the bridge with signs, yelling and screaming. Then after we passed they jumped in cars and ran down to the next bridge, and

---

*The United States Merchant Marine Academy at Kings Point, New York, is one of five federal academies. The others are the U.S. Military Academy at West Point, the U.S. Naval Academy at Annapolis, the U.S. Air Force Academy at Colorado Springs, and the U.S. Coast Guard Academy at New London.

did the same thing. It was quite a deal, grampa's old ship and the guns and so on. There were hundreds of people there and some of them asked what all the shouting was about. So my grandkids told them and everybody joined in waving and cheering."

Exiting the Canal, we saw to our right the Massachusetts Maritime Academy. Their training ship, the *Bay State*, a converted Prudential-Grace "M-type" cargo-passenger ship, was alongside the dock, glowing red in the setting sun. As we steamed out the channel and through the buoys into Buzzards Bay, the sun set ahead of us, turning the smooth water into a mirror of flaming red and yellow that slowly faded to black.

Tom Patterson: "The Cape Cod Canal was a beautiful experience. We were really happy that our crew was able to see all of these canals. I was happy to see it because I remember taking the Liberty ship I was skipper of in the Navy through the Cape Cod Canal. It brought back a lot of nostalgia for me, personally."

Just before 2300 we exchanged pilots, with Capt. Keirnam and Capt. Boslet coming aboard to guide us through Long Island Sound and down to Kings Point. The protected waters of the Sound were smooth and glassy and we had a lovely evening passage with a half-moon and a small sea. The shores on either side of the ship were dotted with small white lights. The moon and the stars were reflected in the water around us. All was at peace with the world. It was a wonderful night to be on the ocean.

Bill Bennett's Crew's News this evening:

History was made today in Massachusetts Bay. At approximately Lat 42-10N, 70-20W, at precisely 1532 hrs EDT, the *Jeremiah O'Brien*, en route Baltimore Maryland via Cape Cod Canal, Manhattan and the Statue of Liberty, met the Liberty ship *John W. Brown*. The *Brown*, en route Halifax, Nova Scotia with Canadian escort vessel, passed abeam with off duty crew lining the rail. Both vessels dipped their U.S. ensigns as a sign of respect while passing. For the great majority of crew on each vessel it was the first time in many decades that any had seen another Liberty ship at sea. It looked marvelous, sparkling with fresh paint, cargo gear secured in a seamanlike fashion and signal flags flying; a sight probably never to be seen again.

We approached Kings Point just after breakfast the following morning. It was a clear, fine, calm day with the promise of warm temperatures. Although the campus fronts Long Island Sound and there is deep water just off the Academy piers, the area was designated as a channel for barge traffic and the Coast Guard wouldn't let us anchor. We steamed in a gentle semicircle across the front of the piers to give everyone a good look at us, then blew our whistle in salute. The Academy's training ship, *Kings Pointer*, a converted survey ship, answered. Our pilot found an anchorage on the other side of Stepping Stone Light, hidden from the campus and not threatening the local barge traffic, of which there was none.

As soon as the gangway was down the Academy Superintendent, Admiral Matteson, and the Regimental Officer, Captain Robert Safarik, came aboard. Bob Black got out his boatswain's whistle and piped them aboard in proper nautical style. After a tour of the ship, they outlined the activities planned for the day: a memorial service in the afternoon, dinner at the admiral's house to which the captain, admiral, chief engineer and chief mate were invited, and, afterward, a cocktail party and awards ceremony at the officer's club with the entire crew invited.

"You can't go home again," said Thomas Wolfe, but sometimes you want to try. For the Kings Pointers on the crew, it was "home" for three of the four years of our college days (as part of the training, one year is spent at sea on merchant ships). It was a Spartan, regimented and difficult time, and intended to be. As with the other federal academies, the curriculum was designed to toughen us up, to discipline our minds and bodies and turn callow youths into officers. Despite the rigors of our undergraduate years, the Academy still was "home," in a way, and we looked forward to our visit.

The cadets manning the launch ashore were friendly, professional and bright, and very young. Had we <u>ever</u> been that young? Riding in from our anchorage, the Academy looked splendid. The wooden piers and covered boat sheds where we learned rowing, sailing and lifesaving had that timeless, weather-beaten look of all structures at the edge of the sea. On shore, behind them, neatly-cut green lawns rose on a gentle slope to the white administration building, the former Chrysler mansion. Its glass-paned doors with black wrought iron grills looked just as they did thirty years earlier. To the right was the magnificent Mariner's Chapel crowned with a gold cupola and a weathervane in the shape of a sailing ship.

The barracks were still there, unchanged and somber-looking, three-story brown stone buildings. Stately deciduous trees covered the campus and lined the walks and paths where we had spent so many hours marching and drilling. Throughout the campus were displayed artifacts of American's maritime tradition, anchors and ships' guns painted white. Inside the buildings large paintings evoked the call of the sea. It was all the same — yet, not the same. The atmosphere seemed different. Was it because it was seen without the onus of grades, exams, demerits, marching and regulations hanging over our heads? The students and administrative staff seemed much nicer than I remembered, but then, visiting from the *O'Brien* gave us something of a celebrity status.

The memorial service was held outdoors behind the administration building at the War Memorial, a bell crowned with a soaring eagle surmounting a large concrete pedestal which honored the 142 Academy cadets killed during World War II while serving in the merchant marine.* The entire regiment of cadets attended, dressed in white uniforms and lined up in formation on the grassy slopes on either side of the memorial. The officers and crew from the *O'Brien* also were there, the captain, admiral and chief mate in their white uniforms. It was a beautiful sunny afternoon with blue skies and still air. The superintendent gave a welcoming speech, followed by Capt. Jahn and ending with Adm. Patterson who delivered a touching eulogy to deceased midshipmen and merchant mariners. Afterward we went to the memorial chapel. Here the pale blue walls with white trim and tall windows overlooking Long Island Sound gave a sense of serenity as we laid a wreath at the altar to honor the merchant marine dead buried at Normandy. The wreath was placed beneath the large book listing

---

*Of the five federal academies, Kings Point is the only one whose students saw action during World War II.

the names of the cadets killed in World War II. It was especially fitting that the Liberty ship *Jeremiah O'Brien*, born of that war, should be there with its crew to honor those who died in the same war to preserve liberty.

The captain and the chief mate were taken on a tour of the Academy's vessel simulator facility. Here we found a ship's bridge inside the building. Today, ships' pilots and masters are trained using computers, three-dimensional projections and state-of-the-art electronics. The effect is to take one through a maneuver-

Capt. Jahn speaking at the memorial service at Kings Point. Photo by Coleman Schneider.

ing sequence on a large, ocean-going ship, complete with unforeseen problems of weather, tides and traffic. Of course, the advantage is that if the trainee makes a mistake, he or she doesn't damage or sink a multimillion dollar ship and its cargo. "Virtual reality" is a term loosely thrown around today, but this was not a game, rather a very serious and effective training program. Being on the bridge of the simulator was just like being on the bridge of a real ship.

"Reminds me of that school I went to in Grenoble," said Capt. Jahn. "But there they use small-scale ships to teach you maneuvering."

Our next stop was the Academy's Merchant Marine Museum. Unique among such facilities, the focus of the museum is on the maritime history of this century, rather than the ancient past. Curator and prolific author, Frank O. Braynard, guided us through the magnificent displays and showed us the fine ship models — freighters, passenger ships, tankers, modern ships, sailing ships — explaining that until the British took it back a few years ago, the museum was the repository of the famed Blue Riband of the Atlantic, known as the Hale Trophy, given for the fastest ship passage from New York to England. For many years the White Star Line had almost perpetual possession of the trophy. It was won repeatedly by Cunard liners such as the *Lusitania, Mauretania, Queen Mary*, and the speed record was held by Cunard ships *Acadia, Scotia* and others even before there was a trophy. When the *SS United States* won the title the trophy was brought to America and eventually found its way to the museum. Capt. Jahn especially enjoyed the models of some of the pre-war freighters, pointing out several types that he shipped on as a youth. "I sailed on ships like that as AB and quartermaster."

Adm. Matteson's quarters were being refurbished so we joined him and Mrs. Matteson in temporary housing located behind the school's main dining hall. Also present were Adm. Patterson, Chief Engineer Dick Brannon, and Adm. F. H. "Hoss" Miller, superintendent of the New York State Maritime Academy and Mrs. Miller. One of Adm. Matteson's hobbies is cooking and he created the evening's fare. Beginning with cold vichyssoise, we progressed to stuffed chicken, green beans, rice and a light raspberry dessert. The food was delicious, the company engaging. Time passed all too quickly as we talked about our voyage and the future of the maritime industry. Then it was time to adjourn to the officers' club.

Set on a small rise just above the water, the Kings Point Officers' Club has a large half-round dining room with plate glass windows overlooking Long Island Sound. Most of the crew were already there when we arrived, enjoying cocktails and canapes. Capt. Jahn gave a short speech, followed by Adm. Patterson and Adm. Matteson. We presented the Academy with a plaque commemorating the *O'Brien's* visit. The hour grew late and eventually we walked down to the pier and caught the launch back to the ship.

Capt. Jahn wanted to get away early on August 17 so everyone was up at the crack of dawn. Before 0630 we had taken aboard about forty Kings Point cadets and instructors as passengers, two pilots, Capt. Bill Clifford and Capt. Lou Dettinelli (both

Kings Point alumni), weighed anchor, given three blasts of the whistle in farewell and were on our way toward Manhattan. In less than an hour we blew the whistle again, saluting Fort Schuyler, the New York State Maritime Academy situated across the Sound from Kings Point. A short time later we received a fax from Adm. Miller:

> It was great to see you last night and to meet the *O'Brien*'s crew. Super evening!
>
> Thanks for the whistle salute as you passed our Nation's "oldest" Maritime Academy this morning.
>
> I don't know if you noticed I was standing (only one) on the sea wall waving as you went by this morning. She was shipshape and Bristol fashion.
>
> Again, great to see you - my best to the crew. They have done a wonderful job <u>and</u> service to our industry.
>
> Smooth sailing,
[signed] Hoss

Tom Patterson: "We were under way by zero six hundred with a number of the regiment aboard and faculty, and went by the New York State Maritime Academy and there on the seawall was Hoss Miller, my dear old friend, waving wildly at us. We gave him three long blasts, a salute to him and a salute to the *Empire State*, his ship that was sitting there."

Then it was through the very heart of New York City, down the East River, under the Brooklyn Bridge, and the other bridges connecting Manhattan to the mainland, surrounded on both sides by skyscrapers, streets, buildings, traffic and millions of people. It was such a unique experience that no one went to breakfast. We were too fascinated with seeing the United Nations building, the World Trade Center, the Empire State Building, the Chrysler Building and the hundreds of other sights and sounds. It was hard to remember we were on a ship; the sensation of traveling through a great city on the *O'Brien* was other-worldly. In many cases we looked directly up the streets, seeing the traffic flow through tall canyons of brick, stone and steel. Ferries and tugboats passed us, blowing their whistles. We answered, our horn echoing off the corridors of Manhattan. We saluted the mayor's residence, Gracie

Mansion, with three blasts, then the South Street Seaport complex with its magnificent sailing ship, *Wavertree.* Clearing the south end of Manhattan at 0740 we began seeing the Staten Island Ferries. Each one

The Jeremiah O'Brien *passing through New York City. Photo by Bill Bennett.*

that passed blew its whistle, saluting the old veteran of World War II. Just off the Battery, close by the Statue of Liberty, we stopped to unload our passengers. They climbed over the side, down our pilot ladder and on to the boat which had followed us from Kings Point.

"The first time I came to New York," said Capt. Jahn, as we watched the cadets leave, "I'd go to an ice cream parlor and get a milkshake. Then I'd sit at a table and drink it real slow, 'cause I was listening to the girls talking all around me with those New York accents. It was like music. I really enjoyed that."

Then we were on our way again, passing under the long arching expanse of the Verrazano Narrows Bridge at 0930. One of our pilots, Capt. Dettinelli, went down to the engine room and spent a half-hour there examining our engine, watching it, and Dick Brannon, operate. At 1030 the pilots debarked, Capt. Jahn ordered the ship to head south and we shaped our course for Cape May and Delaware Bay in a calm sea, under an overcast sky.

By early the next morning we had traveled well up into Delaware Bay, which separates New Jersey and Delaware, and were on our way through the C&D (Chesapeake & Delaware) Canal with Capt. Mead as our pilot. Similar to the Cape Cod Canal in the sense that there are no locks, the C&D Canal joins Chesapeake Bay to Delaware Bay and cuts several hundred miles off a voyage from the northeastern states to the upper Chesapeake and Baltimore, our destination.

The banks of the Canal were relatively low. Elegant homes with well-manicured lawns and water-view restaurants bordered the ship channel. Farther along, much of the country appeared swampy, covered with thick, low vegetation. Occasionally we passed small boat harbors.

The day was warm, the water calm; the cruise was leisurely, the atmosphere collegial. Someone dredged up an old chestnut for the benefit of the pilot. It seems the storyteller was on a ship entering a harbor. The mate on the bow

We paused in sight of the Statue of Liberty to discharge our passengers.

called the ship's bridge on his walkie-talkie to tell the pilot the anchors were ready. A taxi-driver ashore heard the conversation over the radio in his cab, mischievously picked up his microphone and said, "Let go both anchors." The mate complied and, depending on who is telling the story, ran both anchors all the way out pulling the windlass and part of the forecastle off the ship because the ship was still going at full speed, or dragged them across an underwater power cable, or sank the tug that was alongside.

"Yeah, I haven't heard that one for a couple of weeks," said Capt. Mead. "That ship must have had a crew of two thousand because that's how many times I've heard that story.

"But here's one that actually happened to one of our pilots. He was on a Greek ship, an old Liberty like this one. And they were coming up Chesapeake Bay one dark night and he knows it's going to be a long run. So he says to the captain, 'Is there any way to get more speed?' The Greek captain says, 'no.' So our pilot reaches in his carry bag, takes out a newspaper and hands it to the captain, 'Here, might as well read this. We got lots of time.' So the captain is very grateful, "Tank you very much. Tank you.' And he goes over to the speaking tube to the engine room, blows on it, listens a moment, and says, 'Hey, chief, you give five more revolutions, O.K.?' Our pilot hears this and thinks maybe he's on to something. So he reaches into his bag and pulls out a *Newsweek*. 'Maybe you'd like to read this, captain.' The captain goes through the same routine, 'Tank you,' blows in the tube, listens, says, 'five more revolutions.' So my fellow pilot thinks, hey we're making some good speed now. Then he goes to his bag one more time and comes up with a Playboy magazine. Gives it to the Greek captain, who is just overwhelmingly grateful, calls down, 'More, speed. Twenty revolutions.' And the captain goes off to his room to read the magazine. Now the pilot thinks, boy, we're really moving now. This won't be such a long run after all. Then it starts to get light and he looks around at his landmarks and he's nowhere near as far up the bay as he should have been with all this extra speed they're pouring on. Then he looks around the wheelhouse and he sees the speaking tube to the engine room and follows it down with his eyes and sees it was cut off about a foot from the deck. It hadn't operated in years."

Passing under the Francis Scott Key Bridge, named after the author of "The Star Spangled Banner" and marking the entrance to Baltimore Harbor, just before noon, we took on a harbor pilot, Capt. Belcher. The sky was threatening, filled with low, fast-moving clouds pushed by a strong wind. After the day's carefree cruise, the heavy weather seemed to impart a different sense of purpose to the day — the sensation of fulfilling destiny.

The Moran Towing Company provided two free tugs, the *Patricia Moran* and the *Hawkins Point*, which were made fast at each end and we approached downtown Baltimore. As we passed Fort McHenry a large American flag went up. Dottie Duncan: "A highlight of the trip was seeing them raise that giant flag over Fort McHenry. We saw that and some of us started singing 'The Star

Spangled Banner.' That was an emotional moment knowing that was here that Francis Scott Key wrote that song."

Nearing our berth at pier 5 in the inner harbor, we saw before us the sprawl of a modern city with tall, glass-fronted business buildings set around a large harbor. We tied up next to a disused Chesapeake Bay lighthouse, a low, round, red steel tower on a metal frame, which had been removed from the bay and reassembled as an attraction in the downtown area. Nearby was the Baltimore Maritime Museum with the lightship *Chesapeake,* the Coast Guard Cutter *Taney,* and a Tench class submarine serving as focal points. Farther along was Harborplace, a shopping and dining complex consisting of a long low series of buildings offering two floors of shops and restaurants facing the harbor. On a pier facing this complex was the *USS Constellation*, the sailing ship dating from the American Navy of the 1790s.

As soon as the gangway was down we were open for business. Once again, the local authorities wouldn't let us charge admission so we placed the donation barrel right at the top of the gangway. A pleasant surprise was the information that the Masters, Mates and Pilots Union was supplying night mates to the ship.* They would tend the *O'Brien* from 1700 to 0800, allowing the ship's mates to work days only or have time off. This was gratefully received after so many months of constantly being on call and/or on duty.

First on the agenda of many of the crew was dinner ashore. Bill Fairfield, John Borowiec, Marty Wefald and Bob Black lost no time in sampling many of the nearby eateries. Adjacent to the harbor were a number of fine restaurants featuring the famous Maryland crab in every possible style — crab cakes, sautes, hard-shelled crab, soft-shelled crab, crab salads, crab meat in white sauce, chicken with crab sauce. But that wasn't all. We were also within walking distance of Little Italy, an area that dates back

---

*To allow officers time at home in the United States, night-mates and night-engineers are dispatched from local union halls to tend the ship from 1600 to 0800 weekdays and also during the day on weekends and holidays. Of course, we were a non-union, volunteer organization, but the local Masters, Mates and Pilots extended us the courtesy.

several decades in its architecture with many old houses converted into restaurants. Here Al Martino, Lou Casaletto, Brian Goldman, his mom Maxine Kaplan, and others could enjoy fine Italian cuisine — pasta, veal and chicken. Other sights, all within walking distance, included the top floor of the World Trade Center which offered a stunning panoramic view for miles in all directions, Fort McHenry which gave the crew free admission, the National Aquarium, the Maryland Science Center and the Walters Art Gallery. Our location was ideal and we enjoyed frequent walks to these nearby restaurants and attractions.

On August 19, we were closed until after noon for a ceremony held on the pier adjacent to the ship. A platform, podium and public address system were set up near the *O'Brien*'s gangway. Just before eleven the off-duty crew assembled on the pier dressed in blue polo shirts, jackets and baseball caps. The officers wore white uniforms. Also attending were students from the SIU (Seafarer's International Union) school for unlicensed ratings at Piney Point, Maryland. The occasion was the arrival of Representative Helen Bentley of Maryland who was responsible for the "Liberty Ship" bill in 1993 which authorized the sale of the two scrap ships and made our voyage possible. Speeches were given and awards were presented to the ship commemorating the voyage and our arrival in Baltimore. Finally Congresswoman Bentley was introduced. She is a commanding presence and a dynamic speaker. She talked about the importance of American-flag shipping to the country and the significance of the *Jeremiah O'Brien* in symbolizing the industry and American spirit and know-how.

Tom Patterson: "Our reason for calling in Baltimore was to salute Congresswoman Helen Bentley and to thank her for all the assistance she has given with the historic ships and particularly *Jeremiah O'Brien*, getting the Bentley Bill passed which gave us the funds for our repairs. Then Joan Yim, the Deputy Maritime Administrator, spoke and told us how proud the Maritime Administration was of *Jeremiah*, what a good job the ship was doing for the U.S. Merchant Marine and presented us with a plaque. We presented her with a plaque.

"One of the highlights of that welcoming ceremony was the fact that there were fifty trainees from the SIU school, Piney Point Maryland, all in their crisp khakis, Harry Lundberg white Stetsons and lined up like one long row of corn. They were really sharp. And facing them eyeball to eyeball was our crew of fifty-some *Jeremiah O'Brien* crew members with their blue *Jeremiah O'Brien* shirts and hats on. What we had there in one space in one time was two different generations, the new generation being trained to come in and the old generation that shows it can still do the job. And they were all there under the U.S. flag. I just thought that was a great thing to be able to see that and to acknowledge the fact that our merchant marine is not dying, we've got new blood coming in, new ships are going to be built. *Jeremiah O'Brien* is doing its job, highlighting the attention of the country and the world on the fact that this ship not only did its job fifty years ago but it's still doing its job for America today. We just changed our cargo from bombs to a cargo of good will and ambassadorship and our crew are the ambassadors that do this."

It was an inspiring thought, but the sobering reality came in a comment from our ship's agent, a representative of the Norton Lilly, Company. In the previous twelve months they husbanded two hundred twenty-eight ships. Of them all, the *O'Brien* was the only one registered in the United States.

At 1300 we opened the ship to visitors. Unfortunately, there was little or no publicity and no one seemed to know we were there. Our only visitors were those who came to see Harborplace and happened to notice the ship was open. Even so, we had more than 1,000 visitors come aboard by 1700 when we shut down for the day.

Our night mate that evening was Capt. Tim Brown, the president of the International Organization of Masters, Mates and Pilots. It was an honor to have as night mate the president of the largest deck officers' union in the country. He enjoyed the visit and bought several souvenirs in the ship's store. The night mates in Baltimore had all asked for an official discharge from the ship, even though it was for only one day and Capt. Brown was not immune to the sentiment. Everyone seemed to cherish the idea of getting a ship's discharge with *Jeremiah O'Brien* stamped on it.*

"It's not the heat, it's the humidity," is a common expression on the East Coast, especially in the middle Atlantic States. We found out exactly what they meant the next day when the temperature soared into the nineties and the humidity was as thick as a San Francisco fog. Every movement, gesture and action produced perspiration. The "effort" of sitting on deck in the shade caused one to break out in a sweat. Even so, we had 2,500 visitors. Among them were the late Capt. Robert Bryan's sons. Until his death in 1992, Bob Bryan was the Western Region Director for the Maritime Administration and a favorite in the West Coast maritime fraternity. Prior to that, he was Director of Ship Operations for the Maritime Administration in Washington, D.C. His sons are both career civil servants and welcomed the chance to visit the ship their father had talked so much about.

Another visitor was Tom Patterson's brother and his children. Tom's niece became an immediate favorite when, after making several purchases at the ship's store, she said, "If you see my father, tell him I'll be waiting up in Uncle Tom's Cabin."

Sunday was a muggy, lethargic day. One of our visitors was Capt. Oscar Southerland's daughter and grandson. Capt. Southerland was the first master of the *Jeremiah O'Brien* and served on the ship's first three voyages. According to his wishes, his ashes were thrown into the sea during one of the *O'Brien*'s memorial cruises in San Francisco Bay in 1987. His daughter displayed several black and white photos of him in his captain's uniform, off to do his country's bidding during World War II.

Now, the crew was becoming slightly disgruntled with Baltimore. Despite our efforts, we could get no publicity, no advertisements, no indication in the press, radio or TV of our presence. On the other hand, there were complaints because of all

---

*At the termination of a voyage a seaman receives a "discharge" listing the name of the ship, date and port signed on, date and port signed off, and the capacity he or she sailed in. Legally this shows that the contract with the employer is complete, but sentimentally the discharges form a diary of a person's seagoing career.

the people visiting the ship (more than 2,700 that day) and not being allowed to charge admission. Then the crew began worrying about other things such as the upcoming Fleet Week Cruise in October. Would anyone care about the ship once the voyage was over? Would the volunteers that didn't make the trip return to continue the preservation efforts? Who would be allowed aboard the day of arrival and what was the state of the ship's finances? There were no answers. The crew was tired and hot. It was simply normal shipboard griping.

The general unease exploded on an innocent victim. Our ship's photographer, Mike Emery, left while we were in France, but his photo exhibit was still on board, stowed in boxes. While the ship was returning across the Atlantic, Mike arranged for his exhibit* to be displayed at the Transamerica pyramid, a downtown San Francisco landmark. A freight company came down to see where the photos were and arrange for their removal. The crates they were in were too large to take out of the companionway and no. 2 hatch itself would have to be opened to get them out. I agreed to have the ship's crew remove them and set them in a truck if the freight company would provide one. Unfortunately, Capt. Jahn received a fax from Mike instructing Marty Shields, Sam Wood and others to put the photos in boxes and remove them ashore to the freight company. Mike, unfamiliar with the ways of the sea, had made the mistake of wording his fax as if he, Mike, were ordering the crew to do the work for him. The captain was furious, "Who in the hell does he think he is? He don't tell the crew what to do. I do. I'm the captain of this ship." All the rage and pain that had burned for so long over things not related to Mike at all came boiling to the surface. Livid hardly describes it. Capt. Jahn stormed around all day, white-faced and explosive. He gave a direct order that the crew was not to help Mike in any way whatsoever to remove his photographs.

Tuesday, August 23. Departure scheduled for 0830. Mike Emery showed up on board at 0700 looking tired and confused. With his screwdriver, he took the crates apart and, without any

---

*Many of the photos were put into a book, *From Dry Dock to D-Day*, available from Lens Boy Press, P.O. Box 460098, San Francisco, CA, 94146-0098.

help from the crew, removed the photographs and carried the boxes to his waiting station wagon. It was a painful and uncomfortable moment for all.

Mike Emery: "Baltimore was certainly a low point for me. I still have the airline tickets and taxi receipts. But there are no hard feelings. I felt that whatever Jahn ladled on me was nothing compared to what he must have received early in his career."

Sometime during the night the engineers got steam up, preparatory to our sailing. In the early morning we could hear it loudly hissing and hammering as it coursed through cold lines. Somewhere in the ship, water gurgled through pipes like over stones in a brook. Just after breakfast our pilot, Capt. Cudworth, came aboard. We let go our lines, the pilot did a masterful job of turning us around in the inner basin, and we sailed under the Francis Scott Key Bridge and into Chesapeake Bay on a fine, clear day with a light northeast wind and small tufts of white clouds dotting the blue sky.

17

A TEMPERAMENTAL JOURNEY

Once out of Baltimore, we exchanged pilots again. Capt. Cudworth got off and two Chesapeake Bay pilots, Capt. A. Bailey and Capt. G. Quick, came on board. They conned the ship on a lovely all-day trip down Chesapeake Bay. The *Jeremiah O'Brien* rode steadily, with the wind astern. Small low, white clouds drifted lazily across a blue sky. The shore, a mile or two away on our starboard side was made up of vague, low-lying blobs of green land. To port the land was lost in the shimmering line of humidity where sky meets sea.

Just before 2200 we passed over the Chesapeake Bay Bridge-Tunnel, then it was a careful run to the sea buoy keeping sharp watch on a massive coal carrier with a 38' draft steaming close on our port beam at the same speed. At the buoy our companion pointed her bow eastward and we turned south along the coast.

Wednesday, August 24 broke clear and fine with a northeasterly sea and an easterly swell under clear skies. The weather

"Flying bridge weather," off the coast of the southeast United States. Bob Black at the wheel. Photo by Mike Brett.

was noteworthy because we were near Cape Hatteras, notorious for its foul weather and known as "the graveyard of the Atlantic," its shoals a repository to hundreds of shipwrecks. But the gods were smiling on us and the weather continued fine. We passed between the Cape and Diamond Shoals Light, then turned in a southeasterly direction along the coast. Continuing on that course we passed Cape Lookout, then Cape Fear. It was flying bridge weather and we clearly saw that each major cape was marked with a lighthouse, set on a "Texas tower," a tall, spindly steel platform on metal stilts imbedded in the bottom of the ocean. It's a peculiarity of the United States East Coast that the Atlantic seabed is quite shallow, less than a hundred feet, for many miles out to sea. This allows most navigational aids to be solidly driven into the ocean bottom. On the Pacific Coast, by contrast, the ocean is several hundred feet deep within a mile or two of shore.

During the day we received a call on the bridge-to-bridge radiophone from the *Daisy Mae*. She was a dive boat anchored some distance away from us, but on seeing our silhouette recognized a Liberty ship and called to wish us well. Her divers were doing underwater archeological work on the wreck of the *Monitor*, the ironclad that was in one of the celebrated sea battles of the Civil War.

Now, we began preparing the *O'Brien* for our arrival in San Francisco. This meant painting the ship completely from top to bottom, from bow to stern. For the third time this voyage the deck crew went to work with brushes and rollers. Today it was the stack and ventilators on the flying bridge.

Bob Crocker: "She looked as good, if not better, than in wartime. We didn't have time to paint her during the war. She had a lot more rust on her then."

The effects of the long voyage were becoming more apparent. Tempers were short and everyone was irritable. Word came from the home office in San Francisco that a gala celebration was being planned for the *Jeremiah O'Brien*'s return including cannon salutes, a shower of flowers from the Golden Gate Bridge as the *O'Brien* passed underneath, a flyover by vintage planes, brass bands and a ticker tape parade. The day would be capped by a pierside party that would double as a fund-raiser.

The crew was pleased and excited at the news until a fax arrived that set stringent conditions for crew and family tickets, restrictions on who would be allowed to attend and strict regulations on everything from the number of family allowed (2), the price for guests in excess of two, unloading personal gear and every aspect of the return. Most of the crew were furious. They objected to being limited to two passes for families and friends, objected to the restrictions, to the regulations and just about every other point in the fax. A meeting was called in no. 2 'tween deck resulting in a demand that the organization hold another party especially for the crew after the ship arrived. Crew Chairman Nils Anderson would draft a message to the office telling them what the crew demands were. Suddenly it was "Us against them," and "Who do they think they are to treat us like that." "They think we're a bunch of school kids." "They can take their damn party and shove it!"

The shipboard routine continued. The deck department tended to getting the ship painted, the engine department tended to the engine and the generator on no. 4 hatch, the cooks cooked, the radio shack handled messages and the messmen served. One of the "*O'Brien* Twinplex" features that evening was "Casablanca," for the second time that trip. Discussing the movie at dinner Capt. Jahn said, "I'm not going. I won't watch it. I had a crush on Ingrid Bergman, then she up and ran off with that Italian guy. Shacked up with him. I never liked her after that."

The next day we were off the coast of South Carolina. We found we were going to be early (again) arriving in Jacksonville and began slowing the ship down to make the proper arrival time. The weather was fair with a few clouds and the wind from the northeast or astern. This meant that the wind created by the ship moving ahead was negated by the natural wind astern, causing complete stillness on board. The only fresh air the engine room got was from the movement of the ship through the water. At best, it was barely bearable. With no wind blowing in, it was intolerably hot. Kevin Kilduff, the second assistant engineer, complained to the captain about slowing the ship down, "What about all these 70-year-old men in the 120 degree heat?"

But Capt. Jahn was against early arrivals. It was a principle. "He don't run this ship, I do," he said, after telling Kevin we weren't increasing speed.

It was the captain's seventy-ninth birthday and a party was held on the after deck at 1600. Some of the crew had been working for days on a special present for him. When everyone had their beer and drinks, they presented the captain with a metal box. Painted white, it had "*J. O'Brien* Suggestion Box," in black letters on the front. It was locked with a padlock for which there was no key. Turning it over, the captain examined the top, bottom and sides, finally realizing there were no openings or slots in it anywhere. He laughed, a questioning look in his eyes. It wasn't clear if he really understood the significance. Just before dinner Chief Engineer Dick Brannon located a thin piece of black cellophane which he stuck on the lid of the box. At least it then <u>looked</u> like there was an opening.

Bob Crocker: "It was just a good trip down. And to be out on the 3" gun at night, at midnight. We used to be out there on the original trip, two on the bow, two on the stern and two on the bridge. Then the petty officer on watch always relieved for coffee. In the evening, sitting down on deck, nothing had changed, the whales, the dolphins, and the smell of the ocean and the look of saltwater took you right back, just like it was fifty-one years ago."

On Friday, August 26 we took arrival at 0700 with the St. John's Light bearing 240 degrees, ten miles off. Just after 0800 we took on two pilots, Capt. Parker and Capt. Trens, and a docking master, Capt. R. Thumps. Their services, as well as those of the tugs, were donated and Capt. Parker even gave Capt. Jahn a check for $100 as a donation to the ship.

Entering the St. John's river we passed the Mayport Naval Base on our left. Capt. Parker's home fronts the river and we saluted with three whistle blasts as we passed it. His wife came out on the porch and waved. There were several other expensive-looking houses in the lower reaches of the river, then the terrain became swampy with mangroves and low vegetation. Approaching the city, we came into busy industrial areas, freighters loading containers, and large warehouses. Nearing the downtown area we received two tugs from Moran Towing Company, the *D. Moran* and *Cathleen Moran*, and by noon were tied up at the Main Street pier just across the street from the city hall. A Dixieland band was on the pier and struck up on our approach. Our berth was such that we were resting against dolphins that held us off the face of the wharf itself. This necessitated using a sixty-five foot aluminum gangway, provided by the city authorities.

Nearby was a large shopping complex with two air-conditioned floors of souvenir shops, fast food emporiums and clothing stores surrounding an open amphitheater that offered live entertainment. Crossing a nearby bridge, we found a riverwalk, a wooden boardwalk that led one along the riverbank with views of downtown Jacksonville across the water — glass-fronted office buildings and air-conditioned high rises. This was manatee country and the riverwalk had several signs, aimed at nearby boat traffic, cautioning them to avoid getting close to the fragile creatures. Looking at the pictures of manatees on the signs, one couldn't help wonder how ancient mariners could possibly think they were mermaids. Also on the other side were restaurants featuring such fare as alligator tail, marlin terriyaki and gumbo. We were definitely in the south.

There were two major reasons for coming to Jacksonville. The first, as usual, was money; the second was fuel. Going there eliminated the earlier plan to stop in at Miami for bunkers. The fuel barge came alongside the ship just after 0100. The engineer on watch, thinking he could handle the fueling without calling out the chief engineer, connected the hoses and started the process. Adm. Patterson's son, Richard, had joined us in Baltimore. He was sleeping on a cot under the forward port gun tub and heard fuel overflowing through the vent pipes onto the deck. He quickly ran back to tell the engineers. Fortunately, all the scuppers had been plugged with rags and wooden plugs, a standard procedure when fueling, and none got over the side but we awoke to find the foredeck a complete tarpit with black sticky crude oil on the starboard side of number three hatch and the port side of hatches two and three. The engine department spent the next week cleaning up the mess, first with sawdust and wood shavings, then grease remover and finally soap and water. In the end we had to paint over it.

Brian Goldman: "One thing I learned is how to spread sawdust in an effective way to soak up oil. That was amazing."

One additional reason for going to Jacksonville was because Ernie Murdock was once Coast Guard Captain of the Port for that harbor and he wanted to show the ship off to his old colleagues. It was also an opportunity to bring the ship into the Southeast to allow members of merchant marine veterans organizations to view the ship and at the same time generate badly-needed funds. Jacksonville authorities allowed the ship to charge admission ($5) and the Mayport Navy Base Officers' Club sponsored a dinner for the *O'Brien.* But the big money event was that the ship was to be the "Party Boat" for the Offshore Grand Prix Powerboat Races. Charging $100 per person, less $11 a head for a box lunch provided by the Navy, would generate $44,500 for the ship.

Tom Patterson: "We had open house on the ship, and the gate brought in a lot of people. Everything was free to us. That night they took us down to Mayport, the US Naval Station, and they had a wonderful dinner down there. The proceeds from that were donated to the ship. The American Merchant Marine Veterans had made a presentation to us that night of a check for

OIL POLLUTION REACTION PLAN

POSITION	REACTION
Master	Telephone Coast Guard, personal attorney, Time Magazine, pack bags
Chief Mate	Immediately begin reviewing 3rd Mate duties
Second Mate	Cover all liabilities and begin reviewing Chief Mate duties
Third Mate	Feign no knowledge of any events; i.e. carry on a usual
Radio Officer	Upon seeing the news coverage on the TV at the Twin Wheels, say "Hey guys, that's my ship" and buy a round of drinks
Chief Engineer	Respond "Thanks for the beer, Sparks."
1st Assistant	Upon learning of the incident from the Steward Utility the following day, remark "Holy shit, why wasn't I informed?"
2nd/3rd Assistants	Carry on lengthy discussion concerning incompetence of the Deck Department

r:reaction/ab&s93/jlr

This Oil Pollution Reaction Plan was posted in the messrooms after our "spill" at Jacksonville. Clearly, it was written by an engineer.

$4,200 to the ship from all the merchant marine veterans around the country. So our stay in Florida was quite pleasant."

In the afternoon a truckload of supplies for the steward's department came alongside. At first the cooks and messmen began carrying them up the 65' gangway to the ship — fresh fruit, bottled water, milk, canned goods. Then as more crew saw the

At Mayport Naval Base. Bill Rowlands at the helm. In the background aircraft carrier No. 60, USS Saratoga. *Photo by Mike Brett.*

truck was still full, they joined in, then others, including the mates, until there were enough people to form a human chain handing supplies from one to another up the gangway. The truck was unloaded in a short time, an example of volunteerism and the old *O'Brien* spirit.

At 1600 we shifted down river to the Mayport Navy Base to load our passengers and get in position well before the races started the following day.

Sunday, August 28 was hot, muggy and partly cloudy. Just after breakfast, to prepare for the onslaught of passengers that would be viewing the boat races from the *O'Brien,* we set out a table at the foot of the gangway. Stationing two crew members there, with a cash box, change, and tickets for the expected hordes, we steeled ourselves for the deluge. When we pulled up the gangway two hours later a total of sixty-eight passengers were on board. Our $44,500 was suddenly $5,963.

The Navy provided two free tugs, the *C Tractor 5* and the *YTB 832* to take us out of the harbor. Their pilot, Capt. Reynolds, guided us along the beach to a point just offshore of the intended race and adjacent to the center of the "track."

Capt. Jahn, left and Adm. Patterson eyeing the channel as we sail toward the Offshore Grand Prix. Photo by Mike Brett.

We anchored with a few feet of water under the keel, surrounded by a flotilla of small boats, all eager to see the race. Capt. Reynolds said he talked to the owners of the Italian entry in the Grand Prix. They explained that their boat cost $2.5 million to build. The purse for the race was $75,000 and they spent $40,000 just to get the boat to Florida. If only the *O'Brien* could share in some of that money. "Rich man's sport," was a frequent comment heard during the day, in tones of disgust — and envy.

As children of the television era, we are spoiled, with sporting events explained in detail, and close-ups of the start and finish and every occurrence in between. From our perspective on the *Jeremiah O'Brien*, however, the Offshore Grand Prix Powerboat Races were simply a bunch of noisy boats running back and forth in the near distance in front of us. We couldn't tell when a race started or ended. Occasionally a boat would pull ahead of the others, and, often as not, lap them, so you couldn't tell who was winning or who was losing. The most interesting part of the race was the occasional helicopter that followed a boat about ten feet off the water, directly astern, pacing its speed. There was nothing else to see. Behind the boats lay the flat coast of Florida, the only landmarks being a building or two that rose higher than the coastal mangroves.

Tom Patterson's terse comment: "We went down to Mayport after our visit in Jacksonville and picked up sixty-eight passengers, went out to anchorage and they saw these ocean motorboat races. We brought them back in about 4:30 in the afternoon, debarked them, immediately turned the ship around and headed out and for the Canal."

Capt. Jahn was anxious to be underway. Adm. Patterson was anxious to get the ship painted. The chief engineer was complaining that one of his engineers was arguing with everything and didn't do what he was told. It was definitely time to leave. The commanding officer of the naval base came aboard from the tug to say good-bye. He cautioned that there could be a problem with our being painted grey and looking like a Navy ship. Cuban and Haitian refugees were taking to the Straits of Florida in record numbers hoping to be picked up by American Naval and Coast

Guard vessels. Forewarned, we debarked the commanding officer and Capt. Reynolds, took departure at 1730 and continued southward, keeping a sharp lookout. Next stop: Panama.

Dottie Duncan: "Being at sea was real different, not as rough as I thought it would be. The ship needed another messman, at first to Baltimore, then to Jacksonville, then all the way to San Francisco. My dad said, 'This is something that you'll never have an opportunity to do again.' He never gives advice, but he told me to go. It was a great opportunity. Ruth and I were the only two women. We got along well although I didn't know how the men would react."

Dawn revealed a typical tropic sky with tufts of low clouds, warm temperatures and the sea the deepest, bluest blue imaginable.

The heat was really starting to get to everyone. At our 1600 beer break Russ, our chief steward, and second assistant engineer Kevin Kilduff got into a row over beer being handed out. The second seemed determined to provoke Russ. The issue was that Russ quit serving beer at 1645, wanting to make sure it lasted the remainder of the trip. The second seemed determined to set his own agenda which was simply for him to have more beer.

The next day the wind had shifted to the bow, cooling the ship somewhat. We passed through Crooked Island Passage with Eleuretha Island and Cat Island visible to starboard.

Capt. Jahn was in a rare mood. Now he was in a hurry. He checked the speed several times a day, anxious to get home. But it really showed in the devilish glee he took in needling the admiral. Checks issued by the NLSM office required two signatures. Capt. Jahn received blank checks in the mail, signed them, and returned them to San Fran-

> Chief Steward Russ Mosholder made the entire voyage. Born in 1924, he served in the Navy during World War II as a torpedoman and gunner and saw action in five major invasions and two naval battles. In civilian life he worked as a Teamster, driving linen trucks, owned his own restaurant and catering firm, was a salesman for a meat company and, after retiring in 1989, went full time into community service work. He and Ruth Robson now live together in San Diego, California.

cisco. There they were made out to pay expenses and endorsed with a second signature before being mailed. Patterson didn't know this was going on until the captain told him about it after leaving Jacksonville. "I been doing it all trip," said the captain. "And he didn't even know it." Of course, the admiral had a legitimate point in saying there was no control over expenses if the captain didn't know what items he was authorizing with his signature. Capt. Jahn laughed all day about that.

The deck department, in addition to painting, was renewing the white lead and tallow on the mast shrouds. These are the thick cables that run from the edge of the main deck to near the tops of the masts, attaching just at the point where the crosstrees extend from the mast. A compound of white lead and tallow is used to slush them, the tallow acting as a preservative, the white lead providing a nice-looking, clean, long-lasting cover coating. The tallow is heated until it melts, then mixed in a bucket with the white lead. A bosun's chair is rigged with a shackle made fast around the shroud. A sailor climbs in the chair, hooks the bucket of slush to it and is pulled to the top by his shipmates. Using his hands he applies the compound as far as he can reach, then hollers down to have the chair lowered a few feet and applies more slush. This continues until he reaches the bottom. The crew were enthusiastic as this was an "old seafaring chore" not done on modern ships (which don't have masts or shrouds). They lined up to take their turn riding the chair.

Brian Goldman: "Looking at people such as Sam Wood dangling up in the rigging amazed me. He hung around up there, and Bill Rowlands, slushing the cables, and things you just wouldn't expect to see those guys doing. Bill Duncan in the engine room, seventy years old, moved around like he was twenty-five or thirty. Seeing those guys, finding the average age of the crew to be sixty years old, that was really an eye-opener."

Bill Duncan: "Everybody knew what they were doing, everyone was well-qualified to do their assigned job. We had an oiler that came on in Cherbourg that hadn't oiled for thirty or forty years, but within a few days was as proficient as any. David Aris was well-qualified, a chief engineer in the British merchant marine.

Sam Wood rides a bosun's chair as he slushes a shroud on the foremast.

My fireman, Brian Goldman, was very intelligent and very proficient and knew all the basics and what was required and made an excellent fireman. Ed Lingenfield was an old-time oiler and fireman and was able to pick right up again with no problems. We had our engineers, some of whom are sailing today. They were excellent, well-qualified and capable to do what they were doing. And, of course, our deck crew, like our chief electrician, Ed Smith, was one of the most skilled men on the ship. The chief was an old-time engineer and you could trust his judgement completely."

During off hours there was still heated conversation about the ticket situation for the arrival party in San Francisco. Everyone was still upset by the tone of the message sent from the office but the crew was definitely beginning to focus on San Francisco. The captain and the admiral certainly were, with Capt. Jahn anxiously checking our speed every watch and the admiral sending and receiving messages from the home office. Now we heard there was a possibility of a stop at San Diego.

The next day produced a strong, hot easterly wind and partly cloudy skies with small whitecaps dotting a deep, rich blue ocean. As we approached the Windward Passage, the gap between Cuba and Haiti, we suddenly realized that boat people from either country would not be a problem for us. Most of them were in the straits of Florida trying to get to Key West. We were actually several hundred miles away. And, certainly, no refugee with any sense would go from Haiti to Cuba or vice-versa. That would be trading bad for worse in either case.

Capt. Jahn grew more and more anxious. He wanted to arrive at Panama "and go straight on through and get back to San Francisco." He continued checking the ship's speed several times a day and even in the middle of the night.

In the late afternoon the east coast of Cuba became clearly visible. We saw waves breaking on a rocky shoreline, white eruptions of foam against grey-black cliffs topped with green trees. Rounding the east end of Cuba, we changed course to twenty degrees west of south in the late afternoon, bringing the wind abaft the beam and with it, once again, the heat. By the next day the wind was a little more on the beam, but still astern causing the air on the *O'Brien* to be almost still. The engine room and the galley were the least enviable places to be on the ship. A few members of the black gang got a break, though. They continued cleaning up the Jacksonville oil spill on the main deck and got to work on their hands and knees in the relative coolness of the foredeck, cleaning up the black stain with solvents. The deck department was almost finished slushing the shrouds and then it would be back to painting.

Bill Duncan: "The doctor. My first experience with Haslam was when I had a rash between my legs. I was pretty sure it was jock itch. He said, 'let me see,' so I showed him and he said, 'all right, see me tomorrow.' I asked him why and he said because he had to look it up in the book. I thought, gee, this guy is a slow reader. So the next day he says 'yeah, you got jock itch. Just continue doing whatever it is you're doing.' So then, on the way back, the Doc had come down to the engine room a number of times and was interested in what was going on. Some of the guys were showing him how to be a fireman. He became proficient, he was OK. So my fireman went to him one day with a sore throat. Doc quarantined him for three days. So then he came down in the engine room and fired for three days."

Capt. Jahn got an alarming call via radiotelephone from the NLSM office in San Francisco. After confirming that we were going to San Diego after Panama, Chairman of the Board Bob

Blake told the captain that the organization was broke and couldn't afford the additional party the crew asked for after the ship arrived. The "party" was growing out of all proportion to reality.

Crew Chairman Nils Anderson canvassed everyone on board about the arrival party. He sent the following message to our office in San Francisco:

THE CREW HAS BEEN POLLED FROM WIPER TO CAPT & ADMIRAL. WE WILL NOT BE TREATED AS KINDERGARTEN TOTS. WE HAVE GIVEN BLOOD, SWEAT & TEARS FOR UP TO 6 MONTHS FOR THIS SHIP. NOW SOME PEOPLE IN AN OFFICE IN S.F. TELL US THAT OUR FAMILY MEMBERS MAY NOT ALL BE ABLE TO CELEBRATE THIS MOMENTOUS OCCASION WITH US. WE ARE ADAMANT IN OUR POSITION. WE EXPECT TO RECEIVE 200 SPECIAL PASSES FROM PILOT BOAT & WE WILL DISTRIBUTE & FILL IN THE NAMES.

NILS ANDERSON/JIM MILLER, CREW REPS

That brought a radiophone call from Bob Blake to the admiral. The door to the captain's office ("There are no secrets on here, my door is always open.") was closed, but Capt. Jahn told us the Board was upset with Patterson. "Blake gave him 'holy hell' about spending money we don't have. He says they can't afford to throw a party for the crew."

> Nils Anderson was born in 1934 and grew up around the shipyards in Portland, Oregon, watching Liberty ships under construction. A retired firefighter, he became a volunteer in 1993 and worked more than 300 hours on the ship in his first year. Joining the ship in Le Havre, he worked in the engine department and returned with the ship to San Francisco. He lives in Clayton, California.

Warren Hopkins, NLSM board of directors: "I was there when that fax came in, in fact we were having a board meeting at the time. We got Patterson on the radiophone, but he kept fading in and out. What the crew didn't seem to realize was it was a fund-raiser."

To help ease the heat and calm everyone down, the chief steward opened the last of the kegs of Kronenberg Beer acquired during the ride down the Seine. Although it disappeared very quickly it had the desired effect. Tempers were calmed, the heat didn't seem so bad, and we were nearing Panama, a chance for everyone to, once again, experience that wonder of the world.

Nils Anderson: "The verbal repartee that went on over the meal table or as we were going by on the deck was a way of keeping your sanity. You had to play little games with people and they played them back. There was a lot of good-natured kidding between individuals. Some individuals didn't respond to it, so you didn't kid around with them. You were just kind of friendly. Others, why you just dug a little deeper all the time. It was a good experience having to get along with fifty other people. You may not like someone, you may not even want to be around them, but you had to be, and you had to be somewhat civil to them. You'd sit next to them at the meal table or stand a watch with them. We didn't have any problems in those respects. I think it really speaks well of the emotional maturity of the people on board."

Friday, September 2 and the northeast trade winds continued blowing on our port quarter. The east-to-west current was so bad in this part of the Caribbean that at times we had as much as twelve degrees leeway on the ship to keep it on course. The fact that we knew we were being set that much was due entirely to the Global Positioning System (GPS). By taking readings every half hour or hour and plotting them on the chart, we saw the ship being set to the west and compensated. In the days before such systems, when sextants were the state of the art, we wouldn't have known we were off our track line until morning or evening star sights — if weather allowed us to take them.

Adm. Patterson informed us that Jean-Paul Caron and Carl Nolte would be joining us in Panama to make the return voyage to San Francisco. Carl was a favorite with the crew and they looked forward to seeing him again.

On Saturday, September 3 we arrived at Panama just after breakfast. It was overcast and relatively cool as we entered the breakwater at Cristobal. The harbor authorities directed us to anchor to the right of the fairway, which area was designated as the anchorage for ships waiting to transit the Canal. Dropping the anchor we fetched up on the chain and sat and waited. Nearby were several other ships resting at anchor — a modern tanker and two rusty coastal freighters waiting their turn to transit and a large ore carrier waiting for a repair dock. The breakwater was made of large preformed concrete chunks shaped like the jacks that little girls play with. From our distant vantage point they looked like sea lions. To the left of the fairway we saw Cristobal and our berth on the outbound trip. Leading up into the thick mangroves was the channel to the first set of locks at Gatun. The overcast turned to tropical rain, heavy and warm, that continued off and on throughout the day then turned to drizzle. Eventually customs and immigration came aboard and, with them, our agent from Norton Lilly. We were scheduled to move into the Canal at three in the morning.

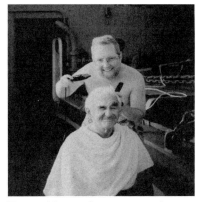

Every ship needs someone who can cut hair. Here Alex Hochstraser wields the clippers over Cliff Hook. Photo courtesy of Alex Hochstraser.

Another letter came from Bob Blake, who was still reacting to the crew's message to him, which was reacting to his message to the ship, which was reacting to . . . :

We have no money to pay for transit costs through the Panama Canal. Our bank account sits at $1,000.00 today, You will have to use the money that you have on hand. The Evening Reception on September 23rd is a fund raiser for the ship and not a party for the crew. As the attached financial statement shows, we already have $570,000.00 in debt. If you want to increase that by $13,000.00 we will comply with your blood sweat & tears. Otherwise, it is one ticket per returning crew member, and one guest per returning crew member.

The reception held Friday night is geared as a fund raiser for debt reduction.

Please note that the parade & time aboard that afternoon are geared for crew's family participation, and entrance to the pier is barred to outsiders.

This whole voyage is a TEAM EFFORT. Many people who were not fortunate enough to make the voyage have given many hours, days, weeks, months & years of their time and effort to make it a success. The returning crew are the only ones receiving complimentary tickets to the evening reception.

There will be no party on Saturday, September 24. We feel the crew will want to be with their families, and we are not in a financial position to have a party at this time. The Volunteer Crew party will be November 11 as planned.

It was like scratching prickly heat, it only made things worse. Fortunately, it was Tom Patterson's seventieth birthday and the party for him on the after deck, with *hors d'oeuvres*, scotch, champagne and beer, was a pleasant diversion. Jimmy Farras brought out a cake shaped like an anchor, covered with blue and white icing. It only had a few candles on it, but Tom blew them out and everyone cheered and wished him well. There was a special dinner, also; tossed green salad, steak, baked potato, cake, ice cream. Despite all the adversity of recent days, we had to admire the admiral's style. After all this time he was still pleasant and gracious and always said the right thing with a smile.

Just before midnight we heard a boat come alongside. Looking down from the main deck we saw a fifty-foot workboat with Carl Nolte and Jean-Paul Caron looking up at us, their bags beside them ready to come aboard. Heaving lines were quickly thrown down, their personal effects pulled aboard and they climbed the pilot ladder and were with us once more. Carl was assigned to the deck department as ordinary seaman on the 8-12 watch. Jean-Paul was put in the engine room as a wiper.

At 0400 on Sunday, September 4, we started our second transit of the Panama Canal. As daylight came the weather slowly changed from an overcast and cloudy twilight to a beautiful morning with balmy tropical air, blue skies and scattered puffs of white clouds. As the sun climbed higher, however, it grew hotter.

Our pilots this time were Panamanian, Capt. Porras and Capt. Sanchez, a reflection of the transition of the Panama Canal from American control to Panamanian control. We seemed to have lost our celebrity status. One was the pilot and the other only a trainee. By 0630 we were through Gatun Locks and into the lake itself. We still received a few salutes from ships going the other way, but not as many as before. As on the previous passage,

the crew spent every off-duty minute on deck, pointing out sights along the way. Approaching the Gaillard Cut we saw a few small thatched houses set on the edge of the jungle. "They belong to the Panama Canal Company," explained the pilot. "If you work for them you can rent one for a dollar a

Through the Panama Canal for the second time this voyage. Thick green jungles and waterfalls. Photo by Bob Black.

month. Most people use them for picnics or once in a while on a weekend."

The heat was relentless. It was 92° on deck at noon, 120° in the engine room, 90° in the mess at midnight, 103° in the radio shack, and in the galley, the coal-burning stove sent the temperature up to rival that of the engine room. Oiler Kenneth Stenburn recalled days that were even worse, though. During the war, ships like the *O'Brien* sailed with their portholes closed so no lights would be seen. Hatches and vents were battened. Ken was a merchant seaman in World War II and sailed on Liberty and Victory ships. "You just did it, that's all."

David Aris: "I think the personnel were at their lowest when there was a hell of a hot and we're running about to Panama and the heat was getting to people."

Jack Carraher: "My God, those men used to come up out of the engine room and they looked like they were death warmed over and not too good a job at that. They were just terrible looking. But they seemed to respond after awhile and I would figure out, well, I think he's alive."

Tom Patterson: "The high temperatures were with us, we anticipated that, but it's never easy, 120 degrees in the engine room and the galley, but we survived."

Dick Brannon: "And, honest to God, Brian Goldman, who is head and shoulders above anybody else, coming through the Canal, we had a hundred, I counted them, we had a hundred bells* coming into Pedro Miguel locks . . . So anyway it was a training program for us. I was only on the throttle about fifty percent of the time, training was the rest of the time. And Brian Goldman came over to me, it was during one of this hundred bell sequences, and he said, 'Hey,' he says, 'you make it look so easy. How come other people are struggling at that throttle and, my God, you make it look so easy. What's the secret?'

"He's fairly young for my analogy so I didn't go into all the sexual implications, I gave him a truncated version of this. 'Brian,' I said, 'There's nothing complicated. It just takes living with it, learning what its capabilities are. It'll respond, it'll do anything. It's the most magnificent engine ever built. No diesel, no turbine, no engine was ever designed in history as well as this engine.'

"And Brian is sharp, he can accept my lectures without a bunch of bullshit, accept it and then apply it. And I'm only passing on to him what the World War I engineers who grew up on these engines taught me. I've absorbed everything they could possibly pass to me and I've passed it on."

Bill Duncan: "The Canal was brutal. I was on the throttle as we entered the Canal coming back, going through the first set of locks. And then we had a delay, anchoring to wait for traffic, so it turned out that I was again on the throttle when we went through the locks on the Pacific side. And we had an awful lot of bells going through there, we had something like forty-five bells in one hour. I said to the chief, 'Damn, that's an awful lot of bells. What the hell's going on?' We found out the older Canal pilots

---

*The engine order telegraph connecting the bridge to the engine room rings a bell in both locations each time the pointer is moved. The commands to change speed are referred to as "bells," a verbal shorthand for "increasing or reducing the speed of the engine."

were training new ones. That was driving us crazy down there. I was completely exhausted by the time we left. That throttle is stiff and hard to manipulate. That was the toughest time I had."

Nearing Pedro Miguel locks we saw crocodiles in the water, swimming lazily away from our approach. At 1500 we exited Miraflores, the last set of locks, went under the Bridge of the Americas like a shot, and, after letting off the pilots, were once again in the Pacific Ocean and homeward bound.

18

STORMY WEATHER

Our first full day out of Panama, Monday, September 5, was Labor Day. The crew honored the day by not performing any labor, other than routine watch-standing and daily duties. The weather was perfect for resting, with fluffy low clouds under a high overcast. A light breeze blew from just forward of the port beam with a low gentle swell coming from the same direction that rocked the *Jeremiah O'Brien* gently, like a cradle, as she steamed along at her usual eleven knots on a west-northwesterly course.

At breakfast Dick Brannon described an infrared temperature detector brought aboard by Dick Currie (who rejoined us in Panama). You could simply point it at a crankshaft bearing and get an instant reading of the temperature. "It's amazing. I've never seen anything like it. Just like star wars."

Adm. Patterson asked, "Does this mean reciprocating engines will be coming back?"

Normally, our coastwise route up Central America and Mexico would consist of a series of straight lines laid down between points two to five miles abeam of major headlands. Because the coast itself is not straight but made up of bays, harbors, lagoons and other indentations, such routing would cause us not to see much land. Also, we would be bucking the Japanese Current, running its way down the Pacific toward the equator. But Capt. Jahn knows these waters. His first trip on this coast was on a tug in 1933 and he has been in every port, down to Chile. He ordered a track drawn on the chart that paralleled the coast two miles off. This kept the ship close to shore and caused us to travel more miles to get where we were going. But it gave us more scenery and the captain thought there was a good chance of picking up a countercurrent close inshore giving us greater speed and more than making up for the straight line approach.

We began to see more and more marine life. A school of tuna passed, large fish, flashing silver and grey as they jumped playfully out of the water and splashed their way along to who-knows-where. Flocks of black and white birds with long, pointed bills dived in the water around the ship. As each one surfaced it swallowed an anchovy or two, then flapped its way into the air, circled and dived again.

At beer break the crew got into casting the movie of the voyage. The rules of the game were that you could select any actor, dead or alive, to play someone on the ship. Each new choice brought a round of laughter: Walter Brennan as Capt. Jahn, E.G. Marshall as Adm. Patterson, Sam Wood played by Charles Bronson, Carl Nolte by Kermit the Frog, Dick Brannon by Jack Lemmon, Alec Guiness would play Jack Carraher and Dom Delouise was cast to play Bob Black.

In the evening we had front seats at a most spectacular sound-and-light show over the shore as we passed the Costa Rican coast. The sky to seaward was perfectly clear with stars showing but on shore large areas of light grey clouds glowed yellow and seemed to vibrate with each thunderclap. From time to time a startling yellow-white flash of multi-forked lightning shot from the base of the thunderheads to the ground. Otherwise, it was a dark night with no moon and the only other lights were those of coastal fishing boats bobbing peacefully on the sea as we passed.

The next day started with thick clouds and drizzly rain but soon cleared to a blue sky and flat calm sea. To starboard we saw the lush green coast of Costa Rica, thick with jungle vegetation and occasional barren brown outcroppings where the coastal hills dropped into the Pacific. Small colorful fishing boats worked offshore, the fishermen waving as we passed. Schools of light-grey dolphin came leaping out of the water toward the ship. They followed for a while, riding the pressure wave at the bow, then disappeared as quickly as they came. Black and white birds with angular wings and long, sharp beaks dove at flying fish, frightening them out of the water in delicate fan-shaped formations as they glided through the air, trying to escape.

Sam Wood was born in 1934. He first went to sea during the Vietnam War, then worked at various jobs in the restaurant and carpentry trade in California. He took a leave of absence from his job as carpenter with the Fort Mason Foundation to make the entire voyage. Beginning as an ordinary seaman, he was promoted to AB. He lives in San Francisco. When interviewed for this book during the voyage he was reading Marcel Proust's *Within a Budding Grove.* "Whenever I go to sea I take Marcel Proust with me. He's great shipboard reading. You can really get into Proust at sea."

The sea water temperature was in the high eighties, making the engine room all but intolerable. The black gang often came up out of their 120° "hell hole" drenched with sweat and looking like they had been through a wringer.

By September 7 we were well along in getting the ship painted. Sam Wood spent the day painting the foremast. Starting at the top he used a roller and manhelper to paint the upper part of the mast and the crosstree. Then he rigged a bosun's chair and rode that down to the masthouse, painting the trunk of the mast. The ship rolled gently and Sam, suspended from the crosstree in his bosun's chair, swung slowly back and forth like a pendulum. He took advantage of this motion by rolling grey paint on one side, then as the ship tilted, pressing his roller against the mast and letting the motion carry him to the other side. It was a clever bit of automation.

We had greased the cargo gear on the way out from San Francisco. The slush was mixed by Bosun Rich Reed. Like many old-time bosuns, his slush was his own formula consisting of various greases, lubricants and "secret" ingredients. Rich's mix was thick and black and rubbed off on everything. Through the trip we had lived with black stains on the flags, clothing and shoes. In port, children accidentally grabbed cargo runners and came up to us with hands covered with black goo. In the heat of the tropics the stuff became thin, leaving a difficult-to-remove black mark at the slightest touch. The crew began referring to it as "Rich Reed's revenge."

Jim Wade remembered, "A youngster and his mother came up to me on the boat deck. The youngster had his hands up in front of him with his fingers stretched out and they were just black. He'd gotten them on one of the cables with all the black graphite and grease lubricant. And it just looked so funny. His mother didn't know what to do, so I took him in right there by the galley and washed his hands off with cleanser. He was French and didn't speak much English but he was afraid to move."

All through the voyage the crew especially enjoyed Phil Frank's Farley cartoons run in the *San Francisco Chronicle.* In the series, Bruce the Raven joined the ship in Panama outbound and made the entire trip with

In the foreground, Sam Wood paints the mainmast, while Marty Shields on the foremast crosstree works on "Operation Raven."

us. Someone suggested we paint Bruce's image on the crow's nest, and what better place for a raven. Catching both the captain and the admiral on the flying bridge, and forgetting the adage "It's easier to ask forgiveness than permission," the chief mate explained the proposal, suggesting it would be a good boost to morale and would fit in with the "nose art" of Miss Jerry O'Brien on the guntub. To his chagrin they both said No. Regrouping, we decided on another tactic. The deck department was still painting the masts, and the crow's nest on the foremast certainly needed it, too. The captain and the admiral seldom went forward but even if they did, it would just be Sam Wood and Marty Shields painting the masts. Besides, someone said, what could they do, fire everybody? Alex Hochstraser was a skilled draftsman and Marty Shields was our professional painter. We had permission from Phil Frank, so Alex could make a stencil and he and Marty could paint the figure when the stencil was drawn in. "Operation Raven" went into effect.

The hot weather continued. The thermometer in the crew's mess showed 95°. In the galley it was over 110°. In the engine room, 110° would have been considered a cold snap. The door to the engine room fidley was so hot you couldn't touch it for longer than a second or two. Hanging laundry in the upper fidley, the first things hung were dry by the time the last were put up.

This is the Voice of the *Jeremiah O'Brien*:
Good evening, San Francisco.
The world over, deck personnel consider themselves to be the elite of seafaring men. Sailors, we call ourselves; we steer the ship,

Bruce gets into the spirit of things. Now if only the rest of us had room service. Courtesy Phil Frank and San Francisco Chronicle.

we handle the mooring lines — lifeboats are in our job description. In a nutshell, we get the ship there and back.

But what happens when the winds don't blow, and the current is in the wrong direction? Enter the black gang, the engineers, the men who toil in inhuman and nearly intolerable conditions deep inside the ship; tending the boilers, oiling the engine, checking, checking, checking the machinery that keeps the ship moving both night and day — whose expertise keeps this engine in top operating condition where breakdown, slowdown, or late arrival is seldom heard.

> Joining the ship in Rouen, Brian Goldman served as the fireman-watertender on the 12-3 watch. Born in 1972, he is a full time student at California Maritime Academy when not working on the *Jeremiah O'Brien*. He was the youngest crewmember during the return trip and lives in Tiburon, California.

In my 45 plus years of mechanical experience, I have never met a more dedicated, knowledgeable and conscientious group than merchant marine engineers. Keep it up, guys, we're homeward bound.

Brian Goldman: "To fight the engine room heat you'd find a fan and sit underneath it. Drink lots of Gatorade. I drank more Gatorade . . . And down there I sweated from more places than I ever knew I had to sweat from."

Bill Duncan: "We provided ourselves with these big coolers with ice water and Gatorade and the wiper that came down for the day shift made sure there was a fresh cooler. We had rags that we wrapped around our heads to keep the sweat out of our eyes. People looked like Arabs down there with towels and rags wrapped around their heads. You'd be down there three hours and drink all the ice water you wanted and never have to go to the

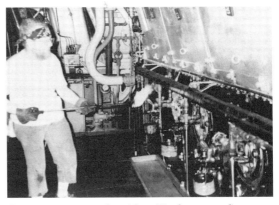

Fireman-watertender Alex Hochstraser fires one of the O'Brien's *boilers. Photo courtesy of Alex Hochstraser.*

bathroom. When not making rounds, you'd find a spot where you could watch your gauges and fires and so on and sit in a breeze. We worked three on and nine off and that made all the difference in the world. But when you came up out of the engine room it was a very exhausting time. You couldn't hold the railings, you had to use a rag or gloves. They were too hot, a hundred and forty-five degrees! You'd climb up on deck and feel like a limp rag. First thing, you come out on deck for the breeze, and then you'd take a shower. The engine gang was probably the cleanest guys on the ship, they took showers two times a day."

Ruth Robson: "I think of Ed Lingenfield and how he was a fireman, down there in that hot world. And it was like when he was back there fifty years ago, doing it again. He must have been in his seventies and he didn't complain. He went down in that hot, hot engine room and took it like a trouper."

While not quite the hell hole the engine room was, the crew working above decks were not basking in comfort. Chipping, scraping and painting steel decks in the hot sun are hard work and the direct sunlight not only sapped strength, the crew had to take precautions to avoid the dangers of heat stroke.

In the evening as we coasted past the town of Champerico, Guatemala, we had another pyrotechnic display. Large grey billowing thunderheads covered most of the shoreline. We heard the thunder and saw the clouds flash brightly in the distance. As it got darker, the entire cloud mass above the coast was brilliantly lit with forked lightning that shot horizontally from cloud to cloud creating an electric grid of white flashes filling almost a quarter of the sky. Then thick white columns of electricity shot straight to the land, backlighting the clouds in eerie pale yellow-grey light. It was an awesome, spectacular show.

The following day was serene and balmy with calm seas and partly cloudy skies. As we approached the Gulf of Tehuantepec we received a weather warning for high winds within 120 miles of the Gulf. Many a ship has been caught in a "Tehuantepecer," the violent winds blowing off the Mexican coast in this area, and suffered severe damage or loss. The prescribed maneuver in such a case is to hug the coastline. Capt. Jahn prudently ordered a course change, a dogleg up into the gulf that would take us away from the center of the potential storm.

The pyrotechnics were even more awesome that night. The coast was spotted with great towering thunderheads that threw off spectacular lightning storms; yet, between these massive storm systems, the sky was clear with stars showing. As we steamed along at ten knots, a thunder cloud slowly moved out from shore toward us, throwing off sheets, bolts and chains of lightning in all directions. It was like a living creature, a huge swirling mass of dark grey cloud angrily throwing off electricity at anything that might be in its path. Another storm cloud appeared ahead to port, equally tall, equally threatening. It was as if the two cloud masses were giant beasts on a forlorn planet, rolling out into an arena, threatening, displaying, challenging each other with their might and power. And we were caught between them. The wind came up, blowing strongly from ever-changing directions. The cloud storms attacked in counterpoint, the one ahead dropping bolts of white lightning on the ocean, the one to starboard glowing angrily and belching ear-splitting thunderous noises. The storm ahead thundered in answer. The cloud mass to starboard spit yellow-white bolts of lightning, one after the other. On shore we could see ugly grey-yellow clouds, funneling their energy in bolts of lightning that shot down to the land. In the flashes, I could see Bob Black, who was at the helm, and through the thunder, I heard him:

> "The wind was a torrent of darkness
>   among the gusty trees,
> The moon was a ghostly galleon
>   tossed upon cloudy seas,
> The road was a ribbon of moonlight
>   over the purple moor,

Born in 1955, Bob Black was one of the younger members of the *O'Brien*'s crew. Joining the ship in Rouen, France, he returned with it, as ordinary seaman, to San Francisco. A skilled cabinetmaker, he spent several years in the Navy and, in 1995, was working toward his mate's license and degree at California Maritime Academy. He and his wife live in Mare Island, California.

> And the highwayman came riding, riding, riding,
> The highwayman came riding,
> > up to the old inn-door."

The natural phenomena in these latitudes inspired others, as well. In one of his finest stories, Carl Nolte wrote:

> It is just before sunset on the coast of Mexico, and time to relieve the watch on the *Jeremiah O'Brien,* homeward bound to San Francisco after its voyage to Normandy. The ship has been out nearly five months, and it won't be long now. The days are getting longer as the ship moves up the coast away from the equator. Earlier in the week, it was dark when the 8 to 12 watch came on. Now, the sun is still up, but barely.
>
> On the bridge, chief mate Walter Jaffee relieves Ray Conrady, the second mate. Jim Miller, an able bodied seaman and the last helmsman of the old watch, turns over the wheel as he always does, exactly on the course with the helm amidship. It is 7:50 p.m. and sometimes in these latitudes, if the conditions are just right, there is a rare light show as the day ends. On a clear, calm night, there is a green flash on the western horizon at the exact moment the ball of the sun sets. You have to be quick to see it. It is over in the blink of an eye sometimes, said Pat Burke, the ordinary seaman of the 4 to 8 watch. It looks like a green flash bulb going off. Sometimes it appears as a green afterglow in the sky. Burke swears he saw the green flash a couple of days ago. It was only the fourth one he's seen in the 10 years in the Navy and aboard this ship.
>
> At sunset or just before, a lookout is sent to the bow. Even in the days of radar and modern electronics, an extra set of human eyes is useful. He stands at the very bow of the ship, watching ahead. Or he may sit in a big brown chair atop a small hatch, like the king of the night on his throne. Behind the lookout is the whole ship, with people reading, sleeping, watching movies, tending the engines. Ahead is the black ocean. It is the simplest job in the world to look out and tell the duty mate what lies ahead. He has a bell mounted behind his chair. If he sees a light to the left, he rings it twice. A light right is one bell. A light dead ahead is three bells. There is a telephone as well.
>
> Mostly there is nothing out there. Coming across the Atlantic, the *O'Brien* seemed to be alone on the midnight ocean. But the other night, off Guatemala, the ship ran through a fishing fleet, so many lights it looked like a floating city.

Sometimes the lights play tricks, appearing and disappearing like mirages. Sometimes the light becomes two and then one again. Often the sea glows with light — phosphorescence given off by tiny sea creatures in the foam churned up by the ship as it moves through the water. In the northern latitudes, their phosphorescence is sharper, like tiny lightning bolts. On the western coast of Mexico it is steady with flashes of brilliance as the bow cuts into the sea. "A beautiful ocean fire dance," said seaman Marty Shields.

Often at night, the lookout will hear a sharp slap, like the sound of a hand hitting the surface of a swimming pool. It is porpoises jumping, diving and swimming around and under the bow of the ship. At night, in the phosphorescence they glow like silvery things, like the drawings of ghosts, like spirits of the night.

There are also electrical storms, especially in the tropics. The Gulf of Tehuantepec is famous for them, and they were there when the ship passed through earlier in the week. The clouds, lit up with flashes, seem to walk on the water with electric legs. There is no sound, no thunder, but sometimes you can smell ozone in the air.

Once, years ago, when George Jahn, now master of the *O'Brien*, was a young seaman standing lookout on a passenger ship on this coast, he saw the rarest sight of all — the whole ship lit up by electricity, as if strings of light had been hung on the masts and the superstructure, blinking and flashing. It was St. Elmo's fire, a sight greatly feared by sailors. That was nearly 60 years ago, and Captain Jahn has not seen it again.

On a recent night, the time came to relieve Bob Black as lookout. "I have nothing for you," he said. "No lights." But he did leave word of a new moon, just beginning to set, Venus, the evening star, Jupiter above that, and the Milky Way across the sky. With binoculars, one could see stars beyond stars.

Bob Burnett: "Being at sea, I don't know if it's getting back to our primal nature or what it is, the peacefulness, the hypnotic effect of the sea and the incredible clear nights, and seeing stars that we generally don't see around the city. An insular nature exists on a ship or boat, you're in your own little world and you have a fairly uncomplicated routine It's peaceful and relaxing on a calm sea."

Dottie Duncan: "Life was so simple out there. Someone says 'porpoise' and everybody runs to the rail to see it. Life becomes simple and uncomplicated and you have time to reflect.

There were no telephones, no calls, no newspapers, no interruptions."

Work continued apace. Bill Rowlands, Jim Miller, Tony Rapp, Carl Nolte, Bill Fairfield and Bill Fenton chipped, scraped and painted red primer. The ship looked like a great grey Dalmatian with red spots. Sam Wood and Marty Shields finished painting the masts.

At noon, Friday, September 9, word went around the ship, "The Raven has landed." On the front of the crow's nest was a full-color painting of Bruce, his wing draped protectively over a keg of brandy. It was quite a magnificent work of art and Alex and Marty were justifiably pleased with their accomplishment. That first day it was difficult to prevent the captain from noticing the unusual number of people walking up to the bow to look at the crow's nest. "Must be a change in the weather," didn't work. The crew was painting coamings, the mainmast, windlasses and the bulwarks. "They want to see how things look when they're freshly painted."

"That must be it," said Capt. Jahn, skeptically.

We saw a Mexican Navy ship coming down the coast. Seeing a grey ship sporting guns cruising along their coast, they immediately turned to investigate. A brief exchange on the radio cleared things up. In fact, one of their

"The Raven has landed." Bruce makes his appearance as official mascot. Photo courtesy of Alex Hochstraser (on right).

officers had been on the *Cuauhtémoc* in Rouen and recognized us. After dipping flags we continued on our separate ways.

The captain was anxious about our arrival in San Diego. Contrary to his usual practice, he wanted to arrive the night before we were due to "let the crew get ashore and unwind." The admiral, on the other hand, wanted to make a grand entrance. One got the feeling that if the admiral said he wanted to arrive early the captain would have insisted on arriving on time. The port call in San Diego was scheduled only because we were now so far ahead of schedule. We needed a place to lay over. The City of San Francisco had set September 23 for the civic celebration and we couldn't arrive until then. The layover would give us a chance to paint the outside of the hull for our arrival at our home port.

Marci Hooper: "Planning the welcome home event took a lot of energy. We were dealing with the mayor's office, the Port of San Francisco, the TV stations, the radio, talking to the ship. Fervor really built after the ship came through the Canal on the way home."

Looking over the bow one morning, the chief mate glanced down at the stem and saw six dolphins riding the pressure wave. They were large, sleek grey creatures swimming in unison, some with one or two large remoras attached to their body, the dolphins' tails just inches ahead of the ship. From time to time all six jumped out of the water in unison while still maintaining their position relative to the ship. More frequently one or two jumped, sometime three or four times in succession as if for the pleasure of it. Occasionally one came out of the water spinning on its axis, twisting, turning and splashing. The captain was making a slow walk around the ship. Looking over the bow he saw the porpoise jump out of the water. He waved at them and said, "Hi there." Then, at each subsequent jump he waved, "How are you? Hello. Hi there." Finally, on some signal or calling they moved off in unison to starboard and disappeared.

As we left the bow, the captain looked up at the crow's nest. "They're doing a good job of getting the ship painted," he said noncommittally, but he was smiling and there was a light in his eyes that said he knew.

Sunday, September 11, we began crossing the Gulf of California toward Baja California. Although there was a refreshing offshore breeze the engine room was still extremely hot due to the sea water temperature which stayed in the high 80s. A heavy rain squall cooled the ship down somewhat and had the added benefit of giving us a good washdown.

The crew was restless and the heat seemed to be getting to everyone. People were quoting the line from the movie *Mr. Roberts* about sailing from tedium to apathy and back again with an occasional sidetrip to monotony. The captain and the admiral sat on opposite sides of the bridge deck at cocktail time, each sipping his drink and looking away from the other. At dinner they avoided talking to each other, even though they sat across from one another at the same table. Maybe the voyage had simply gotten too long.

The captain was concerned about the future of the ship after we arrived and returned to our routine of annual cruises around San Francisco Bay. He echoed many of the concerns of the crew wondering if people would continue volunteering after the "glory" of the voyage to Normandy was over. Strangely, the concern did not seem to extend beyond the immediate future. Perhaps it was difficult for the captain and the admiral to envision a future that did not include them. A noble plan would be to develop an active program to impart their vast experience and expertise to train the next generation of volunteers and turn the ship over to them. In large part due to their efforts, the National Liberty Ship Memorial has grown beyond being "their" ship. The *Jeremiah O'Brien* belongs to everyone now, the volunteers, the public, the nation. The *O'Brien*'s valedictory voyage back to Normandy was a salute to their generation, a brilliant cap to distinguished careers. Perhaps it is an appropriate time to begin the transition to the next generation.

Getting down to the final few days of the voyage brought about a strange mixture of emotions — sadness that the trip was nearly over, joy at returning home to our loved ones, perhaps some frustration over what might have been but wasn't, some missed opportunities. But the dominant feeling was gratitude for being able to be on the great voyage, and a disbelief in our incredible good fortune.

Nils Anderson: "It goes back for me to my interest in steam when I was a little boy. My uncle told me about things like this and then my father worked with the Maritime Commission during World War II and my sister had actually christened one or two of these. So I remember seeing the ships being built, the big prefab sections being lifted around with the cranes. But World War II is a lot of faint, distant memories. This trip really burned it into my mind and made it a lot more meaningful what the United States did for people in Europe. I've read about the merchant marine but until you come out here and spend some time you can't know what people did years ago, going to sea. We shouldn't forget it."

David Aris: "I wouldn't have missed it for anything. When people ask my wife what she thought about me doing this trip, she says, well the *Jeremiah O'Brien* was the only thing that would separate us. And it has, temporarily. But it's something that I'll remember the rest of my life."

Dick Brannon: "This trip is an irreplaceable chunk out of a finite but rapidly passing lifetime. F. Scott Fitzgerald said there are no second chances in life. This is the big chance of the lifetime. There are no more chances. I made it. I did it and I'm very happy about it. I wouldn't have missed it for the world."

Bill Bennett: "The ocean, the water is like a magnet to me. It just keeps drawing me back. But there's also a matter of national pride. I've taken care of that flag back there, always looking pristine when we go into port. That's because I'm showing my country's colors. And I feel stronger about that, since I've been doing it, than when I first came on the trip. So part of the reason I came on this trip was a matter of national pride. Let's show the world what we can do. That sounds corny but that's the way I feel about it. A lot of it, a tremendous amount of it, is the respect for what took place during the 40s. I guess it's true with most people that as they get older they have a better appreciation for life and to see what our fellows had to put up with back in those days, so we honor them, too."

Pat McCafferty: "The nostalgia of it, the adventure, the challenge, plus — this is difficult for me to put into words — but I kinda have this idea that our whole nation needs more volunteers, roll-up-your-sleeves-and-get-things-done attitude and this ship represents a lot of that to me. And it represents that certain things can be accomplished and we're going to have to start giving more back to our country than just taking. The rest of it's the romance of the sea, the adventure, the fun, the *Jeremiah O'Brien . . .*"

That evening the wind shifted from northwest to north. The sea became choppy, but more important, the seawater temperature dropped almost twenty degrees during the night. Suddenly the engine room was bearable. Many of the crew slept under blankets for the first time in weeks.

The next day we passed between Cedros Island and the Baja peninsula. The island was brown, rocky, barren and dry. Its southern end is flat, containing a gypsum processing plant — metal buildings, a pier, white mounds of mineral — and rises quickly to a tall mountain that runs the full length of the rest of the island. Skirting the east coast, we saw an occasional house and a small fishing village at the north end, tucked on the slope of the scrub-spotted mountain where it leveled off before dropping into the sea. We rounded the north point and made our final course change toward San Diego.

The deck department, Marty Wefald, Bob Burnett, Bill Fairfield, Tony Rapp, Bill Rowlands, Marty Shields, Bill Bennett, Sam Wood, Bob Black, Carl Nolte and Bill Fenton, finished painting the main deck. This included rolling out the flat deck surfaces and spraying the bulwarks. Jack Carraher and Ron Smith put the finishing touches on their guns. Since leaving Jacksonville we had painted the entire ship for the third time this voyage. She looked bright and clean, "shipshape and Bristol fashion."

At dinner the crew was in a celebratory mood. After dinner they could be heard singing all through the house,

Poor Monique gets her first taste of America. Talk about culture shock. Courtesy Phil Frank and San Francisco Chronicle.

"Tipperary," "Ole Man River," "Dixie" and other songs well into the night.

Bill Bennett's Crew's News for this evening:

Good evening San Francisco.

After coming off watch at 1600, it is my custom to retire to #4 hatch to enjoy afternoon refreshments with my shipmates. Imagine my concern at finding none present. Have they cancelled our happy hour?

No way! To do so could cause mutiny. No sensible master, least of all skipper and friend, Captain George Jahn, would do so. To cancel, this close to the end of this successful voyage, borders on insanity.

Concern turned to relief shortly, when I discovered the entire off-duty crew crowded onto the fantail enjoying their favorite brand of cool beverage. It seems Marty Wefald had the after decks painted and will not allow any footprints on it. He wants this ship looking very clean as we return home and bos'ns usually get their way. Marty is no exception.

Today's noon data: Lat 28 30N Long 115 14W miles travelled 248, at 10.3 knots. 272 miles to go until San Diego.

Jeremiah O'Brien — out.

After high school, Bill Bennett, AB on the 12-to-4 watch, went to sea in 1947 in the U.S. Coast Guard, serving on the *Falsa,* a buoy tender. He served four years of active duty, nine years in the Coast Guard reserve, and ten years in the Coast Guard Auxiliary. Employed as a maintenance supervisor for Lawrence Livermore Laboratories in Richmond, California, he retired in 1993 on his sixty-third birthday. He and his wife live in Vallejo, California.

Thursday, September 15, came with low overcast and calm seas. The sky stayed hazy and thick all day. Eventually the coast of Mexico became more and more visible through the haze. Soon we saw modern beachfront homes, elegant apartment houses and then a recognizable landmark, the bull ring at Tijuana. Shortly after lunch we took arrival at San Diego and the pilot, Capt. Ryan, came aboard. As we entered the harbor and sailed toward our berth at the foot of Broadway, a few people on yachts waved, a Hornblower dinner boat saluted with its whistle. There were no welcoming ceremonies, bands or folderol. We were just a strange-looking old cargo ship, nearing the end of a long voyage.

19

HOMEWARD BOUND

Our pilot, Capt. Ryan, eased us skillfully into our berth. We docked starboard side to, our bow pointed toward downtown, where tall office buildings glistened in the afternoon sun, mirroring each other's images in their glass sides. At the next pier to our right was the *Yukon,* the tanker we met at the beginning of our voyage, so many months earlier. To our left was a passenger ship terminal with ferries to Coronado and cruise ships to Mexico. Farther along the embarcadero lay the magnificent sailing ship, *Star of India,* her sleek black hull and tall masts evoking memories of the glorious Armada, and the squat white ferry *Berkeley* which houses the San Diego Maritime Museum.

Our brief stay in Panama caused us to be treated as if we had come from a foreign country and Customs and Immigration again boarded. Poor Cliff Hook just couldn't escape his British citizenship and had his passport taken away by the Immigration people. Purser Jim Wade insisted Cliff was part of the crew. But because, as a crew member, Cliff didn't have a visa, he got a notice to appear in court as an illegal alien. Our agent, Norton Lilly & Co., straightened it out the next day, but meanwhile Capt. Hook was restricted to the ship.

The following day was one of crossed communications. We learned that local harbor regulations prohibited any painting at our dock. Our secondary purpose in coming into San Diego, after the need to arrive at San Francisco at a certain time on a particular day, was to touch up the hull. Military Sealift Command (MSC), our host, went to work. Next, we were told there would be a ceremony on no. 2 hatch at 1000. Adm. Patterson changed into his white uniform and stood waiting at the gangway to receive visitors. Ten o'clock came and the only person to arrive was a reporter from the local paper. Meanwhile, remembering that it is always easier to ask forgiveness than permission, the crew began painting the starboard side of the hull from the dock.

MSC cut through the local red tape and later in the day we were given official permission to paint the ship's hull. MSC also loaned us a three-tiered paint float to help paint the offshore side of the ship as well as the bow and stern. Sam Wood, Cliff Hook and Pat Burke, who joined us at Jacksonville, began painting the bow, then worked their way down the port side. Bosun Marty Wefald said the crew consensus was that we shouldn't paint, the ship should look like it's come in from a 20,000-mile voyage. But we wanted San

Top to bottom, Pat Burke, Cliff Hook and Sam Wood paint the bow.

Francisco to be proud of their ship. The painting continued.

San Diego did a good job with public relations. We were in the newspaper and on local television and the visitor count went from 300 to 1,245 after our story was aired. In the evening the bars and restaurants near the harbor were filled with "*Jeremiah O'Brien*, Crew" jackets as they delivered their cargo of good will in their usual friendly manner. Anthony's restaurant had three tables of our ship's ambassadors, the cafe at the harbor tour terminal another two tables and the ethnic cafes of Seaport Village held a few more.

Sunday came cloudy and hazy then settled into partly cloudy with still air and the promise of heat. Thanks to the float provided by MSC the deck department quickly finished painting the hull. A goodly crowd was aboard. We were assisted throughout our stay by the local chapter of the American Merchant Marine Veterans who provided gangway watches and docents. Many of them were old Liberty ship sailors and we often heard their stories:

"During the war I was on this Liberty, and we . . ."

"I'll never forget the time . . . "

"It was the worst crossing you could ever imagine. The waves were so high . . ."

And inevitably, ". . . and we never saw him again."

Monday, September 19, and another day of miscommunications. We were told that "Good Morning, America," would be aboard filming an opening to their show. The crew was told to be on deck early, in their uniform of blue polo shirts and baseball caps, the officers in dress whites. The camera crew arrived but it wasn't "Good Morning, America," but a local cable station, channel 51, doing their morning show. When someone complained about the misinfo.mation, the navy Public Affairs Officer said, "This is the show all the retired flag officers listen to."* That brought several, "So what's" from the unimpressed crew. During the show the captain and the admiral were interviewed as part of the newscast. Later on Capt. Jahn had this to say, "Well, at least

---

*San Diego has probably the largest community of retired Naval officers in the United States.

he [the admiral] makes all the speeches. That way all I have to say is 'you heard it all.'"

The National Liberty Ship Memorial board of directors flew down from San Francisco and held a board meeting in an office alongside the dock. The crew weren't invited but we heard that topics of discussion included the poor way in which the ship was operated, that money had been wasted, opportunities to make money were missed, and so on. The NLSM board would be "straightening things out." The crew's first reaction was, "If they're so worried about expenses, why did they spend the money to fly down here? They could hold the meeting in San Francisco." It was hard to find out just what did happen at the board meeting.

Warren Hopkins, NLSM Board member: "Basically, what it was about was to express our interest in what was happening on the ship, but it turned out to be a report on things that were done right or wrong during the voyage, kind of one of those 'lessons learned' sort of things. Also, we were concerned because we heard the crew's morale was pretty low, and we wanted to assure them that everything was all right."

That evening we held a party in no. 2 'tween deck for the people who helped us during our stay in San Diego — the American Merchant Marine Veterans, Military Sealift Command and San Diego City and Harbor officials. The galley crew did their usual excellent job putting out a menu of shrimp salad, marinated bean salad, baron of beef with red wine sauce, potatoes au gratin, cake, assorted wines, French bread and coffee. Everyone enjoyed the meal. The usual speeches were given and we quickly debarked everyone so we could sail.

At 2200 Capt. Ryan came back aboard, tugs were made fast, and we raised the gangways and let go the lines. We backed slowly away from the dock and everything seemed to be proceeding smoothly when the pilot quietly said, "God damn it." He was looking at the bow tug, "God damn it," he said again. The tug was out of position. Something had happened, perhaps a confused order, and the tug was just maneuvering into position to pull the bow, now rapidly swinging toward the pier, in the opposite direction. But he should have been there all along. Our bow hit the pier with a jarring thud felt throughout the ship. Through clenched teeth, Capt. Jahn said, "I told him she backs to port. I told him the bow would swing." But in the wisdom of his years he didn't say it loud enough for anyone else to hear and he let the pilot continue. We backed into the channel, swung our bow northward and steamed out of San Diego harbor on our way to Long Beach and our rendezvous with the *Lane Victory*.

After reducing speed to make our 0900 arrival (it's hard to believe that we could be early again on a run as short as that from San Diego to Long Beach, but we were) we approached Angels Gate, the entrance to Long Beach Harbor and picked up Capt. Silva, our pilot. He brought us through the breakwater, turned us around with the aid of two tugs and backed the *O'Brien* up the channel toward our berth ahead of the *Lane Victory*. As we neared the ship we saw a large white banner stretched across her midships house with "Welcome Home *Jeremiah O'Brien*" in large black letters. It was a warmhearted and friendly gesture on the part of the *Lane*'s crew, especially touching after the disappointment of their not being able to make the voyage to Normandy.

By 1000 we were alongside and had rung off Finished With Engines. Many old friends from the *Lane* came aboard: Isaac Hayes, Joe Vernick, John Smith, John and Mary Ann Strunck, Hal Runnels, Clint Johnson, Jerry Turner, Don MacLean, Sheila McIntyre. As always, they gave us a grand welcome, with hugs, handshakes and sincere good wishes.

Our first order of business was to assess the damage done leaving San Diego. Fortunately, there were no dents and just a few scratches in the bow near the waterline. Marty Shields attacked it with a roller and a can of grey paint and within an hour had the ship looking like new again. Unfortunately, this wasn't to last long.

There is a group of hobbyists who enjoy building and operating miniature steam engines. Made of brass, stainless steel and chrome, these devices are usually finely-machined works of art, suitable for museum display. A visitor brought one of these small steam engines aboard the *O'Brien*. Our ship's engineers set it up on the main deck, starboard side, aft of the midships house, and connected it to the ship's steam lines. They ordered steam on deck and ran the machine for three hours, all standing around watching the gears and rods turn back and forth, back and forth, up and down, up and down. Occasionally one of them would flip a lever and make it turn in the opposite direction. Then they all stood and watched again, blissful looks of contentment on their faces. The difference between the engine department and the deck department was never so obvious as at times like this. To the deck department, the engine is an absolutely necessary part of the ship, but merely the means of getting you to where you're going. To the engine department, the engine is the prime attraction and getting somewhere is only a side effect of the real interest, which is working with the machinery. It is a difference of focus that neither side can truly comprehend, try as they might.

Like any engine, this devilish little monster needed lubrication and, as with any steam engine, the steam condensed into water and ran down onto the deck, across to the scupper and down the side of the ship, carrying with it a small residue of black oil. The result, to which the engineers were totally oblivious, was a black oil streak down the starboard side of our newly-painted hull, from scupper to waterline. It was a four-hour job in the early morning for the deck department to get the oil cleaned off. Grrr!

Rod Deakin, who worked for KFS, the radio station that generously handled most of our communications at no charge, met us in Long Beach: "Bob Gisslow suggested that I come to Los Angeles and ride with the *O'Brien* on the last leg of her return trip to SF. I saw this as a once-in-a-lifetime opportunity and it didn't have to be suggested twice.

"The first person I met was Admiral Patterson. Bob Gisslow joined up at once and Adm. Patterson asked him to go to the ship's store and get a crew shirt for me. I put the shirt on and was feeling pretty good about that time. Most of the rest of the crew, however, were wondering who this guy was wearing that shirt and they had never seen him before. This led to some comments and I was more than a little embarrassed by the whole thing. But Bob let it be known that I was from KFS and as quickly as it started, the whole thing turned completely around. During the next two days, many of the crew found me and personally thanked me for what KFS had done. From that moment on I was treated as a crew member — as if I had been there the whole time."

Crews News:

This is the Voice of the *Jeremiah O'Brien.*

Bosun Marty Wefald finishes cleaning an oil stain from the side of the hull. Photo by Jo Lawrence.

Good evening, San Francisco.

KFS this is KXCH. Kilo Foxtrot Sierra this is Kilo Xray Charlie Hotel. This call via marine radio is transmitted several times a day by *Jeremiah O'Brien* to marine radio station KFS at Half Moon Bay, near San Francisco. KFS radio has been handling our radio traffic since April 18 at no cost to us. This is a sizeable contribution and is much appreciated.

On board Radio Operator Bob Gisslow, a 7 year volunteer, has the responsibility of all shipboard communications. Some of these are: daily reports to the ship's office; this "crew's news" report; and Carl Nolte's column to the *Chronicle.*

In addition to a communications device known as "SITOR," wherein one computer talks to another computer via high frequency radio, messages are also sent via AT&T high seas operator or, when close to metropolitan areas, via VHF to local marine operators.

Jeremiah O'Brien — out.

Bob Gisslow is a World War II veteran who received his training at Gallups Island Radio School in Boston harbor. He served aboard two Libertys after school and, after coming ashore, was involved in radio and TV repair. Prior to retirement, Bob was an office manager for RCA Radio and Television service. Bob has been a volunteer since 1987 and made the entire Normandy voyage. He lives in San Francisco.

That evening the *Lane Victory* organization had our entire crew to dinner in their no. 4 'tween deck. They have created a remarkable maritime museum there with stunning displays of ship models, uniforms, navigation and engineering instruments, books, brochures, posters and artifacts. Everything is handsomely displayed in glass cases, others are mounted on the bulkheads. It is an outstanding exhibit and visitors tend to linger to be sure they have taken it all in. The *O'Brien* crew wandered around the displays with a degree of envy and some embarrassment at the comparison with the *O'Brien*'s rather pitiful exhibit. The dinner was outstanding, with salads, ham, chicken, green beans, ice creams and cake catered from Ante's, a nearby Dalmatian restaurant. The *Lane* made us feel as welcome as if we were home again.

Two days to home.

Clarence Rocha, at 90 our oldest volunteer, joined us for the remainder of the voyage.

On Wednesday, September 21, at 0600, under an overcast and hazy sky, we sailed from pier 52 with the *Lane Victory* escorting. We cleared Angels Gate and were headed north when we got a dismaying call on the radio from the *Lane*. They were having trouble with a valve on a boiler and would have to pull out of the traffic lane for repairs. There was nothing we could do to help. We proceeded in a calm sea with pilot whales, dolphins and sea lions cavorting playfully around us.

This was our next-to-last day at sea and our last fire and boat drill was held. Those in the crew that made the entire trip, twenty-seven of us, assembled on no. 2 hatch for a crew photo. In front of us we held the American flag, now tattered, that flew at the steaming gaff every day at sea. It symbolized the voyage, the ports, the history, the adventure, the nostalgia and the excitement of this voyage of a lifetime.

Dick Brannon: "It was an outstanding success, mechanically, publicitywise, logisticallywise. This voyage was a unqualified success. We had tremendous enthusiasm from the crowds and we got absolutely a fantastic crew. I've been on ships for many years and I've never seen a more cohesive crew. Everybody, all departments, absolutely dedicated to making the trip a success. Hey, we did it. Great, great, absolutely fantastic. All positives, all positives. And the crew, my God, just speaking for the engine room, we had a fantastically dedicated bunch of engineers."

Brian Goldman (age 22): "I have a whole new respect for age. I came aboard thinking thirty-five, forty was the end of the road and after that you had to become a vegetable in the chair and

The 27 who made the entire voyage, with the 18,000 mile flag. Front row, left to right, Tim Palange, Jim Wade, Bill Duncan, Dick Brannon, George Jahn, Tom Patterson, Bob Gisslow, Walter Jaffee, Ray Conrady. Second row, left to right, Ken Haslam, Alex Hochstraser, Ed Lingenfield, Ed Smith, Russ Mosholder, Pat McCafferty, Greg Williams, Jimmy Farras, Al Martino, Eddy Pubill. Back row, left to right, Bill Bennett, Bob Burnett, Bill Rowlands, Jim Miller, Sam Wood, Marty Shields, Marty Wefald, Jack Carraher and Ron Smith. (Actually, there are 28. Ed Smith left for part of the voyage for medical reasons but returned later).

set in your ways. After coming aboard, I realized that you're not set in your ways after forty. Old, now, to me, is anything over eighty and completely a state of mind. I had a lot of good experiences with the watch, Jeff Speight, the second engineer for forty days. Learned a lot from him, learned a lot from Brannon the chief. Bill Duncan was great to talk to on watch, learned a lot from him, a lot of experiences. For somebody my age, it's been a way to grow up."

Ed Smith: "It was well worth all the effort that every one of us put into it. Jesus Christ, we made friends that will probably be for the rest of our lives because how can you not, living three in a room, and getting that close and talking and all the bullshit. I think, going and coming, it was about the best bunch of guys I've seen in ages. Just everything was fine, no big beefs with anybody, everybody done their job willingly."

Bill Bennett: "I think this trip gave us more than we could have possibly expected. When we left port the original talk was five days of work, one day off, every morning you get up and scrub down the decks and all we need to do is tie up on a dock somewhere. And it turned out different. We worked every day because we wanted to. Then we got over there to England and Cherbourg and Le Havre and Rouen and . . . I think what I'm gonna look back to, and have looked back to many times already, is the gratefulness of the French people. I could not get over that."

Bill Rowlands: "It's worked out well. I enjoyed it, met a lot of interesting people. It was kind of a last hurrah. It wasn't all easy, but the ship functioned well, with the exception of the modern conveniences. I wish I had done more visiting in London and several times, visiting in France, I met a couple of very interesting people. But it was kinda difficult because of the language, and they tried so hard to understand you and it creates a strain. But I'm glad I did it."

Marty Shields: "It was a real interesting experience all around. Standing a watch was just a wonderful experience. It never really became routine, it was just every day, you know, another interesting day. I really believe that it would have been very hard to ever see the countries, England and France, as we saw them, from the old seaports. Cherbourg and the old seaports really made this an outstanding trip, coming into London on the Thames, and going up the Seine, experiences that a lot of people never get to have. And just a lot of good people. I took the opportunity to be at sea and get better at one craft and try to upgrade my license and to practice what I learned. And it really has been a pleasure."

Cliff Hook: "I had real memories of these [Liberty] ships. Something I don't think I appreciated when I was at sea, and only recently have I started thinking about it and reading about it, is that had it not been for these ships I think the war would have been dramatically different. I was only eleven when the war started and we, as kids, very soon accepted it as a way of life. We didn't really appreciate quite what was going on. It's only, perhaps, this year, with the D-Day commemoration finished, that I really started thinking back what a close call it was. The word 'Liberty' now is just the right word, isn't it?"

Jack Carraher: "The response we got in Europe was something I'll be able to talk about for a long time. Of course we hear where nobody cares anymore or things like that, and that our efforts have been in vain. That's not true, not where we were, anyhow. The people were just magnificent. I personally had no negative encounters whatsoever. I'll be able to refute from personal experience anything like that. It was a very positive experience all the way through. I had a great time. Wonderful crew. Officers too. They seemed to have the right attitude, and I can't find fault with any of them. Oh, Rudy used to sing off key occasionally, but he knew a lot of songs, so that was all right. It was a wonderful trip, the crew and the ship went all the way and they were good people to be with. I can't think of a better gang to sail with. They were good shipmates and I think that's the highest praise I can give them. They were very forgiving. [laugh] That carries a lot of weight with me. I felt this was a fun voyage."

Russ Mosholder: "The people I had with me on the ship overall were some of the most wonderful people I've had to deal with in my lifetime. There's been little problems but that's normal. You have that every day you're out in the public. But the age group and the time we spent — I think they're some of the most fantastic people that ever come down. It's been a wonderful, wonderful trip. Like I said, it's the last hurrah but it's been a good last hurrah. I'd do it again. I'll never forget that ship, I can tell you that."

Ruth Robson: "There's nothing about it that wasn't in superlative terms. The people, the trip itself, it was a voyage you could never buy. It was a lifetime experience, something that will be with me for the rest of my life. A year ago I would never have dreamed I would have been so fortunate as to be part of it. It was history. It was the

Ruth Robson retired from a career working for a paint company in Southern California. Her nephew, Ron Robson, managed the *O'Brien*'s ship's store in Europe and Ruth joined the ship in Portsmouth, England, staying on board as store clerk and crew messman for the remainder of the voyage. She and Russ Mosholder now live in San Diego, California.

making of history. It gets more profound the more you think about it."

Greg Williams: "Being on the ship with people that I've known for quite a while, volunteers like Bob Burnett, Bill Rowlands, Jim Miller and the other long-term volunteers, that was wonderful. They all looked forward to it the same as I did. It was something we talked about for years on end and dreamed about but we never actually thought it would happen. And then when it looked like it was going to actually happen, it kind of left us breathless.

"I liked the ports in France, the towns are so nice, especially the villages in France. I have one vivid memory, going through a village, can't remember the name of it, and there were two old people standing in the doorway of their little cottage with the flowers and vines around and they looked so happy and so peaceful and I thought what a wonderful, really idyllic place it was for them to retire. And they don't have to worry about crime or pollution or any of the stuff our elderly people worry about. They just looked so happy. The English countryside that I saw was the most lush, green area that I've ever seen in my life. Spectacular. I took a ride from, it must have been Portsmouth to Winchester, the countryside was just unbelievable."

Sam Wood: "It was more than I could imagine, particularly the work. All the old things, all the old skills, the old jobs that I did in the 60s, I did again, without exception, everything from the slushing to the white lead to the masts to going over the side, everything. All that I've ever done before that was part of the AB's job, I did again, just like reliving the past in a way, a kind of workmanlike way. But, for me, the best thing was going to sea again, just sitting on the fantail reading a book in the quiet of the afternoon after a shower and feeling completely at ease, complete, if you will. I had a lot of worries, I had concerns that were on the shore in San Francisco but I was far removed from it then. I couldn't personally find that kind of contentment in a coffeehouse or in my kitchen or with my lady friend. I could only find it there on the ship. I liked being completely alone and, despite the fact that I was surrounded by crew, I often felt very isolated but it wasn't a bad thing because companionship was there. All I need do was walk forward and I would drink beer with my fellows, but in addition I had this isolation and I enjoyed that, I sought that for whatever reason."

Tim Palange: "It was a lot more than I expected. It was the trip of a lifetime. Some of the highlights were making some new friends overseas and, of course, *La Armada de la Liberté*, I'll never forget that, and Chatham."

Nils Anderson: "The overall experience for me has been kind of bittersweet. I lost my father while we were in the North Atlantic. And you get to know the feelings of other people on the ship and you know that they're truly concerned about you. There was a lot of feeling of family on board there. It was stronger between some than others but you developed a strong bond when you spent that kind of time working with people or sitting reading or whatever you were doing. You got to know people pretty well."

David Aris: "It was fascinating. I will remember it for a long time. I made a lot of friends and it was great to be with a big crowd of Americans and most interesting, most enjoyable, very hot but a great trip, great trip."

Jimmy Farras: "It was great. It was really a good time and my chief cook Al, he was a workhorse in that galley. I couldn't have done it without him and Eddy the third cook. I mean those guys were, they really had no cooking experience other than working. Al's a retired fireman but Al butchered for many years. He was a butcher and that's half the battle as a chief cook's job. He did a lot of butchering for me and that was a big, big, big help.

Jimmy Farras, second cook and baker for the entire voyage, had the job of baking all pies, puddings, cakes, pastries, preparing batter and prepping and cooking meals for breakfast, lunch and dinner. Born in 1954, Jimmy first went to sea in 1975 as a member of the Marine Cooks and Stewards Union. After sailing for five years he attended and graduated from the California Culinary Academy, then went to work as a professional chef. His most recent employment before the voyage was at San Francisco's Balboa Cafe. He lives in Daly City, California.

"One unusual thing about this ship is cooking on a coal-burning stove. I've never experienced that before. That's really something. Al and Eddy and I cooked more than 20,000 meals, which is a lot of cooking, you know, a lot of cooking, especially on a coal burner."

Dottie Duncan: "If I had to name a person that made a difference in the voyage it was Jack Carraher. His personality was just what that ship needed at sea. Jack made me laugh every day, he was just a one man comedy routine, a funny guy."

One of the more mundane chores was packing. It's amazing how many souvenirs and curios one can accumulate in six months. By the time I finished, the boxes, bags, cases of wine and other mementos took up half my room. There was just enough space to get to the bunk and the sink. Every other bit of floor was occupied. The same scene was replicated all over the ship. The smaller crew rooms had no space and their stuff was in the holds — the inside of the ship looked like a floating bazaar.

We received the welcome news that the *Lane Victory* had made her repairs and was underway again. The crew breathed a collective sigh of relief and began a lookout for the *Lane*.

Crew's News:

This is the Voice of the *Jeremiah O'Brien.*
Good evening, San Francisco.
The lucky *O'Brien* did it again. Mooring lines were cast off at 0600 today and your Liberty ship departed San Pedro on schedule. The *Lane Victory* will follow us up the coast later as our escort.

The *Lane Victory* will lead the *O'Brien* under the Golden Gate Bridge in the early morning Sept. 23. *Jeremiah O'Brien,* decked out in signal flags and a large United States ensign, is due under the bridge at 0800.

A moment once again to thank Mrs. Lynette Dwyer for her assistance in securing a grant from Pacific Telesis enabling us to finance this message service.

The crew also wishes to express its gratitude to Mr. Gary North, manager of marine radio station KFS for handling all of our crews news messages at no charge. My personal thanks to you, Gary, for your five months plus, five star performance of recording your voice as the Voice of the *Jeremiah O'Brien.*
Jeremiah O'Brien — out.

Point Concepcion, just north of Santa Barbara, is a line of demarcation on the Pacific Coast. As soon as a ship nears it, it can be sure to pick up a howling northwesterly with accompanying seas and swells. Knowing this, Capt. Jahn built in almost ten hours of extra time to allow for the bad weather. To our astonishment and

We were relieved to hear the Lane Victory was underway again. She quickly caught up. Photo by Bob Black.

amazement we rounded Point Concepcion in an absolute flat calm! The *Jeremiah O'Brien*'s luck was still holding. But, at that speed, we would once again, yes . . . So we began dropping revolutions to make our 0800 arrival at the Golden Gate two days hence.

The crew was in a mood for hi-jinks. Dottie Duncan: "We made this outfit for Nils Anderson one afternoon. We made him the beermeister with an Olympia beer box made into a crown, his scepter was a plumbers helper with a beer can mounted in it and we gave him a cape. He was all in red, white and blue. And he had a big engine room gauge hanging on a chain around his neck."

The "Beermeister," Nils Anderson. Photo by Dottie Duncan.

Russ Mosholder had a special surprise at beer break that evening. Unknown to everyone, he kept one keg of Kronenberg tucked away. He brought it out at 1600 with the proviso that it had to last for two days. The crew was delighted. The keg was tapped and, when halfway empty, put back in the cooler for the following evening.

During the evening a beautiful full moon rose in the early part of the 8 to 12 watch. It was yellow gold, suspended in a clear sky over the gentle dark peaks and valleys of the California coastline. Its reflection was a golden trail on the water, shimmering and radiant, across the sea, from the shoreline to our ship. On the *O'Brien,* the decks were brightly lit with long dark shadows as we sailed across the glassy sea north toward San Francisco and home. The heavens were filled with stars, more stars than seemed possible. All was serene, it was a wonderful voyage, we were at peace with the world, and now, almost home.

Thursday, September 22 — our last day at sea. It was overcast with a high fog but visibility at sea level was good. We passed Point Sur on the morning watch. At 1000 a crew meeting was held to discuss the transition to an idle ship. Hardly anyone listened, we were too excited at the prospect of seeing our families again after being gone for almost six months.

We continued reducing speed and wallowed along at five knots. Passing Carmel the crew looked right up Ocean Avenue, recognizing the landmarks. The rest of the coast was covered with thick green pine and cypress with here and there a stand of redwood. A school of orcas passed, their sharp dorsals knifing through the water, their black and white bodies showing just beneath the surface.

That evening we had the best beer party of the voyage at no. 4 hatch. The rest of the Kronenberg went, then Olympia and Pabst were brought out. Someone produced a bottle of Duggan's Dew of Kirkintilloch, which brought up stories of the Scots chief engineer of the *Inchcliffe Castle.* Amongst other good spirits, there were more stories and singing. "Tipperary" and "We'll Meet Again" vied for most popular, but today, "Auld Lang Syne" held the place of honor. This was followed by the captain's dinner, traditionally served the last night out — steak, bean salad, baked potato, carrots, sour cream, garlic bread, cherry pie, ice cream.

Rod Deakin managed a bit of old-fashioned light signaling that last evening. "Walter Kane is a 'maritime communications consultant' for KFS, meaning he's in sales. He has a keen eye for PR opportunities. During the trip up the California coast from

Los Angeles, Walter contacted me by radio and suggested that it would be a neat idea for us to have a contact between KFS in Half Moon Bay and the *O'Brien* via flashing light while we are steaming in the area. I agree and on Thursday September 22nd, I begin feeding Walter position reports every four hours or so to facilitate our schedule. Around 11:30 p.m. the *O'Brien* is abeam KFS and there's Walter with his headlights flashing away at us. I had already rigged the portable signal light on the starboard side just outside the wheelhouse. We had our chat and it lasted about fifteen minutes. Not one to miss an opportunity, Walter fed this story to the local newspaper in Half Moon Bay and they published it. It sounded like the whole thing was a chance happening but it wasn't."

Bill Bennett's last Crew's News from sea went out that evening:

> This is the Voice of the *Jeremiah O'Brien*.
>
> Good evening, San Francisco.
>
> All day a smiling, congenial, very happy crew of *Jeremiah O'Brien* have been lining the rail gazing at the central California coast. Happy to be home would be an understatement; delighted, would be closer to the truth.
>
> But under it all is this nagging feeling that these shipmates, many of whom we have spent nigh onto six months with, won't be as near again.
>
> Male bonding is a relatively new term. Male bonding happened on this ship — not to exclude our capable, friendly female crew who really pulled their weight — what has happened among the men was truly remarkable.
>
> My initial concern before this trip was: are we going to be a group of grumpy old men, set in our ways, uncooperative, grouchy, do-it-my-way guys — or mature, older people with a single purpose in mind? Maturity won, hands down.
>
> Simply put, we pulled together, strengthened friendships, and we fully accomplished the goals of Normandy '94. As I write, sad to know this trip is almost over, my shipmates are singing: "Auld Lang Syne," on the stern.
>
> What an adventure!
>
> Today's noon data: 196 miles at 8.1 knots; position abeam Point Sur, Monterey County, on our way home.
>
> *Jeremiah O'Brien* — out.

There was one last piece of business to attend to before we arrived in San Francisco — Ron Robson's palm tree which he brought on board before we sailed from San Francisco in April. It was in a pot on the exterior deck behind Capt. Jahn's stateroom. It had weathered the voyage, but just barely. Now only three tiny fronds showed a few inches above the stalk. In fact, the palm looked so poorly, someone bought a new one in San Diego and put it next to the old one. But the allusion had to be played out. When I got off watch at midnight I went straight to the old tree, pulled it out of the pot and threw it over the side. Hopefully, somewhere, Mr. Roberts was smiling down on us.

20

HOME FROM THE SEA

The *Jeremiah O'Brien* took arrival .8 miles off the San
Francisco Light Buoy at 0530, September 23. Shortly
after 0600 Capt. A. Carlier, our pilot, boarded, along with
members of the press, Rich Reed, our bosun from the first part of
the trip, and Capt. Pat Moloney of the Pilot Commission. Russ
Mosholder bought several boxes of doughnuts in San Pedro and
these were now set out at no. 4 hatch along with large thermoses
of steaming coffee. That would be breakfast today. The crew was
at it early. They hadn't had a good American doughnut for many
months.

It was getting light as we went through the main ship
channel toward the Golden Gate. The sky held a high thin grey
overcast. The sun rose under it shooting streaks of red and pink
through the heavens. To our right we saw the white houses of the
Sunset district climbing San Francisco's headlands, the dark streets
and light houses looking like a chess board by Dali. To port was
rocky Point Bonita, the green Marin headlands and, in the distance,

Point Reyes. Astern, the *Lane Victory* kept pace, a few hundred yards off. Miles ahead, the Golden Gate Bridge was dimly seen, dwarfed by the land on either side. Another boat came alongside and Frank Jordan, the Mayor of San Francisco, climbed aboard.

But before we met the welcoming parade, we had to say a last good-bye to two supporters and friends of the *Jeremiah O'Brien*. Outside the Golden Gate the ship slowed, a short ceremony was held on the stern and two wreaths were dropped into the sea, one in memory of the recently deceased Thomas Crowley, President of Crowley Maritime, longtime member of the NLSM Board of Directors and staunch supporter of the *Jeremiah O'Brien*. Tom Patterson: "Without Tom Crowley, there would be no *O'Brien* sailing today." The second bouquet was in memory of Janet Doyle, our "Wendy the Welder," who painted the figures on the forward guntub and gave so much of herself to the ship. We watched in silence as the flowers drifted astern and out to sea.

Ahead, we saw a large flotilla of boats coming out the Gate — President Roosevelt's yacht, the *Potomac,* fireboats from San Francisco, Oakland and other ports in the Bay, the historic hay scow *Alma,* the steam tug *Hercules,* a replica square-rigger that had come from Hawaii for the event, and hundreds of motorboats, yachts, tugs and excursion boats.

Karen Kamimoto: "The day the ship came in, I drove along Land's End and then the Presidio and there were cars parked all over the place at seven in the morning. It was surprising how many people were there, all along, hundreds of people. By seven-fifteen Fort Point was closed because it was full. I drove along Crissy Field and along the Marina Green, it was a great sight to see all these people, young, old. I just really felt proud of everybody."

Rod Deakin: "It is now 07:30 a.m. on Friday, September 23rd. We are about five miles outside of the Golden Gate. It's overcast with some clearing through which sunlight is pouring. There are some six fireboats and maybe 200 other vessels, large and small, accompanying us into San Francisco. I am on the flying bridge surveying this scene. I look toward Ft. Baker and notice a light flashing. It's not sending anything intelligible — just flashing more or less randomly. So just for the fun of it, I train the big signal light on the port side of the bridge toward this flashing light and turn it on. I send '?' twice. Back comes the light with "Welcome home *Jeremiah O'Brien*" in perfect code. This guy knows the code but not the protocol for light signaling. No matter, I reply 'Thanks, it's good to be home.'"

As we approached the Gate Bridge the boats surrounded us, the fireboats shooting foaming sprays of water in giant arcs. Now the bridge was quite large, just ahead of us, then we were looking up at it. We saw people on the bridge waving and cheering. American flags and welcome home banners hung from the railings. The square-rigger fired her antique brass cannons, the *Lane Victory* answered with her ship's guns and then we shot ours (being berthed close to Hollywood, the *Lane* has learned how to "fire" her guns, movie-style, with butane. While in Long Beach Jack Carraher and Ron Smith took a few lessons). On our after deck Eddy Pubill, Bill Bennett, Pat Burke, Alex Hochstraser and several others spread out our largest American flag.

Eddy Pubill helps with the American flag as we return home to San Francisco. Photo by Bill Bennett.

At the other edge of the flag, left to right, Pat Burke, Carol Fisch and Alex Hochstraser. Photo by Bob Black.

A small part of the fleet that greeted us on our arrival at San Francisco. Photo by Bob Black.

The *Jeremiah O'Brien* passed under the Golden Gate Bridge at four minutes after eight, the first time in five and a half months, fifteen ports and more than 17,000 miles that we were late for anything. Capt. Jahn said, "Give 'em the whistle." I blew three long blasts. A deafening cacophony of toots, honks, blasts, squeals and peeps erupted and thousands of red carnations showered down on us from the bridge. Capt. Jahn turned to me and with misting eyes, said, "Welcome home, Walter." I was too choked up to answer.

We steamed toward the San Francisco waterfront amidst a thousand rainbows of spray from the fireboats' nozzles. The *Jeremiah O'Brien* could hardly be seen, sometimes, through all the spray. Soldiers at the Presidio fired a nineteen gun salute. The *O'Brien* rode slowly past the Embarcadero, the long curving waterfront in the heart of San Francisco that had seen countless thousands of ships in her day. Each pier evoked a different, now-nonexistent, American-flag company — Pacific Far East Lines, States Line, Pope & Talbot, United Fruit Company, States-Marine Lines, Isthmian Steamship Company. A tug from the Suisun Bay Reserve Fleet came alongside with Frank Johnston, Western Region Director of the Maritime Administration on board. Adm. Patterson grabbed his battery-powered bull horn and thanked them for the wonderful job the Reserve Fleet had done in preserving the *O'Brien* during her thirty years on "scrap row," and for all they had contributed to help make the voyage possible.

The *Lane Victory,* a few hundred yards astern, escorted us in, then docked at her berth. We paraded past the World Trade Center in the Ferry Building, then under the Oakland Bay Bridge

In the crow's nest Bruce had a spectacular view, but his lady friend flew the coop. Courtesy Phil Frank and San Francisco Chronicle.

Part of our reception committee, Anna Falche, left, Ernie Murdock and Marci Hooper. Photo courtesy of NLSM.

and turned back in a large arc toward San Francisco. All around, on land and water, were American flags, welcome home banners and cheering, waving people. Traffic on the Bay Bridge slowed to a crawl. Boats of every description swarmed around us, churning the water, remniscent of the Solent so many months earlier. Helicopters flew overhead, their clatter all but drowned by the foghorns, whistles, bells, shouts and cheers. At pier 7, a fishing pier near the Ferry Building, some government workers on their coffee break put up a huge sign that said "MARTY!" in honor of our bosun, Marty Wefald, a computer analyst for the Forestry Service before he retired and ran off to sea again. We approached our berth at pier 27, two tugs alongside, fore and aft. On the pier a large crowd of family members and *Jeremiah O'Brien* volunteers was gathered. A gigantic billboard proclaimed, "WELCOME HOME, *SS JEREMIAH O'BRIEN*."

Bev Masterson: "I was there when she came home. I made arrangements for the volunteers to greet her. There were oodles of people at homecoming, dignitaries, bands, lots of people. All of the families and friends that were there were so happy and

The billboard to beat all billboards.   Photo courtesy of Jean Yates.

thrilled that she did it. It was just like waiting on the dock during the war when the men came home. Many people thought we wouldn't get out of San Francisco. I was thrilled to death that she got over there and back in one piece. She looked great, she was all clean and the crew was happy to get home."

Bruce McMurtry: "I was there when you came in. Being on the pier and people asking if you were really on the crew was thrilling. It was a real proud moment watching her come back in and just a real, real good feeling."

Ron Robson: "I was very, very proud. Proud to be involved, proud and happy for those on the ship. It was encouraging to see the political faces and the high profile people and the local government officials. The real excitement was when it came alongside the pier. It was impressive to see the *Lane,* the helicopters, the armada that escorted the ship in. But it meant more to see the faces of the crew, to see their exhaustion and exuberance."

We slid alongside, astern of the *Lane Victory,* to the sounds of cheers, boat whistles, and two brass bands. Mooring lines went out fore and aft, and soon we were fast. All the crew, except for the engine watch, were up on deck waving to friends and family and tossing down some of the flowers that covered the ship. Up

At Last — Our Ship Comes In

Mike Martino (left) and Jim Anderson waved flags as the O'Brien passed under the Golden Gate Bridge

Rowers tipped their hats to the O'Brien as a tugboat pushed it toward its berth at Pier 27

PHOTOS BY MICHAEL MALONEY/THE CHRONICLE

Crowds, Boats and Parade Hail Historic Voyage

By Carl Nolte
Chronicle Staff Writer

The last seagoing Liberty ship came home to San Francisco yesterday from a remembrance of World War II and received a welcome fit for a war hero.

An armada of boats and ships greeted the Jeremiah O'Brien under the Golden Gate Bridge shortly after daybreak, the crew of the old ship was treated to a parade through the financial district at noon and was feted at a party last night.

It was a bit overwhelming to the crew, and to Captain George

THE TRIP HOME
A VOYAGE ON THE JEREMIAH O'BRIEN

More on the O'Brien
SEE PAGE A15

Jahn, the 79-year-old master of the O'Brien who took the 51 year-old ship and its volunteer crew on a historic five-month

O'BRIEN: Page A13 Col. 3

Admiral Thomas Patterson greeted grandson Wilson Deane, 4

Our home town paper gave us grand coverage on our return, capturing the spirit of the occasion. From the San Francisco Chronicle.

San Francisco Chronicle

THE VOICE OF THE WEST

EDITORIALS

The Jeremiah O'Brien Sails Home in Triumph

THE VOYAGE of the Jeremiah O'Brien is nearly over. The doughty veteran of World War II, heading home from England, Normandy and points in between, is due beneath the Golden Gate Bridge at precisely 8 a.m. today.

If for some inexplicable reason the ship happens to arrive 15 seconds later than that, we can expect Captain George Jahn to apologize and say that he hopes no one was inconvenienced by the delay.

For the fact is, everything has gone with uncanny skill and precision ever since the 51-year-old Liberty ship let go its lines at Pier 70 on April 18 and sailed to France.

The trip was memorable not only for the 50-plus crew members on board the O'Brien but for those who followed the dispatches from Carl Nolte, the Chronicle staff writer who put aside his shipboard chores each day to send out progress reports. Readers shared in the life aboard ship as the O'Brien sailed down the Pacific Coast, through the Panama Canal and across the Caribbean Sea and the North Atlantic.

There will be opportunities today for a closer look at some who made it possible. Crew members will parade this noon through the Financial District and will be honored tonight at a reception on Pier 27.

Whether in the engine room in tropical heat, in the galley, on the bridge or elsewhere, those entrusted with the O'Brien's mission came to appreciate what a remarkable craft was put together in only 56 days. In World War II the O'Brien joined in making the landing in Normandy a triumph in mankind's long struggle against tyranny.

"Simple and totally reliable," said retired Rear Admiral Thomas Patterson, chairman of the O'Brien's Normandy expedition.

And so the O'Brien was, as would be acknowledged even by those who supplied the ship with "Norwegian steam" — sweat labor performed by crewmen who used muscle power to do much of the work managed with the push of a button on more modern vessels.

It was a crew comprised mostly of grandfathers, veterans of the Merchant Marine in the days when German U-boats stalked their prey and sent many of the O'Brien's sister ships to the bottom of the Atlantic. But there were also some comparative youngsters as well, along with the in-betweeners like Nolte, who was too young to take part in World War II but old enough to endure Army service in Korea.

In an earlier era, those who shared the five months and five days the O'Brien was at sea or in friendly ports would have been called "tars." It seems appropriate to lengthen the word slightly and acknowledge, in a world where too much is imperfect, that they may more properly be described as "stars."

'Norwegian steam' — muscle power to do much now performed by the push of a button

We even rated the lead editorial. It was good to be home.

The engine room revolution counter at the end of the voyage.

on the flying bridge I walked over and held out my hand to Capt. Jahn. "We did it," I said as we shook hands. "Yep, we really did," he said warmly.

Then, slowly and deliberately, he said, "Ring her off." I walked over to the telegraph and swung the handle from full ahead to full astern four times, then stopped in the final position. We both watched the engine room answer. The pointer came to rest. "Finished With Engines."

Finished With Engines. Photo by George Bonawit.

EPILOGUE

The voyage was over but the celebrations were just beginning. The bands played, the politicians made speeches, the television and news media recorded the scene. The crew were huddled with families and friends and didn't pay much attention. But the politicians had a fine time.

Then it was time for the ticker tape parade. We climbed into vintage cars — Packards, Fords, Pierce-Arrows, Hupmobiles — military vehicles and motorized cable cars festooned with balloons, signs and red, white and blue bunting. Just as we drove out of the piershed, it began raining. That didn't stop us. We drove through the financial district right at lunch hour when the largest turnout could be expected. Blue and white balloon arches framed the streets. Despite the rain, San Franciscans came out to see the crew from their ship. People held up signs, "Welcome home mateys, Thanks for Liberty," and ran out to shake hands. We were stunned. We knew there would be a celebration, but the scope of our welcome home was beyond anything we might have

This scene was replicated on the dock by dozens of crewmembers eager to see their loved ones after almost 6 months. Courtesy Tom Meyer and San Francisco Chronicle.

imagined. From the cannon salutes to the flower cascade, the victory water parade, the brass bands and now this outpouring of

Tom Patterson and George Jahn lead the crew down the gangway after arrival. Photo courtesy NLSM.

affection, the smiles, cheers, people standing in the rain just to greet us and welcome us home — we were literally stunned. Somehow, even after the enthusiastic receptions we received everywhere on the voyage, we didn't expect it here at home. At first we waved tentatively at the people standing on

One of the vintage autos in our ticker tape parade containing George Fleharty, National Maritime Museum Association president and Robert Blake, chairman of the NLSM Board. Photo courtesy of NLSM.

This Packard holds Capt. Jahn, Dick Brannon and the author. Photo courtesy NLSM.

the sidewalks, and they enthusiastically waved back. Then we waved at the people standing at windows and waving in the upper floors of buildings. Soon street vendors were handing us little flags and we waved those. They cheered and we cheered back. By the time we returned to the piershed we were hoarse and our arms were wet from waving at everyone in the rain. It literally rained on our parade, but the atmosphere and goodwill were pure sunshine. Ironically, the rain stopped at about the same time the parade ended, the sun came out and it was a beautiful day in San Francisco.

Bill Duncan: "The reception we got on arrival, that was unexpected. I didn't think that we would be received like that. Coming home was reminiscent of the way we were received in Europe. There was a tremendous turnout and it was impressive because they stayed out there in the rain. That's the way it was during the war. . ."

Many of the crew got to ride motorized cable cars under arches of blue and white balloons. Photo courtesy NLSM.

This is the Voice of the *Jeremiah O'Brien*

Good afternoon, San Francisco. And thank you for the marvelous reception that you gave us as we arrived home today.

Jeremiah O'Brien and the *Lane Victory* are moored at pier 27 north of the Bay Bridge, and are open to visitors this weekend.

I, Bill Bennett, able bodied seaman, hope that you have enjoyed this message service as much as I have enjoyed sending it. Please continue with your support of this Liberty Ship Memorial. Financial support is much needed as well as hands-on work on the ship. Please call 415-441-3101 and see how you can help.

This will be the final message from *Jeremiah O'Brien* on Normandy '94.

Jeremiah O'Brien — out.

That evening was the infamous champagne reception and party. After all the excitement and burning up of the airwaves about who got how many tickets, the pier was wide open and anyone recognized as a crew member was allowed in with whoever was with them, regardless of how many they were. The piershed was elegantly laid out with formal bars, ice sculptures, tables with white linen tablecloths, silverware and massive buffets, all catered by the Westin St. Francis, one of San Francisco's leading hotels. Swing music was provided by the Rex Allen Big Band and dining and dancing went on until late in the evening. Many of the crew spent the time renewing old acquaintances and polishing their trove of newly-acquired sea stories. The momentous day came to a happy end and we could finally go home with our families.

Home. It seemed almost strange not to have the ship as "home." For five and a half months we ate, slept, worked and lived on the ship. The sound of the engine, the vibration of the

WELCOME HOME

The front of the invitation to the party shows the O'Brien in Rouen.

S. S. JEREMIAH O'BRIEN

Welcome Home
S.S. Jeremiah O'Brien
September 23, 1994

S.S. JEREMIAH O'BRIEN
NORMANDY '94 VOYAGE
WELCOME HOME CELEBRATION
FRIDAY, SEPTEMBER 23, 1994
5:30 to 9:30 p.m.
Pier 27 • **The Embarcadero** • **San Francisco**
Dancing to the Sounds of
THE REX ALLEN BIG BAND

One of the tickets which, thankfully, turned out not to be a problem.

Bruce punctuates the end of the voyage by dotting the final eye.   Courtesy Phil Frank and San Francisco Chronicle.

propeller, rolling from side to side in a seaway, the gurgling of steam pipes in the early morning, the smells from the galley, grey paint, grease, oil, sawdust, slush, beer break, movies in no. 2 'tween deck, movies on no. 2 hatch, the warmth of the engine room on a cold day, the night watch on the flying bridge under a full moon in the tropics — all these would be missed. As happy as we were to be with our loved ones again, we all left a little bit of our hearts on the ship and we would never be quite the same as before.

There were other events later on. The San Francisco 49ers invited us to a game at Candlestick Park as their guests and at halftime we came out on the field to the thunderous standing ovation of a packed stadium. As the band played, a huge American flag was spread on the field. World War II vehicles paraded around the infield and photos of the *O'Brien* flashed on the giant screen. On Veteran's Day, November 11, a volunteer party was held, sponsored by the NLSM. This was the first reunion, with everyone renewing acquaintances from the ship and trading reminiscences and sharing photographs. Each voyage crew member was presented with a special certificate and a medal for being part of the voyage, the gifts of François and Odette Le Pendu. François made the San Francisco to Le Havre trip and thoroughly enjoyed himself, often entertaining the crew with his stories of growing up in France and his impersonations. After he returned home, he fell seriously ill, but he was determined to live long enough to see the whole voyage through. He did, and sat by, smiling, as each member came up and received his memento. It was his final gesture to the ship and crew that he loved so well.

At a gala event, attended by Mayor Jordan and a large crowd of well-wishers, the Maritime

We were featured during the half time ceremony at a 49ers game.

Left to right, Bill Duncan, François Le Pendu and Ed Smith. François was dearly loved by all the crew. Photo courtesy Bev and Wes Masterson.

Administration, in recognition of Capt. Jahn's achievements, promoted him to the rank of Rear Admiral in the United States Maritime Service. And again, crew and volunteers mingled in happy reunion, reminiscing about the trip.

But the voyage really ended the night of the party on the pier. From that point, after being together for almost six months, we each went our separate ways, returning to "real life." The voyage of a lifetime was over but the camaraderie, the visitors, the events, the excitement, the serenity and beauty of the ocean and the ship would live on in our memories.

Anna Falche: "There's nothing in my life that I can say has been more rewarding than going out and raising money for this ship and working for this ship. It was really the crew. Everybody's dedication to this, what it stands for, the historical part, is probably the most important of all. That all of our school kids have the opportunity to see a World War II vessel, to see what we stand for, to educate young people today about the war is very important, and that this ship is maintained in top-notch condition for our youth and our schools."

For the next several months, it was uncanny how much unfinished business there seemed to be on board. On any day, members of the Normandy crew found reasons to "stop by the ship for a few minutes." We wandered around the silent decks where there had been so much activity, saw the dark galley and the empty rooms and the silent engine and a part of each of us wished we were still out there.

Even now, months later, everyone still feels a piece of them will always be on the ship. We all think about it — can never forget it — the trip of a lifetime. Never again will there be an historic occasion to match D-Day + 50 Years, nor a gathering of ships to match the Armada, or the cheering crowds, the tears, the gratitude, the thanks, the feeling of unity among the crew and our old Allies. We were proud of the fact that we sailed a fifty-one-year-old ship, with a volunteer crew whose average age was near seventy, halfway around the world and back. It was thrilling to be part of the return to Normandy and, fifty years after the liberation of Europe, celebrate the triumph of freedom and liberty.

Anna Falche: "This was a commemorative voyage. That's what I liked about the whole drive to get the ship over there. It had nothing to do with fun or fabulous parties. We didn't plan fabulous parties, all that was planned was going to Normandy. It was never done for glory. Nobody spent fifteen years getting the ship ready for glory. It was done for the love of those that were lost, for the history, and the veterans and the merchant marine."

That is really what the voyage was all about. And, through the *Jeremiah O'Brien*, that love and commemoration continue. They always will.

APPENDIX A

THE PROPOSAL

PROPOSED ANNIVERSARY VOYAGE OF THE
S.S. JEREMIAH O'BRIEN

This is a proposal for the 50th anniversary voyage of the *S. S. Jeremiah O'Brien*. This voyage will include the three major ports of San Juan, Puerto Rico; South Portland, Maine; and Omaha Beach, Normandy. These ports represent significant chapters in the long life of the O'Brien and the life of Merchant Seamen. October 12, 1992 will see the arrival of a flotilla of historic vessels in San Juan Harbor to celebrate the quincentennial of Columbus' landing in the Americas — the most significant maritime event of the millennium. The O'Brien has been invited to take part in this momentous occasion. June 19, 1993 marks the 50th anniversary of the O'Brien's launching in the New England Shipyard Corporation's yards at South Portland, Maine. Our presence there is both welcome and desired. June 6, 1994 represents the 50th anniversary of the landing of the Allied Expeditionary Force at

Normandy. The O'Brien made eleven trips across the English Channel in support of the D-Day landings — surely her finest hour. It is altogether fitting and proper that she return to Normandy for the occasion. It is very likely that the O'Brien would be the only ship participating in this anniversary which actually participated in the invasion.

The following is a draft of those things necessary to achieve this goal, given the understanding that more detail will be needed and that more assistance is absolutely necessary.

I. FINANCIAL PLANNING

A. Dept payment to Bethlehem should be raised above the required $12,000.00 per year to at least $18,000.00 per year in order to liquidate this debt prior to departure.
B. Fund raising -
    1. Grants - require research and a good grant writer.
    2. Events - specifically designed to raise money for this purpose.
    3. Corporate Solicitation Committee - should target specific corporations, individuals and societies. Each Committee member should be assigned liaison with such societies, etc. Specific assignments will avoid wasted effort and the embarrassment of duplication.
C. Loan guarantors - bases for such:
    1. Revenue in Port.
    2. Slop Chest.
    3. Cruises in major ports.
    4. May Seaman's Memorial Cruise to be held at whatever port we are visiting in May.
    5. If possible, anticipated costs should be funded before departure.

II. RESTORATION AND REPAIR - PRIORITIES

    1. Deck - wheelhouse and monkey bridge.
       - radar, Loran and radio as necessary.

2. Engine - restoration (cleaning) of reserve feed tanks.
   - installation of marine sanitation device.
   - installation of oil/water separator.
   - schedule preventive maintenance.
   - pull tail-shaft; repair shaft and liner as necessary.
   - repair rudder as necessary.
3. Stwds - reassess 'tween decks storage and refrigeration capacity.

III. CREWING

A. Tenure of volunteers must be respected.
B. Liaison necessary for support from:
   1. Unions
   2. Maritime Academies.
   3. Medical personnel (M.D.s).
C. Expect to need maximum of 100 in crew.
D. Should consider extra housing, canvas racks, cots on deck in warm weather, 'tween decks 3 and 4.
E. Licensing: all officers should be licensed if possible.
F. Training:
   1. Investigate the possibility and ramifications of having the vessel certified as a public nautical school ship.
   2. Engine Department and Deck Department must be familiar with equipment.
   3. Training periods advisable.
   4. "Gold Crew/Blue Crew."
   5. Crew requirements: Southbound crews will require passports, vaccinations, visas. Airline tickets must be arranged for arriving and departing crews. Crew ID cards will be required for Customs on all arriving crewmembers to verify exit point.
G. Incentives
   1. Crew jackets.
   2. Belt buckles.

3. 75-hour guest rule use or lose on this cruise.
4. Reliable organizational link for all crewmembers who stay behind (e.g., newsletter, update meetings, etc.)

IV: PORT DIRECTORS

A. Duties:
1. Schedule visits.
2. Arrange donation of pilots.
3. Arrange donation of berths.
4. Arrange donation of tugs.
5. Arrange for water, oil, electricity, telephones, food delivery and other necessary services.
6. Facilitate crew arrival and departure.
7. Assist with transportation to and from ship.
B. Must provide liaison with:
1. Government offices.
2. Coast Guard.
3. Port Authorities.
4. MarAd representatives.
5. Provide constant liaison with O'Brien's representative in San Francisco.
C. Responsible for scheduling social events and cruises.
D. Arrange for banking at his/her particular port.
E. Should be provided with video-slide show to aid in these duties.

V. GOVERNMENT AGENCY LIAISON - SAN FRANCISCO BASED

A. Need strong liaison with:
1. U.S. Coast Guard (*Note bene*: The Coast Guard Bark "Eagle", a sail training vessel built nine years before the *O'Brien* is currently on a voyage from New London, Connecticut to Sidney, Australia for that country's bicentennial. She will very likely be in Puerto for the quincentennial of Columbus' landing.)

2. U.S. Maritime Administration.

3. U.S. National Park Service.

4. U.S. Navy.

5. Other agencies with jurisdiction over ports with available berths.

VI. CLUBS AND PUBLICITY.

A. Alumni of Maritime Academies.

B. Propeller Clubs.

C. Association of Port Authorities.

D. Association of Port Engineers.

E. Council of Master Mariners.

F. Naval Armed Guard Association.

G. Shipyard Employees Association.

H. Possibilities of broadcasts from vessel in major ports - mostly radio expected due to cost.

I. Maritime Historical Societies in United Kingdom, Puerto Rico, Nova Scotia and Vancouver.

VII. OPERATIONS LEVEL

A. San Francisco based reps - every department must have one.

B. Support from local shipyards.

C. Network to support port visits (material and crew needs must be well defined).

VIII. POSSIBLE CARGOES

A. None - the only cargo we can carry is Slop Chest stores.

IX. FUEL

A. Estimated at $330,000.00.

B. $22.00 per barrel.

X. NATIONAL TRUST

A. Imperative we join as a member organization.
B. Should investigate National Maritime Heritage insurance.

PORTS OF CALL ON 50TH ANNIVERSARY VOYAGE

Los Angeles	Savannah	Long Island Sound [1]
San Diego	Charleston	Newport, R.I.
Corpus Christi	Wilmington, N.C.	Portsmouth, R.I.
Galveston [2]	Morehead City, N.C.	Providence, R.I.
Houston	Norfolk, Va.	Cape Cod [3]
Port Arthur	Newport News	Boston (Charleston Navy Yard)
Beaumont	Richmond	Castine, Maine [4]
Lake Charles	Yorktown	South Portland, Maine
New Orleans	Washington, D.C.	Machias, Maine
Passcagoula	Piney Point	Newfoundland (Bay of Fundy)
Mobile	Annapolis	Nova Scotia
Panama City	Baltimore	United Kingdom
Tampa	Philadelphia	Normandy
Key West	Chester, Pa.	Portland, Oregon
San Juan, P.R.	New York, Fort Schuyler	Vancouver, Wa.
Miami	Hoboken	Seattle, Wa.
Ft. Lauderdale	Albany	Port Canaveral
New London		
Jacksonville		
Brunswick		

[1.] United States Merchant Marine Academy.
[2.] Texas Maritime Academy.
[3.] Massachusetts Maritime Academy.
[4.] Maine Maritime Academy.

On the voyage through the Gulf of Mexico and the East Coast, it would be best to by-pass some ports and visit them on our return. We will visit the Northwest last before returning home. We will gladly consider any port considerations which we have overlooked.

RESPECTFULLY SUBMITTED December 10, 1987:

ERNIE MURDOCK
Chief Engineer

CAPT. GEORGE M. TUTTLE, JR.

MARCI HOOPER
Second Purser/Storekeeper

KEVIN D. KILDUFF
Third Assistant Engineer

SUSAN KRELLE
Engine Department

Appendix B

Normandy Committee
NLSM Board of Directors

The NORMANDY '94 Committee:

Robert Blake, Chairman, NLSM
Gerald Bowen, Military Vehicle Collector's Club
Norman Burke, Corporate Finance
Douglas Dickie, Chief Engineer
William P. Duncan, Crewing Committee
Capt. C. E. Gedney, Industry & Union
Arthur J. Haskell, Budget
Marci Hooper, Business Manager, NLSM
Capt. Walter W. Jaffee, History
Capt. George Jahn, Master
Fred Kaufman, Shipyard Repair
Warren Hopkins, Corporate Liaison
Frank Martell, Insurance Representative
Ernie L. Murdock, Vice Chairman
Ugo Nardi, Treasurer

Cdr. Franklin S. Nelson, Medical
Capt. Carl Otterberg, PR and Scrap Ship Committee
RADM Thomas J. Patterson, Chairman
John Pottinger, Crew Representative
Charles Regal, Publicity Chairman
Capt. Paul Reyff, Washington Representative
Ed Roberts, Military Vehicle Collectors Club
Capt. Hank Simonsen, Legislative Chairman
Wes Staratt, PR Consultant
BGEN Robert Tripp, U.S. Army Liaison
William E. Vaughan, Legal Chairman
L. Col. William Voortmeyer, U.S. Army Liason
Don Watson, Medical Department

The National Liberty Ship Memorial Board of Directors

Dennis Arnett
Charles Audess
Robert Blake
Richard Brannon
Norm Burke
Bill Duncan
Anna Falche
Chick Gedney
Arthur Haskell
Warren Hopkins
Capt. Saunders Jones
Gunnar Lundberg
Ernie Murdock
RADM T. J. Patterson
Capt. H. Simonsen
Don Watson
William Vaughan, of counsel
Capt. Francis X. Johnston, Maritime Administration,
    ex officio.

APPENDIX C

BUDGET

	Pre-Sail 1/1/93-4/3/94	All Operations 4/4-10/9/94	Program 1/1/93-10/9/94
Administration			
Staff & Admin	$33,000	$67,000	$100,000
Temp. Employee	$6,400	$17,600	$24,000
Office Supplies	$3,000	$7,000	$10,000
Travel Expenses	$15,000	$15,000	$30,000
Subtotal	**$57,400**	**$106,600**	**$164,000**
SHIP PREPARATION			
#Ship Repair (HR58)	$200,000		$200,000
#Drydock (HR58)	$500,000		$500,000
USCG-ABS	$200,000		$200,000
*Strip Ship	$10,000		$10,000
*Ballast	$20,000		$20,000
*Inclining	$2,000		$2,000
Subtotal	**$932,000**		**$932,000**

OUTFIT

#Liferafts	$52,000		$52,000
*Cargo Handling Gear	$20,000		$20,000
#Emergency Suits	$104,000		$104,000
#Linen Supplies	$28,000		$28,000
#Mattresses	$6,000		$6,000
#Crockery & Glassware	$2,500		$2,500
Subtotal	**$212,500**		**$212,500**

Insurance Premiums	$50,000		$50,000

CONSUMABLES

*Food	$97,240		$97,240
*Deck & Eng. Supplies	$50,000		$50,000
#Medical Supplies	$10,000		$10,000
Subtotal	**$157,240**		**$157,240**

VESSEL OPERATIONS

Voyage Repairs		$50,000	$50,000
*Tug Assists (50%)		$42,000	$42,000
Canal Tolls		$31,900	$31,900
*Pilotage		$20,000	$20,000
*Fuel Oil		$482,130	$482,130
*Lube Oil		$25,000	$25,000
Subtotal		**$651,030**	**$651,030**

Crew (52 persons)			
Travel		$100,000	$100,000
Uniforms	$10,000		$10,000
Subtotal	**$10,000**	**$100,000**	**$110,000**

ENTERTAINMENT & GIFTS		$50,000	$50,000
CONTINGENCY (15%)	$189,285	$159,730	$349,015

TOTAL	$1,451,185	$1,224,600	$2,675,785

*In Kind   # In Hand

As of 1/9/94

In Kind	$768,370.00
In Hand	$902,500.00

Funding Required	$1,004,915.00

APPENDIX D

MERCHANT MARINE MEMORIAL ENHANCEMENT ACT OF 1993

103D CONGRESS
1ST SESSION

H. R. 58

To authorize the Secretary of Transportation to convey vessels in the National Defense Reserve Fleet to certain nonprofit organizations.

IN THE HOUSE OF REPRESENTATIVES

JANUARY 5, 1993

Mrs. BENTLEY introduced the following bill; which was referred to the Committee on Merchant Marine and Fisheries

---

A BILL

To authorize the Secretary of Transportation to convey vessels in the National Defense Reserve Fleet to certain nonprofit organizations.

1 *Be it enacted by the Senate and House of Representa-*
2 *tives of the United States of America in Congress assembled,*
3 **SECTION 1. SHORT TITLE.**
4   This Act may be cited as the "Merchant Marine
5 Memorial Enhancement Act of 1993".
6 **SEC. 2. CONVEYANCE VESSELS.**
7   (a) AUTHORITY TO CONVEY.—The Secretary of
8 Transportation may convey without consideration all
9 right, title, and interest of the United States in 2 vessels
10 described in subsection (b) to any nonprofit organization

534

2

1 which operates and maintains a Liberty Ship or Victory

2 Ship as a memorial to merchant mariners.

3   (b) VESSELS DESCRIBED.—Vessels which may be

4 conveyed under subsection (a) are vessels which—

5   (1) are in the National Defense Reserve Fleet

6   on the date of the enactment of this Act;

7   (2) are not less than 10,000 displacement tons;

8   (3) have no usefulness to the Government; and

9   (4) are scheduled to be scrapped.

10   (c) CONDITIONS OF CONVEYANCE.—As a condition of

11 conveying any vessel to an organization under subsection

12 (a), the Secretary shall require that before the date of the

13 conveyance the organization enter into an agreement

14 under which the organization shall—

15   (1) sell the vessel for scrap purposes;

16   (2) use the proceeds of that scrapping for the

17   purpose of refurbishing and making seaworthy a

18   Liberty Ship or Victory Ship which the organization

19   maintains as a memorial to merchant mariners, to

20   enable the ship to participate in 1994 in commemo-

21   rative activities in conjunction with the 50th anni-

22   versary of the Normandy invasion; and

23   (3) return to the United States any proceeds of

24   scrapping carried out pursuant to paragraph (1)

3

1   which are not used in accordance with paragraph

2   (2).

3   (d) DEPOSIT OF AMOUNTS RETURNED.—Amounts

4   returned to the United States pursuant to subsection

5   (c)(3) shall be deposited in the Vessel Operations Revolv-

6   ing Fund created by the Act of June 2, 1951 (65 Stat.

7   59; 46 App. U.S.C. 1241a).

8   (e) DELIVERY OF VESSELS.—The Secretary shall de-

9   liver each vessel conveyed under this section—

10   (1) at the place where the vessel is located on

11   the date of the approval of the conveyance by the

12   Secretary;

13   (2) in its condition on that date; and

14   (3) without cost to the Government.

15   (f) EXPIRATION OF AUTHORITY TO CONVEY.—The

16   authority of the Secretary under this section to convey ves-

17   sels shall expire on the date that is 2 years after the date

18   of the enactment of this Act.

O

APPENDIX E

SEAMEN'S DUTIES

Duties of the sailors as prepared by Bosun Rich Reed before the voyage:

SEA WATCHES

This is the way three man watches were stood on the *Jeremiah O'Brien* fifty years ago and the same way watches are stood to-day!!

Three watches 12x4 4x8 8x12 three men to a watch 4 hours on 8 off.

Each watch has certain duties, the 4x8 is responsible for bridge sanitary, and the 8x12 is responsible for sailors sanitary. During the day watches sailors on watch, but not on the wheel or lookout will work on deck with the Bos'n.

Lookout and standby are usually just used on night watches, however, lookout may be called by the Captain or Mate on watch at any time. Deck work on watch will be Monday thru Friday, on weekends the watch will lay below.

Watch standers will rotate duties during the watch spending approximately 1 hour and 20 minutes at each duty. Rotation will be wheel watch, lookout, and standby.

12x4 Watch

	1st Wheel	1st Lookout	1st Standby
0001	rel. 8x12	rel 8x12	rel. 8x12
0100			rel. lookout
0120	to stby	rel. wheel	
0220	rel. lookout		
0240		to stby	rel. wheel
0330		call 4x8	
		rel. lookout	

AFTERNOON WATCH -- Called at 1120 hrs. Eat lunch, and then at 1200 the first wheel goes to the bridge, and the other two watchstanders turn to on deck for work as per the Bos'ns instructions.

2nd wheel K.O. at 1300 and to wheel at 1320
3rd wheel K.O. at 1420 and to wheel at 1440
1st wheel K.O. at 1430 to make coffee for afternoon coffeetime.
Call 4x8 watch at 1530.

12x4 does not have sanitary assignments. Mandatory deck work on watch Monday thru Friday, lay below on weekends.

Report fire watch to Mate when relieving the wheel on A.M. watch.

4x8 WATCH
SUNRISE AND SUNSET WATCH

	1st wheel	1st lookout	1st standby
0400	rel 12x4	rel. 12x4	rel. 12x4
0500			rel. lookout
0520	to stby	rel. wheel	
0620	rel. lookout		
0640		to stby	rel. wheel
0720		Call 8x12, Bos'n and Daymen.	

Lookout should be K.O. at daybreak. Last standby and lookout will do bridge sanitary. This will include washdown of flying bridge, chart room, and wheel house. Sweep, swab, dump garbage, dust, polish brass, wash windows, and making sure you don't wake the Captain are all responsibilities of the 4x8.

Afternoon watch, lookout starts at sunset or when Mate calls. Deck work from 1600 to 1630 by the two sailors not on the wheel. 2nd wheel should eat supper early and relieve his partner early so that he has time to order and eat. Call 8x12 watch at 1930 hrs.

8x12 WATCH

0800 hrs. 1st wheel to bridge and relieve 4x8 helmsman. The other two sailors will begin sanitary work at 0800. Sanitary consists of cleaning the deck department common areas and crew rooms. Deck heads will be swept, sanitized, and swabbed, and garbage emptied. Commodes and sinks will be cleaned and scoured, and mirrors will be wiped clean. The Bos'n and Carp. room will be swept and swabbed and garbage emptied. If the 4x8 and 8x12 are below then you will not be responsible for their rooms. The passage way deck in front of the crew rooms will also be swept and swabbed.

0920 hrs 2nd wheel to bridge. 1st wheel on deck to work for Bos'n.

0940 hrs 3rd wheel makes coffee for gang.

1020 hrs 3rd wheel secures sanitary gear and relieves wheel at 1040. 2nd wheel turns to on deck.

1120 hrs call 12x4 watch

	1st wheel	1st lookout	1st stby
2000	rel. 4x8	rel. 4x8	rel. 4x8
2100			rel. lookout
2120	to stby.	rel. wheel	
2220	rel. lookout		
2240		to stby.	rel. wheel
2330		call 12x4	
		rel. lookout	

Report fire check to mate when relieving wheel.

Note: Normally 8x12 Ordinary Seaman does all the sanitary work, and the A.B.'s work on deck, when not steering. One A.B. may be called off sanitary in the morning if needed on deck.

LOOKOUT

FROM SUNSET TO SUNRISE, OR WHEN CALLED BY THE CAPTAIN OR MATE. THIS MAY BE IN A RESTRICTED VISIBILITY SITUATION, OR IN A HEAVY VESSEL TRAFFIC SITUATION.

REPORT EVERYTHING !!!!! EVEN IF YOU ARE NOT SURE OF A LIGHT REPORT ANYTHING YOU THINK YOU SEE.

ALL TARGETS OR NAV. AIDS ARE REPORTED IN POINTS RELATIVE TO THE DIRECTION OF OUR VESSEL. 11 DEGREES TO A POINT 32 POINTS ON THE COMPASS.

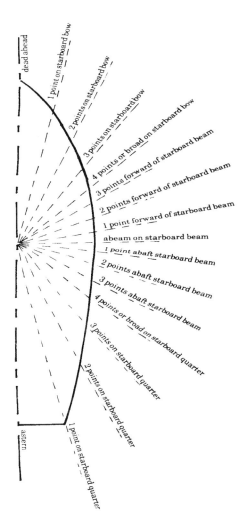

SLOPS AND DITTYBAGS

Work clothes — recommend all cotton, this will be a warm weather trip. A lot of poly and synthetic materials don't breathe, creating more perspiration and not letting you cool off. Bring good lookout clothing warm socks and parka and ear covers. You may only need this gear for a few weeks, but it's worth having. Insulated coveralls are good either Carhards or Sears are good brands. Rain gear will not need to be a real heavy gauge since we will not be in the northern latitudes. Helly Hansen in the best brand for work, but it's expensive. Rainboots from West Marine are great because they have a real good arch support. Work boots and shoes, wear what's strong and comfortable. Really recommend shoe inserts or pads. You will be spending months walking on unforgiving steel decks, not to mention the time standing on wheel watches and lookout.

Bring a suit bag to keep your going ashore clothes in. Stash your clothes in it and keep it hanging in your locker. The bag will protect your clothes from the rest of your work clothes and the salt air. Bring plastic hangers, the cheap ones you find in Longs or Payless. Plastic hangers won't scrape on the metal rung in the locker when the ship rolls, and they won't corrode like metal and get rust on your clothes. X-tra washcloths or small towels are good to line the shelves in your locker. They will keep things from shifting around when the ship moves.

Bring flashlights, a 2 or 3 cell for using on deck, and a small pocket light to have with you on the bridge. Bring lots of batteries.

Bring a small backpack or a fannypack. These are great for taking ashore if you plan to go shopping or smuggle gold back home.

Bring a laundry bag or an old pillow case to use as one. Stow your dirty stuff in the bag and you can carry the whole thing to the laundry room.

Writing paper, pens, calculator (to figure out your overtime and payoff). Don't worry about stamps, they won't do you any good in a foreign country. If you bring a walkman, look into buying external speakers that fit into the earphone jack.

DO'S AND DON'TS

Many people live in a small area aboard ship, so personal adjustments are necessary to maintain sanitary conditions and livability.

"What will you have?" the messman asked
as he stood there, picking his nose.
"Give me hardboiled eggs, you son of a bitch,
You can't get your finger in those."

Don't wear "go aheads" or sandals in the messroom
Don't wear underwear t-shirts or tank tops in the messroom.
Don't wear your hat in the messroom.
Don't sit on another person's bunk unless given permission.
Don't bring your work in your foc'sle no tools, oily rags, paint brushes or work projects. Your foc'sle is another man's home.
Don't whistle on the ship.

Do call the watch on time.
Do keep quiet in the passageways at all times.
Do respect the space of your foc'sle partner.
Do relieve your partner on time.
Do keep your foc'sle clean and bunk made up.

APPENDIX F

NORMANDY '94 SPONSORS

CORPORATE SPONSORS

Acme Toilets
Administrateur En Ehet Des
    Affaires Maritimes Quartier De
    Rouen
Affaires Maritimes
After The Battle
Airtouch Communications
Alden Electronics
American Bureau of Shipping
    Robert Tozier
American Merchant Marine
    Veterans
        John M. Lockhart
        Richard D. Mallett
American President Companies
    American President Lines
Aqua Treat Chemicals, Inc.
    Edwin M. King

Ass. Maquettistes Et Modelistes Du
    Havre
Associated British Ports
    Southampton
Association Francaise Des
    Capitaines De Navires
Association of Maryland Pilots
    Capt. Avis T. Bailey
Baltic Exchange
Bank of America
Bank of the West
Bartenders Unlimited
Bass Tickets
Bay and Delta Towing
    Capt. Jack Going
    Capt. Steve Ware
Benicia Historical Society
Cable Car Charters
California Parking
Caterpillar Engine Division
    Tom Lawrence, President

Chambre De Commerce Et
  D'Industrie De Cherbourg-
  Cotentin
Champion
Chatham Maritime
  English Estates Medway
Chef D'Etat Major De La Marine
Chevron Shipping Co.
  Thomas Moore, President
  Dennis Arnett
City and County of San Francisco
  Board of Permit Appeals
    Ike Felzer
  Office of Protocol
    Sherri Ferris, Deputy Chief
      of Protocol
  Port of San Francisco
  San Francisco Fire Dept.
  San Francisco Traffic Dept.
The City Club
Cliff's Variety Store
Coast Marine & Industrial Supply
Cogema
Compagnie Generale Maritime Le
  Havre
Communaute Urbauine De
  Cherbourg
Conseil General (Caen)
Conseil General (Saint-Lô)
Conseil Regional De Haute
  Normandie (Rouen)
Conseil General De La Seine-
  Maritime (Le Havre)
Conseil General De La Seine-
  Maritime (Rouen)
C.P.P.M.A.
Creative Automotive Consultants
Crowley Maritime Corporation
Crowley Maritime Services
DBSA (Le Havre)
Direction Interregionale Des
  Douanes De Rouen
Director Des Ports Et De La
  Navigation Maritimes
Dirigeants Commerciaux de France

Discount Fabrics
Domaine Chandon
Douanes (Cherbourg)
Double T
Dutra Dredging
  Bill Dutra
  Robert Johnston
Egghead Software
  Ellen Wallis
Entertainment Line
Etretat
Event Security
Fletcher Challenge Paper Company
Fondation Nationale (Paris)
Ford (Cherbourg)
Forest Terminals Corporation
Foster Poultry Farms
  Shirley Keyser
Foster Wheeler Corporation
  Energy Equipment Group
    Robert A. Whittaker
Franciscan Winery
General Engineering and Machine
  Works
The Glencannon Press
  R. B. Rose, Publisher
Green Glenn
Green Valley
Groupement European De
  Professionnels Du Marketing
The Harbor of Portland
  Board of Harbor Commissioners
    Alfred W. Trefry III,
      Harbor Master
Hansen Machine Works
  Mr. & Mrs. Duke McMillan
HMS Belfast
Homer J. Olson, Inc., Contractors
Huttons International Ltd.
  E. J. Newman, Southampton
IBM Almaden Research Center
  Jim Cannon
  Dan Sainsbury
IMPACT Lighting
Imprinerie Hebert

Independence Petroleum
  Anna Falche, President
Inter. Regional Des Affaires
  Maritimes Nord-Normandie
International Longshoremen and
  Warehousemen's Union
    George Romero
International Organization of
  Masters, Mates & Pilots
    Capt. Timothy A. Brown,
        International Pres.
    Capt. Paul Nielsen
International Stationary Steam
  Engine Society
    Paul R. Stephens, Chmn.
Jacques Pierot Jr. & Sons, Inc.
  Sven Juul
  Bill Mollard
Jacobson Transfer
Jess Jones Farms
  Jess Jones
John Plumer & Partners Maritime
  Ltd.
    Colin Akers
    John Drury
    Jeremy Heyhoe
KABL 960 AM
Kiwanis
  Cherbourg
KFS World Communications
  Rod Deakin
  Timothy S. Gorman
  Ken Jones
  Walter Kane
  Gary North
  Lou Tozzi
L'Armada De La Liberté
  Patrick Herr, Pres.
Le Pilotage Hauturier
  Capt. Charles Gallerne
Levi Strauss
The Lions Club
  Cherbourg
Lloyds Register
M. Rosenblatt & Son, Inc.

Maersk Stevedoring Company
  Michael Pourgaulg, Director
  Cletis Raiford
Maire De Rouen
Maire D'Isneauville
Maire Du Cherbourg
Maire Du Havre
Marine Fireman's Union
  Henry Disley
Marine Nationale
Marine Terminals Corporation
The Maritime Royal Artillery
Matson Navigation Co.
  C. Bradley Molholland
McAllister Towing Company
McCune Audio/Visual/Video
MEBA/NMU District #1
  Rusty De Roussett
  Frank Leahy
Michael Emery Photography
Michael Hensley Party Rents
Ministere De L'Equipement, Des
  Transports Et Du Tourisme
Montague Spragens Lithographers
  Richard S. Tough, President
Moran Towing Corporation
MTMC Oakland, CA
  Col. Douglas Foye, USA.
  Cdr. Donald T. McBurney, USN
  Charles Tillotson
National Archives, Pacific Region
  Dan Neiland
  Neil Thomsen
National Cargo Bureau
  Capt. Fraser Sammis
National Maritime Historical
  Society
    Peter Stanford
National Maritime Museum Assn.
  Daria Booth
  Russ Booth
  Kathy Lohan
  Jana Sheldon
Navy League

Nestle Beverage Company
  Virginia S. Banals
North Peninsula Wind & Percussion
  Ensemble
Normandy American Cemetery
Norton, Lilly & Co., Inc., Steam-
  ship Agents
    John Griffith, CEO
    Michael A. Ross, President,
      Panama
Norway House, Merchant Marine
  Seamen's Service
    John Pederson
Ormacom
Otis Spunkmeyer, Inc.
  Kenneth Rawlins, President
P & O Containers
  Southampton
P & O Lines
P & O Orient Lines
Pacific Gas and Electric Company
Pacific International Rice Mills,
  Inc.
    Bruce Rolen
Pacific Merchant Ship Association
Pacific Telesis
Panama Canal Commission.
  Gilberto Guardia, Administrator.
  Ray Laverty
  Capt. Ove V. Hultin, Pilot
Pastorino Farms
Patrick Media Group
The PBN Company
Peachy's Puffs
Pernod S.A.
Pier 23 Cafe
Pier 39
Pilotage De La Seine
Pilots Greenhithe
  Capt. C. B. Lukehurst
Polaroid Corporation
  Lize Greene
Port Autonome De Rouen
Port Autonome Du Havre
Port De Cherbourg

Port of London Authority
Portland Docking Masters, Inc.
  Capt. Jim Mooney
  Capt. Howard Wentworth
Portland Pilots, Inc.
  Capt. Granville Smith, President
Prefecture De La Manche (Saint-
  Lô)
Prefecture Maritime (Cherbourg)
Pretet De Region De Haute
  Normandie Pretecture (Rouen)
Pride of Baltimore
  Capt. Robert C. Glover III
R. Kassman Piano
Raytheon
  Graham & James
Redmond O'Colonies (Town Crier)
Regional Des Douanes Du Havre
The Rex Allen Big Band
Rotary Cherbourg
Rotary Club Val De Saire
Rough and Ready Island
  Richard Brocchini
  Tom Salmon
Royal Naval Association
  Atlasta Hall
Royal Navy
  London
  Portsmouth
Sailor's Union of the Pacific
  Gunnar Lundeberg, President
San Diego Bay Pilots Association
  Capt. Eric Ireland
San Francisco Chronicle
San Francisco Dry Dock
  Paul Gates
  Carl Hanson
San Francisco Towers
San Pellegrino
Seafarer's International Union
  George McCartney
Shell Oil Company
  Shell Refinery, Martinez
    Bob Andrews
Societe Des Regates Du Havre

Societe D'Importation Et De
Commission
Societe Thann Et Mulhouse
Solaehar
Sous-Prefecture (Cherbourg)
Sous Pretet, Sous Pretecture (le
Havre)
South End Rowing Club
Stan Flowers Co., Inc.
 Stan Flowers
State of Maine
 House of Representatives
  Herbert Adams
 Maine Maritime Academy
  T. S. State of Maine
  Capt. Jerry Cummings
SuperShuttle
Tarke Warehouse
 Tim Stine
Team One Construction
Television France 1
Thorpe Marine Services
 R. James Thorpe, President
3M Photo Color Systems Division
 Bob Chapman
Transports Mertz
Tosco Refinery
U. S. Maritime Administration
 Capt. Frank Johnston,
  Western Regional Director
United States Merchant Marine
 Academy Alumni Association
  San Francisco Bay Chapter
United States Navy
 Mare Island Naval Shipyard
  John Logue
  Al Norton
  James Rookwood
 Naval Air Station Alameda
  CWO David Cradit
 Naval Station, Treasure Island
  RADM Ernest Tadeschi
 USS Samuel Gompers
  Captain Charles Gervin
  BTR 2 Hitchcock

  BT 2 James Wetherington
  BT John Cilatson
  Chief Richard Kappler
  M Mate Frank Spritzer
  M Chief Wink Crag
  M Chief Steve Kealey
  M Chief George Smith
  Capt. Thomas Rose, marine
  pilot
  Capt. Terry Ruff, marine pilot
  Capt. Edward F. Johnston
U. S. Merchant Marine Veterans
 World War II
  Joe Vernick, President
  John Smith, Vice-President
  Jerry Werner, 2nd V.P.
Ville De Puteaux
Waterfront Transportation Project
Westar Marine Services
 Mary McMillan
 Wendy Morrow
Western Scenic Studios
The Westin St. Francis
Wilmes Co.
Worms Services Maritimes
 Pascal Doucet

INDIVIDUAL SPONSORS

Tony Abela
Theresa Abela
Walter Abernathy
Lawrence Adams
David Adkins
Ralph Ahlgren
Tom Alexander
Langdon Alvord
Bob Anderson
Gene Anderson
Nils Anderson
Vivienne Antal
Rudy Arellano
David Aris
Sam Armijo
Charles Audet

Myra Baillie
Captain William Barton
Laure Beauvallet
Ward Beckwith
Lucien Bedu
Bill Bennett
Congresswoman Helen Delich
    Bentley
            David Richardson
Kathleen Berge
Barry Bertillion
Rita Bertillion
Peter Blake
Robert E. Blake, Jr.
Ed Blanchette
Betty Borowiec
John Borowiec
Dennis Bouey
Ken Bower
Richard Brannon
Larry Brown
Jim Buehler
David Bulkley
Patrick Burke
Norman Burke
Bob Burnett
Del Campbell
Terrance Carraher
John Carraher
John Carroll
Andy Casper
Stella Chin
Bill Cilia
Dean Clements
Monica Conrady
Raymond Conrady
Pierre Cole
Charles P. Comes
Jim Conwell
Nancy Crowe
Thomas Crowley, Jr.
Richard Currie
Darwin Curtis
Bill Cuzzens
Robert Davidson

Congressman Ron Dellums
Jeff Detels
Walter Deuring
Fred Dewing
Paul Dempster
Doug Dickie
Gene DiMartini
Mitzi Doninelli
Janet Doyle
Dick Dunbar
Dottie Duncan
William Duncan
William Fairfield
Anna Falche
Jimmie Farras
Sherri Ferris
Bill Fenton
Tom Field
Patrick Figari
John D. Fitzgerald
Mr. & Mrs. Daniel Flambard
George C. Fleharty
Jerry Friedrich
Chick Gedney
Jim Gillis
Bob Gisslow
Erik Gize
Brian Goldman
Mr. & Mrs. Richard N. Goldman
Larry Gomes
Lyle Guipre
Bruce Handler
Gladys Hansen
William J. Harris, Sr.
Jim Hart
Arthur Haskell
Sheldon Hawk
Erica Henri
M. L. Henry
Paul Higgins
Richard Hill
Bob Hiller
George Hobbs
Neil Holmgren
Harold Hoogasian

Clifford Hook
Jean Hook
Marci Hooper
Warren Hopkins
Susan Horsfall
Jane and Stewart Hume
William Hussell
Bob Imbeau
Cora Imbeau
Beverly Immendorf
Jack Immendorf
George B. Immisch
Daniel Jackson
Bob Jacobson
Alberta Jacobson
Walter Jaffee
George Jahn
David Jamison
P.J. Jamison
George Jasen
Rudy Jasen
Chuck Jennings
Buzz Jones
Frank X. Johnston
Steven Jellinek
Arlene Jellinek
Sanders A. Jones
Myriam Jouanny
Kim Kaddas
Ephiram Kaufmann
Roy Keisling
Kevin Kilduff
Paul Fritz Koenig
Charles Koffler
Bill Kramer
Bill Krasnosky
Carl Kreidler
William Lally
Walter Lapsley
Jo Lawrence
Karine Le Mauff
Francois Le Pendu
Mr. Lerouvillois
Ruth Levy
Herb Lewis

Ed Lingenfield
Robert Lion
Ed Lodigiani
Jack Loomis
Ruth Malone
Ed Mandin
Al Martino
Bev Masterson
Wes Masterson
Bill Mayer
Robert McEntee
Vincent McGarry
Bill McGee
Patrick McGinn
Thomas McKenzie
Bruce McMurtry
Mr. & Mrs. Bernard Sarandas
    Metharam
David Meyer
Daryl Meyer
Joe Milcic
Hans Miller
Jim Miller
Herb Millspaugh
Charles Mitchell
Gene Mooney
Charles Mooney
J. E. Moore
Kay Morgan
Russ Mosholder
David Mosholder
David Mowat
Ernie Murdock
Jim Murray
Ken Murray
Adele Murray
Ugo Nardi
Bob Nelson
Frank Nelson
Alice Neverman
Alex Newbold
Robert Neilsen
Carmela Nilan
Cliff Nilan
Carl Nolte

William Nusser
Kerry O'Brien
Charles O'Neill-Jones
Francis J. O'Neill
Stephen Olijaynyk
Bill Oliveri
Carl Otterberg
Nell Otterberg
Ray Palacin
Tim Palange
Maud Paléologue
Ann Patterson
Thomas Patterson
Philip Patton
John Paul
Mr. & Mrs. Lionel Pelfresne
Patricia Pelfresne
JaMel Perkins
Otis Phelps
Mr. & Mrs. Herbert Pierre
Julius Pleshakov
Howard Polansky
John Pottinger
Nancy Powers
Michael Pritchard
Ray Radovich
Charles Rapp
Tony Rapp
David Rarvin
Rich Reed
Charley Regal
Andrew Remus
Paul Reyff
John Rivers
Ed Roberts
Ron Robson
Clarence Rocha
Robert Rock
Dennis Rodd
John Rodgers
Bruce Rolen
Ramon Romero
Nick Rommel
Bill Rowlands
Adrian Ruddell

Lawrence Reugg
Drew Sallee
Byron Samuel
Glen Sanders
Taryn Sapienza
Bill Sawyer
Norman Schoenstein
Arnold Sears
Elliott Secondari
Richard Secondari
Michael Shane
Hank Simonsen
Phil Sinnott
Sam Skelly
Valerie Skordin
Bill Smith
Ed Smith
Ronald Smith
Michael Smith
Otto Sommerauer
Jeff Speight
William V. Spiker
Christian Stark
Mary Steinberg
Ralph Stevens
Alma Stout
Ed Sturken
Lou Switz
Art Taber
Mary Louise Taber
Adm. & Mrs. Ernest Tedeschi
Jim Thompson
Michael Thurman
Charles Todd
Harvey Tollesen
Muriel Tolliday
Miller Tomback
Laura Tordsen
Ernie Tordsen
Moe Torres
Ed Tostanoski
Michael Tran
Bob Tripp
Bill Vaughan
Sondra Vaughan

Joe Verhalen
Ed Von der Porten
Saryl Von der Porten
Bill Voortmeyer
Jim Wade
Jim Walsh
Frederick Warhanek
Terence Watson
Janet Watson
Don Watson
Martin Wefald
Rich Westerfield
Walt Willard
Greg Williams
Bill Williams
Irene Williams
Bill Wilson
Homer Winter
Sam Wood
Mary Woodward
Jean Yates
Elliott Yellin
Marion Young

Appendix G

The Normandy Voyage Crew

Name	Position	Voyage Leg
Ahlgren, Ralph	Oiler	Le Havre-San Francisco
Alexander, Tom	Oiler	Panama-London
Anderson, Gene	Oiler	San Francisco- Le Havre
Anderson, Nils	Wiper	Rouen-San Francisco
Arellano, Rudolph	Messman	San Francisco - London
Aris, David	FWT	Le Havre-San Francisco
Bara, Stanley	3rd Asst. Eng.	Jacksonville-San Francisco
Beckwith, Susannah	Storekeeper	Cherbourg-Rouen
Bennett, William	AB	ALL
Black, Robert	Deck Utility/OS	Rouen-San Francisco
Borowiec, John	Messman	Portland-Jacksonville
Bosch, Maria	Wiper	London-Le Havre
Brannon, Richard	Chief Engineer	ALL
Burke, Norman	Oiler	San Francisco-Panama
Burke, Patrick	Deck Utility	Jacksonville-San Francisco
Burnett, Robert	Carpenter	ALL
Callahan, Joseph	Deck Utility	San Francisco-Portsmouth
Cannady, William	Oiler	Le Havre-Baltimore
Caron, Jean-Paul	Wiper	Panama-San Francisco
Carraher, John	Messman/Gunner	ALL

Casaletto, Louis	Messman	Rouen-San Francisco
Concannon, William	Oiler	San Francisco-Portsmouth
Conrady, Monica	Storekeeper	Portsmouth-Le Havre
Conrady, Raymond	Second Mate	ALL
Conwell, James	AB	San Francisco-Le Havre
Crocker, Robert	Messman	Portland-Jacksonville
Cumming, John	Engine Utility	Jacksonville-San Francisco
Currie, Richard	FWT	San Francisco-London, Baltimore-San Francisco
Dewing, Fred	2nd Asst. Eng.	Portsmouth-London
Dickerson, William	Third Mate	Portsmouth-London
Dow, Gary	Engine Utility	Portland-Baltimore
Duncan, William	Deck Engineer 3rd Asst. Eng.	ALL
Duncan, Dorothea	Storekeeper/ Messman	Portsmouth-London Portland-San Francisco
Emery, Michael	OS	San Francisco-Cherbourg
Fairfield, William	AB	Le Havre-San Francisco
Farras, James	Second Cook	ALL
Fenton, William	OS	Jacksonville-San Francisco
Fitzgerald, John	AB	Jacksonville-San Francisco
Franklin, Wallace	3rd Asst. Eng.	Kings Point-Baltimore
Geronimo, Lou	Third Mate	Le Havre-Portland
Gillis, James	3rd Asst. Eng. 2nd Asst. Eng.	San Francisco-Panama Panama-Portsmouth
Gisslow, Robert	Radio Operator	ALL
Goldman, Brian	FWT	Rouen-San Francisco
Goldwaithe, Lawrence	Oiler	Le Havre-Baltimore
Gregory, Alvin	Storekeeper	Cherbourg-Rouen
Haslam, Kenneth	Doctor	ALL
Hill, Richard	Oiler	San Francisco-Le Havre Baltimore-San Francisco
Hobbs, George	2nd Asst. Eng.	London-Le Havre
Hochstraser, Alex	FWT	ALL
Hook, Clifford	OS./AB	Le Havre-San Francisco
Hooper, Marci	Business Manager	Portsmouth-Cherbourg
Jaffee, Walter	Chief Mate	ALL
Jahn, George	Master	ALL
Jellinek, Arlene	Storekeeper	Cherbourg-Le Havre
Jellinek, Steve	FWT	London-Le Havre
Jennings, Charles	Messman	London-Portland
Keinanen, Sven	Third Mate	London-Le Havre
Kaplan, Maxine	Storekeeper	Portland-Jacksonville Long Beach-San Francisco
Kilduff, Kevin	2nd Asst. Eng.	Le Havre-San Francisco

Kinsella, Tim	Asst. Radio Op.	Southampton-Le Havre
Kreidler, Carl	Gunner	San Francisco-Le Havre
Lawrence, Jo	Storekeeper	Portsmouth-London
Le Pendu, François	Engine Utility	San Francisco-Le Havre
Linderman, John	AB	Rouen-Portland
Lingenfield, Edgar	FWT	ALL
Londos, Erika	Storekeeper	Portsmouth-London
Lyse, Peter	Third Mate	San Francisco-Portsmouth
Martino, Allen	Chief Cook	ALL
Masterson, Wes	AB	London-Le Havre
Maus, William	3rd Asst. Eng.	Panama-Le Havre
McCafferty, Patrick	Messman/Utility	ALL
McMurtry, Bruce	OS	San Francisco-Portsmouth
Miller, Hans	3rd Asst. Eng.	San Francisco-Panama
Miller, James	AB	ALL
Mosholder, Russell	Chief Steward	ALL
Mooney, Charlie	Wiper	London-Le Havre
Mooney, George	Oiler	London-Le Havre
Noiseux, Robert	FWT	San Francisco-London
Nolte, Carl	Deck Utility/OS	San Francisco-London
		Panama-San Francisco
Otterberg, Carl	Staff Captain	European ports
Otterberg, Nell	Storekeeper	European ports
Palange, Tim	2nd Asst. Eng.	ALL
	1st Asst. Eng.	
Patterson, Ann	Storekeeper	Portsmouth-Le Havre
Patterson, Thomas J.	Commodore	ALL
Phelps, Otis	Third Mate	Portland-San Francisco
Pubill, Eduardo	Third Cook	ALL
Radovich, Raymond	OS	London-Le Havre
Rapp, Tony	Deck Utility	Jacksonville-San Francisco
Reed, Richard	Boatswain	San Francisco-Le Havre
Reidy, Edward	Wiper	Le Havre-Panama
Rivers, John	Storekeeper	Portsmouth-London
Robson, Ron	Store Manager	Portsmouth-Le Havre
Robson, Ruth	Storekeeper/	Portsmouth-San Francisco
	Messman	
Rodd, Denis	Oiler	Panama-Chatham
Rowlands, William	AB	ALL
Schneider, Coleman	Messman/Utility	San Francisco-Panama
Sears, Arnold	Wiper	San Francisco-London
Shields, Martin	OS	ALL
Sinnott, Philip	AB	San Francisco-Le Havre
Smith, Edward	Deck Engineer	San Francisco-Chatham
		Rouen-San Francisco

Smith, Michael	Deck Utility	Portsmouth-London
Smith, Ronald	Messman/Gunner	ALL
Sommerauer, Otto	Gunners Mate	San Francisco-Le Havre
Speight, Jeff	2nd Asst. Eng.	Le Havre-Baltimore
Speight, Barbara	Storekeeper	Cherbourg-Le Havre
		Portland- Baltimore
Steenburn, Kenneth	Oiler	Jacksonville-San Francisco
Steinberg, Mary	Wiper	San Francisco-Chatham
Taber, Arthur	Storekeeper	Portsmouth-Le Havre
Taylor, Nathan	Deck Cadet	San Francisco-Rouen
Vincenzo, Frank	Oiler	Le Havre-Baltimore
Von der Porten, Edward	Storekeeper	Portsmouth-London
Von der Porten, Saryl	Storekeeper	Portsmouth-London
Wade, James	Purser	ALL
Warren, Dirk	Engine Cadet	San Francisco-Rouen
Wefald, Martin	A. B./Bosun	ALL
Williams, Greg	Messman/Utility	ALL
Williams, Bill	Oiler	Portsmouth-Le Havre
Wood, Samuel	OS./AB	ALL
Worthy, Stephan	1st Asst. Eng.	San Francisco-Panama
Yates, Jean	OS	San Francisco-Le Havre

DOCENT VOLUNTEERS IN EUROPE:

Addie, Ted
Banks, Arnold
Cole, Pierre
Curtis, Darwin
Dallas, Charles
Egan, Michael
Fawcett, Bernard J.
Guikink, Hans
Hook, Jean
Tofield, Robert
Turner, Ron
Wartenberg, Charles

BIBLIOGRAPHY

Blackburn, Graham. *Overlook Illustrated Dictionary of Nautical Terms.* Woodstock, N.Y.: The Overlook Press, 1981

Brouwer, Norman J. *International Register of Historic Ships.* Annapolis, Maryland: Naval Institute Press, 1985.

Haws, Duncan and Alex Hurst. *The Maritime History of the World - 2.* Brighton, Sussex.: Teredo Books, Ltd., 1985.

Medway News, Friday, 25 March, 1994. Medway Dockyard Supplement.

Sawyer, L.A. and W. H. Mitchell. *The Liberty Ships.* London: Lloyds of London Press, 1985 (second edition).

Wall, Robert. *Ocean Liners.* Secaucus, New Jersey: Chartwell Books, Inc. 1977.

Index

559